Pimps, Wimps,
Studs, Thugs
and Gentlemen

ALSO BY ELWOOD WATSON

Searching the Soul of Ally McBeal*:*
Critical Essays (McFarland, 2006)

Pimps, Wimps, Studs, Thugs and Gentlemen

Essays on Media Images of Masculinity

Edited by Elwood Watson

McFarland & Company, Inc., Publishers

Jefferson, North Carolina, and London

LIBRARY OF CONGRESS CATALOGUING-IN-PUBLICATION DATA

Pimps, wimps, studs, thugs and gentlemen : essays on media images
of masculinity / edited by Elwood Watson.
    p.   cm.
Includes bibliographical references and index.

ISBN 978-0-7864-4305-5
softcover : 50# alkaline paper

   1. Masculinity in motion pictures.   2. Masculinity on television.
3. Masculinity in popular culture — United States.   4. Mass media
and culture — United States.   5. Masculinity — Social aspects —
United States.   6. Masculinity — Political aspects — United States.
I. Watson, Elwood.
PN1995.9.M34P56   2009
791.43'6521— dc22   2009016891

British Library cataloguing data are available

On the cover: Will Smith in *Seven Pounds* (2008) Columbia
Pictures/Photofest

Manufactured in the United States of America

McFarland & Company, Inc., Publishers
  Box 611, Jefferson, North Carolina 28640
   www.mcfarlandpub.com

To all my contributors for their immense patience
as this project has slowly but surely evolved

Table of Contents

Introduction

This collection of essays explores the diversity and pluralism personifying the phenomenon of contemporary images of masculinity. In an era where the nation has elected it first African American president, such a book is more timely than ever. President Barack Obama is the personification of contemporary masculinity. Smart, sexy, dashingly handsome and cool, he is embodiment of the type of twenty-first century contemporary man. For so long, we have viewed masculinity through a visual and literary lens. Movies, television, and in many cases, magazines and books, were seen as the vehicles that represented the varied ways that the American man, as well as the international man, were depicted. As our culture and technology has evolved, we have seen the proliferation of contemporary masculinity mediated through the internet. Masculinity is multifaceted. The American man has always been a figure of study among diverse parties: women, other males, psychologists, sociologists, and academics in general. However, over the past several years, there has been considerable examination of the American male.

At no time in American history have we seen as much media attention given to men from all walks of life, involved in various professions, diverse educational levels, all races and ethnicities. While there has been a plethora of scholarship discussing American women and feminism from multiple perspectives, outside of Michael Kimmel, Sam Femiano, Mark Justad, and a few others, there has been very little work done discussing contemporary American men and masculinity as it relates to the mediated version of manhood.

By the early 1990s, men's studies became an academic discipline at a handful of colleges and universities across the United States. Unlike women's studies, men's studies initially failed to garner mass attention or support. It was during this decade that the public witnessed a number of male dominated events like the "sensitive, caring guys" festival and the October 1995 Million Man March led by controversial minister Louis Farrakhan that called on black men to be more responsible to their families and communities. We also saw the development of various men's movements such as Promise Keepers (the Christian organization that asked its members to become more responsible fathers and husbands). While these events and organizations were inspirational on the surface, critics argued that such movements seemed to be based on shame and humiliation.[1] Perhaps this accounted for neither event nor organization having any long-term success.

However, by the latter part of the 1990s, with the Clinton/Lewinsky scandal, and then the 2000 Democratic nominee Al Gore's alpha male image, and Republican nominee George W. Bush's cowboy ruggedness, the issue of male behavior and contemporary masculinity in general had become a topic of considerable interest for a number of Americans. The American male is under enormous scrutiny and pressure to conform to the rapidly changing mores and customs taking place.

A growing number of men have become frustrated, disenfranchised, and confused. Fewer men are attending college, and increasing numbers are dropping out of society altogether. Men have increasingly resorted to television and the internet, where they are finding themselves depressed, sedentary and increasingly isolated.[2] This has undoubtedly taken a toll on many men who have been conditioned by their parents, their communities and society at large to be breadwinners and heads of their households. As Susan Faludi argued in her book *Stiffed: The Betrayal of the American Man*, men have been "mythologized as the ones who make things happen, so how can they began to analyze what is happening to them?"[3]

The idea for this book grew out of a conference that I attended in Atlanta in 2006. I was part of a four-man panel discussing the state of the contemporary American man. The discussions were riveting and the panel received such positive responses that I decided to explore the topic further.

The following chapters represent products of interdisciplinary links among English, history, religion, American studies, film and theatre, communication and rhetoric, sociology, philosophy, women's studies, cultural studies, and men's studies, to note a few. The collection explores a large sphere across a body of cutting edge theory and research in academia. Moreover, it presents a significant range of diverse cultural perspectives.

For example, discussions of men of all races and various occupations are included. Issues such as race, class, sexuality, religious prejudice, miscegenation and homophobia are explored. A number of examples and messages are discussed. One assumption that can be taken from these essays is the fact that masculinity is diverse. There is no single definition of masculinity.

The majority of chapters address the societal pressures under which men find themselves in our society: pressure to conform, to excel, to be masculine, to be sexually strong, yet remain in touch with the feminine side. The contemporary adult male is expected to be one helluva man! As evinced in the essays, the stereotypes associated with African American men can often differ with those of Italian or Asian men. We also can see that many men, irrespective of intellectual ability or professional setting, often responded in various fashions to the pressure that masculinity imposes. Some of the men do so with a level of coolness, while others are more likely to succumb to fear or pressure, or both.

The first part of the book looks at the issue of racialized masculinity and its various manifestations. Historically, the stereotypical image of Italian men in the media has primarily been one of crime fighters, boxers (Jake LaMotta, Rocky Balboa), mafia hit men (*The Sopranos*), and detectives (*Columbo, Donnie Brasco, Goodfellas*).[4]

While all of these representations have been presented in a largely respectful light and have shown varying degrees of heroism, there is one Italian American image that has tended to embody all the grotesque traits of a gangster from a Martin Scorsese film while ostensibly acting on the side of angels. The vigilante, known as "the Punisher," is coarse because he embodies sexism, violence, and apish traits. He directs his anger and murderous impulses against his fellow mafia men to sanitize the Italian American community by killing every gangster he can get his hands on. He is the equivalent of a character straight out of 1970s exploitation films like *Dirty Harry* or *Death Wish*.

"The Punisher" first originated in the Amazing Spider-Man collection, appearing as an anti-hero, before graduating to his own comic book and two feature films. In the essay "The Dilemma of the Italian American Male," Marc DiPaolo examines the most extreme examples of the punisher by exploring his actions and motivations in a broader context by comparing him to less exploitative portrayals of law enforcement. DiPaolo concludes by examining the contemporary state of Italian Americans, their acculturation in American society, and considers to what extent their position is similar, yet different, from the lives of Italian Americans on film and television in the current day.

Since the early 1990s, a number of movies (*Falling Down* with Michael Douglas and *American X* with Edward Norton) depicted angry, disillusioned and dysfunctional middle and upper class white males (WASPs) as men who were rabidly being consumed by the breakneck speed of consumerism and rapidly changing American social, cultural and economic demographics. While 1950s books and later movies like *The Organization Man*[5] and *The Man in the Gray Flannel Suit*[6] showcased white males who were seemingly well-adjusted despite their unrelenting embracing of conformity, more contemporary films have focused on the largely oxymoronic image of the supposed deviancy, yet normalcy, of the professional white male.

Daniel Mudie Cunningham discusses how racial whiteness is a mask — a fantasy position — that illuminates its subjects but simultaneously renders them invisible because of the difficulty in viewing whiteness in its transparent state. Cunningham's essay, "Patrick Bateman as 'Average White Male' in *American Psycho*," further states that the identity of Bateman, played by actor Christian Bale, is positioned as "average," despite his murderous attempts to escape a fate. According to Cunningham, it is the very privilege embedded in Bateman's heterosexual white masculinity that perpetuates his average persona. The essay culminates in demonstrating how Bateman's averageness renders him invisible.

Better Luck Tomorrow was an indie film that received rave reviews at the Toronto International Film Festival in 2003. Many critics lauded the movie's portrayal of Asian American masculinity, a topic that had not previously received the same level of attention as male images of other ethnic men of color. Film critics Elvis Mitchell and Roger Ebert praised director Justin Lin for "presenting three-dimensional, positive portrayals of Asian American characters." Despite its R rating, the movie was successfully marketed as a teen movie by primarily focusing on the narrative of five Asian American youths who resided in an upper middle class southern California suburb.

In her essay "Ambivalence, Desire and the Re-Imagining of Asian American Masculinity in *Better Luck Tomorrow*," Ruthann Lee examines Justin Lin's film. Her essay argues that legacies of colonialism and current forms of neo-imperialism produce particular forms of Asian American masculinity that privilege certain imaginings of gender, family ethnicity and nationality. Lee argues that the film, shaped by Asian American cultural politics, contests historically constituted stereotypes of Asian Americans. She further contends that *Better Luck Tomorrow* simultaneously reinscribes normative, hierarchical and exclusionary forms of cultural identity while deconstructing ambivalent representations of middle-class Asian American masculinity in commercial film.

While the images of the paranoid, hot-headed, dysfunctional white male and the ever acclimating upwardly mobile Asian male are a relatively new topics to many, such stereotypes have long been historically associated with black men. In fact, in 1965, Daniel Patrick Moynihan, senator from New York, wrote of the famous (or infamous, depending on how people viewed it) *The Negro Family: The Case for National Action*.[7] Among the concerns reported was the condition of African American men, specifically those who were the product of female headed households. According to Moynihan, black men were unable to exhibit "the essence of the male animal" because strong African American women denied black men the right to strut like bantam roosters and four-star-generals. This supposed transgression on the part of black women threatened not only the strength of black families but the nation's manpower. Essentially, the report rendered black men and women as enemies to themselves and to the nation.

In his essay "The Black Interior, Reparations and African American Masculinity in *The Wiz*," Jesse Scott examines this film with a cult following among many in the African American community. It is Scott's credible assertion that *The Wiz* has not received the appropriate critical acclaim that it deserves. Moreover, he argues that the movie was far ahead of its time and that it provided valuable psychic messages for African American men when it premiered in 1978 and still does so today.

One fact that is far from reflective or inspirational is the ever-present image of buffoonery of black manhood in the media. From the wide-eyed cooning of 1930s actor Stepin Fetchit and blackface routines of entertainer Al Jolson, to the array of minstrel shows that were commonplace prior to the mid–1940s, the image of the buffoonish, dancing, shucking-and-jiving black man has been a fixture in the American mind-set. Cooning and shiftlessness are the subject of Valerie Palmer-Mehta and Alina Haliliuc's essay "*Flavor of Love* and the Rise of Neo-Minstrelsy on Reality Television." Using the theory of minstrelsy, they provide a close textual analysis of the first season of the reality program *Flavor of Love*.[8]

They argue that Flavor Flav's representation on the program represents a form of neo-minstrelsy and, as such, serves as a threat to black sociopolitical power and contemporary understandings of black masculinity. Their insightful conclusion is that what should not escape our attention is the fact that while Flavor was briefly embraced as a politically irrelevant television character, he was previously marginalized and demonized in his role as a member of Public Enemy, a radical, militant black male rap group of the late 1980s and early 1990s. They conclude that mainstream America has readily embraced Flavor and his retrograde reality program, which suggests a recurring and troubling ambivalence towards black masculinity. Images of black masculinity are embraced when those images serve to reinforce the status quo and often villified when attempting to attain political relevancy.

Another issue that has aroused considerable attention, suspicion and in a number of cases, outright anger toward black men, is the topic of interracial relationships. Indeed, throughout American history, the topic of black men and white women has always been one of taboo. Crossing racial lines of demarcation was seen as a cardinal sin. Such relationships were never supposed to be imagined or discussed, let alone exist in real life. Nonetheless, much has been made of the relationships between black men and white women over the last period of the last quarter of a century. A number of scholars including Estelle Freedman, John D' Emilio,[9] and Kevin Mumford[10] have discussed the various intricacies associated with such unions. By far, more black men date and marry white women than at any time in American history. The topic is one of debate in a large number of households, workplaces, and any other place where people gather to discuss news and gossip. Attitudes range from indifferent to intense passion to outright disgust. With the decline of overt, violent racism and the gradual changing of such attitudes, many black men have continually sought relationships outside of their race. This fact seems to have caused considerable consternation among a segment of black women and white men as well.

In his essay "Jungle Fever: Bold, Beautiful and Unnecessarily Maligned," Daryl A. Carter looks at the many controversies that surround such interracial unions. Carter's essay examines the historical relationships between the black men and white women, why these relationships seem to be more common-place than white men/black women couples and whether there are reasons — economic, aesthetic, supposed physical prowess or other factors — that affect whether black men seek out relationships with white women and vice versa.

One arena where black men have been seen with increasing frequency is in the film industry. black male film stars have always represented the diversity of black manhood. From the 1950s and '60s, when Sidney Poitier graced the silver screen as Hollywood's first black superstar, he was seen as a stunning matinee figure and a phenomenon of sorts. Americans of all races were delighted by his magnetic presence on the screen. Poitier's popularity among his peers in the film industry was apparent as evidenced by his best actor Academy Award for his performance in the 1963 film *Lillies of the Field*. In 1967 and 1968, Poitier was the number one box office star in Hollywood. In 2002, the Academy of Motion Pictures awarded Poitier with an honorary Oscar for his significant contribution to American film and for what they saw as his intelligent body of work.

Over the past 40-plus years, there have been only been a few black actors, such as Denzel Washington and Samuel Jackson, who have reached or exceeded the same level of cinematic success as Poitier. Another black actor who has managed to do so is Will Smith. In fact, following in Poitier's footsteps, Smith has been the number one box office star in the world for the last several years. In his essay "Celebrity Culture and Racial Masculinities: The Case of Will Smith," David Magill examines Smith's success, from his multifaceted role in *Six Degrees of Separation* to his hit comedy *Fresh Prince of Bel-Air*. Magill explores Smith's star identity and his ability to assuage the fears of white America through the fantastic resolution of America's racial contradictions while concurrently acknowledging black anxieties regarding whiteness and power.[11]

The second part of this book explores the issue of contemporary mediated performance and the cultural politics of masculinity. Throughout history, the subject of math has been seen as a masculine oriented discipline.

Despite this fact, male mathematicians have only recently begun to take central stage in contemporary popular culture as reflected in a number of books and films featuring them. *A Beautiful Mind, Good Will Hunting, Pi, Fermat's Last Theorem, Proof, Enigma, Straw Dogs, The Curious Incident of the Dog in the Night-time, The Da Vinci Code*, and *Numb3rs* are just a few examples of recent movies that that have focused on the topic of mathematics and its relation to masculinity.

In their essay "Constructions of Mathematical Masculinities in Popular Culture," Marie-Pierre Moreau, Heather Mendick and Debbie Epstein examine the issue of the "mathematical man" in film and television, as well as in fiction, documentary and reality genres. They argue that in such a climate, mathematicians are constructed as "other" and that such constructions are gendered as well as "raced," classed, and sexualized. They astutely explore the fact that the mathematicians in these texts and spheres are almost invariably men and, more often than not, their masculinities are associated with undesirable characteristics such as mental health disorders (obsessional behavior to schizophrenia), lack of social skills, sternness of lifestyle, and personality. Moreover, the authors argue that while cultural representations of the mathematical man appear to disrupt some of these tropes, they simultaneously serve to reaffirm the limits within which masculinities can go astray.[12]

While mathematics has largely been associated with male masculine identity, the issue of hegemonic, rugged masculinity has often been a recurring theme in the literature that discusses white men of the early frontier, particularly, the interior west. As historical records document, due to European colonization of the Americas, the various nations and tribes of indigenous American Indians that once spanned the continent have experienced domination, exploitation, extermination, assimilation, displacement, and marginalization. Author Sherman Alexie addresses these issues from a contemporary perspective in his 1996 novel *Indian Killer*,[13] a dark murder mystery. Alexie presents a critique of the hegemonic forces of white masculinity and superiority through the depiction of several male characters whose identity and psyche suffer from the effects of white hegemony, particularly that of alienation and injustice.

In her essay "Killing Off White Hegemonic Masculinity in *Indian Killer*," Jane E. Rose argues that the murder of white males represents the killing off of white hegemonic masculinity and all that is associated with it: sexism, racial superiority and dominance, contamination and corruption of Indian culture, and the inevitable transformation of Indian masculinity. She further explores an in-depth analysis of the cultural critique of white American and hegemonic masculinity that Rose sees as underlying Alexie's depiction of Smith's quest for self-identity and the murdering of white males.

Warfare has certainly been a subject that has been associated with men. Military men have been viewed as masculine men. The American soldier has often been the personification of masculinity. He is seen as strong, tough, and time after time displays his uncompromising tenacity. However, as time has progressed, such an impervious image has been challenged and frequently reconstructed. While American soldiers were viewed as valiant and victorious in World War II, the Korean War and most other wars, there was a large degree of ambivalence surrounding the Vietnam War. It was an event that left an indelible stain and deep resentment in the hearts and minds of many Americans.

Since the Vietnam War, there have been efforts to reestablish cultural models of masculinity that were at the center of American narratives during World War II. Vietnam War soldiers were in search of ontological acceptance by American society. They wanted to be heroes. They wanted their deeds to be honorable and valorous. Without this verbal recognition, they could not come to parity with their fathers' generation. Reaction to Vietnam was abnormal, or at least atypical, from previous wars in which Americans had been involved. There was an urgent desire to redefine the outcome of the conflict. Hollywood decided to address the Vietnam issue in films such as *The Deer Hunter* and *Coming Home*.

In his essay "Narrative's Role in Constructing Masculinities in *We Were Soldiers*," Bradley Smith examines the attempt by author Leo Braudy to redefine previously held assumptions about the war. In *We Were Soldiers*, Smith argues that, like a few other novelists, Braudy desperately attempts to legitimize the masculinity of Vietnam War soldiers. Moreover, he demonstrates how the role of the narrator can be crucial in such an effort.

Masculine men in war and related topics have always been of primary concern in American life, and have received some degree of critical attention in American literature. To date, this has not been the case with respect to men and the cult of domesticity. In literary studies, as in masculinity studies, American manhood has typically been defined as an escape from home and family. The seemingly recent appearance of the phenomenon of the househusband, and of fictional representations of this phenomenon since the 1990s, raises very thought-provoking questions concerning meanings of domesticity and the intersection of masculinity and housework.

In her essay, "Masculinity and Domesticity in *A Home at the End of the World* and *Househusband*," Helena Wahlström investigates representations of men as homemakers/housewives/househusbands in two contemporary American novels: *Househusband*[14] and *A Home at the End of the World*.[15] Throughout her essay, Wahlstrom makes the reader question why such figures appear at precisely this point in American history and think about the relationship between the contemporary househusband and the history of the housewife. She concludes with an insightful perspective on the limits of both masculinity and domesticity at a certain point in American history.

Race, sex, class, and gender in fiction are always topics of considerable interest. Sexism in contemporary literature is a topic that has mostly been obscured. Reviewers of Jonathan Franzen's *The Corrections* (2001)[16] character-ized it as a hybrid novel that combined the feminine domestic novel with the masculine edge associated with the social novel. However, after the "Franzen Affair," the spectacle that erupted after the author's snide remarks about Oprah's Book Club reestablished strict gendered boundaries. *The Corrections'* failure to function as both simultaneously masculine and domestic provided valuable insight into the gendered, raced, and classed tensions that inhabit and define twenty-first-century American masculinities, literature and domes-tic culture. The case in particular, highlighted contemporary American mas-culinity's negotiation of domesticity.

Using the Franzen–Oprah Winfrey enmity as a case study in American authorship and masculinity, contributor Kristin Jacobson, in her essay "Anx-ious Male Domesticity and Gender Troubled *Corrections*," examines contin-ued attempts by critics and authors to distance masculinity from the "taint" of the femininity, particularly as manifested in representations of "domestic masculinity." When placed alongside contemporary American political char-acterizations of domesticity, one can observe masculinity's sustained invest-ment and success in resisting hybridization with "low," "mass" or otherwise "feminine" cultures (even as it produces hybrid or mediated texts). In other words, this case argues that exploring or celebrating such examples of post-modern hybridity alone is not enough. We must also consider how hybrid ties like domestic masculinity circulate in the public sphere. Jacobson con-trasts such boundaries policing with Clarissa Sligh's artwork and Michael Nava's mystery novel *Rag and Bone*.[17]

Jacobson argues that this collection of contrasting texts attempts to cre-ate alternative mediations between American masculinity and domesticity. By comparing the Franzen-Oprah contretemps with these texts, Jacobson's essay analyzes the complicated etiquette required for negotiating the patriarchal structures related to gender difference and conceptions of domestic masculin-ity within American communities.

Images of masculinity domestic or otherwise, are a mainstay in the films of playwright and author Neil LaBute. Branded by some as the most impor-tant playwright to emerge in the last decade, La Bute's plays explore how male bodies signify social and historical processes. In his most critically acclaimed theatrical works — *bash: latterday plays* (1999), *The Shape of Things* (2001) and *Fat Pig* (2004) — we witness male protagonists wrestle with specific definitions of masculinity within their respective bodies. A suitable analysis of LaBute presents his works as performed and embodied on stage, and not solely words on the page. In his essay, Marc Shaw examines the issue of male performance in each of LaBute's aforementioned works and examines the extent that the media and other external sources influence both genders in sexual, psychological and other emotional manners.

One event where issues of sex, psychology and raw emotion was rampant was the media-saturated first trial of former Heisman trophy winner and pro athlete O.J. Simpson. The initial Simpson trial brought all of the darkest elements of human nature — greed, lust, violence, racism, sexism, murder, perverse voyeurism — to the forefront of the mainstream media. Overnight Simpson evolved from being a beloved media darling to a big, bad, brutal, pathological murderous boogeyman. The former racially neutral prince charming became a polarizing figure who evoked passion from people from all walks of life.

The trial became an economic bonanza for the mainstream media. Networks made megabucks, careers were launched and in some cases revived. Mainstream print journalism, tabloids, television and radio followed the first trial with viral intensity. By doing so, they also focused on the historically retrograde racial stereotypes that have been associated with black men for centuries — violence, sexual deviancy, violence against women, supposed arrogance. The acquittal of Simpson in his first trial furthered stroked the flame of racial animosity. Some people argued that it contributed to the further marginalization of black men in American society. The second Simpson trial garnered very little if any such level of unhinged passion. In my essay, "O.J. Simpson: Tabloidized, Sexualized, Racialized and Largely Despised," I explore how O.J. Simpson was psychoanalyzed through racial, economic, media and gender prisms.

One area where the forces of race, gender and economics frequently intersect is the field of sports. There is no doubt that athletics is a profession that where physical prowess and fitness are essential. The athletic man is viewed as male, rugged, and domineering. One factor that is seldom associated with athletes is the issue of homosexuality. While there have been a few Broadway plays such as *Eight Men Out* that have examined the issue of a gay sports player, it is a topic that is *discussion non grata* for many people. Over the past several years, baseball has had to confront the issue of gay men in its ranks. The topic was sensationalized in the summer of 2001 when the gay and lesbian magazine *Out* editor-in-chief, Brendan Lemon, announced that he had been having an affair with a pro baseball player who was fairly well known in the sport.[18] In the spring of 2002, chat rooms, sports magazines and radio talk shows became deeply immersed with the rumor that Mike

Piazza, catcher for the New York Mets, was actually the mysterious lover of whom Lemon spoke. After persistent denials and no evidence to link him, the media began to focus on other topics of the moment.[19]

These incidents point to a social, political, and cultural moment in American professional sports, and American culture in general. The significant number of gay men in professional sports, and in this case, baseball, can only go publicly unacknowledged for so long. With the continual arrival of gay male baseball players onto the public stage, American popular culture may be moving towards a significant unmasking of western masculine illusion.

In her essay "Major League Baseball and the Cultural Politics of Sexuality," Rachelle Sussman explores a variety of media outlets and pundits that covered these stories as well as popular baseball sites that have made such gossip relevant. Sussman focuses on baseball, its significance as America's pastime, and how it harkens back to the time of unblemished "good ol' days" for some Americans. She further concludes that in many ways, baseball has come to represent a societal and cultural arena of demarcation between normal and unacceptable. Sussman attempts to help us fully understand the current state of masculinity by exploring how the mainstream media represents hegemonic mediated, masculinity gay culture and its relationship to America's pastime.

The contemporary twenty-first century American male is an individual who is scrutinized more than ever before. This intellectually engaging and diverse collection of essays has been assembled to admirably discuss the advantages, situations, challenges, and dilemmas of the contemporary mediated man.

Notes

1. Daniel Jones, *The Bastard on the Couch: 27 Men Try Really Hard to Explain Their Feelings About Love, Loss, Fatherhood and Freedom* (New York: William Morrow, 2004). 22–23.

2. Jones, *The Bastard On The Couch.* 25.

3. Susan Faludi, *Stiffed: The Betrayal of the American Man* (New York: William Morrow, 1999).

4. *The Sopranos, Columbo, Donnie Brasco* and *Rocky Balboa* were just a few of the many Italian American characters that were immensely popular among the public.

5. William Whyte, *The Organization Man* (New York: Simon and Schuster, 1956).

6. Sloan Wilson, *The Man in the Gray Flannel Suit* (New York: Simon and Schuster, 1955).

7. Daniel Patrick Moynihan, *The Negro Family: The Case For National Action* published in The Moynihan Report and The Politics of Controversy Trans-action Social Science and Public Policy Report (Cambridge: MIT Press, 1967).

8. *Flavor of Love* was an immensely popular, yet retrograde reality television program

that starred former rap star Flavor Flav who was a member of the militant rap group Public Enemy.

   9. Estelle Freeman and John D'Emilio, *Intimate Matters: A History of Sexuality* (Chicago: University of Chicago Press, 1998).

   10. Kevin Mumford, *Interzones: Black/White Sex Districts in Chicago in the Early Twentieth Century* (New York: Columbia University Press, 1997).

   11. Will Smith, according to *Entertainment Weekly* and several other similar publications, is the most consistently bankable star in Hollywood.

   12. G. Lloyd, *The Man of Reason: "Male" and "Female" in Western Philosophy* (London: Routledge, 1993).

   13. Sherman Alexie, *Indian Killer* (New York: Warner Books, 1996).

   14. Ad Hudler, *Househusband* (New York: Random House, 2002).

   15. Michael Cunningham, *A Home at the End of the World*. New York: Farrar, Strauss and Giroux, 1990.

   16. Jonathan Franzen, *The Corrections* (New York: Farrar, Straus and Giroux, 2001).

   17. Michael Nava, *Rag and Bone* (New York: Berkeley Prime Crime, 2002).

   18. Brendan Lemon, "Letter from the Editor" (http://www.out.com/html/edletter 90.html 2001; accessed January 2002).

   19. Toby Miller, "Out at the Game: The New Look of Sports"; (http://chronicle. com/weekly/v47/i49/49bo1401.htmchronicle; accessed August 2002).

Bibliography

Alexie, Sherman. *Indian Killer*. New York: Warner, 1996.

Cunningham, Michael. *A Home at the End of the World*. New York: Farrar, Straus and Giroux, 1990.

Faludi, Susan. *Stiffed: The Betrayal of the American Man*. New York: William Morrow, 1999.

Franzen, Jonathan. *The Corrections*. New York: Farrar, Straus and Giroux, 2001.

Freeman, Estelle, and John D'Emilio. *Intimate Matters: A History of Sexuality*. Chicago: University of Chicago Press, 1998.

Hudler, Ad. *Househusband*. New York: Random House, 2002.

Jones, Daniel. *The Bastard on the Couch: 27 Men Try Really Hard to Explain Their Feelings About Love, Loss, Fatherhood and Freedom*. New York: William Morrow, 2004.

Lloyd, G. *The Man of Reason: "Male" and "Female" in Western Philosophy*. London: Routledge, 1993.

Moynihan, Daniel Patrick. *The Negro Family: The Case for National Action*. In *The Moynihan Report and the Politics of Controversy Trans-action Social Science and Public Policy Report*. Cambridge, MA: MIT Press, 1967.

Mumford, Kevin. *Interzones: Black/White Sex Districts in Chicago in the Early Twentieth Century*. New York: Columbia University Press, 1997.

Nava, Michael. *Rag and Bone*. New York: Berkeley Prime Crime, 2002.

Whyte, William. *The Organization Man*. New York: Simon and Schuster, 1956.

Wilson, Sloan. *The Man in the Gray Flannel Suit*. New York: Simon and Schuster, 1955.

Part I

Racialized Mediated Performance and Contemporary Masculinity

1

The Dilemma of the Italian American Male

Marc DiPaolo

"There's nothing extraordinary about American gangsters," protested [James] Bond. "They're not Americans. Mostly a lot of Italian bums with monogrammed shirts who spend the day eating spaghetti and meat-balls and squirting scent over themselves ... greaseballs who filled themselves up with pizza pie and beer all week and on Saturdays knocked off a garage or drug store so as to pay their way at the races."
— Ian Fleming, *Diamonds Are Forever* (1956)

GENNIFER FLOWERS: Well, I don't particularly care for [Governor Mario] Cuomo's ... uh ... demeanor.
GOVERNOR BILL CLINTON: Boy, he is so aggressive.
FLOWERS: Well, he seems like he could get real mean.... I wouldn't be surprised if he didn't have some Mafioso major connections.
CLINTON: Well, he acts like one. [laughs]
— Transcript of a telephone conversation tape-recorded in late 1991 and released by *The Star* tabloid newspaper in January 1992.

The Immigrant Stigma of the Mafia Don

As David Chase's landmark HBO television series *The Sopranos* came to an end, select television critics proclaimed it "the greatest TV show of all time," columnist Peggy Noonan called it "a masterpiece," and — despite some dissatisfaction with the open-ended finale — there was great public mourning over the passing of the gritty crime soap opera. However, a solid contingent of Italian Americans were just as glad to see yet another mass-media portrayal of their people as degenerate Mafia killers fade into memory. Traditionally, American movies and television shows featuring those of Italian

descent in "non–Mafia" roles are few and far between. The restaurant own-
ers of *Big Night* and *For Roseanna*, the various fake Italians played by Chico
Marx, and the military men in *Crimson Tide, Band of Brothers,* and *From Here
to Eternity* are the exceptions that prove the rule. Fortunately, while Sylvester
Stallone's character Rocky Balboa spent a brief stint as hired muscle for Italian loan sharks, he was too nice to break legs to collect on loans and quit the
Mafia early in the first *Rocky* movie to become a professional boxer. In addition, a small-but-notable subset of Italian American characters on film and
television *fight* crime rather than *commit* crimes. Though not Italian American himself, actor Peter Falk played the brilliantly intuitive homicide investigator Lt. Columbo in the 1968 telefilm *Prescription Murder*. He continued
to play the character for decades afterward in a series of *Columbo* television
movies, continuing to outsmart rich, establishment villains who underesti-
mate his intelligence because his slovenly appearance tricks them into thinking that he is a poor, unintelligent, immigrant cop. Film and television
followed up with further examples of noble Italian American police officers,
including Al Giardello, Yaphet Kotto's half–Italian American, half–African
American protagonist from *Homicide: Life on the Streets* (1993–1999), space
station security chief Michael Garibaldi in the science fiction series *Babylon
5* (1993–1998), and portrayals of real-life Italian crime fighters in the movies
Serpico (1973), *The Untouchables* (1987), *Rudy: The Rudy Giuliani Story* (2003),
and *Donnie Brasco* (1997).

    While all of these crime fighters are presented in a respectful light, and
are shown exhibiting varying degrees of heroism, there is one Italian American crime fighter who has all of the grotesque traits of a gangster from a Martin Scorsese film, while ostensibly acting on the side of the angels. The
vigilante known as the Punisher is just as coarse, sexist, violent, and apish as
any character from *Goodfellas* (1990), but he turns all of his anger and murderous impulses against his own people in the Mafia, hoping to sanitize the
Italian American community by killing every last gangster he can get his hands
on. He is a character right out of a 1970s exploitation film like *Dirty Harry*
(1971) or *Death Wish* (1974), but first appeared as an anti-hero in *The Amazing Spider-Man* comic books in 1974 before graduating to his own comic
book and two feature films. It is the extreme example of the Punisher that I
am most concerned with exploring here. I intend to place his actions and motivations in a broader context by comparing him to less exploitative portrayals
of Italian law enforcement, especially Lt. Columbo and Joe Pistone (a.k.a.
Donnie Brasco). Finally, I will examine where Italian Americans are, in the
21st century, in their process of enculturation in American society and consider to what extent their position is mirrored by, and diverges from, the lives
of Italian Americans as represented on film and television up to this point.

Italians vs. Italians: The Dilemma of the Italian American Crime Fighter

As refreshing as it is to see Italian Americans presented as upstanding citizens, and while many of these characters are well-written and superbly acted, a fascinating dramatic and sociological tension is created on any occasion when one of these Italian crime fighters is ordered to pursue an Italian criminal. In some ways, watching an Italian cop incarcerate an Italian criminal is a cathartic experience. It makes the average middle-class Italian hope that such a story dramatizes, symbolically, the fact that Italians no longer need to turn to crime in order to survive and thrive in America, and can put their underworld stigma behind them — and I say "stigma," rather than "past" as statistically, very few Italian Americans turned to crime, either in order to survive prejudice and a lack of job opportunities, or to recreate the Sicilian mafia on U.S. shores.[1] On the other hand, the extent to which Italians still exist somewhat on the margins of American society makes one wonder if the Italian cop isn't being too hard on one of his own. After all, despite the fact that many members of other disenfranchised groups certainly have even less access to the so-called "American Dream," Italians do not have the same job opportunities as the individuals who compose the white, Anglo-Saxon, Protestant community that still thinks of itself as the rightfully privileged American mainstream. If such is the case, then is an Italian crime fighter who arrests and/or kills Italian criminals some kind of Italian "Uncle Tom?" The issue comes up time and again in crime dramas featuring Italians, and is at its most compelling in stories featuring the Untouchables, Donnie Brasco, Columbo, and the Punisher.

One of the first notable real-life Italian crime fighters is Frank Basile, a man who understood underworld culture and joined Eliot Ness' squad of Untouchables during the Prohibition era to help bring down the empire Al Capone built on illegal alcohol trafficking. While Ness and Oscar Fraley do not do much to develop Basile's character in their book-length account of the mob war, they express admiration for Basile and terrible anger at Capone for ordering Basile's murder. Presumably, Capone targeted Basile for assassination because he was angry that Basile worked against his own people. Capone may have also felt it would be easier to get away with killing a mere Italian than a member of the U.S. Treasury Department (although he would later try to kill Ness as well). Basile is not widely remembered by the American public, and is hardly a household name, but he was the inspiration for Andy Garcia's character in Brian De Palma's *The Untouchables* (1987). In the film, Garcia is a dedicated member of the team who had attempted to distance himself from Italian criminals, and from his Italian heritage, by changing his name from Giuseppe Petri to George Stone. Sean Connery's character, Irish cop Jim Malone, admits to having some prejudices against Italians, and calls Capone's men Dagos and WOPs, but admonishes Stone for changing his name, and insists on affectionately calling him Giuseppe. Stone, thankfully, is more fortunate than the real-life inspiration for his character and survives to see Capone jailed for tax evasion. The film presents Stone as being a more righteous Italian American than Capone mainly because Capone is a cruel, murderous, unelected "head" of Chicago, and Stone is bravely defiant of Capone's unjust rule. Consequently, the film virtually sidesteps a very natural audience caveat that few Americans feel that Prohibition was a just or enforceable law, and that Capone was merely providing the public "what they wanted."

Joseph D. Pistone, an American of Sicilian extraction and another real-life crime fighter, helped bring down New York's Bonanno crime family by operating undercover as one of their number for six years during the late 1970s. Pistone's book *Donnie Brasco*, named after the alias he assumed while working undercover, inspired the Johnny Depp vehicle *Donnie Brasco* (1997), the independent film *10th & Wolf* (2006), several fiction novels featuring the further adventures of Donnie Brasco, and the short-lived television series *Falcone*. Consequently, Pistone has become as much of a folk hero in the annals of crime drama as he is a real person, prompting *New York Post* entertainment critic Linda Stasi to complain of his ubiquitous presence. In the film *Donnie Brasco*, Depp plays Pistone as a figure who spies upon his fellow Italians with great reluctance. He relates strongly to mob culture and is in danger of embracing the gangster personality. He feels like a Judas figure when he betrays his mobster friend "Lefty" Ruggiero. He also butts heads with his "white," establishment superiors in the FBI. However, the Joe Pistone in the book *Donnie Brasco* is vastly different from the one in the film. Pistone's own written account of his feelings — both at the time he was undercover and since — seems far less conflicted. In fact, Pistone appears almost detached in his attitude towards the two hundred criminals that were indicted for crimes based on evidence that he gathered. Aside from voicing disapproval of their lifestyle, their corrupting influence, and their lack of intelligence, Pistone claims to have felt neither malice nor great sympathy for those he spied on. At the conclusion of *Donnie Brasco*, he writes:

> People wanted to know whether I felt I was on a mission to clean out the Mafia because I'm Italian-American.
>
> I didn't carry out the mission on behalf of upstanding Italian-Americans. I wasn't an ethnic policeman.... I would have accepted any undercover assignment against any group the FBI targeted.
>
> I am proud about how it turned out, however.

Italian-Americans have told me they are proud that I had the courage to do it and that I showed the nation that not all Italians side with the Mafia....

Now we know the Mafia is not invincible.

It is also clear that the Mafia preys on Italians as well as other people....

On the other hand, some people asked, "How could you have done it to other Italians?"

I don't feel that way. I busted a group of people involved in illegal activities.

Not viewing the probe from an ethnic point of view was important for keeping proper perspective. Another reason the investigation was successful was that I knew, no matter what I did, that I was not going to reform anybody in or around the Mafia, that the people I was getting close to were going to lie, steal, cheat, and murder whether I was there or not. My goal was to gather evidence for later prosecutions. I was not a social worker [407–408].

Pistone likes the film adaptation of his book very much, and has not, to my knowledge, voiced objections to Depp's portrayal of him as more conflicted than he lets on in the book. It is possible that both portrayals of Pistone are, to an extent, true. However, they are almost irreconcilably different, and represent two different, believable reactions for someone in Pistone's position. The Pistone in the film sees what he is doing as a crime against his own people and feels guilty for it, while the Pistone of the book sees the case in terms of law-breakers versus law abiders and feels no such conflict. Both reactions are fascinating.

Barry Harvey, himself a former undercover agent and a twenty-four-year veteran of the Pennsylvania State Police's Organized Crime Division in Philadelphia, has also noticed the discrepancy between the book and the film and believes that the truth is somewhere in between. However, he suspects that Pistone feels the most guilt over the fact that the several of the individuals who brought him into the inner circle of the mob — not knowing that he was an undercover agent — were later killed by other gangsters as punishment for the mistake. As Harvey explained in an October 8, 2008, e-mail to me, "I have personally used individuals such as Lefty who I certainly did not care for but still had some reservations about using them and what would happen to them.... [W]orking undercover requires lies and deceit. You must 'like' someone no matter if you do or not if that person is useful. Relationships are formed, and just because someone is a criminal does not necessarily mean they are not likeable. I will never forget a long-term undercover assignment I had in which I became friendly with a group of people and one in particular. At the end of the investigation when this one person was arrested, he cried and told me 'I thought we were friends.' ...[So] even if Pistone did not like Lefty he knew that he, Pistone, would be directly responsible for Lefty's death. Maybe that is where the 'guilt' comes from [more than from being Italian like Lefty]."

Unlike Pistone, Lt. Columbo only infrequently found himself investigating Italian criminals. An evil vineyard owner and wine connoisseur played by Donald Pleasance in *Any Old Port in a Storm* (1973) springs to mind as a rare Italian adversary. However, Columbo's Italian heritage has been mentioned repeatedly during the course of the series, and is often the subject of light-hearted humor. One of the most memorable conversations in the history of the show takes place between Columbo and his Italian American dentist, Dr. Perenchino, in the story *Columbo: Candidate for Crime* (1973). As Perenchino examines Columbo's wisdom teeth and listens to opera playing on the radio, he launches into a monologue about anti–Italian prejudice in America: "Ah, when people talk about Italians, do they think cops, dentists, tenors? The Pope, not even? The Pope is Italian, ain't he? They think ... they think *Mafiosa, Mafiosa, Mafiosa.*"

At the time the episode was broadcast, the Pope *was* Italian: Pope Paul VI. The script (written by Irving Pearlberg, Alvin R. Friedman, Roland Kibbee, and Dean Hargrove from a story by Larry Cohen) involved a senatorial hopeful (played by Jackie Cooper), killing his controlling campaign manager and blaming the death on members of the underworld whom he has sworn to bring down. Amusingly, when Dr. Perenchino hears on the radio that the famous public figure was killed, he predicts that the real killer will likely be a rich white guy who tries to pin it on the Mafia. As Columbo leaves the dentist's office to begin his investigation, Perenchino says, "You are an Italian cop. No matter who you catch for this murder, they're still gonna say it's the Mafia and that you're covering for them.... Take my advice, lieutenant, change your name!"

Columbo has no comment. Nor does he change his name. He merely proceeds to prove that the senator was the killer and makes a successful arrest at the end of the episode. Interestingly enough, Perenchino is convinced that, as an Italian American on the police force, Columbo is in constant danger of becoming a victim of his own ethnicity, but the series never presents Columbo's status on the force, or his reputation, as being threatened by his class or culture. In fact, Columbo's entire *modus operandi* works because he follows Sun Tzu's dictum, "Appear strong when you are weak and weak when you are strong." He appears weak, but his position in the fabric of the criminal justice system, and in American society, is secure. He is able to fool his criminal adversaries into underestimating him by pretending to be on the margins of society when, in actuality, he commands the respect of his superiors and the power to jail white-color criminals who, in the real world, oftentimes *would* be beyond the reach of a mere working-class homicide investigator. In fact, Columbo is unassailable, even when wealthy murderers, like the psychiatrist played by Gene Barry in *Prescription Murder*, are friends with the district attorney, or use bribes or threats to shake Columbo off their trail. Columbo is never taken off the case, and never faces an opponent too rich or politically powerful to buy his way to freedom. Indeed, this almost counterintuitive consistency of outcome makes some viewers wonder if Columbo is secretly wealthy himself, has some kind of politically invincible ally, or if his whole persona as a frumpy, poor, cop is a put-on and he's not even really Italian but secretly some rich, white guy himself who only pretends to drive a broken-down car and wear a hand-me-down raincoat when he's off-duty.

In many ways, the Punisher is not as compelling a figure as either Pistone or the fictional Columbo, but the twisted caricature of Italians that he represents is worth discussing, even if the comic books in which he appears are not on the same level of "popular art" quality as the *Columbo* television series, and his films are not as stellar as the Mike-Newell-directed *Donnie Brasco*. The Punisher has appeared in two eponymous films, a direct-to-video release in 1989 featuring Dolph Lundgren as the Punisher and a theatrical release in 2004 starring Thomas Jane in the title role. In addition to the films, the Punisher has appeared in cartoons and video games, and has inspired a number of novelty T-shirt designs and action figures. Originally created as an adversary for Spider-Man in "The Punisher Strikes Twice!" *The Amazing Spider-Man* #129 (1974), Frank Castiglione is a Vietnam veteran, ex-Catholic seminarian, and former New York City cop who went crazy after the Costa crime family gunned down his wife and two children during a family picnic in Central Park, Manhattan. Wishing that he had died with his family, Frank donned a black Kevlar suit with a white skull emblazoned on the chest, adopted the identity of The Punisher, and declared a one-man war on crime. After successfully avenging his loved ones by slaughtering the mobsters who played a role in their deaths, he continued his campaign to protect other families from the horrors he suffered by killing every violent criminal he felt was beyond the reach of the deeply flawed (and perhaps too liberal) criminal justice system.

The Punisher's story has a visceral appeal to anyone of non–Italian descent as an indulgent, *id*-unchained revenge narrative, and he is interesting to Italians as one of the few Italian comic book "heroes" (with Tony "Iron Man" Stark, the sexy magician Zatanna, and Helena "The Huntress" Bertinelli as three of the few exceptions), but he is a exploitative character that raises unpleasant questions about crime, racism, immigration, and war in American society. These questions are all disturbing, and the answers the Punisher tries to give are still more disturbing, but they are worth considering in greater detail here.

The Punisher as Self-Hating Italian American

Punisher stories tend to walk a fine-line between trying to evoke audience sympathy with the character, and attempting to justify his mad quest, while others try to assume a more ironic, satirical, or critical distance. The 2004 film goes to great lengths to justify Castle's murderous campaign against Howard Saint by having Saint responsible for the deaths of Castle's *entire extended family*. In the film, Saint sends his hired killers to the Castle family reunion and they machine gun everyone in attendance. The film also strives to justify Castle's decision to quit the police force and take the law into his own hands. Castle is also unwilling to go to the police or the judiciary system because (in the extended cut of the film released on DVD in 2006), his African-American partner, Weeks, helped Saint find and eliminate Castle's family members. Saint is also, presumably, the richest man in Tampa, and has the police in his pocket. Unlike Columbo, who is influential enough in the criminal justice system to bring down any criminal he finds evidence against, so no matter how wealthy that "perp" is, Castle is powerless to fight crime within the system. Therefore, he removes his policeman's badge and becomes a vigilante.

While the police are not always evil in the Punisher universe, they are often ineffective. The Lundgren film, for example, portrays the police as weak and inefficient, but not corrupt. In that version of the story, Louis Gossett Jr. plays Castle's former partner, Jake Berkowitz, who is a decent man who hopes to capture Castle and get his friend treatment for mental illness. When Berkowitz is finally reunited with his former partner, he cries when he sees just how much of the humanity has been burned out of Castle's eyes. Louis Gossett Jr.'s acting in the scene is superb, and it makes the film worth watching for that segment alone. His character also provides a heart, humanity, and decency to a film that is otherwise cynical and coldhearted. He is the moral center of the story, and his perspective represents a genuine alternative to the worldview offered by the mentally ill Punisher. Since Berkowitz exists as a goodhearted cop in the Lundgren film, the movie raises the possibility that the Punisher could have, if he wanted, fought crime more mercifully and within the system, alongside his old friend. The excuse the Punisher uses that he alone can fight crime has even less resonance in the comic book universe, in which characters like Spider-Man and Daredevil are arguably just as effective at fighting crime while still being merciful.

The Punisher's creator, Gerry Conway, wrote Spider-Man, Wonder Woman, and Batman comic books throughout the 1970s and 1980s, has written television scripts for TV shows such as *Hercules: The Legendary Journeys* and *Matlock,* and recently became the co-executive producer for *Law & Order:*

Criminal Intent. According to Conway, he came up with the basic premise and look of the Punisher, and artist John Romita finalized the design for penciller Ross Andru to draw in the final comic book. As Conway explains, "My idea of the Punisher was that he was a guy who was driven by his need for vengeance but was not so driven that he couldn't see what was going on around him." Conway did not intend to present the Punisher as insane, but acknowledges that writers who have written the character since have done so.

Interestingly, Conway never referred to the character as anything but the Punisher, but writer Steven Grant made the always swarthy figure an Italian in 1986's *The Punisher # 1.* Grant's script revealed that the Punisher was born Frank Castiglione to Sicilian immigrants living in New York, Mario and Louise Castiglione. The parents Americanized the family name to "Castle" in 1956, when Castle was six. Since Frank had an Italian surname for the first few years of his life, and then saw his surname changed at an impressionable age, the change probably contributed to his conflicted feelings about his own ethnicity.

Future writers, such as Mike Baron, expanded upon the Punisher's Italian background by revealing that Frank Castle was a Roman Catholic, and that he briefly studied to become a priest but left the seminary when he discovered that he had difficulty forgiving those who confessed to committing grievous sins during the Sacrament of Confession (see the 1989 graphic novel *The Punisher — Intruder*). It was later revealed that Castle met his future wife, Maria Falconio, after leaving the seminary, and enlisted in the Marines and served in Vietnam, after his marriage. By making the Punisher a former seminarian, the comic book achieved three things: it added a layer of characterization to a fairly one-dimensional figure; it tapped into the evocative hypocrisy best exemplified by Michael Corleone in *The Godfather* films of the churchgoing murderer, and it gave the Punisher a history of religious zealotry that transferred from traditional Catholicism — which has come to embrace a "consistent life ethic" over the past several decades, opposing the death penalty, abortion, and euthanasia — to a harsh, fanatical mission to kill virtually every career criminal he encounters.

Mike Baron is one of the writers who have written the Punisher in a highly sympathetic light, and he is not the only creative figure at Marvel Entertainment who seems to regard the character with a measure of understanding, perhaps even a little admiration. According to Ari Arad, an executive at Marvel Studios who worked on the 2004 film adaptation, the Punisher is not insane, but a man whose morality is so different that it makes him a pariah. "His system of ethics, his moral code, is very different from most people's, but it is specific and it exists. He doesn't kill innocent people. He has a benchmark for people that deserve to die and he's going to kill them, but it is not an arbitrary benchmark and it is not one that he violates."

Somehow surviving all of his run-ins with criminals, and never successfully being contained by the police, the Punisher's war on crime has lasted (in the fictional timeline of his comic book adventures) for thirty years. Law enforcement characters within his comic book adventures have charged him with the deaths of *thousands* of criminals. While the character exists in a universe of superheroes, he himself is not supposed to have any superpowers, but his longevity and invincibility cannot be accounted for by normal means (not even his nifty Kevlar body armor), so certain writers have suggested that he has been granted supernatural abilities, possibly by the devil (as suggested in Garth Ennis' *The Punisher: Born*), to wage his war for so long. While the Punisher is an equal-opportunity killer, having slain street gang members, corporate criminals inspired by the Enron offenders, Muslim terrorists, and members of the Italian, Irish, Japanese, and Russian mobs, he has the most personal anger for the Italians, because it was they who killed his family. Consequently, the adventures in which he squares off against the Mafia are the ones that have the most dramatic resonance.

For example, in "Red X-Mas," writers Jimmy Palmiotti and Justin Gray introduced a close circle of Mafia widows who decide to avenge their husbands' murders by putting a contract out on the man who killed their husbands — Frank Castle. Ringleader Regina Napolitano, who lost three consecutive mates to Castle's crusade, talks the other widows into contributing $5,000 a piece to hire a female assassin from Sicily named Suspiria (the name is an in-joke nod to an Italian horror film directed by gore-master Dario Argento). The leather-clad S&M sexpot Suspiria fails to kill Castle and, in an ironic twist, the two later become lovers because of their mutual love of carnage. In the meantime, Castle tracks down and kills Regina, and warns the other widows to donate several thousands of dollars to charity and leave the country or he will hunt them down one by one. As he puts it, "Just because you married a bunch of greaseballs, doesn't make you gangsters. I'm giving you a stay of execution."

In the Boaz-Yakin-scripted film adaptation starring Dolph Lundgren, Castle's vendetta against the various Italian crime families has weakened their hold on the city to the extent that the Japanese Yakuza is able to move in on their territory. While the Punisher is initially delighted to see a gang war brewing and jokes that he can finally go on vacation and let the Yakuza finish off the Italians for him, he feels compelled to help his enemies when Yakuza boss Lady Tanaka kidnaps the children of all of the Mafia dons and threatens to sell them into slavery. The Punisher reluctantly teams up with the same gangster who ordered his family killed, Gianni Franco (played by Jeroen

Krabbe), in order to rescue the children, who he sees as innocent of any wrongdoing and undeserving of being punished for their fathers' crimes. At the end of the film, the Punisher rescues the children, but kills Franco in front of his own son, Tommy. The Punisher warns Tommy not to grow up to be like his father. "You're a good boy, Tommy. Grow up to be a good man ... because if not, I'll be waiting."

This horrifying and evocative scene in the film inspired a variety of similar scenes in later comic books in which the Punisher, dressed in the garb of Santa Claus, would kill criminals in front of children and then pause to explain to the shocked little ones, "They were naughty." The unsubtle message is, "Be good little children, or the Punisher will come to get you."

Because the Punisher is such a one-note character, he tends to be at his most interesting when he is sparing lives, rather than taking them, but he is still more iconic in his "boogeyman of the underworld" persona than he is a three-dimensional character. That is why, when screenwriter Michael France was assigned to write a first draft of a screenplay for the 2004 adaptation of *The Punisher*, he felt the challenge was to make the character fresh when the "'you killed my family — prepare to die' story and character had been done a thousand times." France felt that the key to the character was the fact that, on the one hand, Castle enjoyed killing criminals, and on the other, he hated his existence as the Punisher and would "trade anything at all to have his family back." To tackle this duality in the Punisher, France rewrote the origin story a little, placing Castle in the same conflict that Joe Pistone faced in the film *Donnie Brasco*. In France's version, Castle was an undercover FBI agent and family man who had infiltrated the Mafia and was enjoying both his existence as a mobster and as a husband and father. Unsure who "the real Frank" was, father or gangster, Castle decided to quit the FBI and leave the evil influence of the Mafia behind. Unfortunately, his extraction from the field doesn't go well, his cover is blown, and his old associates seek revenge by killing Castle's family. As France explains, "Frank Castle the family man dies with his family and he reverts to the man he's been pretending to be for years while undercover: a completely ruthless psycho who goes after the mobsters who killed his family."

France's idea played up the Punisher's Italian identity and blurred the distinction between Castle and the gangsters he fought by making Castle the son of a mobster. "I had another character angle which was so dark I understand why [it didn't make it into the final film]. In the movie, Frank's father is a lawman played by Roy Scheider. But in my drafts, I established that Frank's father was actually a hitman in New York City named "Il Punisco" — "The Punisher." — and Frank was always ashamed of that. He joined the FBI to prove that he wasn't at all like his father — but the fact is, he was such a good killer that every day he was on the job as an undercover cop, he was proving that he was exactly like his father."

The film as eventually made seemed reluctant to engage in Italian stereotyping, avoiding revealing that, according to the comic books, Castle's birth name was Castiglione. It also dropped France's idea for the Punisher's father as Il Punisco, and changed the guilty party responsible for the Castle family killings from the Costa family to Howard Saint, a figure who is presumably not Italian even though he is played by Italian American actor John Travolta. While Italian villains are not present, other villains in the film are far more stereotypical, including a steroid enhanced Russian assassin similar to *Rocky IV*'s Ivan Drago, and the Toro Brothers, Hispanic gangsters inspired by the Spider-Man villains the Lobo Brothers. Still worse, the film features a psychotic gay assassin named Quentin Glass and Saint's bloodthirsty wife, Vivian, who coaxed her husband into having Castle's entire family killed instead of just putting a hit on Castle himself.[2] The presence of these villains in particular is a nod to yet another stereotype with a questionable foundation in fact — that the modern-day Italian American male has an unfortunate tendency toward prejudice against feminists and gay men. Despite the fact that the audience is meant to feel somewhat sorry for Vivian and Quentin in the end, when they fall victim to Castle's elaborate (and cruel) revenge scheme, their respective sexual orientation and gender cast the film's already politically incorrect sensibilities in an even darker light. Interestingly, in making the villains a multi-ethnic cast of stereotyped villains instead of a group of Italians, the film goes from being potentially offensive to Italians, and prejudiced against Italians, to potentially offensive to women, gays, Hispanics, Russians, and other groups who might see themselves in the Punisher's sleazy rogue's gallery. And, as much as the Punisher hates his own people, this is not the first time he has slaughtered unflatteringly portrayed members of other minority groups. Therefore, the recent Punisher film is not the first film to seem racist against ... just about everyone.

The Punisher as a Racist Vigilante

Unlike the Punisher, who kills plenty of non–Italians, but who reserves a special hatred for his own people, the Irish-American vigilantes Connor and Murphy MacManus featured in *The Boondock Saints* (1999) are functionally protectors of the Irish-American community in Boston. After hearing a sermon during Sunday mass about the importance of fighting evil in society, the MacManus twins defend the local Irish bar from being shaken down by Russian Mafia extortionists. They kill the gangsters in self-defense and become neighborhood heroes. Afterwards, the MacManus brothers go on a killing spree, focusing their attention on purging Boston of the Russian and Italian mobs, but claiming to be against all criminals who prey upon the innocent. Like the Punisher, the Boondock Saints are religious fanatics who think God is on their side when they kill criminals. While these "Boondock Saints" are briefly pursued by a gay FBI agent played by Willem Dafoe, his character ultimately comes to see the wisdom of their actions, and does not arrest them. There is some indication that he even joins them at the end of the film.

The Boondock Saints was written and directed by Troy Duffy, who reportedly felt compelled to write the screenplay as a form of therapy after he saw a murdered woman being removed from an apartment across the hall from him. As Duffy explained in an interview:

> I decided right there that out of sheer frustration and not being able to afford a psychologist, I was going to write this, think about it. People watching the news sometimes get so disgusted by what they see. Susan Smith drowning her kids ... guys going into McDonald's, lighting up the whole place. You hear things that disgust you so much that even if you're Mother Teresa, there comes a breaking point. One day you're gonna watch the news and you're gonna say, 'Whoever did that despicable things should pay with their life' [http:/ /en.wikipedia.org/wiki/The_Boondock_Saints].

Duffy's rage at the sight of the murdered woman is understandable, and I admit that my own upbringing in a safe, middle-class, Orthodox Jewish neighborhood in Staten Island prevents me from feeling the immediacy of crime in the same way that Duffy experienced it. He was forced to live in an apartment building in which ugly crimes were committed. I was not. Nevertheless, there is a disturbingly racist overtone to the film *The Boondock Saints*. In fact, one of the Italians who ultimately joins forces with the MacManus brothers against his own people, tells a racist joke in which a genie solves all of white America's "problems" by teleporting all Hispanics to Mexico and all blacks back to Africa. The joke is not only mean-spirited, but makes one wonder if the Boondock Saints are not performing the same function as the genie, only by killing minorities instead of deporting them. The symbolism of the MacManus brothers as guardians of American "whiteness" is particularly ironic if one considers the fact that, when the Irish first came to America, they were greeted with terrible racism from the whites who already lived here, and were the targets of NINA ("No Irish Need Apply") laws, just as the Italian immigrants were considered "non-white" and discriminated against as well. So the anger and hatred that the Boondock Saints level against immigrants who came to America after them seems hypocritical in the extreme.

And the Boondock Saints are not alone in this hypocritical racism.

Indeed, while Italian Americans as a whole are reportedly left-leaning

Democrats, a few too many of those who live on Staten Island have, in my own personal experience, a surprising tendency towards being arch conservatives that are particularly prone to racism. They look back upon the "old neighborhood" in Brooklyn where they and their parents and grandparents lived before the family relocated to Staten Island, see that the apartment buildings that they had kept up so well have fallen into disrepair under the stewardship of Russian, Muslim, Hispanic, or black newcomers, and they feel nothing but anger and confusion about the new minorities who have taken over what used to be "little Italy." These Italians forget that they were once poor minorities, too.

This perspective is a contentious one, especially since the many Italian Americans who are not prone to racist feelings do not deserve to be painted with the same broad brush as those who do. Also, arguably, there is an inconsistency in any article that disavows one stereotype (the mafia stigma) while reinforcing another (the racist Italian American). However, while there are statistically few Italian Americans in the mafia, the question of Italian American racism is raised consistently and convincingly enough in the media, and in sociological works, that it seems harder to refute. Recent articles published online at the Italian American Digital Project (www.i-italy.org) have taken a strong stand against Italian and Italian American racism. These articles and blog posts have been largely supportive of the Presidential candidacy of Barack Obama, have criticized anti-immigration rhetoric in Italy and the United States, and have attempted to determine the extent to which the media coverage of the 1989 murder of African-American teenager Yusef Hawkins in Bensonhurst justifiably painted the Brooklyn Italian American community as essentially racist.

Significantly, Martin Scorsese and Robert DeNiro have both directed films that were based on true stories in which an Italian American male faces his own prejudice, and the prejudice of his peers when he contemplates dating a black woman —*Mean Streets* (1973) and *A Bronx Tale* (1993). These films hint that anti-black sentiments are common in Italian American communities. In addition, Spike Lee has nailed Italian Americans to the wall for being anti-black, and has been strident enough, and persistent enough in his criticism that he has been accused of being himself racist anti–Italian and painting them in too broad, and negative a brush. (For example, Lee's attempt to cast an Italian American cop as *moderately* likeable *despite* being racist in the 2006 film *Inside Man* is still a bitter pill for many Italian American viewers to swallow, as the police officer, once again, is a racist Italian American.)

On the other hand, Lee may well be right to be as persistent and as critical as he is of Italian Americans. Some sociologists have documented a phenomenon of recurrent cases of antiquated notions of race in the Italian

American community. For example, Jennifer Guglielmo explores the inexplicable, and frustrating, tensions between Italian Americans and other minorities, especially African-Americans, in the introduction to her book *Are Italians White? How Race Is Made in America* (2003):

> *Italians are niggaz with short memories.* In late June, 2002, Chuck Nice, an African American deejay at WAXQ-FM in New York City casually made this remark on-air while hosting an early morning talk show. Within days, a response came back. The Order of the Sons of Italy in America, the oldest and largest organization of Italian Americans in the United States, announced that it was "puzzled by such a statement and the station's refusal to do an on-air apology. We understand that Mr. Nice is an African American, but we don't understand why it is wrong for a white person to call an African American that name, but okay for an African American to use it to describe white people." What the organization's spokesperson saw as so offensive was not the entire phrase, just the epithet, which made no sense since it was used by an African American to describe whites. What they seem to have missed, however, was how this radio host was calling Italians out on their particular whiteness: Italians were not always white, and the loss of this memory is one of the tragedies of racism in America [1].

The forgetfulness that both Nice and Guglielmo describe is particularly hard to forgive in light of the fact that, while Italians faced prejudice and obstacles in light of their status as immigrants, their suffering as marginalized Americans is miniscule in comparison to what African-Americans have gone through, from the age of slavery up through the present. As Malcolm X wrote in *The Autobiography of Malcolm X* (1965):

> How is the black man going to get "civil rights" before first he wins his human rights? If the American black man will start thinking about his human rights, and then start thinking of himself as part of one of the world's great peoples, he will see he has a case for the United Nations. I can't think of a better case! Four hundred years of black blood and sweat invested here in America, and the white man still has the black man begging for what every immigrant fresh off the ship can take for granted the minute he walks off the gangplank [806].

While I agree with Malcolm X's point wholeheartedly, in my experience, most Italian Americans either don't understand what he is saying, or are too offended by his argument to consider the possibility that it might be true. Italian Americans from Staten Island forget that they, like the blacks, have suffered from prejudice. They forget that the early Italian Americans in America were *allies with the black activists of the late eighteen hundreds and early nineteen hundreds*, and that Italians were famously lynched in New Orleans They also forget that they, in comparison to African-Americans, have suffered little. Instead, Staten Island Italian Americans in particular wonder why they were able to class-jump from a one-room apartment in Bay Ridge to a semi-attached home in Staten Island while other minorities seem mired in poverty, incapable of making such a class jump. This kind of thinking leads to Staten-Island Italians wishing that the old neighborhoods would somehow be "cleaned up" by the Italian equivalent of the Boondock Saints, or the Punisher. These sentiments are harsh and despicable, and shared by the vast majority of Italian- and Irish-Americans I knew growing up in Staten Island. Many of these same Staten Islanders, not coincidentally, were big fans of *The Punisher* comic book growing up.

Ironically, such horrible sentiments have been most effectively countered by a voice for tolerance that comes from the unlikeliest of quarters, the Irish-American, right-leaning Fox News personality who bills himself as a moderate when he is anything but ... Bill O'Reilly. Using personal memories and anecdotal evidence rather than statistics, O'Reilly nevertheless gives a reasonable response to Italian Americans like those I grew up around, who blamed the wrong people for the deterioration of the neighborhoods they used to live in. As O'Reilly writes in *The O'Reilly Factor: The Good, the Bad, and the Completely Ridiculous in American Life* (2000):

> The attitude of my [prejudiced] friend's parents came, I think, from the history of our lily-white town. Levittown was populated in the 1950s, mostly by whites who fled Brooklyn after World War II. This sudden exodus was caused by evil real estate agents. They began buying up small apartment houses and moving black families in. This was not an enlightened plan to promote integration and harmony among the races. They knew that many Irish, Italian, and Jewish families would succumb to prejudice-and to well-placed rumors-by selling their row houses in a panic.
>
> That's how "blockbusting" began. Real estate prices dropped drastically in many working-class sections of Brooklyn. The real estate people, the block-busters themselves, snapped up the houses cheap. Then they subdivided them, squeezing two black-families into a one-family structure. One thing led to another, and the quality of some neighborhoods spiraled downward fast. The agents, now acting as landlords, made a killing on rent but provided little maintenance.
>
> I know what I'm talking about because my family experienced it. My grandfather meticulously maintained his home on West Street in Brooklyn because he owned it. The black families coming into these areas usually could not afford to own. As renters, they reasonably expected their landlords to be responsible for maintenance and repairs. Few of these landlords bothered. Maintenance cut into profits.
>
> Naturally, many of the blocks owned by blockbusters began to deteriorate. Some whites blamed the black renters for this decline, but they were looking only at the surface. The slums had been created by blockbusters, and they were never really held accountable. Setting one race against another, they used fear and prejudice to make money, not caring that well-kept, peaceful neighborhoods were destroyed [156–157].

While there is evidence to support O'Reilly's claims, such a reflection on the creation of "bad neighborhoods" rarely filters into popular crime narratives, be they *Punisher* comic books or episodes of *NYPD Blue*, which are more concerned with depicting the punishment of an individual criminal for a particular crime than with looking at the root causes of poverty, crime, and race and class divisions. Only the comic book *Green Lantern/Green Arrow*, written during the activist 1970s by Dennis O'Neil, dares to show a superhero (the Robin-Hood-like Green Arrow) join a gang of minorities in attacking a fat, white businessman for being a slum lord rather than depict a super hero defending a "respectable businessman from an unreasonable mob." It is a striking, progressive image, watching the Caucasian Green Arrow condemn the greedy white businessmen, but it is, again, the exception that proves the rule. Far more common in the world of comic books is the sight of the Punisher acting as racial purist, killing a black or Hispanic mugger/rapist in an alley after the grotesque criminal accosted a pretty white woman at the point of a switchblade. Iconic, and disturbing, scenes such as those demonstrate why, arguably, the Punisher reflects and amplifies the tendencies of conservative readers to, in a racist fashion, scapegoat entire groups for the problems of society without thinking of meaningful ways of dealing with poverty and crime. Obviously, the white-supremacist, wish-fulfillment fantasy of the Punisher is not a meaningful way of thinking about how to fix the problems of the decaying inner cities in America, but many reactionary readers seem to think it is.

Unfortunately, a lot of the men who write stories for the Punisher do not appear to be aware of the racist dimensions of the character. Some are, and present him as a villainous or satirical figure. Other stories are written by people with ambivalent feelings for the character and the result is a work that is hard to decode as either racist or satirical, but that seems to lean towards racism, like the uncomfortable viewing experience that is Scorsese's *Taxi Driver*. But a lot of Italians love the Punisher comics as much as they love the movie *Taxi Driver*, and I am suspicious of the motives of fans of both works of pop art. Why, exactly, do they love these stories so much? Can this love be healthy? And what is an alternative to this kind of narrative of black/Italian hostility?

Eddie Murphy has a famous comedy routine where he makes fun of Italian Americans for investing too much in the myth of Rocky Balboa, and accuses the film series of race-baiting and escalating tensions between blacks and Italians because three of Rocky's main opponents are formidable African Americans whom audience members are invited to root against. While I see where he is coming from, the friendship that Rocky eventually cultivates with Apollo Creed in *Rocky III* and *IV*, the training he does under Tony Burton, the affection he gives to Little Marie's son Steps, and the respect he ultimately gives the Mason "the Line" Dixon, who defeats Rocky at the end of *Rocky*

Balboa, is an infinitely preferable model of black/Italian relationships than those seen just about anywhere else in the popular media.

And, coming at it from another angle, unlike most Italian American characters in film, Rocky has the advantage of being *a really nice guy*.

Amazing!

The *Rocky* films are not perfect, but they are the best we've got so far outside of the genre of the crime film, and the respective legacies of *The Godfather* and *The Punisher*.

The Legacy of the Punisher

The Punisher comic books belong to the same disturbing pop culture family as 1970s and 1980s slasher movies, exploitation crime films, and rape revenge narratives like *I Spit on Your Grave*. Film historians have argued that these exploitation films were a natural outgrowth of the horrors of the Vietnam War, as well as a backlash against the "Love Generation," and all endorsed a conservative worldview. Unsurprisingly, in the contemporary political environment created by the Iraq War, the Punisher is back and Quentin Tarantino is gleefully trying to resurrect the 1970s exploitation film in *Grindhouse*. And everything old is new again.

And what of the Italian Americans of the Iraq war generation?

Who are they and what is their relationship to this grotesque character?

In recent years, the growth of the discipline of Italian American studies in academia has inspired the writing of several excellent books about the Italian American experience by members of the "baby-boom" generation. These works, which include Robert Viscusi's *Buried Caesars* (2006) and Alfred Lubrano's *Limbo* (2004), have used autobiographical anecdotes, historical research, and sociological data to chronicle the journey of enculturation that many Italian American families made over a period of several generations. Such works invariably begin with a discussion of the arrival of the main wave of immigrants at Ellis Island and follow the displaced Italians to urban centers such as Rochester or Brooklyn, where they survived in an alien land by clustering together in "Little Italy" neighborhoods and toiling in jobs involving hard physical labor and unjustly low pay. From such humble beginnings, these working-class Italians saved enough to send their children to college, or to enable their progeny to begin their own small businesses. Within the span of two or three generations, many Italian Americans felt that they had finally achieved the much-vaunted American Dream when the descendents of immigrants began trading in their one-bedroom city apartments for (semi-attached) homes in the suburbs of places like New Jersey and Staten Island.

Both Viscusi and Lubrano speak of the present-day Italian American as a middle-class figure, often a college professor in the humanities, or an executive with one home in Park Avenue and another in Tuscany, who is weary of the immigrant stereotype of the Mafia don that haunts the Italian American public image and who has a love-hate relationship with films like *The Godfather*. For these authors, the greatest problem facing their contemporaries are identity issues tied up with the fact that, as financially and socially successful as Italian Americans are, they do not feel "at home" anywhere. For Lubrano, the feeling of "Limbo" is one of class. Italians who were the first members of their family to graduate college never felt at home in the Protestant, middle-class communities they moved into (or the "WASPy" occupations they entered), nor could they ever feel at home again in the working-class communities they left behind. According to Viscusi, national identity remains the most contested problem as Italian Americans are still not truly accepted either by the Italy they left behind or the America they came to. As he writes:

> ...consider the difficulties immigrant Italians needed to face in developing a discourse of their own entitlement in the millennial European project called *America* [after the Italian explorer Amerigo Vespucci]. These new arrivals in no way could identify themselves directly with the ruling peoples. The Anglo-Americans had resisted the entry of the Irish Catholics. But now these groups began to cooperate in the definitive marginalizing of the Italians, who found themselves forming, and still do, a part of the vivid and highly decorated frame of American society, along with the blacks, the Latinos, and the Eastern European Jews. Naturally, a society as mobile as that of the United States always has room to absorb some members of these border peoples into the operating centers, but much larger proportions remain, as before, to a greater or lesser degree visibly tattooed with their tribal or racial otherness. For Italians this exclusion has been less rigid than for blacks or Latinos, but more rigid than for Jews and Irish Catholics. In short, to the regional and class divisions of Italy has been added in the United States the machinery of ethnic boundary markers. The borders are such that Italians who cross them must do so at the risk of losing their own possibilities of historical self-awareness.
> ...Not surprisingly, many Italians have refused to pay this price [146–147].

Despite the obvious anxiety in evidence here, the general narrative arc presented by both books suggests that, despite the presence of many obstacles — such as anti–Catholic bigotry, first-generation immigrant poverty — the Italians have succeeded in improving their lot in America with each successive generation.

As Viscusi observes,

> Italians now come to New York, not to organize garbage trucks and cocaine dealers, but to represent major manufacturers, traders, and banks. They have offices along Park Avenue. They win lucrative contracts to build bridges and

pipelines all over the world.... From Greenwich, Connecticut, to Palo Alto, California, Italian American professionals have the financial and educational capital to appreciate the finer — that is, the more socially dominant — meanings of the word *Italian*.... These graduates of Stanford and Harvard do not resemble the candy store bookies and Brooklyn torpedoes who populate American Mafia films. As Italian Americans move toward the notion that *Italian* means something central and authoritative, their impatience with the immigrant stigma grows. Some spend huge amounts of money protesting the Mafia mythology. Others simply buy themselves villas in Tuscany [31].

However, despite the fact that previous generations of Italian Americans have seen their quality of life improve, and have seen the creation of a class of Italian Americans who can afford to buy a house in Tuscany, this is the first generation in which Italians appear to be losing ground in their quests to finally achieve, and retain, their status as full-fledged Americans while holding on to their Italian heritage. Lubrano and Viscusi both effectively end their discussion with the "baby-boom" generation, and do not consider how members of Generation X, or the Millennial Generation, have fared in the face of additional problems such as the dissolution of the American family, the political polarization of the Culture Wars and the War on Terror, and the slowdown of the American economy. Naturally, all of these issues plague the baby boomers as well, but they are having a particularly disastrous effect on young Americans in general, who have not yet made their careers or begun their families.

Even as Rudolph Giuliani failed his 2008 bid to become the first Italian (and the second Roman Catholic) U.S. president, middle-class suburban Italian families seem to be fighting to keep up with their mortgages, health care and utility bills, and debt from college loans and credit cards used to help keep the family up with inflation. The financial strain has caused many Italian Americans in their twenties and thirties to wonder why they bothered going to college when all that is open to them is a middle management job that involves sitting in a cubicle in an understaffed office entering data into a computer for more than forty hours a week with no health benefits and no chance of promotion. Truly, they are members of the Generation Debt described by Anya Kamenetz in her 2006 book of that title. As such, many Italian Americans wonder whether they will ever earn enough money so they can marry, buy a house of their own, or have children, and some males lament the possibility of ever meeting a woman who has not been so scarred by her parents' divorce that she is even willing to consider marriage. Also, while Italians have traditionally not been big drinkers, reserving their alcohol intake for a glass or two of wine at dinner, the younger generations of Italian Americans have taken, in recent years, to succumbing to the youth party culture and, on Staten Island, are now part of a demographic of "Northeast ... white, middle-class, teenage" Catholics who are "one of the highest demographics of underage drinkers" who "drink, and drink savagely" (Zailckas xv).

It is also interesting to try to trace the migratory patterns of Italian Americans, many of whom cannot afford to be homeowners, but do not feel at home returning to the apartment buildings their families owned in the past, since new ethnic groups have moved in and the neighborhoods are less "Italian," or, in the case of Greenwich Village, far to expensive for most. However, the richer Italians are part of an intriguing white-flight pattern. Some have moved off of Staten Island over the years, searching for greener pastures in New Jersey, joining other former Brooklyn residents who bypassed New York's least famous borough. Other Italians moved to Florida, but later grew tired of Florida and decided to take a home in North Carolina. (Local lingo dubs these North Carolina transplants from Florida "half-backs" because they moved half-way back to Brooklyn.) Despite these maneuvers, there is a general sense among Staten Islanders that there's no place to move *to*. Partly due to economic factors, partly due to a lack of imagination or a general sense of fear, they feel fundamentally trapped on Staten Island, as if it were some kind of black hole. They are not very interested in Italy, or most of the rest of the country, or even Manhattan, which is expensive and a pain to commute to given the lack of subway access, affordable parking, and the erratic bus schedule. If they do move, they want it to be to another "Little Italy," for fear that, should they try moving to a town without a sizable Italian populace, they will be greeted with disdain by the non–Italian neighbors. In addition, as Italians disperse across America, it becomes harder to maintain their traditional culture in any meaningful way — especially when, thanks to falling Italian and Italian American birthrates — there are fewer and fewer birds of the same feathers to flock together. It is even difficult sometimes to eat "real" Italian food when the closest thing Italian Americans living in rural or suburban areas can find to Italian food is Olive Garden (!) or whatever Wal-Mart chooses to stock in its generic ethnic foods isle.

Given that they are facing this situation, Italian Americans of today might consider the possibility that American society, and the American Dream, is in need of serious reform. As they face this reality, it might behoove them to remember that, as bad as their problems are, there are other groups suffering far more serious calamities in the United States, who never succeeded in making the class jump that they did in the first place, and who might reasonably feel that worrying about a "middle class squeeze" constitutes living a charmed life. Italian Americans might finally embrace a life of progressivism and activism in a way they haven't done in decades. On the other hand, Italians caught in such a squeeze may buy into racist propaganda that only outsourcing of jobs to India or illegal immigration from Mexico are to blame for their woes, and feel their inclination towards prejudice magnify into full-blown racism.[3] And they may become still more conservative and reactionary as a culture.

Italian Americans are at a cross-roads. Since there aren't any media representations of Italians *as we are today*, that speak to our current situation, we need to come up with a new vision of who were are in the twenty-first century, what we stand for, how we want to relate to members of other cultures and other races, what kind of Italians we want to be, and what kind of Americans we want to be. Since so many of the Italian Americans shown on film and television are not Italian Americans as *we actually are*, but Italian Americans as the rest of the country *needs us to be* to satisfy their own fantasies — larger-than-life gangsters as mythic symbols of "the modern urban cowboy" who act on the needs of the *id* in ways that mainstream America, with its overdeveloped *superego*, cannot — there are few popular culture role models for who we are and what we really represent. However, in some ways, even the most sensationalistic figures of Italians presented in the mass media offer us possible models of our current situation, and no Italian figure is more interesting to me, and more apropos of our situation at the moment, than the figure of the Italian American member of law enforcement. As an image of Italian Americans from a previous generation who has endured in this one, Columbo continues to serve as the best example of an Italian American in popular culture that is currently available to us — if one were inclined to look to fictional characters for inspiration, of course.

Columbo is a creature of intellect who understands how society works. He spends his time fighting the corrupt, white-color criminals who undermine our democratic system and exploit the poor instead of wasting his time scapegoating the disenfranchised and the desperate. He treats other police officers with warmth and respect, whether they are Italian, African-American, or any other race or ethnicity. He is also comfortably American, comfortably Italian, and does not hate himself or anyone else. He is a great male role model for young Italian men.

The Punisher, on the other hand, represents Italian Americans at their worst: anti-feminist, homophobic, racist, self-loathing, Catholic zealots who are caught up in the pro–Mafia/anti–Mafia polemic and unwilling to see themselves, and the world, in a broader, more enlightened context. The Punisher represents a retreat into a fantasy patriarchy in which he is the Caesar in the "Old Italian" tradition and wants to exert his will to make a new "Little Italy" in America where all other races need not apply for residence, and only Italians who have never been in the Mafia are allowed entrance.

If anything, the Punisher may still serve us well as an example of what not to do as a next step for the Italian American community, and the individual Italian American male... The Punisher represents a warning to us not to make any of the choices Frank Castle made. He is an illiterate moron who thinks that all of society's problems can be solved with the barrel of a gun. As appealing as the Punisher's anti–Mafia stance might be to some of us, the Punisher is, ultimately, wrong about crime, wrong about women, wrong about race, and wrong about Italians.

The last thing that Italian Americans should be interested is in imitating a dead-end character like him. In the end, despite their flaws, Italian American men are better than that, and should act accordingly.

Special thanks to the following readers for their insights and opinions: Barry Harvey, assistant professor of criminal justice, Alvernia College; Catherine Porzio, professor emeritus of English, New York City Technical College; and Marc Lucht, assistant professor of philosophy, Alvernia College.

Notes

1. According to Barry Harvey, a twenty-four-year veteran of the Pennsylvania State Police's Organized Crime Division, it is difficult to ascertain how many (and what percentage) of Italian Americans were a part of the mafia throughout its history, from the Prohibition era to the present. "As the mafia is a 'secret' organization it usually is very difficult to determine accurate numbers. There are members and then there are associates. Most figures are merely estimates by law enforcement agencies or writers who specialize in organized crime.... [However, t]here is no doubt that the percentage of Italian Americans belonging (actually "made members") to the mafia is very small." As Harvey observes, "The original mafia came about as a pseudo government when there was none in Sicily. The local don was the most respected man in the village and functioned as a government would. The mafia, or men of respect, formed around this don to perform services for the community. It was a tradition and part of the heritage. When groups of Sicilians and Italians immigrated to the United States they found themselves living in overcrowded cities where once again the real government ignored them so the men of respect once again became very powerful in the little Italys etc. They viewed themselves as honorable men bringing with them a tradition, rules, and a structure. For the most part these men were looked up to in the neighborhoods.... They would not exist if they were not supported by the public through the use of their "services" and through the support and respect of the Italian/Sicilian people who live in the neighborhoods. So on the one hand they do not like the depiction of all Italians as mafia but on the other hand the mafia is supported and held up as something special in the neighborhoods where they thrive."

2. According to Barry Harvey, "One of the unique things about the Mafia is that they are a criminal organization with tradition and rules, a code of conduct if you will, ways of doing things. Unlike some portrayals, they are not random killers. They do not kill people's wives and families even to get even. They accept the fact that they can be killed at any time as part of their 'occupation' but wives and families are usually off limits. They are very specific killers. So the depiction of them killing a family and then this Punisher taking revenge on them is very far from the truth."

3. These are likely contributing factors to the problem of employment in America, but I am surprised at the extent to which some Staten Islanders seem to express jealousy

of (and hostility to) exploited migrant workers, impoverished illegal immigrants (to whom President Bush rightly wished to grant amnesty), and Third World peoples. My casting these workers as victims may, in a sense, be as much of an unenlightened, prejudiced perspective as casting them as "job thieves," but I speak out of equal concern for their well-being, as well of the well-being of out-of-work Americans, while anti-immigration talk tends to label non–Americans as somehow subhuman and worthy of contempt in a manner that deeply disturbs me.

Bibliography

Abnett, Dan, and Andy Lanning. *The Punisher: Year One.* New York: Marvel Comics Group, 1994.

"Army of One: Punisher Origins." *The Punisher.* Special Features. Lions Gate Films, DVD, 2004.

Baron, Mike, and Erik Larsen. "The Iris Green Saga." *The Punisher.* vol. II nos. 21–25. New York: Marvel Comics Group, 1989.

Beck, Bernard. "The Myth That Would Not Die: *The Sopranos,* Mafia Movies, and Italians in America." *Discovering Popular Culture.* Ed: Anna Tomasino. New York: Pearson Education, 2007. 122–130.

"The Boondock Saints." http://en.wikipedia.org/wiki/The_Boondock_Saints

Busiek, Kurt, and George Perez. *JLA/Avengers* (1 of 4). New York: Marvel Comics, September 2003.

"Candidate for Crime." *Columbo: The Complete Third Season.* Starring Peter Falk and Jackie Cooper. Teleplay by Irving Pearlberg, Alvin R. Friedman, Roland Kibbee, Dean Hargrove. Story by Larry Cohen. Universal City, California: Universal Studios Home Entertainment, 2005.

Conway, Gerry, with Ross Andru and John Romita, Sr. *Amazing Spider-Man* #129. "The Punisher Strikes Twice." New York: Marvel Comics Group, February 1974.

Conway, Gerry, with Tony Dezuniga. "Death Sentence." *Classic Punisher.* New York: Marvel Entertainment Group, 1989.

DeFalco, Tom. *Spider-Man: The Ultimate Guide.* New York: Dorling Kindersley, 2001. 84–85.

Ennis, Garth, with Darick Robertson. *The Punisher: Born.* New York: Marvel Entertainment Group, 2004. Ennis, Garth, with John Severin. *Punisher: The Tyger.* New York: Marvel, February 2006.

"First Blood." Directed by Ted Kotcheff. Written by Michael Kozoll, William Sackheim, and Sylvester Stallone. Starring Sylvester Stallone. 1982. Artisan DVD, 2002.

Fleming, Ian. *Diamonds Are Forever.* London: Penguin, 2002. 23 and 231.

Fraction, Matt, and Ariel Olivetti. *The Punisher War Journal: Civil War.* New York: Marvel Comics Group, 2007.

Gerbner, George. "Reclaiming Our Own Cultural Mythology: Television's Global Marketing Strategy Creates a Damaging and Alienate Window on the World." *In Context: A Quarterly of Humane, Sustainable Culture, Ecology of Justice,* no. 38 (Spring 1994): 40.

Guglielmo, Jennifer. "White Lies, Dark Truths." *Are Italians White? How Race Is Made in America.* Ed: Jennifer Guglielmo and Salvatore Salerno. New York: Routledge, 2003.

Grant, Steven, and Mike Zeck. *The Punisher.* Vol. I, nos. 1–5. New York: Marvel Comics Group, 1986.

Jones, Gerard. *Killing Monsters: Why Children Need Fantasy, Super Heroes, and Make-Believe Violence.* New York: Basic Books, 2002.

Kamenetz, Anya. *Generation Debt: Why Now Is a Terrible Time to Be Young.* New York: Riverhead, 2006.
Lubrano, Alfred. *Limbo: Blue-Collar Roots, White-Collar Dreams.* Hoboken, NJ: John Wiley and Sons, 2004.
Mahedy, William P. *Out of the Night: The Spiritual Journey of Vietnam Vets.* Cleveland, OH: StressPress, 1996. 41, 46–47.
Malcolm X, "A Homemade Education," from *The Autobiography of Malcolm X.* Reprinted in *The Conscious Reader*, 10th edition. Ed: Caroline Shrodes, Marc DiPaolo, et al. New York: Pearson, 2006. 806.
Ness, Eliot, and Oscar Fraley. *The Untouchables: The Real Story.* New York: Pocket, 1957, 1987.
O'Reilly, Bill. *The O'Reilly Factor: The Good, the Bad, and the Completely Ridiculous in American Life.* New York: Broadway, 2000.
Ostrander, John, and Gary Frank. "Bullets and Bracelets: Diana Prince and the Punisher in *The Final Thrust*." New York: Marvel Comics, 1996.
Palmiotti, Jimmy, and Justin Gray (writers); Mark Texeira and Paul Gulacy (pencils). "Red X-Mas" and "Bloody Valentine." *The Punisher: Very Special Holidays.* New York: Marvel, 2006.
Pistone, Joseph D., and Richard Woodley. *Donnie Brasco.* New York: Penguin. 1987. 407–408.
The Punisher. Directed by Mark Goldblatt. Written by Boaz Yakin. Starring Dolph Lundgren, Louis Gossett Jr., and Jeroen Krabbe. 1989. Live/Artisan DVD, 1999.
The Punisher. Directed by Jonathan Hensleigh. Written by Jonathan Hensleigh and Michael France. Starring Thomas Jane and John Travolta. Lions Gate Films, 2004. (An extended edition was released by Lions Gate in 2006.)
"The Punisher." http://en.wikipedia.org
"The Religious Affiliation of Comic Book Character Frank Castle, The Punisher." http://www.adherents.com/lit/comics/Punisher.html
Seeton, Req, and Dayna Van Buskirk. "Screenwriting Punishment with Michael France." UGO Screenwriter's Voice, http://screenwriting.ugo.com/interviews/michaelfrance_interview.php
Skal, David J. *The Monster Show: A Cultural History of Horror.* New York: Faber and Faber. 1993.
"Transcript: The Flowers/Clinton Tapes — Accuracy in Media." http://www.totse.com/en/politics/political_spew/clintonc.html
The Untouchables. Directed by Brian DePalma, written by David Mamet, starring Kevin Costner, Robert DeNiro, and Sean Connery. Paramount Pictures, 1987.
Viscusi, Robert. *Buried Caesars and Other Secrets of Italian American Writing.* Albany: State University of New York Press, 2006.
Zailckas, Koren. *Smashed: Story of a Drunken Girlhood.* London: Penguin, 2004.

2

Patrick Bateman
as "Average White Male"
in *American Psycho*

Daniel Mudie Cunningham

> The white man is sealed in his whiteness.
> The black man in his blackness.
> — Frantz Fanon, *Black Skin, White Masks*[1]

In *Black Skin, White Masks*, Frantz Fanon analyses the psychic and social processes that can lead black subjects to internalize an inferior self image. The title of his landmark study refers to black skin as a signifier of social and cultural worth — or perceived non-worth, as the case may be — and the way in which whiteness can be symbolically attained if a black subject learns its language. To learn the language of whiteness, its appetites and discontents, Fanon implies that black subjects must appropriate a white position, adopt a mask of privileged whiteness, because "it is from within that the Negro will seek admittance to the white sanctuary."[2] It is in the very nuances of Fanon's own language that we can begin to piece together the shards of porcelain that make up the masks of privileged whiteness. If the subject is "sealed" by the color of their skin, surely whiteness is a kind of mask or envelope that binds its contents. The body's surface and all its racial markings are, in Fanon's schema, the limitations of identity, because identity at least in Cartesian terms has been regarded as the stuff, not of the body, but of the mind.

Racial identity, for Fanon, is paradoxical. Race is marked by the visibility of the flesh, but as an internalized entity, it has not yet seen the light of day. If whiteness is an internalized "sanctuary" that can only be accessed "from within," whiteness becomes an invisible entity because of its perceived cul-

40

tural privilege. As a "sanctuary," whiteness takes on a set of spiritual or otherworldly connotations. Whiteness is a place of rest, a place where the light supposedly shines brighter. In this schema, a black subject can only approximate the norms that constitute whiteness. And to approximate whiteness, a subject must first understand that the act of claiming whiteness entails a belief in the following declaration: "I am white: that is to say that I possess beauty and virtue, which have never been black. I am the color of daylight."[3]

Whiteness has held a privileged position in Western culture because it connotes beauty, virtue and light. Blackness has often been associated with the 'dark' side of life, or as cultural critic Ruth Frankenberg states, "crime is 'black.'"[4] Frankenberg is referring to the way crime has a representational lineage of being associated with the menace of darkness or evil. Specifically, the racial signifier of blackness has often been represented as a suspect identity and is, therefore, more likely to engage in criminal behavior. Of course, whiteness has been linked to criminal behavior, especially in the way whiteness has enforced itself as supreme and dominant at the expense of so-called inferior races. This essay will examine the film *American Psycho* (2000) and its protagonist Patrick Bateman: a spectacle of whiteness as serial killer criminality contextualized within the exceedingly privileged context of late 1980s American corporate surfaces and greed.

My reading of *American Psycho* uses a backdrop of social and cultural privilege, drawing upon Carol Clover's concept of the "average white male" by arguing that one does not necessarily need to be poor or working class to be average. Being part of a privileged class grouping can ensure "averageness," and by extension, paranoia, self-loathing and madness. Played by Christian Bale, Bateman is trapped in an ongoing cycle of keeping up with the break-neck speed of consumerism and it is precisely this immersion in surfaces that produces an identity trapped as average. Bateman performs conspicuous consumption to fit in and be assimilated within his circle of privileged peers. Whiteness is thus represented as serial self-sameness and ensures Bateman's perpetual erasure and invisibility.

In my analysis of *American Psycho*, I will argue that racial whiteness is a mask — a fantasy position — that illuminates the subject, but simultaneously renders them invisible because "whiteness can be difficult to see."[5] In her reading of Fanon's work, feminist theorist Diana Fuss argues that "'white' defines itself through a powerful and illusory *fantasy* of escaping the exclusionary practices of psychical identity formation."[6] Fuss is speaking to the process by which whiteness comes to be a privileged signifier in a binary schema. Unless it is called attention to, whiteness is an unmarked and generic signifier for human. Whiteness may attempt to remain an invisible and generic signifier, but it is only because whiteness is constantly attempting to negotiate and reinforce its own self-worth that it calls attention to itself as a paranoid identity, forever approximating its own set of values.

Whiteness is invisible because it is perceived as the unmarked norm by which otherness is constituted and thus marked. Like a drawing outlined in invisible ink, whiteness only reveals itself when its surface is scrutinized under specific conditions. The contradiction here is that whiteness is invisible because it is unmarked, while it is simultaneously rendered visible by its mask-like qualities. Whiteness calls attention to itself while simultaneously positioning itself as substanceless. Whiteness is, therefore, an unmarked surface that is marked as it begins to gain self-recognition as a raced entity. Whiteness is a "sealed" mask that reveals as much as it conceals.

Masked, Watermarked

Based on Bret Easton Ellis' notorious novel of 1991, *American Psycho* takes delight in the sheer surface of things in order to critique or satirize those very surfaces. *American Psycho* emphasizes the literal and symbolic masks that conceal and inevitably reveal the identity of the white subject. Bateman is a Wall Street trader whose life is not simply privileged, it is indulgent. Bateman, named after Norman Bates from Hitchcock's *Psycho* (1960), epitomizes all the ideals that attend straight white masculinity: he is exceedingly handsome, possesses a muscular body, attracts beautiful sexual partners, his career requires very little effort or work but makes him wealthy and powerful. He is in a position to indulge every materialistic desire, which includes a regular cocaine supply, a rigorous beauty regime, a spectacular apartment decorated with chic furnishings, and a wardrobe consisting of designer gear.

Perhaps it is because Bateman has everything, but lacks cultural or social importance, that he sets out to be a serial killer. It seems that Bateman is disenchanted with being perceived as ordinary, invisible and (as one of his colleague remarks) "a dork" that he begins his rampage of, not mergers and acquisitions, but "murders and executions." The first person Bateman kills is Paul Allen (Jared Leto), a smug executive who is more successful in Bateman's eyes. For example, Allen is always able to get a table at Dorsia — the most exclusive restaurant in the city — and whenever Bateman has tried he has been unsuccessful. That Allen continually mistakes Bateman for another colleague, Halbestram, only makes matters worse and further illustrates Bateman's social invisibility. When Allen refers to him as Halbestram, Bateman comments in voiceover:

> Allen has mistaken me for this dickhead Marcus Halbestram; it seems logical because Marcus also works at P&P and in fact does the same exact thing

I do. He also has a penchant for Valentino suits and Oliver Peoples glasses. Marcus and I even go to the same barber, although I have a slightly better haircut.

Allen's mistake bothers Bateman, but instead of correcting him, Bateman bludgeons him to death with an axe in a later scene. When Bateman elicits the services of two prostitutes he introduces himself as Paul Allen, delighting in the performance of a man apparently more successful, powerful, sexually potent, and, most importantly, dead.

The temporary blurring of Bateman's identity with Allen's demonstrates how Bateman's identity as interchangeable and somewhat assimilated among his corporate peers to the extent that he is literally and metaphorically indistinguishable. In the film's opening scene, Bateman obsessively grooms himself with the latest range of skin care products, acknowledging in a voiceover that his identity is not grounded or "real":

> There is an idea of a Patrick Bateman; some kind of abstraction, but there is no real me — only an entity, something illusory. And although I can hide my cold gaze and you can shake my hand and feel flesh gripping yours, and maybe you can even sense our lifestyles are comparable, I simply am not there.

Bateman acknowledges he is generic, a product of consumerism in exactly the same way he is a consumer of products: a fact highlighted by the constant reference to brand names and products. The facial products are a metaphor for of Bateman's mask of sanity that is about to slip. The use of facial masks is his flimsy attempt to purify or rejuvenate a self that can never be clean; the products are meant to enhance the face allowing it to shine brighter that before. But Bateman continues to be invisible, concealed, nothing. The way he peels away the facial mask visually suggests he is peeling away a layer of skin, taking off a mask, only to reveal zero-degree nothingness, an identity in crisis and subject to transparency. Richard Dyer argues that

> light shows through white subjects more than through black, so that they appear indeed illuminated and enlightened, but this is also a problem, since it is capable of rendering the white subject as being without substance altogether.[7]

Brightly lit to emphasize Bateman's transparency, the translucent facial mask reinforces his substanceless, revealing an identity defined as "some kind of abstraction ... some kind of entity, only illusory."

Though attractive, Bateman is as generic as the mass-produced consumables he uses, items sold on an empty promise of individuality, authenticity, and exclusivity. The Marxist term "pseudoindividuality" is applicable in that it refers to how mass culture creates a false sense of individuality in consumers through advertising and popular culture, especially in images that directly address the consumer as an individual, when in fact it is speaking to a mass audience. Instead of being noticed, Bateman is one of countless other white executives who live and work in an identical manner. All the white male characters are alike in that they share similar suits, haircuts, accessories, and even names. In one of very few scenes where Bateman is actually on a date with his "supposed fiancé" Evelyn (Reese Witherspoon), he reveals the motivating drive to maintain his lucrative Vice President position is based purely on conformity:

> EVELYN: Patrick we should do it.
> PATRICK: Do what.
> EVELYN: Get married, have a wedding.
> PATRICK: No, I can't take the time off work.
> EVELYN: Your father practically owns the company; you can do anything you like, silly.
> PATRICK: I don't want to talk about it.
> EVELYN: You hate that job anyway; I don't see why you just don't quit.
> PATRICK: Because, I ... want ... to fit ... in.

The extreme levels to which this careerist conformity manifests, is evident when Bateman and his colleagues compete for the most impressive business card. In reality their business cards are almost identical and only differentiated by very subtle gradations of whiteness, paper stock, typography, and embossing. Each card reveals that they all hold a Vice President position, further evidence that his job may be lucrative but hardly unique. When they are flaunting their business cards in a kind of macho "pissing contest," Bateman becomes visibly distressed that his card is not nearly as impressive as Paul Allen's card. Studying the card, Bateman's brow becomes beaded with sweat. In voiceover, he says, "Look at that subtle off-white coloring, the tasteful thickness of it. Oh my God, it even has a watermark." That Bateman is impressed with its watermark is significant, because a watermark by definition is "a figure or design impressed in the fabric in the manufacture of paper and visible when the paper is held to the light."[8] The temporal opacity of a watermark, dependent on light for visual clarity, is an apt metaphor for Bateman's whiteness. The historically embedded connotations of whiteness and light, according to Dyer, have the effect of "advantaging white people in representation and of discriminating between and within them, but also of suggesting a special affinity between them and the light."[9] Bateman may be advantaged in so many ways by his whiteness, or by light, but like a watermark he is rarely "discriminated between and within" his colleagues, affecting a kind of erasure that comes to light as his greatest fear: average-ness. What may seem an advantage for an entire culture of white representation can affect average-ness when individuality becomes an assimilable procedure enacted through maniacal consumption. It is because Bateman is a carbon copy of his colleagues that he is often mistaken for them, a mistake he never rectifies because he acknowledges his invisibility: "I simply am not there."

Disembodied Self-Loathing

Bateman is paradigm of whiteness as invisible. The main reason Bateman is never visible to himself or others is that his identity as a privileged white male is camouflaged by the surfaces around him. His apartment in the American Garden Building on West 81st Street in New York City (though really a set in a Canadian warehouse), is almost entirely white and bathed in sunlight: an over-clean container of surfaces analogous to his own translucent identity. Bateman's privilege and prestige is the very thing that slowly brings him unstuck, forcing a detachment from himself and others. Bateman's detachment and invisibility is emphasized through his confessional voiceover.

The voiceover makes Bateman visible only to the audience — he is still very much invisible to those around him because his identity as a white male already produces him as such. The narration perpetuates Bateman's invisibility *and* interiority because a voiceover is disembodied from its referent: the person to whom it relates. The person is heard but not always seen in a voiceover. As a cultural norm whiteness is similarly disembodied and invisible. Dyer writes, "White people need to see their particularity. In other words, whiteness needs to be made strange."[10] One of the first steps towards making whiteness visible is identifying white as unique, different and not merely a cultural norm.

Bateman does indeed see his particularity — as "illusory" — but never attributes it to his whiteness, let alone his masculinity. Bateman certainly makes strange his identity as he becomes a menacing serial killer, but his whiteness is an assumed norm, in much the same way that his maleness and heterosexuality are assumed to be normative and privileged. At times throughout the film Bateman makes passing comments that call into question the racism or sexism of those around him. In context, his comments are merely hollow sound bytes that are not taken seriously by those to whom he speaks them. Bateman attempts to project an image of social awareness in conversation, but is really just mimicking politically correct views that ultimately aim to counter the culturally central position of white heterosexual masculinity. It is arguable, even with his satirical intentions that anybody really listens to him at all. Perhaps such views are not supposed to be articulated by the straight white male, because in all actuality the assumed privilege of the straight white male is the reason such views have come to pass. Who really wants to listen to the self-aggrandizing claims of a man who, on the surface, appears to have it all? Bateman's slogan-like political correctness is therefore an empty reminder that the exact opposite is true: he is racist, classist, homophobic, and misogynistic. While he may be a racist, he worships African American pop star Whitney Houston, whose song *The Greatest Love of All* appears in the film's diegesis and is accompanied with Bateman's elaborate commentary on its brilliance. As a star who was especially popular in the late eighties setting of *American Psycho*, Whitney is a popular culture phantasm and perhaps not racially marked for her African American identity as much as she is by the seductions of fame and celebrity. Whitney is just as illusory and unreal as Bateman.

Bateman's professed hatred of others is really an implied form of self-loathing. Like an empty brandscape, Bateman is "simply not there." In many respects self-loathing is a defense mechanism that protects the subject from being the target of others' hatred or prejudice. Cultural critic Annalee Newitz writes, "white identity is doomed to remain trapped in a cycle of self-torture and self-celebration."[11] Newitz is pointing out the way in which white identity has become a self-conscious identity, and wracked by internal contradictions. Is it is our upsetting history of white power and racism that has produced such guilt and defensive behavior? Whatever the case, Newitz claims that "white racial self-consciousness is based on various forms of divisiveness and self-loathing."[12] Bateman certainly does not practice a literal form of self-torture, but there is a direct relationship between his fractured view of himself, and the way in which he relates to (or kills) others.

Cut Down to Size

Since its inception, the aim of whiteness studies has been to destabilize the unquestioned, unmarked authority of white identity. Paradigmatically, the figure to bear the interrogative scrutiny of whiteness scholars was the straight white male. Certainly this was not the first time the straight white male was under fire because the feminist project had already ensured balls (if not heads) were rolling. One film that initially resonated with critics of whiteness was *Falling Down* (Joel Schumacher, 1993) because of the way it represented straight white masculinity as an identity in crisis. The protagonist D-Fens (Michael Douglas) is so frustrated and disillusioned that he gradually descends into madness, brought about because of the supposed injustices directed at him. D-Fens is wanted by the police after a series of crimes, however, he cannot reconcile that he is a wanted man: "I'm the bad guy?" D-Fens is incredulous because he passes through black and Hispanic communities in Los

Angeles, where crime is commonplace. Furthermore, D-Fens is an average white working-class male, whose identity revolves around his position as a failed father, husband and worker.

Film critic Carol Clover defines D-Fens within the orbit of the average white male who is perceived as "infinitely endowed with wealth and privilege but in the real individual case, running on fumes: nerves fraying guilt, and down to an insurance policy."[13] More specifically, the average white male is the man who, by virtue of being white, should not be confronted by his normativity; it should be assumed, innate, and unquestioned. Clover writes, "The Average White Male is the guy who theoretically owns the world but in practice, in this account, not only has no turf of his own but has been closed out of the turf of others."[14]

Patrick Bateman, for all intents and purposes is not an average white male. If we compare him to D-Fens, it is obvious that class divides them. Bateman is a self-described yuppie with all the perks of an executive lifestyle, while D-Fens is a working class citizen, who might have occupied relative comfort had it not been for his series of marital and nervous breakdowns. What they do have in common is a crumbling white identity that has somehow traded automatic privilege and power for defensiveness, self-consciousness, paranoia, self-loathing, and madness. Both Bateman and D-Fens are all of these things to lesser or greater degrees, and it is these characteristics that are linked to the way they perceive their identities as straight white males. While Bateman may not on first glance occupy a position of average-ness based on a marker of class, his greatest fear seems to be the fact that he really is just an average guy with money. Take away the cash and very little exists, because as he himself surmises, he is illusory and not there, unless like a watermark he is held to the light for closer inspection and scrutiny.

I am focusing on this concept of average white masculinity in relation to *American Psycho*, because it is a concept that proliferated on screen during the late 1990s and early 2000s when *American Psycho* was adapted for the screen. Edward Norton's character Jack in *Fight Club* (David Fincher, 1999) is comfortable in his Ikea-furnished paradise, but it is this very comfort that induces his pathological insecurities. Kevin Spacey's seemingly ordinary character Lester Burnham in *American Beauty* (Sam Mendes, 1999) also occupies a position of relative comfort in his upper-middle-class environment, but it does not exempt him from a mid-life crisis where he transcends his ordinariness through a drastic and somewhat comic lifestyle makeover. The film's tag-line "Look closer" suggests that one must confront and uncover what lies beneath the surface of ordinary, respectable, average white masculinity. Another film to emerge at this time, *The Man Who Wasn't There* (Joel Coen, 2001), is centered on the persistent ordinariness and metaphoric invisibility of barber Ed Crane (Billy Bob Thorton). While the dominant racial whiteness of this vision of late 1940s suburban America is heightened by the black and white cinematography, it is Ed's acknowledgement that he is ordinary and invisible, that propels the film's drama. In one scene he says in voiceover: "I was a ghost. I didn't see anyone. Nobody saw me. I was the barber." Moreover, the recurring theme of the film is stated in one simple line of dialogue: "the more you look the less you see," which counters *American Beauty*'s insistence that one must "look closer" into themselves if they are to change the banality of their everyday realities.

In *American Psycho* the figure of the average white male is represented through a satire of both corporate male identity and the 1980s — a decade renowned for being characterized by greed. The things this figure might be capable of being or doing are represented through the most extreme worst-case scenario because satire allows such exaggerations to appear plausible, or at least entertaining. On another level *American Psycho* hints at a deepening level of madness for the average white male, whereby all of Bateman's crimes are perhaps imagined — a series of over-the-top crimes unconsciously invented to make him feel more important than he really is. Whenever Bateman is about to murder someone, a shot is included of his image is depicted in a reflective surfaces (mirrors or glass predominately), suggesting his crimes are imagined and illusory. Whether or not his crimes are real or imagined is never really stated, but exists in the film as a tension, a mere possibility. Ellis' novel leans more towards a perception that Bateman imagines his crimes, because as the narrative comes to its rather non-eventful climax, Bateman's hallucinations have greater resonance, and his internal confusion is represented in more explicit terms.

In *Bad Girls and Sick Boys*, feminist cultural critic Linda Kauffman draws analogies between a number of disparate cultural productions by writers, artists and filmmakers, all of whom employ the mechanics of fantasy to represent their subject. In one chapter, "Masked Passions," Kauffman dissects the debates central to the novel *American Psycho*. Written before the novel was adapted for the screen, Kauffman argues against critics who had condemned the novel as pornographic and identifies it more as a satire more about the processes of fantasy and consumption, than it is about serial killing. Kauffman identifies the key tenets of the novel: "the compulsion to repeat, an addiction to representations, and the analogy between serial killing and serial consumption."[15] If *American Psycho* is indeed concerned with the analogy between serial killing and serial consumption, then it is obvious that Bateman's obsession with commodities is, in large part, responsible for his emergent serial killing. He sees them as linked, if not the same thing. They both necessitate the accumulation and fetishization of things or bodies.

Bateman is also addicted to representations, because they enable him to construct an *image* that oscillates between a successful executive and a seemingly successful (if not unstable) serial killer. But it seems that he is also addicted to the popular, though waning representation of straight white masculinity as privileged and powerful by virtue of birth and/or wealth. Initially Bateman unconsciously falls for the trappings of whiteness, and is lured into a false sense of security. It is only when he exhibits signs of being average, that he must execute those who are inferior and visibly average along class lines (prostitutes, the homeless) or those, like his colleague Allen, who challenges Bateman's superiority by emphasizing an identity that doesn't simply fit in as much as it is erased under the weight of being average. For Bateman, average-ness is to be feared at all costs, because if you are rich, straight, white, and male, there is nothing more threatening or humiliating than being cut down to size. And if you have access to a chainsaw and a modicum of bloodlust, being cut down to size is an attractive prospect, not for self, but other.

What *American Psycho* demonstrates is that privileged whiteness is increasingly being represented as an identity that can no longer claim access to privilege simply on the grounds of race. Even when whiteness and privilege go hand in hand, as they do here, it becomes clear that race and class must be separated out and examined for the way they function independent of one another, as much as for the way they overlap. Patrick Bateman's privilege paradoxically marks him as average, rendering his sealed whiteness marked and masked, his visibility threatened by a desire to fit in and become subject to complete erasure. The vapid excess of his white male corporate identity cannot save him from being one of the most average serial killers represented on screen. Bateman may appear to have it all, but as he states himself, "I simply am not there." His privileged whiteness is represented in a manner that is identical to the other white male executives around him — and for this reason, Bateman's identity is an ongoing disappearing act.

Notes

1. Frantz Fanon, *Black Skin, White Masks* (New York: Grove, 1967), 9.

2. *Ibid.*, 51.

3. *Ibid.*, 45.

4. Ruth Frankenberg, "Local Whiteness, Localizing Whiteness," in *Displacing Whiteness: Essays in Social and Cultural Criticism*, ed. Ruth Frankenberg (Durham, NC, and London: Duke University Press, 1997), 7.

5. Rebecca Aanerud, "Fictions of Whiteness: Speaking the Names of Whiteness in U.S. Literature," in *Whiteness: Essays in Social and Cultural Criticism*, ed. Ruth Frankenberg (Durham, NC, and London: Duke University Press, 1997), 37.

6. Diana Fuss, *Identification Papers* (New York and London: Routledge, 1995), 146.

7. Richard Dyer, *White* (London and New York: Routledge, 1997), 110.

8. *Macquarie Essential Dictionary* (Sydney: Macquarie University NSW, 1999), 913.

9. Dyer, *White*, 84.

10. Dyer, *White*, 10.

11. Annalee Newitz, "White Savagery and Humiliation, or A New Racial Consciousness in the Media," in *White Trash: Race and Class in America*, ed. Matt Wray and Annalee Newitz (London and New York: Routledge, 1997), 152.

12. *Ibid.*, 133.

13. Carol Clover, "*Falling Down* and the Rise of the Average White Male," in *Women and Film: A Sight and Sound Reader*, ed. Pam Cook and Philip Dodd (Philadelphia: Temple University Press, 1993), 145.

14. *Ibid.*, 144.

15. Linda Kauffman, *Bad Girls and Sick Boys: Fantasies in Contemporary Art and Culture* (Berkeley: University of California Press, 1998), 255.

Bibliography

Aanerud, Rebecca, "Fictions of Whiteness: Speaking the Names of Whiteness in U.S. Literature." In *Displacing Whiteness: Essays in Social and Cultural Criticism*, ed. Ruth Frankenberg. Durham, NC, and London: Duke University Press, 1997.

Clover, Carol. "*Falling Down* and the Rise of the Average White Male." In *Women and Film: A Sight and Sound Reader*, ed. Pam Cook and Philip Dodd. Philadelphia: Temple University Press, 1993.

Dyer, Richard, *White*. London and New York: Routledge, 1997.

Fanon, Frantz. *Black Skin, White Masks*. New York: Grove, 1967.

Frankenberg, Ruth. "Local Whiteness, Localizing Whiteness." In *Displacing Whiteness: Essays in Social and Cultural Criticism*, ed. Ruth Frankenberg. Durham, NC, and London: Duke University Press, 1997.

Fuss, Diana. *Identification Papers*. New York and London: Routledge, 1995.

Kauffman, Linda. *Bad Girls and Sick Boys: Fantasies in Contemporary Art and Culture*. Berkeley: University of California Press, 1998.

Macquarie Essential Dictionary. Sydney, Australia: Macquarie University, 1999.

Newitz, Annalee. "White Savagery and Humiliation, or a New Racial Consciousness in the Media." In *White Trash: Race and Class in America*, ed. Matt Wray and Annalee Newitz. London and New York: Routledge, 1997.

3

Ambivalence, Desire and the Re-Imagining of Asian American Masculinity in *Better Luck Tomorrow*

Ruthann Lee

I first viewed *Better Luck Tomorrow* (*BLT*) at the Toronto International Film Festival in 2003. During the screening, I experienced a range of conflicting emotions that were largely informed by my social and political location as a queer, feminist, second-generation Asian Canadian–identified video maker and activist: disappointment at the lack of depth in the portrayal of female characters and centrality of a (hetero)masculine narrative in the film — combined with feelings of elation and vindication; I was enthralled at the film's conventionally stylish presentation — its "hip" soundtrack, the slick editing — this certainly was not the gritty independent Asian American cinema of the early 1980s. I took delight in the highly taken-for-granted context and witty in-jokes that could perhaps only speak to a certain Asian diasporic audience and community — interestingly enough, one I felt that I belonged to.

Featuring a mostly Asian American cast, director Justin Lin's independently produced feature length film premiered at the Sundance Film Festival in 2002. It was hailed by well-known U.S. film critics such as Elvis Mitchell and Roger Ebert for "presenting three-dimensional, positive portrayals of Asian American characters."[1] Although it carries a restricted rating, *BLT* has been successfully marketed as a "teen movie" by focusing primarily on the narrative of five Asian American male youth who reside in an upper middle-class area of suburban Southern California. Notably, *BLT* is the first Asian American film to be distributed by MTV films.

What the film and my varied reactions to it signal to me now is an arrival at a significant historical and political conjuncture — an important moment in transnational cultural politics that illustrates the uneven, shifting relations of capital and identities. The production of *BLT* reflects the rise of the visibility of Asian Americans — it is a site of contestation and pleasure where the ambivalence and possibilities for transnational political identities are played out. It can therefore be read as a text for interrogating new performances of cultural citizenship in the United States.[2] If, as Aihwa Ong contends, "diaspora politics describe not an already existing social phenomenon, but rather a social category called into being by newly empowered transnational subjects,"[3] I am interested in how *BLT* can be a site for foregrounding newly organized intersections of race, class, gender, sexuality, and nation within the structures of late global capitalism.

The political visibility of Asian Americans can be interpreted as a historically specific performative act in its transnational processes — which includes the self-representation of Asian Americans in globalized forms of media — that produce citizens as cultural subjects. May Joseph points out that "political visibility makes it possible to stake claims for cultural legitimacy because it operates on a sense of belonging within the state. It deploys strategic identities in the interest of cultural citizenship."[4] Joseph also highlights that

> ...the enactment of political visibility, is neither transparent nor the only avenue through which complex identities express themselves as citizens. On the contrary, such a performance of visibility hinges on the very North American notions of self and its relation to the social [1998, 357].

It is thus important to recognize that individualist notions of entitlement inherently shape and inform Asian American claims to cultural citizenship and thereby affect forms of transnational politics and organizing in significant ways.

If we understand the category of "Asian American" to be a political one, in other words, a constructed diasporic identity — how is it being constituted? Who are these newly empowered transnational subjects of capital that are being imagined and produced? I draw on Avtar Brah's considerations of diaspora whereby "[d]iasporic identities ... are networks of transnational identifications encompassing 'imagined' and 'encountered' communities."[5] According to Brah, the concept of diaspora problematizes the notion of fixed origins while acknowledging a "homing desire" that is distinct from desiring a "homeland."[6] In a similar way, Purnima Mankekar contends that

> [t]he term *disapora* foregrounds a field of relationships with a *homeland*, with the homeland signifying an imaginative, and occasionally imagined, space of

struggle, and ambivalence. Diasporas are marked by shifting relationships with homelands, relationships that are sometimes, but not always, configured in terms of nationhood [1999, 733].

What are the homing desires — the wishes to belong to a home and/or to a nation — projected by the young Asian American men in *BLT*? In what ways are representations of masculinity and inflections of gender and sexuality being deployed in the film? How might these reflect Asian American claims to cultural citizenship — in particular, the struggle for recognition, legitimacy, and cultural capital?

David L. Eng's seminal text, *Racial Castration: Managing Masculinity in Asian America*[7] provides an insightful preliminary investigation of Asian American masculinity by applying psychoanalytic analysis to the reading of various Asian American literary texts. Eng explores how the formation of Asian American sexual identity is haunted by white heteronormative codes and assumptions.[8] Other analyses of Asian American masculinities are presented in volumes such as *Asian American Sexualities: Dimensions of the Gay and Lesbian Experience*, edited by Russell Leong[9] and *Q&A: Queer in Asian America*, edited by David L. Eng and Alice Y. Hom.[10] These groundbreaking collections make crucial links between the theoretical intersections of race and sexuality by investigating the emergence of queer Asian diasporas. However, scholars such as Jasbir K. Puar importantly note that "[t]he genealogies of 'queer' and 'diaspora' share a particular absence: neither foregrounds complicities with concepts of the nation-state."[11] Constructions of queer diasporas may rest upon claims to cultural nationalism via quests for sexual roots and origins. Puar thus advocates the investigation of identity formations that take into account questions of transnationality — to enable more nuanced understandings of the ways in which subjects are *unevenly* produced along the lines of race, class, gender, sexuality and nation.

Oscar V. Campomanes urges scholars to recall that Asian American studies emerged from anti-imperialist movements of the 1960s, specifically in opposition to the Vietnam War.[12] Campomanes insists on the necessity to view American race relations from an international perspective by considering the transnational currency and hegemonic constructions of Asian American identity within the U.S. history of cultural politics:

> We need to chart the powerful effects of these rhetorical conventions in condoning the self-erasure of U.S. imperialism and their consequences for those who were absorbed through neocolonial and postcolonial annexation: Filipinos, Hawaiians and Pacific Islanders from 1898 onward, Southeast Asian refugees in the 1970s (albeit on a different order, but still connected to the flexing of imperial might). This is a task that requires initiative and collabo-

rative work among us, given the politically forbidding and logistically overwhelming aspects of the subject [1997: 538].

For Campomanes, it is necessary to historicize differently located Asian
American subjects in order to challenge the myth of U.S. "innocence" in its
processes of racialization, which are most evident in popular immigrant assim-
ilationist narratives.

BLT privileges certain representations of Asian American identities and
experiences, reflecting a complex host of historical, geo-political and socio-
economic factors that have generated internal hierarchies within the category
"Asian American." These conditions have bracketed certain possibilities of
representation in commercial films such as *BLT*. The prominent representations of privileged classes of Chinese, Korean and Japanese Americans in the
film further obscure the "heterogeneity, hybridity, multiplicity" and differences that constitute Asian American identity.[13] For example, while the most
of the characters' ethnicities are not specifically named in the film, the main
actors are visibly East Asian.[14]

I remain somewhat hesitant to center the analysis of an Asian American
film. As Campomanes notes, scholars of Asian American studies often ignore
the global context of U.S. imperialism in Asian American historiography. The
tendency of Asian American studies has been to "domesticate" questions of
U.S. nationality and nation-building whereby claims upon U.S. nationality
are made on behalf of constituent racial and ethnic difference but only to "contribute" to the exceptionalism of the U.S. as a pluralist "nation of nations."[15]
It should therefore be acknowledged that "the country with which Asian
Americans seek to affiliate by birth and circumstance has been, and continues to be, a major imperialist player on the global scene."[16] Following Grewal and Kaplan, if "the term *transnational* can address the asymmetries of the
globalization process,"[17] I wish to apply a framework of transnationality to
examine the social, political and global economic conditions that have shaped
the emergence of new forms and representations of Asian American masculinity in *BLT*.

In this essay, I take up cultural theorist Gina Marchetti's view that
because films are *discourses*, that is, constructed objects of signification rooted
in particular social environments — their meanings arise from the institutions
(both within the film industry and beyond it) and the historical, cultural, and
social circumstances that frame their production.[18] Cultural texts such as film
provide raw material for the examination of the ideologies of race, gender and
sexuality. Moreover,

> like all discourses, they are concrete manifestations of the ideological sphere
> and share in all of the struggles for power, identity, and influence what polit-

ical theorists like Antonio Gramsci saw as part of the construction of hege-mony within any given society at any particular historical juncture.[19]

I also take into account Purnima Mankekar's argument that "[w]hile political and economic developments do not overdetermine the meanings of cultural texts, they participate in the conditions of possibility for the cre-ation, circulation, and reception of these texts."[20] I contend that *BLT* itself reflects a movement between social history and filmmaking and can be his-torically situated within its material conditions of production and reception.

Asian Boys in White Suburbia: Situating Better Luck

By tracing the incursion of identity politics within American popular culture, I wish to highlight the shifting constructions of diaspora that are being articulated by a new, largely second-generation of Asian American filmmakers. Renee Tajima describes that the origins of Asian American film are linked to the civil rights movement and the Vietnam War, mainly as a cinema of opposition and criticism.[21] Thus, since the late 1960s, the abiding concern of Asian American filmmakers has been to reclaim subjugated his-torical narratives. Not surprisingly, the earliest Asian American films were of the documentary type. Throughout the 1970s, many Asian American film-makers worked in experimental genres; by the mid–1980s, the consolidation of Asian American media organizations promoted Asian American artists to branch into commercial industries with documentary or narrative work. Throughout the 1980s and 1990s, three major styles emerged in Asian Amer-ican films: documentaries made for public television, low-budget feature films with limited theatrical release, and film school products showing more tech-nical accomplishment and potential for mainstream U.S. marketability.[22] This era includes work by second-generation Asian American filmmakers such as Justin Lin, a UCLA School of Film and Television graduate who wrote, pro-duced and directed *BLT*.

Lisa Lowe argues that

> ...the making of Asian American culture may be a much less stable process than unmediated vertical transmission of culture from one generation to another. The making of Asian American culture includes practices that are partly inherited, partly modified as well as partly invented; Asian American culture also includes the practices that emerge in relation to dominant rep-resentations that deny or subordinate Asian and Asian American cultures as "other" [1997, 65].

If second-generation Asian American filmmakers have mediated verti-cal transmissions of culture, they have also been informed by horizontal cultural practices. These horizontal influences might include seemingly disparate social movements — for example, gay and lesbian, labor, feminist, Third World, anti-racist, etc.— that are shaped by competing forms of U.S. multiculturalism, nationalism and notions of citizenship.

How might these identity movements affect the commercial representation of Asians in American film? How might they provide both possibilities and limitations for the (re)imagining of Asian American masculinity in an era of late capitalism? In what ways do the legacies of colonialism and current forms of neo-imperialism manifested through neoliberalism and transnational capital shape this particular story of racialized suburban youth in America?

According to Lin, the premise of *BLT* is

> a film about growing up in modern American suburbia and the angst and anger that are often nurtured in this environment. I was intrigued by how violence goes hand-in-hand with the oppressive nature of identity politics. In my exploration of these themes, I synthesized and incorporated much of what is seen in the news regarding teen violence, and continually found myself drawn to the same notion; that certain acts of violence — particularly those involving youth and/or ethnic minorities stem from a basic human need: the desire to belong.[23]

Lin also explicitly states that

> as an Asian American filmmaker, I wanted to make a movie that was real and non-apologetic, one that resisted the standard stories and stereotypes of recent Asian American cinema.... While the film heavily deals with identity politics, I tried to steer clear of being didactic or polemic.[24]

Rather, the film draws attention to the ironies and contradictions inherent to identity politics for Asian male diasporic subjects in postmodern America, characterized by a mixture of ambivalence and desire.

In brief, *BLT* is about a group of Asian American teenagers who reside in an upper middle-class suburb of L.A. The main perspective of the film is voiced through the character of Ben Manibag (played by Parry Shen), an extremely intelligent 17-year-old who is intent on graduating at the top of his class and gaining acceptance to the best Ivy League university. Rather than being motivated by economic need, Ben leads a double life of mischief and petty crimes along with his two friends, Virgil (played by Jason Tobin), a brilliant yet socially inept character and Virgil's cousin, Han (played by Sung Kang), a brawny, silent type who expresses his frustrations through violence directed at Virgil — in order to diminish the pressures of perfection. Ben, Virgil and Han befriend Daric (played by Roger Fan), the senior valedictorian and another archetypal overachiever and perfectionist. Daric leads the group into an increasingly dangerous set of scams that escalate from selling cheat sheets to stealing computer equipment to eventual dealings in drugs and guns and the group gains notoriety as a suburban gang.

The boys' nemesis is Steve (played by John Cho), the boyfriend of Stephanie. Stephanie is also Ben's romantic interest. Steve attends a nearby private-school and embodies the ideal Asian American man; he is wealthy, accomplished, academically brilliant (having been accepted to numerous Ivy League schools), conventionally attractive, and his (hetero)masculinity is affirmed by his suggested relationship with a white female classmate. When Steve asks the boys to rob his parents' house in order to "give them a wake-up call," the boys collectively decide to teach him a lesson. They deem Steve to be an arrogant, ungrateful and spoiled son. However, the night of the planned confrontation with Steve spins out of control, ending in his very symbolic and horrifically violent murder by the four other boys. The ending of the film remains intentionally open-ended and "morally ambiguous."[25]

I wish to trouble the notion of *BLT* as a "morally ambiguous" representation of Asian American masculinity by foregrounding the current climate of Asian American cultural politics. Like Purnima Mankekar, I am concerned that "the very term diaspora, as deployed in academic and popular discourse, is rooted in discourses of gender and kinship based on heterosexual privilege."[26] Other scholars recognize that the concept of diaspora relies on notions associated with the biological family as representative of community and nation. Because the concept of diaspora is frequently linked to the naturalization of heterosexual relations, I seek to examine how *BLT* both disrupts and maintains complicity with dominant constructions of gender, race, class and sexuality. Thus, I wish to highlight how notions of belonging in the diaspora are constrained and enabled under intensified flows of transnational capital in the contemporary period.

Disrupting the Model Minority Stereotype

An interesting feature of *BLT*'s promotional posters is the labeling of each of the central characters as teen caricatures such as "the boyfriend," "the girlfriend," "the clown," "the muscle," "the mastermind," and "the overachiever." These social archetypes make reference to conventional (white) American teenage stereotypes and transfer them onto an Asian American context. The list perhaps signals a purposeful attempt to shift and expand mainstream imaginings of Asian American identity. Such insertions work to reconfigure and complicate — albeit in very limited ways — dominant understandings of Asian American teenagers in popular culture by supplementing an existing "model minority" stereotype with new ones.

Lisa Lowe, Aihwa Ong and others have discussed the historical consti-
tutions of the "model minority" stereotype by linking it to the emergence of
successful capitalist states in Asia. Such an emergence has necessitated global
restructuring for U.S. capital, exacerbating American anxiety about Asia.
Throughout the twentieth century, the Asian immigrant has been configured
as an internal threat to the national body — the yellow peril — illustrated most
blatantly in the classification of Asian-origin immigrants as nonwhite "aliens
ineligible to citizenship" as articulated in late nineteenth and early twentieth
century U.S. immigration laws. However, this image has more recently shifted
to pose Asians as the domesticated model minority. While on the one hand,
Asian states are conceived of as external competitors in overseas imperial war
and in the global economy, on the other, Asian immigrants remain an essential racialized labor force within the domestic national economy. The racial
formation of Asian Americans has thus been established by state categorization and the social challenges to those categorizations.[27]

The more recent emergence of the "model minority" stereotype that portrays Asian Americans as the most successfully assimilated minority group is
explicitly addressed and contested in *BLT*. Accordingly, the popularity and
commercial success of *BLT* with American film critics and non–Asian audiences could arguably be attributed to this easily-understood and digested
form of opposition, particularly in a mainstream liberal American context.
To refute the film's intentional disruption of the model minority myth of
Asian Americans would be considered not politically correct. Furthermore,
this commercial success reflects Gina Marchetti's view on the historical depictions of Asians in Hollywood cinema:

> Hollywood used Asians, Asian Americans, and Pacific Islanders as signifiers
> of racial otherness to avoid the far more immediate racial tensions between
> blacks and whites or the ambivalent mixture of guilt and enduring hatred
> toward Native American and Hispanics [1993, 6].

Although *BLT* provides tentative opportunities to explore the more
volatile and complicated issues of relationality among differently racialized
diasporic groups in the U.S., on the whole, inter-racial relationships depicted
in the film fail to exceed a normative white-Asian binary.

Bad Boys? Emerging Asian American Masculinities

In *BLT*, the boys' parents (who are presumably first-generation Asian
American immigrants) are conspicuously absent from the film; however, their
influence is indicated in various ways, perhaps most obviously in the way that
social mobility is understood by their sons to be acquired through higher
education. As Ben states in an early voice-over, "Our straight A's were our

alibis, our passports to freedom. Going to a study group could get us out of the house until four in the morning. As long as our grades were there, we were trusted." Virgil and Han's characters give further indication of the boys' sense of loyalty toward their parents (for example, Virgil articulates enormous fear of his father's reaction to the idea that he could be legally arrested for participating in the beating of another student; Han's brusque response to Steve's plan to betray his parents is: "that dude's fucked!").

In the film, Daric recognizes that identity politics can work to his advantage. For Daric, acquiring social status is a game. He thus chastises Ben for working at a local fast-food joint and invites him to participate in a money-making scheme of selling and distributing cheat sheets to other students. Daric also crushes Ben's sense of pride at making the high school basketball team by writing a school newspaper article about affirmative action and school sports, for which he wins a journalism award. Daric informs Ben that it is obvious that he is the "token Asian" on the team, destroying Ben's innocent belief in American meritocracy.

Daric lives alone in a large house; we are informed by Virgil that Daric's parents reside in Vancouver, reflecting what Ong describes to be an increasingly common family arrangement of "flexible citizenship" among affluent classes of Hong Kong professional migrants.[28] All of the main characters in *BLT* reside in an upper middle-class suburb of L.A., demonstrating the establishment of Asian communities in formerly white neighborhoods. Ong also notes:

> By locating themselves in white suburbs rather than in Chinatown, and by making a living not as restaurant workers but as Pacific Rim executives, well-to-do Asian newcomers breach the spatial and symbolic borders that have disciplined Asian Americans and kept them on the margins of the American nation. This "out-of-placeness" of new Asian immigrants reinforces the public anxiety over the so-called thirdworldization of the American city, a term that suggests both economic and ethno-racial heterogeneity, over which white Americans are losing control [1999, 100].

In *BLT*, this white American suburban anxiety is reflected in a scene where the boys arrive uninvited to a neighborhood party. Although the boys are mocked by a racially mixed group of young men from their school (interestingly, there is another visibly male Asian student in the group), the group is clearly led by a white student who taunts Ben's group by inquiring why they're not "at Bible study." When the white student directly targets Daric with the racist insult: "Who are you trying to be? A Chinese Jordan?" Daric becomes enraged and draws out a gun, which he points at the white student and the crowd of observers. A fight ensues and the white student is left unconscious. All four of the boys participate in his beating.

At first glance, the boys' possession of a gun can be read simply to function as phallic symbol — a compensatory device that stands in for the lack of masculine power held by Asian American men and an indication of the social capital that the boys lack. Following Ong,

> [l]ong viewed as coolies, houseboys, and garment workers, but now upgraded to members of a law-abiding and productive model minority, each new wave of Asian immigrants has to contend with the historical construction of Asian others as politically and cultural subordinate subjects [1999, 101].

Ong further contends that many Asian Americans seek to convert symbolic capital into cultural capital in the attempts to attain higher social standing in Anglo-American circles. This includes the acquisition of class markers, such as name-brand clothing, automobiles, real estate, art and other kinds of property. The arrival of wealthy Asian immigrants poses challenges to white Americans' understanding of themselves as privileged American citizens, who should take no back seat to foreigners, especially Asians. But, as Ong asks, "will the accumulation of cultural, and not just economic, capital by these well-heeled immigrants change such nativist perceptions?"[29]

In addition to the phallic symbol of desired normative masculinity, the boys' possession of the gun can also be read as a reflection of how forms of white militarized (hetero)masculinity are rewarded and sanctioned by neo-imperial states. As M. Jacqui Alexander argues, advanced-capitalist states systematically construct discourses and policies to consolidate heterosexism and white supremacy in ways that actively socialize loyal citizens.[30] In the film, the gun also stereotypically reveals how dominant constructions of masculinity in the U.S. are organized hierarchically according to race. After the fight scene, the boys quickly escape from the party in Han's car. In this getaway scene, another vehicle with two racialized — possibly Latino — young men pull up and travel beside Han's car. Virgil (who remains oblivious to the interaction occurring with the young men in the other vehicle) maintains a run-on dialogue that presents the Asian boys' initial feelings of exhilaration and power. However, when the Latino boys make threatening gestures and flash their (larger) gun at Han, Daric, and Ben, the Asian boys are made aware of their comparatively inferior level of masculinity. This scene reveals the relational aspect of racialized masculinities between men and the constructed and performed nature of such identities. Arguably, however, the scene may also reinforce the "hyper-machismo" stereotype of Latino males.

Steve repeatedly requests the purchase of a gun from the other boys in the film but significantly never receives one — his character doesn't require a symbolic device to stand in for masculinity. However, Steve indicates a feeling of resentment about his subject positioning. During a scene in which Ben accompanies Steve to a batting cage, Steve asks Ben if he is happy. Ben replies that he doesn't know and throws the question back to Steve — is Steve happy? Steve bitterly replies, "I'm very happy. Isn't it obvious? I have everything: loving parents, top grades, Ivy League scholarships, Stephanie.... So fucking happy, I can't stop it." Steve explains: "It's a never-ending cycle. When you've got everything you want, what's left? You can't settle for being happy, that's a fucking trap. You've gotta take your life into your own hands, you've gotta break the cycle. That's what it is. Breaking the cycle." For Steve, breaking the cycle turns on a plan of self-destruction. Maintaining the power associated with an idealized Asian American heteromasculine identity thus propels the boys' unexpected and unsettling journey, resulting in Steve's tragically symbolic murder.

Racialized Heteronormativity and Competing Masculinities

Gina Marchetti describes that a vast majority of the historical depictions of Asian sexuality in Hollywood film can be inextricably linked to "yellow peril" ideologies. One of the most powerful characteristics of these yellow peril discourses is the sexual threat of contact between the races. Early representations of Asian male sexuality in Hollywood feature scenarios that depict fantasies of the Asian male as a danger to white women, which, as explained by Marchetti "tend to link together national-cultural and personal fears, so that the rape of the white woman becomes a metaphor for the threat posed to Western culture as well as rationalization for Euroamerican imperial ventures in Asia."[31] Hollywood film narratives also typically illustrate fantasies of the exotic Asian woman luring and seducing the white male. Representations of sexuality have thus been a crucial aspect of defining Asian otherness in film. *BLT* works to both reinforce and reconfigure these representations in various ways.

In a sense, the symbolic threat of the Asian American male to white women is reconfigured in *BLT*. The white woman appears to reconstitute Asian American masculinity in the film when the boys hire a white female sex worker as Ben's seventeenth birthday gift. The sex worker takes full charge in the scene, informing Ben of the rules of her practice, including the fact that she always leads. The white woman is clearly in control of her own sexuality and Ben willingly accepts. Her overt sexuality confers the boys' sexual innocence and passivity. Later in the scene, the failure of Asian American men to attain dominant (hetero)masculinity is re-emphasized when Virgil pulls out his gun on the sex worker, who subsequently flees from the hotel room.

The film thus reinscribes more recent configurations of racialized sexu-

ality in which Asian men are imagined as largely asexual, as described by
Richard Fung:

> Asian men ... have been consigned to one of two categories: the egghead/wimp,
> or — in what may be analogous to the lotus blossom-dragon lady dichotomy —
> the kung fu master / ninja / samurai. He is sometimes dangerous, sometimes
> friendly, but almost always characterized by Zen asceticism. So whereas, as
> Fanon tells us, "the Negro is eclipsed. He is turned into a penis. He *is* a penis,"
> the Asian man is defined by a striking absence down there [1996, 183].

In the film, we are told that Stephanie is rumored to have starred in a
pornographic video. Virgil and Ben watch the video but they are unable to
discern the truth of the matter. Aside from this reference (which is presumably left unresolved as a means of providing comedic relief), Asian women
are essentially not portrayed in sexually explicit ways in *BLT*, particularly in
relation to white women. I relate this observation to Gayatri Gopinath's con-
tention that heterosexual women have come to embody the idea of the pure,
traditional home in discourses of diaspora. Gopinath argues that women's
bodies are crucial to nationalist discourses; in particular, the regulation of
women's sexuality by men can be viewed as an effort to preserve and maintain cultural essence and identity.[32] We can see that in *BLT,* "discourses of
belonging and nationhood are fundamentally gendered and (hetero)sexual-
ized."[33] In particular, Ben's desire and protectionism for Stephanie[34] can be
read as his desire to find a "home" and/or nation in attempt to secure his own
(hetero)masculine identity as an Asian American male diasporic subject.

In a related way, Steve's heterosexuality is carefully monitored by Ben,
who chastises Steve for having a secret relationship with "Barbie." Ben's disapproval of Steve's relationship with a white woman indicates a cultural nationalist perspective, in which loyalty to "Asian" culture is conflated with the
responsibility of reproducing community and the nation through heterosexual relationships.

Unearned Innocence and Ambivalent Desires

In *BLT,* paradoxes of racial stereotyping are revealed in the fact that the
boys are never charged for their violent assault on the white male student at
the party. Ben is at first convinced that the four of them will be caught, since
most of school is aware of the incident. However, in the following week, the
boys are never accused of the crime. In a sense, the Asian American model
minority stereotype has worked to their favor by granting them unearned
innocence.

In the same way, the boys collectively maintain their silence about Steve's murder. Towards the end of the film, however, Virgil attempts to commit suicide. At the hospital, Daric approaches Ben in a distraught and frantic manner, clearly preoccupied with fears of being caught for Steve's killing. In this scene, Ben is interestingly positioned as the morally superior character in relation to Daric. Ben's closing voice-over indicates that he feels complacent about not knowing what will happen next and merely hopes for better luck in the future. His momentary sense of security, however, seems to rely on the awareness that keeping silent will work in his favor — the boys will most likely not be suspected of murder or violence, given their previous experience of failing to encounter accusations of criminality. Ben's moral ambivalence signals his position of privilege in relation to other racialized subjects and reflects conflicting nationalist and diasporic logics that configure Asian American men as ambivalent citizen-subjects.

The destruction of Steve's character — who, by expressing the most cynical view of social conformity, had significant potential to become an active social critic in the film — signals some disheartening limits and constraints of a (re)imagined Asian American diasporic masculinity in the film.

Conclusion: Homoerotics and the Unspeakable

By way of conclusion, I wish to read into more subversive possibilities and what I will refer to as "unspeakable" sexualities in *BLT*. There are definitive moments of homoeroticism between the characters in various scenes, suggesting some insurgent potential in the representation of Asian American male identity and understandings of subjectivity. Steve's sexuality, in particular, is ambiguously portrayed. For example, during the scene in which Steve expresses disinterest in taking Stephanie to her high school formal, Ben inquires whether or not Steve is "a fag or something." Rather than replying directly to Ben's question, Steve responds with a steady gaze and asks, rhetorically "what do you think?" Steve also makes several suggestive homoerotic remarks towards Daric in the film, such as "how's your stroke?"

While I have argued that the overall effect of representation in *BLT* has reinscribed dominant understandings of (hetero)masculinity in the Asian American diaspora, I have also tried to show that such representations have themselves been shaped by a broader historical and socio-economic context of Asian American cultural politics in the contemporary period. As Russell Leong remarks:

> In the United States, the myth of Asian Americans as a homogenous, heterosexual "model minority" population since the 1960s has worked against exploration into the varied nature of our sexual drives and gendered diversity. Asian

Americans "are presumed to practice the typical values of individualism, self-reliance, the work ethic, discipline, and so on." Our mythical successful assimilation is used to pit us against other minority groups such as African Americans and Latinos. In terms of sexuality, the model minority view simply denies diversity as an issue [1996, 3].

Additionally, following M. Jacqui Alexander's insight in that "loyalty to the nation as citizen is perennially colonized within reproduction and heterosexuality,"[35] it seems unlikely that the project of making Asian American homosexual identity intelligible to a commercial audience in the U.S. could be imagined in this particular film. However, I wish to pursue these alternative readings of Asian American masculinity that are presented in *BLT* such that possibilities for understandings of male homoeroticism and homosexuality are not foreclosed.[36]

In this story of racialized suburban male youth in the U.S, we can trace ways in which the legacies of colonialism and current forms of neo-imperialism produce particular forms of Asian American masculinity that privilege certain imaginings of gender, family, ethnicity, and nationality. These constructions are inherently shaped by Asian American cultural politics, which contest historically constituted stereotypes of Asian American men. However, the film simultaneously reinscribes normative, hierarchical and exclusionary forms of cultural identity. Grewal and Kaplan importantly note that "social and political movements are cosmopolitan and class-based, generating new sites of power rather than simply forms of resistance."[37] This investigation has sought to think through and map out some of the uneven and complex ways that new subjects emerge in an era of late global capitalism. By locating and deconstructing representations of Asian American masculinity in commercial film, I have aimed to trouble and complicate the rather static cultural nationalist conceptions of racial identity prevalent in Asian American discourses that center the heterosexual, middle-class, American-born, English-speaking male subject. The ambivalent positioning and desires expressed by subjects in *BLT* thus illustrate a number of limitations but present some subversive possibilities for the (re)imagining of Asian American diasporic masculinity.

I would like to thank Jesook Song and Alissa Trotz for their insights and feedback on earlier versions of this essay.

Notes

1. See the film's website, which features extensive promotional material, commentary by the director, and an interactive forum for movie fans at http://www.betterluckto morrow.com.

2. In a U.S./Latino context, Renato Rosaldo (1999) has coined the term "cultural citizenship" to describe a negotiation over belonging, and over political power within a multi-ethnic, modern nation-state. I use the term "cultural citizenship" to refer specifically to struggles of self-identified and self-organized diasporic communities to make interventions in the larger U.S. cultural domain. This relates to the older concept of identity politics, which emerged from post–World War II civil rights movements and can be simply defined as the self-naming and self-identification of individuals and communities around a common identity category in order to make a political intervention. However, unlike identity politics, interventions made on behalf of cultural citizenship are not necessarily focused on the state, but can also encompass broader struggles over issues of representation. See Monika Kin Gagnon (2000) for a useful and related discussion of art and "cultural race politics" in a Canadian context.

3. Aihwa Ong, "Cyberpublics and Diaspora Politics Among Transnational Chinese," in *Interventions* 5, no. 1 (2003), 88.

4. May Joseph. "Transatlantic Inscriptions: Desire, Diaspora, and Cultural Citizenship," in *Talking Visions: Multicultural Feminism in a Transnational Age*, ed. Ella Shohat (New York: MIT Press, 1998), 357.

5. Avtar Brah, *Cartographies of Diaspora: Contesting Identities* (London and New York: Routledge, 1996), 197.

6. *Ibid.*, 197.

7. David L. Eng, *Racial Castration: Managing Masculinity in Asian America* (Durham, NC: Duke University Press, 2001).

8. As pointed out by Grewal and Kaplan, however, although psychoanalysis can be a powerful interpretive tool, it "has struggled with its universalizing tendencies" (2001, 667). Moreover, if the study of transnational relationships addresses questions related to the political economy of the family, psychoanalysis is limited by its Eurocentric biases that "can often be marshaled to reproduce nationalist formations" (Grewal and Kaplan 2001, 668). Eng's analysis of the constitution of Asian American masculinity is largely constrained by a nationalist framework in his examination of social relations.

9. Russell Leong, ed. *Asian American Sexualities: Dimensions of the Gay & Lesbian Experience* (New York: Routledge, 1996).

10. David L. Eng and Alice Y. Hom, eds. *Q & A: Queer in Asian America* (Philadelphia: Temple University Press, 1998).

11. Jasbir K. Puar, "Transnational Sexualities: South Asian (Trans)nation(alism)s and Queer Diasporas," in *Q & A: Queer in Asian America*, ed. David L. Eng and Alice Y. Hom (Philadelphia: Temple University Press, 1998), 407.

12. Oscar V. Campomanes, "New Formations of Asian American Studies and the Question of U.S. Imperialism," in *positions* 5, no. 2 (Fall 1997): 523–550.

13. Lisa Lowe, *Immigrant Acts: On Asian American Cultural Politics* (Durham, NC, and London: Duke University Press, 1996).

14. The film informs us that the character of Stephanie (played by Karin Anna Cheung)— who is labeled "the girlfriend" on the movie bill — is Chinese American; her ethnicity is subtly revealed when her character reveals a newly acquired tattoo that inscribes her "Chinese name." Notably, however, Stephanie is a Chinese American adoptee — we are shown that Stephanie was adopted by a wealthy white American family. While this particular storyline is not explored in much depth within the film, it does propose significant complications to more conventional Asian American identity narratives and underscores a powerful transnational relationship entailing China and the United States, for which there is an emerging body of feminist literature (for example, see the collection edited by Toby Alice Volkman, 2005).

15. Campomanes, 530.

16. *Ibid.*, 533.

17. Inderpal Grewal and Caren Kaplan, "Global Identities: Theorizing Transnational Studies of Sexuality," in *GLQ: A Journal of Lesbian and Gay Studies* 7 no. 4 (2001), 664.

18. Gina Marchetti, *Romance and the "Yellow Peril:" Race, Sex, and Discursive Strategies in Hollywood Fiction* (Berkeley: University of California Press, 1993).

19. Marchetti, 7.

20. Mankekar, 748.

21. Renee Tajima, "Moving the Image: Asian American Independent Filmmaking 1970–1990," in *Moving the Image: Independent Asian Pacific American Media Arts*, ed. Russell Leong (Los Angeles: UCLA Asian American Studies Centre and Visual Communications, 1991): 10–33.

22. For an extensive historical review of Asian American independent film and video, see the volume edited by Leong (1991)—particularly the essay by Tajima (1991).

23. See http://www.betterlucktomorrow.com/html/index.php?id=about&ImgId=05&banid=notes.

24. *Ibid.*

25. Writer and director Justin Lin has commented: "It was never my interest to show cause and effect, right and wrong. Instead, I wanted to be true to the characters. The morally ambiguous denouement is directly related to the moral confusion of the characters. More than that, however, it was extremely important for me to create a dialogue after the film's closing credits rather than give the viewer a traditional narrative closure. I'd much prefer the film to raise questions rather than present some sort of "answer" (see http://www.betterlucktomorrow.com/html/index.php?id=about&ImgId=05&banid=notes).

26. Mankekar, 734.

27. Aihwa Ong, *Flexible Citizenship: The Cultural Logics of Transnationality* (Durham, NC, and London: Duke University Press, 1999).

28. *Ibid.*

29. *Ibid.*,101.

30. M. Jacqui Alexander, "Erotic Autonomy as a Politics of Decolonization: An Anatomy of Feminist and State Practice in the Bahamas Tourist Economy," in *Feminist Genealogies, Colonial Legacies, Democratic Futures,* ed. M. Jacqui Alexander and Chandra Mohanty (New York: Routledge, 1997): 63–100.

31. Marchetti, 3.

32. Gayatri Gopinath, "Nostalgia, Desire, Diaspora: South Asian Sexualities in Motion," in *Theorizing Diaspora*, ed. Jana Evans. Braziel and Anita Mannur (Oxford, UK: Blackwell, 2003), 263.

33. Mankekar, 734.

34. Interestingly, although Stephanie is neither portrayed as stereotypically submissive nor domineering or evil, her character development is largely limited to constructing the (hetero)sexualities of Ben and Steve.

35. Alexander, 64.

36. And here I will make note of Eng and Hom's important observation concerning mainstream cultural representations of Asian American diasporic identities: "where dominant images of the emasculated Asian American men and hyperheterosexualized Asian American women collide — the Asian American lesbian disappears" (1999, 1).

37. Grewal and Kaplan, 671.

Bibliography

Alexander, M. Jacqui. "Erotic Autonomy as a Politics of Decolonization: An Anatomy of Feminist and State Practice in the Bahamas Tourist Economy." In *Feminist Genealo-*

gies, Colonial Legacies, Democratic Futures, ed. M. Jacqui Alexander and Chandra Mohanty. New York: Routledge, 1997, 63–100.

Better Luck Tomorrow, http://www.betterlucktomorrow.com [accessed April 8, 2005].

Campomanes, Oscar.V. "New Formations of Asian American Studies and the Question of U.S. Imperialism." *positions* 5, no. 2 (Fall 1997): 523–550.

Eng, David L. *Racial Castration: Managing Masculinity in Asian America*. Durham, NC: Duke University Press, 2001.

_____, and Alice Y. Hom, eds. *Q & A: Queer in Asian America*. Philadelphia: Temple University Press, 1998.

Fung, Richard. "Looking for My Penis: The Eroticized Asian in Gay Video Porn." In *Asian American Sexualities: Dimensions of the Gay & Lesbian Experience*. Russell Leong, ed. New York: Routledge, 1996, 181–198.

Gopinath, Gayatri. "Nostalgia, Desire, Diaspora: South Asian Sexualities in Motion." In *Theorizing Diaspora*, eds. Jana Evans Braziel and Anita Mannur. Oxford, UK: Blackwell, 2003, 261–279.

Grewal, Inderpal and Caren Kaplan. "Global Identities: Theorizing Transnational Studies of Sexuality." *GLQ: A Journal of Lesbian and Gay Studies* 7, no. 4 (2001): 663–679.

Joseph, May. "Transatlantic Inscriptions: Desire, Diaspora, and Cultural Citizenship." In *Talking Visions: Multicultural Feminism in a Transnational Age*, ed. Ella Shohat. New York: MIT Press, 1998, 357–367.

Kin Gagnon, Monica. *Other Conundrums: Race, Culture, and Canadian Art*. Vancouver: Arsenal Pulp, 2000.

Leong, Russell, ed. *Asian American Sexualities: Dimensions of the Gay & Lesbian Experience*. New York: Routledge, 1996.

_____. *Moving the Image: Independent Asian Pacific American Media Arts*. Los Angeles: UCLA Asian American Studies Center and Visual Communications, 1991.

Lowe, Lisa. *Immigrant Acts: On Asian American Cultural Politics*. Durham, NC, and London: Duke University Press, 1996.

Mankekar, Purnima. "Brides Who Travel: Gender, Transnationalism, and Nationalism in Hindi Film." *positions* 7, no. 3 (1999): 731–761.

Marchetti, Gina. *Romance and the "Yellow Peril": Race, Sex, and Discursive Strategies in Hollywood Fiction*. Berkeley: University of California Press, 1993.

Ong, Aihwa. "Cyberpublics and Diaspora Politics Among Transnational Chinese." *Interventions* 5, no. 1 (2003): 82–100.

_____. *Flexible Citizenship: The Cultural Logics of Transnationality*. Durham, NC, and London: Duke University Press, 1999.

Puar, Jasbir. K. "Transnational Sexualities: South Asian (Trans)nation(alism)s and Queer Diasporas." In *Q&A: Queer in Asian America*, eds. David L. Eng and Alice Y. Hom. Philadelphia: Temple University Press, 1998, 405–422.

Rosaldo, Renato. "Cultural Citizenship, Inequality, and Multiculturalism." In *Race, Identity, and Citizenship: A Reader,* eds. R. Torres, et al. London: Blackwell, 1999, 254–61.

Tajima, Renee. "Moving the Image: Asian American Independent Filmmaking 1970–1990," In *Moving the Image: Independent Asian Pacific American Media Arts*, ed. Russell Leong. Los Angeles, UCLA Asian American Studies Center and Visual Communications, 1991, 10–33.

Volkman, Toby Alice, ed. *Cultures of Transnational Adoption*. London: Duke University Press, 2005.

4

The Black Interior, Reparations and African American Masculinity in *The Wiz*

Jesse Scott

The very essence of the male animal, from the bantam rooster to the Four-Star-General, is to strut.

Daniel Patrick Moynihan, The Negro Family:
The Case for National Action[1]

The Wiz is a massive pop-cultural coda to the black civil rights movement. It feels like the celebratory hurrah of Hollywood late-coming role in a "Sesame Street" style of affirmative action and it moves to the last few beats of funky R&B before Spike Lee and the hip-hop revolution takes over.

Hank Stuever, "Michael Jackson on Film:
No Fizz After The Wiz"

Daniel Patrick Moynihan's *The Negro Family: The Case for National Action* (1965) commonly referred to as The Moynihan Report helped to initiate what has become "a perennial crisis of black masculinity whose imagined solution is a proper affirmation of black male authority"(Harper x). Subsequently, African American men have come to be represented as simultaneously endangered and endangering — as victims of and menaces to U.S. society. These warnings have help develop a popular cultural discourse that represents the vast majority of African American men as leading "sorry" lives. Yet, there are thousands upon thousands of ordinary African American men, who remain largely invisible in our popular cultural discourse. Even as academic study about African American men steadily increases, the visibility of the ordinary African American man remains nearly invisible. As a recent series, "Being a Black Man," published in *The Washington Post* in 2006 observes:

More than 50 years after the publication of Ralph Ellison's *Invisible Man*, black men appear more visible than ever — a freshman senator from Illinois, Barack Obama, is the American Idol of national politics, and Will Smith is perhaps the most bankable star in Hollywood. Yet black men who put their kids through college by mopping floors, who sit at home reading Tennyson at night, who wear dreadlocks but design spacecraft, say it sometimes seems as if the world doesn't believe they exist [Ballard and Roberts].

Being an ordinary African American man, as *The Washington Post* series suggests, does not offer one greater visibility and seemingly does little to displace the notion that African American men lives are the source of a perpetual crisis that threatens not only their communities, but the nation at large. *The Washington Post* series does not and nor do I intend to suggest that there is not a population of African American men who are indeed in some form of crisis, but that the popular cultural discourse does not acknowledge the diversity of African American men's lived experiences. The challenge, then, for ordinary African American men is to identify a space beyond the "sociological and fantasy discourses," where they are most frequently imagined, in which they can embrace what they know to be true and meaningful about their existence (Alexander 2). Poet and scholar, Elizabeth Alexander identifies one such space in her idea and/or metaphor of the black interior which she defines as a:

> metaphysical space beyond the black public everyday toward power and wild imagination that black people ourselves know we possess but need to be reminded of ... tapping into this black imaginary helps [African Americans] envision what [they] are not meant to envision: complex black selves, real and enactable black power [2].

Alexander's black interior advocates introspection as a reparative endeavor that allows African Americans to survey their public and private lives and carry out the imaginative and critical work necessary to heal and sustain African Americans living in a racially hostile terrain. While Alexander specifically address the black interior's usefulness to artists, the black interior constitutes a crucial reparative space worthy of being pursued by all African Americans and perhaps especially so for ordinary African American men.

Throughout this essay, I use the terms reparation(s), reparative and remedy throughout this essay in light of developments in the late 1990s when scholarly attention to and activism for reparations for African Americans' experiences of slavery and Jim Crow proliferated and entered the public discourse. As a result of these developments, the popular, though misinformed, an understanding of the various campaigns for reparations are primarily about the pursuit of money has taken hold in the public imaginary. However, campaigns for reparations have never been just about money but instead, about efforts to repair all facets of African Americans' lives. In many ways some of the most critical reparations are those that cannot be secured through the nation's courts or its legislature but instead, are self-made repairs that require, in this essay, that African American men identify and dwell in the black interior. Alexander's black interior does not advocate embracing patriarchal ideals of masculinity as the way to affirm African American men, thus this concept challenges prevailing notions that the remedy for African Americans' and their families is the ascendancy of African American men as suggested in the above epigraph whose source is Daniel Patrick Moynihan's infamous *The Black Family: The Case for National Action.*

Though seldom invoked directly, Moynihan's report and its influence continues to resonate in contemporary conversations about the condition of African American families and especially African American men some forty years later. Popular representations of African American men reiterate Moynihan's belief that the African American family is a "tangled web of pathology." The source of this pathology is African American women and mothers who prevent African American men from being the bantam roosters and Four-Star-Generals that Moynihan identifies as the essence of normative masculinity. In Moynihan's view, it is African American men and the nation who suffer the most from this so-called black pathology. Since Moynihan's influential report was released the popular representation of African American has linked African American men to the term crisis. This representation has so thoroughly saturated the contemporary public discourse about African American men that the so-called crisis has become regarded as an incurable condition that has created a significant population of sorry African American men.

This essay explores the so-called sorry state of African American men by examining the 1978 film, *The Wiz,* which has not received the critical engagement that it deserves, as a film that attempts to represent the difficulties that ordinary African American encounter as they pursue identifies that accurately reflect they are and who they aspire to be as men.[2] While *The Wiz* reflects the influence of Moynihan's claims about African American women and men, both films suggest that African Americans and particularly African American men need something more Moynihan's remedy of patriarchy expressed through avian and militaristic metaphors, if ordinary African American men are to be healthy, affirmed and successful men, fathers and husbands.

Rerouting the Yellow Brick Road

Contrary to the celebratory applause that my epigraph offers, *The Wiz* was not treated as a popular cultural coda for the 1970s, when it was released; nor has it been regarded as such in African American film criticism. Despite the critical dismissal of *The Wiz*, the film offers an important allegorical treatment of ordinary African Americans, but particularly African American men living in the wake of the Civil Rights movement.[3] The film registers the paradox of the 1970s for many African Americans who "find themselves more highly integrated into American life more than ever before, and yet in many ways, thoroughly as segregated as at any time during this century, wealthier than at any time in our history, yet increasingly economically isolated and impoverished; more visible in public life, yet more alienated and angry" (Holt).

This analysis of African Americans' social and economic position in the 1970s resonates with the findings in *The Washington Post*'s 2006 series, "Being A Black Man." In light of these prolonged anxieties about the lived experiences of ordinary African American men, it is crucial to consider the implications of changing the film's setting from Kansas to Harlem, with Oz functioning as New York City at large in the 1978 cinematic adaptation of the original 1975 Broadway production of *The Wiz*. The Broadway production retains the original setting of Kansas that appears in both Frank Baum's 1900 book, *The Wonderful Wizard of Oz* and its adaptation into the film *The Wizard of Oz* in 1939. *The Wiz* relocates the narrative's setting from Kansas to Harlem and as result not only does the film signify on Baum's original narrative but also highlights the significance of African Americans' migration to and experience of the urban north.

In the African American literary and filmic imaginary, "Harlem has been a metonymic projection into the dimension of meaning articulated in the vocabulary of place ... a cultural text for continual retelling and exegesis, palimpsest or scriptural field for literary figuration" (DeJongh 210). Just as *The Wizard of Oz* calls for a reexamination of what the American Dream means for Midwestern agrarians, *The Wiz* explores what the American Dream and its pursuit entails for urban African Americans. The relocation from Kansas to Harlem, then, also seeks to debunk the myth of the urban north as more promising than the agrarian south, from which African Americans had migrated en masse in the 1920s and 1940s. *The Wiz* suggests that African Americans carry the scars and the idea of racism in their bodies. In the film Oz — New York City — constitutes an attempt to imagine a space where racism does not and thus, a space in which both opportunities for self-affirmation and upward mobility exist for African Americans. However, in *The Wiz*, Harlem and other locations within New York City becomes a space that imprisons those such as Tinman, Cowardly Lion, Scarecrow and Herman Smith/The Wiz. For Dorothy, who has never been south of a 125thstreet, Oz becomes the space where she is sent to repair her views of family and motherhood.[4] *The Wiz*, with its all African American cast, also suggests that inhabiting such a space does not displace the implications of the ways in which the intersections of race, gender and class have always impacted African Americans' lives. Thus Dorothy's ambivalence about motherhood combined with the sorry condition of African American male analogs reflect Moynihan's anxiety over the supposed displacement of the appropriate gender roles in African American families, a displacement that left African American men injured and thus unable enjoy the natural right of all men to strut like bantam roosters and Four-Star-Generals.

If Only I Could Be a Rooster

Moynihan's reference to bantam roosters and Four-Star Generals provides a useful lens to interpret Scarecrow, Tinman, and Cowardly Lion's sense of injury and Dorothy's response to these injured African American male analogs in *The Wiz*. Even as *The Wiz* reflects the influence of Moynihan's reading of African American men existing in a state of crisis, the film attempts to problematize Moynihan's remedy, aspiring to embrace patriarchy, as the appropriate or even viable remedy for African Americans. While Moynihan acknowledges that racism played a critical role in producing the crisis that he identifies, he fails to recognize that patriarchy does not adequately address racial injury as much as it exacerbates, what at the time of the report's release were, largely unacknowledged gender dynamics produced by African American men an women's gendered experience of slavery, Jim Crow and contemporary expressions of racism more generally. Ultimately, *The Wiz* read as a cultural narrative is not invested in Dorothy's self-affirmation, as the film's opening sequences suggest, but rather what Moynihan's report advocated, the repair of African American men. Dorothy character, then, becomes a means for representing the healthy relationship between African American women as mothers and wives with African American men. Dorothy's successful return home depends upon her ability to repair her companions, Scarecrow, Tinman, and Cowardly Lion and to dispose of the powerful and destructive African American matriarch, represented through the character of Evillene, in *The Wiz*. What follows, then, is a close and intertextual reading of the relationship between the African American male analogs and Dorothy as they journey to what the group has been encouraged to believe is the great and powerful patriarch, The Wiz.

A Mind Is a Terrible Thing to Waste

Surrounded by abandoned tenement buildings, trash and a gang — The Crows, Scarecrow is ensnared in a seemingly hopeless situation. Daily, Scarecrow begs The Crows to liberate him so that he can pursue his quest for a brain, intellect development. The Crows ignore Scarecrow's requests and mock the western philosophy, strips of shredded books used as his stuffing, that Scarecrow espouses as rationale for why he should be emancipated from their tyranny. The scene invokes African American experiences in the south and the ritual lynching of African American men. The Crows, however, have no intention of doing bodily harm to the Scarecrow — theirs is a more insidious violence as they insist that Scarecrow waste his intellectual potential. The gang seeks to discipline Scarecrow by forcing him to recite the Crow Commandments, "Thou shall honor all Crows. Thou shall stop reading all bits of paper. Thou shall never get down off the pole." The Crow Commandments invokes the laws that forbid educating slaves. Scarecrow's desire for knowledge that will help him interpret the discourses and institutions that shape his life signifies on the slave narrative.

With its emphasis on literacy and freedom, African American slave narratives document that for many African Americans literacy was understood as an essential path to freedom. Douglass's *Narrative of the Life of Frederick Douglass, an American Slave* revealed powerfully the rationale for criminalizing educating slaves. In his narrative he shares that his Master rebuffed the Mistress for instructing Douglass, warning her that, "it is unlawful as well as unsafe to teach a slave to read" (275). Free of the actual chains of slavery that bound Douglass, *The Wiz* asks with its opening the exchange between Scarecrow and The Crows asks what happens when African Americans, freed from the slavery that bound Douglass, embrace the logics and politics of plantation slavery. Put differently, the Crows' insistence that reading is useless, even dangerous for Scarecrow because it only leads to discontentment takes on an especially haunting reminder of the ways in which the residues of slavery continue to injure contemporary African Americans. The Crows reinforce Scarecrow's subjection at their hands through a song whose refrain "you can't win child, you can't get out of the game" that aims to disabuse Scarecrow of any aspirations toward freedom.

Their insistence that "reading is stupid" suggests that a Eurocentric education does not promise liberation from "the game" that race and racism create. When Scarecrow quotes Bacon and Cicero, the crows respond, "Bacon once over lightly please" and "Cicero row row your boat."[5] The Crow's dismissal of education and western thought fails because they do not offer Scarecrow an alternative that will emancipate him. The Crows attempt to discipline Scarecrow by displacing his hope with nihilism. For The Crow's so-called book knowledge is less valuable than what they perceive to be real knowledge — street smarts. Though they are not tethered to a pole, they are seemingly unable or as their commandments and anthem suggest, unwilling to find opportunities than their present location provides. The Crow's chorus to Scarecrow's song is revealing for what it says about their loss of hope.

The Crow's are even more disadvantaged than Scarecrow because, unlike him, they are hopeless. The Crow's chorus, like The Crow Commandments, reflects their disillusionment with their inability to realize the promise of upward mobility. The Crows are suspicious, and perhaps justifiably so, of optimistic political discourse that promises substantive change. There is little difference between the Crow's logic and Moynihan's rooster logic, for both seem destined to produce more Scarecrows — analogs for some African American men who will be trapped by the convergence of race, class and gender ideologies that alienate African American men from themselves.

The Crows, then, become symbolic of a potentially negative family dynamic, one that subjugates its members and does not encourage an exploration of alternatives constructions of the self. Importantly, this negative dynamic is not explicitly linked to African American women as it is in Moynihan's analysis of African American families. Despite the Crow's negativity and their relentless efforts to disillusion him, Scarecrow gives no indication that he intends to abort his efforts to liberate himself physically and intellectually. His encounter with Dorothy will help him to realize, contrary to The Crow's assertions, that Scarecrow's pursuit of knowledge can indeed help him to win opportunities for improving his life.

You Make Me Feel Like a Natural Man

On Coney Island, Tinman and his wife Teenie lose their jobs at the Midway because they are outdated mechanical carnies. Tinman "quickly made plans for the future, but ... was felled by my fourth wife, Teenie ... *crushed* in my prime!" With her head wrapped in the familiar red scarf accompanied by a broad grin on her dark face, Teenie embodies the nineteenth century popular representations of the Mammy stereotype. Her grin in this instance seems to indicate the pleasure she enjoys in triumphing over her husband, The Tinman. Teenie does not speak, unlike The Crows who tormented Scarecrow, her silence gives Tinman's assertion that his position "under" Teenie, as a seat cushion, "one that he assumed all too often" greater poignancy, while simultaneously demonizing African American women. Tinman's and Tennie's actual jobs at the carnival are unclear, but it is probable that they were displayed as oddities, their difference placing them outside of the human family. Tinman's resting place under Teenie perhaps conveys the unnaturalness of African Americans in light of Moynihan's rooster theory, for it is Teenie who stands and struts triumphantly as Tinman languishes.

Tinman's description of Teenie resonates with Moynihan's description of the pathology that emerges from matriarchal family structures and its impact, "a crushing burden on the [African American] Negro male." Tinman's response, expressed through song, reveals that this burden has left him devoid of feeling. Tinman's song, "What Would I Do I Could Feel" posits that Tinman's reparation depends upon his ability to feel.

Tinman's lament also reveals that he shares Scarecrow's desire for knowledge and that such knowledge is part of becoming self-affirmed. Tinman's encore song, "Slide Some Oil to Me," expresses his desire for mobility and reiterates his desire for knowledge. Not only does Tinman iterate his desire to be vulnerable — human — but also, that such vulnerability constitutes a form of restoration. Beneath his tin exterior, there exists an interiority that remains just beyond Tinman's reach. It is introspection that comes with the embrace of vulnerability that will help Tinman determine the best path for him to pursue. Tinman recognizes that it was his maker, the dominant culture that neglected to give him a human body, especially a heart and thus Tinman identifies the historical stereotyping of African American men as predatory, brutal, mentally inferior and hypersexual beast — inhuman — as the injury that leaves him in a state of disrepair. Tinman's body and Scarecrow's underdeveloped mind articulate the legacy of slavery and the bodily and psychic injuries it produced. Unlike Moynihan's insistence on the strutting rooster model of manhood, Tinman desires an identity that does not limit him to colorful but largely symbolic displays of power. His desire for the mobility that will allow him to pursue a heart stands in stark contrast to the "rolling stone" description so often attached to African American men. In ways that are perhaps to subtle, *The Wiz* advocates pursuing the black interior as opposed to advocating patriarchy as a meaningful form of reparation.

To Be King

Though Scarecrow, Tinman and Lion's experiences are different they are linked by their sense of incompleteness and/or inadequacy as men. Lion shares with his fellow travelers that he has been officially "exiled in disgrace" from the jungle for being IOBK, Incapable of Being King. Just as Tinman's position under Teenie speaks to the failures of the African American family (according to Moynihan), so too does the Lion's exile. In *The Wiz*, gender expectations for African American men's dominance are expressed through animal imagery. Stymied in his "natural" expression of superiority and privilege, Lion is the outcome of men who are denied their natural right to strut and roar; the king of the jungle is banished because he is not manly enough to perform his kingly duties. Lion does not reveal whom, if anyone replaces him as King. However, *The Wiz*, rehearsing Moynihan's arguments in *The Black Family: The Case for National Action*, suggests that it is matriarchy, represented as Evillene in the film.

Banished, by Evillene, for his weakness, Lion takes refuge in one of the several lion statutes outside the New York Public Library. Literally, Lion is a shell of a man. Discovered by Dorothy, Tinman and Scarecrow, Lion does not respond to them with a ferocious roar, but rather a campy performance in which he declares that he is "...a Mean Ole Lion." Lion does not strut, but instead he prances and swishes his tail while he looks into mirror. Toto, Dorothy's dog, further emasculates Lion by biting his tail, which sends Lion into tears. His response then reiterates his unfitness to be king.

Like Tinman squashed under Teenie, Lion proves to be weak. Lion's behavior is less an indication of cowardice as it is the suggestion of a non-heteronormative identity. In *The Wizard Oz*, the Cowardly Lion says "life is sad ... when you're born to be a sissy." The connotation of sissy changes across time and community — sissy becomes a term that is linked to not only weakness, but homosexuality in African American parlance. Arguably, then, Lion is incapable of being king (IOBK), not only because he is cowardly, but also because he is perceived to be gay. Homosexuality is generally thought to be incompatible with African American masculinity, thus to be gay is not to be an African American man in many African American communities.[6] My reading of Lion does not intend to suggest that if in fact he is gay that his sexual identity invalidates his masculinity, but rather to acknowledge that African American gay men are stigmatized as aberrant subjects and thus ridiculed with a greater degree of scorn than African American men who possess other "deficiencies" in many African American communities. Dorothy and friends, however, embrace Lion and provide him with an accepting community.

After calming Lion, the group extends an invitation to join their quest for the Wiz. During the group's conversations, Lion reveals that his birth name is Fleetwood Coupe de Ville, Fleet for short. Lion's name, a combination of two different models of Cadillac automobiles, signifies both an emphasis on style and economic status. Lion's name perhaps explains his proclivity for preening and prancing; moreover, his behavior also suggests that he has been encouraged to invest in style over substance and as a result. Lion might, then, be read as a dandy, a negative description of African American men who attempt, with disastrous effects, to imitate white behavior associated with the upper classes. Put differently, Lion possesses style but lacks any form of capital to prove that his style signals anything other than his own vanity. In light of Moynihan's fears and their expression in *The Wiz*, Lion's subsequent discussion with the group offers potential insight into his designation of IOBK.

Cowardly Lion tells the group that his "mama would be so proud of him" but never mentions his father. Lion's story suggests that he may be the product of a single parent home headed by a mother, which according to Moynihan is the source of the pathology that produces men represented in *The Wiz* Moynihan's report emphasizes the nuclear family with strong fathers who ensure that young men "learn ... their biologically given maleness"; the absence of the father leaves the male child exposed to and defenseless against the negative influence of the mother's femaleness. According to Moynihan's logic, Lion lacks the appropriate male influence or education; ostensibly, which leaves him unable to fulfill his manly/kingly duties when he reaches adulthood. Out of the void of effective African American men, African American women emerge as the king and queen of the jungle. In *The Wiz* Dorothy emerges as the most competent subject and thus the responsibility for navigating the journey to Oz falls to her. Again, I want to emphasize that Dorothy's quest for self-affirmation and her quest to return home is secondary to repairing Scarecrow, Tinman and Lion's mind body split that leaves them damaged and incomplete. Dorothy becomes a surrogate mother and wife whose primary job is to encourage sooth and empower the men who could be her children and husband. With the help of the ultimate patriarch, The Wiz, Scarecrow, Tinman and Cowardly Lion, hope to be transformed into "real" men.

Matriarchy as Disease

While the Moynihan report acknowledges that African American men are challenged by political and economic practices, Moynihan suggests that African American women have become not only "too strong for their own good" but also, they have become "malignant growths" in the lives of African American men (Harris 110). *The Wiz* reflects Moynihan's arguments and suggests through Dorothy, that appropriate mothering is a significant part of the reparations that African American men require. The film opens with Dorothy ambivalent about accepting a new job that would move her away from Harlem and require that she teach older children. Dorothy's ambivalence about changing jobs masks a deeper and more troubling ambivalence. Dorothy neither believes that she posses the maternal feelings necessary to start her own family, nor is she interested in cultivating those feelings. Dorothy's ambivalence about family and motherhood propels her to Oz.[7] In Oz Dorothy becomes a surrogate mother to Scarecrow, Tinman, Cowardly Lion. In this surrogacy Dorothy practices being a mother that produces African American men capable and ready to inhabit their biological maleness. That is she must be a mother without becoming a malignant force in the lives of African American men. Unlike Teenie, whose oppression renders Tinman physically and emotionally numb, Dorothy acquiesces to his request that she "slide some oil to him." Dorothy liberates Scarecrow from the pole that holds him in bondage and lifts him from the ground, where he falls after his initial attempts at independence. She encourages Scarecrow, telling him that he is the "product of negative thinking" and encourages him to reject The Crows outlook. Dorothy's ability to envision Lion as a "different kind of Lion" encourages him to believe that he will reclaim his rightful position as King.

The film, then, contrasts Dorothy's mothering against Evillene's excessive and unchecked power which produces misery and despair in the lives in which she has influence and control. Moreover, with The Flying Monkeys' and The Crows under her control along with everyone else, Evillene occupies the throne that the ill-prepared Lion left vacant. In Lion's absence, Evillene emerges as both the King and Queen of Oz. *The Wiz* presents Evillene's power as an anomaly — unnatural and dangerous — that threatens to destroy African American families by producing sorry-ineffectual African American men. The film suggest that what is at least equally disturbing is the potential of Evillene's power to destroy African American women, like Dorothy, who can be disciplined into celebrating African American men's pursuit of patriarchy.

Beyond Apologies

Dorothy does not encounter the urban sexually and socially virile African American men that populate films such as *Shaft* and other Blaxploitation films of the 1970s or the safe African American men that Harry Belafonte and Sidney Poitier portrayed in the previous decades. Instead, Dorothy's men are the ordinary that populate Ntozake Shange's choreopoem, *for colored girls who have considered suicide the rainbow is not enuf.* Scarecrow, Tinman and Lion, however, are not the men that are the source of scorn and frustration expressed in the lady in blue's soliloquy on sorry African American men. It is Herman Smith, the man behind the mask that is The Wiz, who emerges as the object of African American women's displeasure and the men that Moynihan's report identifies as proliferating at an alarming rate in African American communities.

Herman Smith/The Wiz enters into a contract with Dorothy, Scarecrow, Tinman and Lion that stipulates that in exchange for eliminating Evillene, thus securing Smith's position as the "King" of Oz, that The Wiz will grant their individual wishes. Duped by the Wiz's style and powerful performance, the group, despite their misgivings, accept the contract. Initially, Smith/The Wiz refuses to include Dorothy's companions, however she refuses that offer. The Wiz's resistance to recognizing Scarecrow, Tinman and Lion suggest that it is not only Evillene, that threatens him, but other African American men who are in pursuit of the power that comes from achieving a sense of wholeness. Herman Smith/The Wiz truly is all strut and style for he does not possess the power or resources to execute the contract in good faith. His dishonesty in that realm is, of course, reflective of his dishonesty with himself. Like Dorothy's companions, the Wiz is in a state of disrepair. It is only when the group returns, victorious, to Oz expecting to have the terms of their contract honored that they discover the truth about that the "great and powerful" Wiz. The group finds Herman Smith/The Wiz in his bed cowering under the covers. Herman Smith/The Wiz as Dorothy proclaims is "nothing but a phony." The Wiz can only offer the dreaded apology identified in Shange's choreopoem, "I'm Sorry, I'm Sorry, I'm Sorry, everything they say about me is true, I got no powers."

The Wiz is Herman Smith — an ordinary black man from Atlantic City, New Jersey. Despite the Civil Rights movement, which Smith/The Wiz references, he has not yet become a signatory to what was supposed to be a new social contract, one in which the exclusion of non-whites has been amended. Herman Smith/The Wiz recounts his failures to be elected to any political office saying that he couldn't even win the office of dogcatcher. As a result of Herman Smith's failed attempts he lands in Oz, where the folk are impressed and mesmerized by the hot air balloon, part of his that brings him to Oz. As an ordinary African American man, Smith's/The Wiz's inability to ascend the political ladder suggests that meaningful strutting — biological maleness — power eludes many ordinary African American men. In Oz, his spectacular style gave the appearance that he was the equivalent of Moynihan's bantam rooster and Four-Star-General, a real man.[8] *The Wiz* suggests that living as an ordinary black man means living in a sorrowful state. Film scholar Donald Bogle argues that as the Wiz, Richard Pryor gives one of his "least effective and least funny performances" (Bogle 265). Pryor's performance is not humorous because beneath the film's infectious soundtrack, the film and its characters present a disturbing portrait of African American men. The challenge that *The Wiz* and other films focused on the condition of African American men face is how to offer a narrative exploration of ordinary African American men's lives that goes beyond visually representing the popular discourse that posits African American masculinity to exploring ways in which the problems that trouble African American men, women and families might be addressed. *The Wiz* attempts to do such work, albeit not as successfully as it might have had the film's screenwriter resisted scripting African American women as the source of African American men's challenges. Herman Smith/ The Wiz possesses all of the flaws that other three African American male analogs imagine themselves to possess, a lack of self-awareness, compassion, courage, intellectual capacity and an obsession with style. While Dorothy rejects the Wiz's apologies and pleas for them to stay because he "lives there all alone in terror that someone will find out [that he's] a fraud" she does not, as Evillene would have, belittle him or destroy him.

Instead, Dorothy reveals to Scarecrow, Tinman, and Lion that they already possess what they had sought from the Wiz. Their problems, it would seem, stem from domineering African American women, negative/colonized thinking and limited conceptions of masculinity — all of which circulate in the prevailing discourse about African American men. Their intellect, courage, and their emotive potential have simply been hampered by internalizing the negative and narrow conceptions of blackness and gender. Ultimately, they must find the resources to become the men that they always already were despite the negative circumstances that framed their lives. Tinman, free from overbearing women such as Teenie, will have the emotional space and physical freedom that he needs to develop into a man who is strong and sensitive. Scarecrow's desire for an intellectual development is in itself evidence that he is capable of doing the work necessary to make his dream a reality.

In her serenade to Lion, Dorothy instructs Lion to be a "lion in his own way." Her compassionate teaching allows the Lion to reclaim his birthright. Adding their voices to the song, Scarecrow and Tinman affirm that Lion is not a cowardly lion, but a lion. In the final chorus the Lion expresses his new found self-affirmation as he declares triumphantly that, "I am a lion." When Lion reclaims his place in the jungle, the film suggests that he will be a different kind of Lion, one that understands that domination is not the only way to gain and exercise power. Dorothy's comrades are compassionate, brave, strong, ordinary African American men. Damaged, but not destroyed or beyond reparation especially that which comes from dwelling in the black interior.

For Dorothy, a man's ability to admit his state of disrepair, combined with his willingness to pursue remedies, is preferable to men such as Herman Smith/The Wiz who takes refuge behind "an imposing array of masks, acts, and facades" in an effort to perform a strong and powerful African American masculinity (Richard and Billson 4).[9] In *The Wiz*, the strut embodied by the bantam rooster and Four-Star-General, is embodied in the silver Afro studded head symbolic for the 1970s macho African American male, Herman Smith is truly sorry.[10] Unmasked and faced with the prospect of being ousted from Oz for being IOBK, Herman Smith/The Wiz asks Dorothy if she will assist him. Her reply is simple and powerful, "I don't know what is in your heart ... begin with letting people see who you are." The exchange reiterates the value of Tinman's desire for vulnerability as it leads to introspection that facilitates discovering a self that is worth revealing to others.

Dorothy's affirmation of Scarecrow, Tinman, and Cowardly Lion's displaces the need for Herman Smith/The Wiz to grant their wishes. Dorothy launches into "If You Believe," in which she reinforces her earlier statement about believing in yourself. Dorothy's insistence that her companions do not need a wizard to make them men retains the spirit of *The Wizard of Oz*, which in the end, celebrates ordinary people. However, there is a critical difference in The Wiz's ending. In *The Wizard of Oz*, Dorothy's companions, including the witches and the wizard, are people that return home with her because they are a part of her family and community. In *The Wiz*, however, Dorothy's companions literally vanish. The film moves to its conclusion with Dorothy singing "Believe in Yourself" accompanied by Glenda the Good Witch. During this scene, Glenda is surrounded by a group of African American babies. The lyrics of "Believe in Yourself" combined with the visual imagery in the scene reveals that Dorothy's surrogate experience with Scarecrow, Tinman and Lion have not only repaired her companions but also, the experience repaired her ambivalence about family and motherhood. Repaired, Dorothy returns to Harlem where she ascends the steps of Aunt Em's house. The film's ending suggests that Dorothy will soon be opening the door to her own home and family.

As an allegory for the condition of African American men, *The Wiz's* ending ignores the realities of African American men lives on which the film comments. Reading Scarecrow, Tinman, Cowardly, Lion and the Wiz composites of real African American men means that they do not fade into oblivion or that they are so easily repaired and lived happily after. *The Wiz's* ending is especially disturbing because Herman Smith/The Wiz's inability to understand the necessity of introspection leaves him without a sense of direction, a sorry state of existence that will produce to more empty promises and apologies. Abandoning Herman Smith/The Wiz at the end of film, undermines what I identify as the film's efforts, albeit troubled, to advocate the reparative potential of ordinary African American men "actively engaged in struggles to transform [themselves within the context of] social structures of domination ... that constrain, restrict and suppress the full development of the *human* personality" (Mutua x). The final image of Herman Smith/The Wiz combined with the disappearance of Scarecrow, Tinman and Lion, ordinary African American, works against the film's efforts to displace the popular notion that African American masculinity is destined to be represented and experienced as crisis.

In light of the vanishing African American male analogs and the perplexed Herman Smith/The Wiz, I want to close this essay with an imaginative leap and suggests that these characters, offered as representative of actual African American men in *The Wiz*, might very well been amongst the many African American men who responded to Minster Farrakhan's call for the Million Man March, a day of atonement for African American Men.[11] In the twenty-seven years between the release of *The Wiz* and The Million Man March and Spike Lee's cinematic representation of that cultural event in the film, *Get on the Bus*, African American men continue to signify the dire condition of African Americans as evidenced by their disproportionate rates of incarceration, unemployment, poor academic performance and new HIV and AIDS cases. These statistics among others have helped to usher in and sustain a discourse that represents African American men as simultaneously endangered species and enemies of the state, a variation of Moynihan's claims in *The Black Family: The Case for National Action* in 1965.

Notes

1. See http://www.dol.gov/oasam/programs/history/webid-meynihan.htm for the full *The Black Family: The Case for National Actions* report minus the charts and graphs included in the original. All references to *The Black Family: The Case for National Actions* are drawn from this source.

2. *The Wiz* was regarded as failure when it was released and has been regarded as such in African American film criticism. Even as African American film theory and criticism proliferate — in particular, regarding the significance of the city to African American film — *The Wiz* remains largely unaccounted for in African American film history. Produced by Motown Productions and released by Universal Pictures, *The Wiz* cost $24 million to make and brought in only $13 million during its original theatrical release; the film, like its titular character, is generally regarded as a flop.

3. The film adaptation of *The Wiz* includes a number of key changes in addition to geography. Diana Ross replaced Stephanie Mills as Dorothy. Dorothy was no longer a prepubescent girl but a young kindergarten teacher worried about taking a new job and moving out of Harlem. Audiences were not impressed with Ross's portrayal. The film is regarded as one of award-winning director Sidney Lumet's failures.

4. See Jacqueline Stewart's *Migrations to the Movies: Black Cinema and Urban Modernity*, Paula J. Massood's *Black City Cinema: African American Urban Experiences in Film*, and Farah Jasmine Griffith's *Who Set You Flowin; The African American Migration Narrative*. Stewart's and Massood's work documents the emergence and importance of the city in African American film. Griffith's work treats the significance of migration in African American literary tradition. Griffith's safe spaces are open to men and women and can be both healing and injurious as they function as retreats or encourage complacency.

5. All quotations from *The Wiz* are attributed to the screenwriter Joel Schumacher.

6. For a variety of engagements with the issues of homosexuality in African American communities see the following: Simms-Constantine, Delroy. *The Greatest Taboo: Homosexuality in Black Communities*. (New York: Alyson Books, 2001); Roscoe, Will and Stephan Murray, *Boy-Wives and Female Husbands: Studies in African-American Homosexualities*, (New York: Palgrave, 2006); Boykin, Keith. *Beyond the Down Low: Sex Lies and Denial in Black America*. (New York: Avalon, 2005).

7. *The Wiz* opens with Aunt Em celebrating the birth of her first grandchild and the value of family more generally. Dorothy retreats to the kitchen, in song, "Can I Go On," she contemplates her lack of maternal feelings. Later in the kitchen Aunt Em confronts Dorothy about the job offer and essentially gives Dorothy an ultimatum, saying that it is time for Dorothy to create her own home and family.

8. The emphasis on style, particularly as an activity that trumps real political engagement and power, is reinforced in the film by a scene that shows a group of people, ostensibly some of the same people who work for Evillene, outside who respond to the Wiz's fickle demands for changing the fashionable colors. The colors change from red, to green, to gold finally. The color scheme suggests the faddishness of African dress and perhaps even interest in Africa as a particular expression of African American style in the 1970s.

9. See Kelley, Robin D.G. *Yo' Mama's Dysfunktional!: Fighting Culture Wars in Urban America.* (New York: Beacon Press, 1998). In Kelley's introduction and in Chapter One he offers an extended treatment of the implications of the cool pose and its limitations as a theory for understanding African American masculinity.

10. I am indebted to my co-panelist, Carmen Gillespie, at the 2000 Annual Meeting of the Popular Culture/American Culture Association in New Orleans for her astute observation about the significance of the silver Afro-clad head in *The Wiz*.

11. I develop this argument in a chapter that examines reparations has been a gendered discourse. I use *The Wiz* and *Get on the Bus* as two contemporary popular cultural examples in my forthcoming book, *Not Just Money: African Americans, Reparations and Cultural Narratives.*

Bibliography

Alexander, Elizabeth. *The Black Interior.* St. Paul, MN: Graywolf, 2004.

Ballard, Tanya, and Ju-Don Roberts, eds. "Being a Black Man." *The Washington Post*, 2006. <http://www.washingtonpost.com/wp-srv/metro/interactives/blackmen/blackmen.html>

Bogle, Donald. *Toms, Coons, Mulattoes, Mammies and Bucks.* New York: Roadhouse, 1994.

Carbado, Devon. "Black Male Racial Victimhood." *Callaloo* 21 no. 2 (1998): 337–61.

Cassuto, Leonard. *The Inhuman Race: Racial Grotesque in American Literature and Culture.* New York: Columbia University Press, 1997.

DeJongh, James. *Vicious Modernism: Black Harlem and the Literary Imagination.* New York: Cambridge University Press, 1990.

Dwyer, Owen. "Interpreting the Civil Rights Movement: Place, Memory, and Conflict." *Professional Geographer.* 52 (4) 2000, 660–671.

Earle, Neil. *The Wonderful Wizard of Oz in American Popular Culture; Uneasy Eden.* Lewiston, NY: Edwin Mellen Press, 1993.

Eyerman, Ron. *Cultural Trauma: Slavery and the Formation of African American Identity.* New York: Cambridge University Press, 2001.

Harris, Trudier. "This Disease Called Strength: Some Observations on the Compensating Construction of Black Female Character." *Literature and Medicine* 14 no. 1 (Spring 1995), 109–126.

Harper, Phillip. *Are We Not Men?: Masculine Anxiety and the Problem of African-American Identity.* New York: Oxford University Press, 1996.

Henderson, Carole. *Scarring the Black Body: Race and Representation in African American Literature.* Columbia: University Press of Missouri, 2002.

Holloway, Steve. "Identity, Contingency, and the Urban Geography of 'Race.'" *Social & Cultural Geography.* Vol. 1, No. 2 (2000), 197–208.

Jackson, Elvin Holt. "Reconstructing Black Manhood: Message and Meaning in Spike Lee's Get on the Bus." *College Language Association* 47 no. 4 (June 2004): 409–26.

Lumet, Sydney. *The Wiz.* Los Angeles: Columbia Pictures, 1996.

Mitchell, Don. "Cultural Landscapes: Just Landscapes or Landscapes of Justice?" *Progress in Human Geography* 27, 6 (2003). 787–796.

Murray, Rolland. "The Long Strut: Song of Solomon and the Emancipatory Limits of Black Patriarchy." *Callaloo* 22, no. 1 (1999): 12–133.

Mutua, Athena, ed. *Progressive Black Masculinities.* New York: Routledge, 2006.

West, Cornel. *Race Matters.* New York: Vintage, 1993.

5

Flavor of Love and the Rise of Neo-Minstrelsy on Reality Television[1]

Valerie Palmer-Mehta and *Alina Haliliuc*

Scholarly research on reality television has proliferated in recent years.[2] Despite a growing body of literature, research that focuses specifically on the representation of African American masculinity is still in its infancy and only very recently has gained some momentum.[3] Derosia's analysis of racialized criminal male bodies on *America's Most Wanted* (236–58), Orbe et al.[4] and Kraszewski's examinations of black male stereotypes on *The Real World* (179–96), as well as the recent examinations of black fatherhood by Smith (393–412) and of performances of black identity by Dubrofsky and Hardy (373–92) are notable and recent exceptions. The record-breaking celeb-reality[5] television show, *Flavor of Love*, starring Public Enemy rap star, Flavor Flav, provides a unique opportunity to contribute to this growing body of literature. While previous scholarship has offered present-day readings of reality television as either reproducing or challenging stereotypes about black men, our analysis inserts *Flavor of Love* in a larger network of texts in order to offer a historically informed understanding of the contemporary cultural work done by this show. In doing so, we also hope to answer Nakayama's call to explore the implications of racialized masculinities for "the entire social scene" and, thus, to contribute to the broader literature on American masculinity (113).

The rhetoric surrounding the debut of Flavor Flav's (born William Jonathan Drayton, Jr.) most recent[6] reality television venture was less than noteworthy, failing to portend the record-breaking ratings and popularity the program would soon garner. Indeed, *Reality Television Magazine* introduced the show with the following headline: "*Flavor of Love* Offers Up the First Reality TV Vomit of the Year." Despite the disparaging introduction, *Flavor of Love* quickly cultivated a cult following. The final episode of the first season became the highest rated program in the history of the cable television station VH1 at the time. Additionally, it was ranked as the number one program out of all basic cable programming in the 18–49 demographic, and the number two program of all cable programming following *The Sopranos,* garnering nearly six million viewers. Hoping to capitalize on the popularity and profitability of the program, VH1 subsequently produced a second season of the program.[7]

Flavor of Love is based on the popular ABC reality dating program, *The Bachelor,* in which one man enjoys a bevy of women vying to be selected as his potential wife. Flavor makes a direct comparison between the shows when he states on the debut program, "I know ya'all heard of the show *The Bachelor.* Flavor Flav is the black-chelor!" Despite their similarities, there are some important differences between the two programs. To date, all the nine bachelors featured on *The Bachelor* have been white and without children, criminal records, or drug problems. Flavor Flav (hereafter Flavor) is the first African American bachelor. At the time of this writing, he has seven children and two grandchildren, as well as criminal record and a history of drug abuse. While the men on *The Bachelor* take their cadre of women to extravagant venues for their dates, Flavor is shown taking the contestants to such sites as Red Lobster and the roller skating rink. Additionally, Flavor tests the contestants by making them think they are going on a date but instead he drops them off at various locations to work while he watches their performance on a video monitor. Some might argue that *Flavor of Love* functions as a parody of *The Bachelor,* and the ways in which *The Bachelor* idealizes the traditional heterosexual relationship. Although there may be potential in such a reading, the troubled history experienced by African Americans in U.S. culture complicates interpretations that ignore issues of race or deal with racial issues only by comparison with *The Bachelor.* Hooks in particular raises difficult questions regarding the intersection of race and the sphere of representation: "Opening a magazine or book, turning on the television set, watching a film, or looking at photographs in public places, we are most likely to see images of black people that reinforce and reinscribe white supremacy" (1). The influence of mediated images compounds such concerns, as Orbe et al indicate: "because of the power of mediated images, characterizations of African Americans are never neutral" (Orbe, Warren, and Cornwell 19). The stakes are high in the realm of representation, as African Americans struggle to attain identities of dignity in a culture that historically has impeded such efforts. Because of this history and enduring practice of maligned representations of minorities, our analysis expands the intertextual reading to a diachronic perspective, to include the U.S. tradition of minstrelsy and Flavor's Public Enemy persona.

Flavor's presence on reality television has been particularly troubling for fans who were introduced to Flavor as the hypeman of the black nationalist rap group, Public Enemy (PE), which was inducted into the Long Island Music Hall of Fame in 2007. Dubbed "music with a message," PE took the music industry by storm in 1988 with one of the most famous and influential hip-hop albums, "It Takes a Nation of Millions to Hold Us Back."[8] Although the group's zenith was inarguably the late 1980s, PE continued to release records throughout the 1990s, and the most recent album at the time of this writing, *Rebirth of a Nation,* was released in 2007. The group's revolutionary antigovernment, pro-black music stresses pride and empowerment as it raises critical questions regarding the status and future of African Americans. As rap's original "hypeman," Flavor roused the audience and provided a complement to Chuck D, lead rapper of the group. The original group members also included DJ Terminator X and Minister of Information Professor Griff who was backed by the Security of the First World (S1W). As PE was achieving significant momentum and influence, a scandal emerged in 1989, when Professor Griff was accused of making anti–Semitic statements in an interview with the *Washington Post.* Chuck D fired him from the group even though Professor Griff publicly stated that he was misquoted and his remarks were taken out of context. This event roused ire with some fans who perceived Chuck D as capitulating to the interests of his label, but others read in the decision a desire to maintain the groups' ethical social stance. In contrast to the heavily commercialized rap common on the airwaves at the turn of the twenty-first century, PE became famous for its anti-establishment sociopolitical messages that focused on transforming the situation of African Americans. PE was at the forefront of bringing crucial social issues to the airwaves, as Ollison indicates: "The music of Public Enemy was like a call to arms in the battle for black cultural relevancy and political empowerment" (par 1). At the same time, critics saw the group's music as incendiary, and encouraged record stores and radio stations to boycott their albums. As the group's popularity and influence grew, so did the attacks against them. In 1990, PE was mentioned in an FBI report to the U.S. Congress regarding "Rap Music and its Effect on National Security."

Fans who were introduced to Flavor in the context of PE cannot ignore the seeming transformation he has undergone. Once the man who hollered, "Don't Believe the Hype" Flavor's new role on *Flavor of Love* seems nothing but hype.[9] Carlson indicates that some have viewed Flavor's comeback as inherently counter to the struggle for black empowerment: "What is a group to do when its mentors leave the revolution for reality TV?" Even Chuck D, the mastermind behind PE, has expressed concern regarding Flavor's performances on reality television, suggesting that they are not in alignment with the group's political aims, which sought to enhance black socio-political power and to critique the kind of stereotypes Flavor was becoming. Indeed, the PE song, "Burn Hollywood Burn" specifically addresses the clownish roles African Americans have been forced to play by Hollywood.[10]

The shift in Flavor's representation, from a politically potent musician to a vacuous television star, and the shift in the public's attitude towards him, from vilification to approval, raises some troubling questions about the kinds of images of black masculinity the broader culture validates. Placing Flavor in the context of the history of minstrelsy in America, as well as in dialogue with *The Bachelor*, and his former image as PE rapper, lends insight into this situation. In what follows, we provide an overview of minstrelsy and the Sambo character in U.S. popular culture to demonstrate the minstrel figure's tenacity and its resemblance to Flavor. As Boskin states, "no comic figure played to wider audiences, received more thunderous applause, or lasted as long in the popular theatre. No other immigrant stereotype came close to Sambo's popularity or expressive grin" (10). We then compare the representation of Flavor on the first season of *Flavor of Love*, on the one hand, to those of the lead on the eighth season of *The Bachelor* and to Flavor's PE persona, on the other, in order to demonstrate Flavor's parallel to the minstrel figure. We selected the eighth season of *The Bachelor*, featuring the bachelor Travis Stork for two main reasons. First, this season ran concurrently with the first season of *Flavor of Love*. Second, Stork typifies the kind of man featured on *The Bachelor*. In situating Flavor in comparison with the original show, with his PE persona that brought him to public notoriety, and with the older history of minstrelsy, we argue that Flavor on *Flavor of Love* reflects a commodified, hyper-racialized image of African American masculinity that harkens back to the minstrel era and undermines, through parody, progressive conceptualizations of black masculinity.

Minstrelsy in the U.S. Culture

Emerging in the north around 1830 as a form of white, working class entertainment, minstrel shows were pervasive and well attended in nineteenth century America (Lott "Blackface" 3–34). The first minstrel act is attributed to Thomas D. Rice who, performing in Pittsburgh, created the song and dance routine that became known as "Jim Crow." Although Rice commenced this cultural form, the first group to specifically identify as "minstrel" was Dan Emmett's Virginia Minstrels, who started performing at the Chatham Theater in 1843 (Lhamon 57). Typically, minstrel shows featured white men donning blackface, appropriating what they deemed to be black cultural practices in a vulgar commodification of black masculinity and an exploitation of racist ideology. Performing a caricature of black masculinity (and sometimes femininity), minstrels smeared burnt cork to darken their faces, wore ragged clothes, and employed a southern drawl and broken language to mimic the verbal style of southern plantation culture. Humor was employed to portray the minstrel figure as a fool, however without the wisdom conferred upon the medieval fool. As Boskin indicates, the medieval jester was accorded a "touch of wisdom and perspective — and thus the ability to manipulate humor for higher ends" (9). In contrast, the minstrel figure was denied these qualities and "accorded the follies of foolishness" (9). The minstrel character was rarely given a rational function or the ability to influence his social world. While the minstrel shows are a thing of the past, the caricatures they promoted still have a presence in contemporary popular culture.[11] Coleman argues that these "racial stereotypes ... are known for their longevity and permeation throughout mainstream popular culture" and that such caricatures are prevalent even today (43).

Popular culture has long been a site of contested meaning, where the collective fears and desires that emerge in a culture are struggled over and negotiated. Minstrel theater was a key location where anxieties possessed by the dominant culture were symbolically addressed at the expense of African Americans. The minstrel show appropriated black culture for white commercial and socio-political interests, and "divested black people of control over elements of their culture and over their own cultural representation generally" (Lott, *Love* 18). The shows circulated around racist humor and buffoonish images that undercut African Americans at a time of political and social uneasiness in the U.S. Although the minstrel shows carried on long past abolition, at the time of their debut, the shows worked to allay whites' misgivings over the inherent moral dilemma embedded in slavery by positing it as a benevolent institution (Coleman 35). By making black men appear childlike and deferent to white authority, the shows also served to assuage fears of an unstable social climate seen as a potential result of the increasing presence and power of blacks in American culture (38–39).

In addition to responding to political concerns, the shows represented an "obsessive curiosity and envy over Blackness" (Coleman 41) as white audiences sought to know more about the African American population, but always from a distance and on their own terms. Finally, the minstrel show functioned to distance whiteness from blackness. Coleman underscores the ideological opportunism embedded in this distancing: "If African Americans are deemed in any way analogous to Whites, what then would this sameness be saying about the dominant group? What impact would an admitted equality, even if such an admission was confined to symbolism, have upon the institutions of racism and supremacy?" (28–29). The exaggeration of differences between blacks and whites, thus, served to buttress oppressive social institutions and practices as it dehumanized and disempowered African Americans.

Minstrelsy was symptomatic of many underlying social issues, one of which was whites' fears of the potential power of black males. The degraded images of black masculinity provided by the minstrel show enabled whites to negotiate their fear of and fascination with the African American male, while maintaining ultimate symbolic control over him (Lott "Blackface" 13). Humor provided the vehicle through which this was accomplished. English argues, "humor is never innocent" because "comic practice is always on some level or in some measure an assertion of group against group, an effect and an event of struggle, a form of symbolic violence" (9). Boskin provides insight regarding how humor in minstrel shows functioned to oppress:

> To make the black male into an object of laughter, and conversely, to force him to devise laughter, was to strip him of masculinity, dignity, and self-possession. Sambo [a minstrel figure] was, then, an illustration of humor as a device of oppression.... The ultimate objective for whites was to effect mastery: to render the black male powerless as a potential warrior, as a sexual competitor, as an economic adversary [14].

The humor evoked by the shows functioned to reinforce the in-group (whites) and to marginalize the out-group (blacks) by creating a buffoonish caricature of black masculinity that required dependence on the in-group. By making black men the object of laughter, the minstrel show worked to undercut the political and social potential of black masculinity.

Perhaps the most pervasive masculine form in the history of minstrelsy is the Sambo. As Boskin indicates, "as the American jester, Sambo was found everywhere, in every nook and cranny of the popular culture" (10–11). He was marked by his willing subservience and loyalty to whites and by his "distorted, heavy dialect" (Coleman 42). Coleman states that this faithful, docile character "was often depicted as a house servant who sang, danced, strummed the banjo," but he also "was superstitious and would lapse into trickery and dishonesty" (42). The Sambo figure dressed in raggedy clothes or plantation garb, but he also wore "finely tailored, yet incredibly gaudy, excessive clothing" (41). Because of his "unabashed loyalty, and fun loving, amusing nature, the Sambo became a hailed character in minstrel theater" (42). Sambo was depicted as childlike and "as children are given to impetuous play, humorous antics, docile energies, and uninhibited expressiveness, so too one could locate in Sambo identical traits" (Boskin 13). Ultimately, Sambo functioned to disempower black masculinity by infantilizing black men, and making them appear deferent to white authority. Sambo represented "an extraordinary type of social control, at once extremely subtle, devious, and encompassing. To exercise a high degree of control meant also to be able to manipulate the full range of humor; to create, ultimately, an insidious type of buffoon" (13–14).

The Brutal Buck was another popular theater character in the nineteenth and early twentieth centuries. In contrast to the docile Sambo figure, the Brutal Buck caricature galvanized the fear that, simmering under the easy-going outward appearance of some black males was a predator who had a desire for revenge and a propensity for violence. The Brutal Buck represented the insurrectionist potential in black men, and served as a symbolic justification for maintaining tight control and power over African Americans. Additionally, this figure typified whites' anxieties over black male sexuality. The Brutal Buck was portrayed as possessing an unbridled sexuality that was supposedly waiting to be unleashed on white women. This stereotype had a presence in theater as well as early American film. Bogle advises that D.W. Griffith, filmmaker of the infamous *Birth of a Nation*, capitalized on the "myth of the Negro's high-powered sexuality, then articulated the great white fear that every black man longs for a white woman" (14). The stereotype cultivated a fear of black males in U.S. society that functioned to justify white domination, as the Brutal Buck was positioned as "a pure predator that was eventually put down, subdued, or killed, through a great show of White force (superiority)" (Coleman 44). By creating a figure that fostered a sense of black masculinity as violent and fearsome, minstrel culture promoted a context in which black men could be viewed as potential predators and thus apt victims of ostensibly justifiable white violence.

Ultimately, images of the Sambo and Brutal Buck figures strategically functioned to reinforce white hegemony and black marginality, as the negative caricatures posited African American masculinity as vacillating between either threatening or childlike. Both stereotypes fractured notions of black men as productive and desirable equals. Although the twentieth century saw the demise of the minstrel show, these stereotypes still emerge in contemporary American culture. Demonstrating that these images are still with us, Orbe, Warren, and Cornwell provide a disturbingly precise example of the Brutal Buck stereotype on contemporary cable television. The authors analyzed the representation of four black men who were among the 45 cast members in the first six seasons of the reality television program, *The Real World*. Included in their investigation were the episodes of the characters' respective seasons and the images featured in the special, "Most Dangerous *Real World* Episodes." Interestingly, "although African American men constituted less than 9% of all cast members, they were featured in over 50% of the 'most dangerous' segments presented in the 7-hour marathon special" (111). The authors found that contemporary media stereotypes on *The Real World* represent African American masculinity as "inherently angry, physically threat-ening, and sexually aggressive" (112) and that the show worked to "reinforce existing societal stereotypes that regard Black men as dangerous creatures that deservedly invoke fear in others" (119). Drawing on similar episodes, Kraszew-ski comes to comparable conclusions, underscoring how black masculinity is portrayed as violent and sexually out of control, and explicitly comparing this construction to the stereotype of the Brutal Buck (189–94). Because the pro-gram is framed as based on the "real world," Orbe, Warren, and Cornwell argue that its characterization of black masculinity is particularly troubling as "everyday discourse of real people ... is used to create a media text that works to reinforce existing personal stereotypes that the media helped to cul-tivate in the first place" (119).

In her examination of the alleged criminals portrayed on *America's Most Wanted*, Derosia found a similar representation of black masculinity. Derosia's study found that Latino and black men are disproportionately portrayed as the criminal suspects on the program and white people are overrepresented as law enforcement. Additionally, violent crimes were disproportionately depicted on the program, feeding into people's fear of being a victim of vio-lent crime. This fear is exacerbated when the show focuses on random acts of violence, which intersects with the overrepresentation of people of color as suspects of crimes. Consequently, "reality-based television programs give a false impression of the extent of the threat of random violent crime ... and especially target white viewers' fears of people of color as the most likely per-petrators of that violence" (242). Drawing largely on examples that feature black males, Derosia argues that typical programs play on white people's fear of racially marked others and "suggest not only violent ... tendencies but also visually encode a highly sexualized" representation of black male bodies (247).

The above reviewed research of black masculinity on reality television indicates that the minstrelsy-based image of the Brutal Buck still permeates contemporary media culture. It is important to point out that these represen-tations emerged from outside of the African American population as Cole-man indicates: "Minstrelsy is important to us for the purpose of documenting the *stereotypes Whites created of Blacks* and how they found their way into mass media" (39). Prompted by the knowledge of such harmful representations of black masculinity as violent, two prominent members of the rap scene, Rev. Run (born Joseph Simmons) and Snoop Dogg (born Calvin Broadus) aimed to change the television scene. As coproducers of their own reality television shows, *Run's House* and *Snoop Dogg's Father Hood*,[12] Simmons and Broadus wanted to disrupt the stereotypical imagery of violent black men by showing their own families on reality television. Such shift in representation led Smith to argue that the two RTV programs revived the tradition of *The Cosby Show*.

Instead of violent black men out of control, *Run's House* shows the rapper Rev. Run "presiding over discussions about education, empty nesting and child anger management," (395) while *Father Hood* teaches the viewers "lessons in humility and success through education" (407).

While both the world of television production and that of academic scholarship have paid praiseworthy attention to counteracting the image of the Brutal Buck, we argue that similar efforts have not been made to analyze and counteract minstrelsy-originating images of black masculinity that are equally detrimental. In the next section, we demonstrate that Flavor on *Flavor of Love* eschews the Brutal Buck image, but reinforces the stereotype of the Sambo. In so doing, it reinforces the scene of reality television as a form of neo-minstrelsy that — with two notable exceptions — vacillates between the Brutal Buck and Sambo caricatures.

When we compare Flavor in *Flavor of Love* with both *The Bachelor* and Flavor's PE persona, we are presented with a gap, a distance that centers whiteness, domesticates, through commodification, revolutionary rap, and casts blackness as deviant. While other reality television shows also have marked blackness as deviant, none have done it in such a politically debilitating manner. The source of derision on *The Flavor of Love* consists of those characteristics and behaviors of Flavor that mirror the Sambo minstrel character and comically distances the bachelor from normative standards of courtship and masculinity. The viewers learn the norms of courtship and masculinity through both the implicit invitation to a generic comparison with *The Bachelor*, and through depictions of the contestants' reactions to Flavor's behavior.

"I'm the Black-chelor"—The Alterity of Blackness

One central generic convention of the shows is presenting a desirable bachelor. In *The Bachelor*, the men are white, predominantly in their early thirties, and presumably attractive. They have no children. None have criminal records. All possess good jobs, impressive college pedigrees, or are heirs to fortunes. The eighth bachelor, Dr. Travis Stork of the 2006 *The Bachelor*, graduated Magna cum laude from Duke University. He is an emergency room doctor at the Vanderbilt Medical Center. Dr. Stork never has been married, has no children, and is thirty-three years old. He dresses in modest clothing in subdued tones and his pictures on the website show him in fashionable, expensive suits which one might wear in a professional setting. The other bachelors dress in a similar fashion.

In comparison, Flavor is the first African American bachelor, albeit on his own, separate reality dating program (there has yet to be a man of color featured on *The Bachelor*). Flavor dresses in vibrant colors such as fuchsia and bright green. He often wears a top hat and sports a walking stick. Sometimes he dons a king's robe or a helmet with horns. He is never seen without a large clock hanging around his neck like a necklace, even when he is on the tennis court. He also wears a grill.[13] Additionally, at the time of the first season, Flavor was forty-six years old and had six children[14] and two grandchildren. In case the audience does not know how many children Flavor has, he tells them on the third episode entitled, "A Friend of Flav's is a Friend of Mine." Flavor states, "Ya'all know me. Now I got six kids. I want four more before I die. Definitely I want a woman who is good with kids."

For those who have been following Flavor's reality television career, specifically the program *Strangelove*, it was revealed that Flavor is in arrears in his child support. Flavor also possesses a criminal record, related in part to his struggle with drug addiction. For viewers unfamiliar with his past, the program takes the time to inform them. On the debut program, "Dimplez," one of the contestants, states: "I told my parents about being on the show. And they said, "Oh no, oh no." But I tried to explain that Flavor Flav is no longer an addict and he may or may not be taking care of his children, I don't know. His record is behind him. And he's romantic at heart." While the extra-contextual information on *The Bachelor* posits Dr. Stork as heroic, Dimplez's comment suggests that Flavor is a parent's nightmare. Her remark that Flavor is a romantic at heart hardly compensates for the damaging information about his struggle with addiction and his lack of support for his children. On the contrary, it centers the elements of the Sambo caricature: Flavor appears as a negligent father, unable to resist drugs and take care of his children, who gets himself into trouble not because he is violent or threatening, but because he is not strong enough to lead a normal life.

This lack, in the forms of laziness and deficiency of intelligence — notorious characteristics of the Sambo — is depicted in the show by the use of nicknames. While the men on *The Bachelor* take the time to learn all of the contestants' names, Flavor gives the women nicknames, such as Hoopz, by which they are known throughout the series. Flavor explains his decision to nickname the contestants on the debut program: "Alright yo check this out. Your man Flav, he is not good with names at all. So what I gonna attempt to do is give each one of ya'all a nickname so that way I can remember it." Then, directly speaking to the audience at home, Flavor states, "And the reason why I picked nicknames is because I knew I wouldn't remember their real names, and nicknames I might can remember easier." The idea that Flavor cannot remember names feeds into "the fixed idea that black men are 'all brawn and no brains,'" a stereotype that traverses time and space, from the Sambo caricature to the contemporary black male sports hero (Mercer 178).

While the men on *The Bachelor* represent the best looking, brightest and most marketable (so to speak) of white masculinity, Flavor hardly represents the same for African American masculinity. Rather than showcasing the best looking, smartest, and most accomplished black male, Mark Cronin, the show's European American creator, writer, and producer has presented, comparatively, an avidly clownish character with questionable parental skills and a criminal background.[15] In juxtaposing the images of masculinity — which is inevitable since generically the programs are similar and Flavor's remarks (e.g., "I'm the black-chelor") directly cultivate a comparison — an implicit message is sent about the centrality of whiteness and the alterity of blackness. As Dickinson and Anderson argue, "white masculinity (like whiteness itself) works its magic in part by constantly refusing positive definition, forcing others to tell white masculinity what it is through a process of differentiation and negation" (275). The representations of masculinity on the two programs present a romantic, idealized version of white masculinity and position black masculinity as clownish and a deviant Other. Indeed, on an *XXL Magazine* message board, one respondent referred to *Flavor of Love* as the "ghetto bachelor,"[16] clearly differentiating the universality and centrality of whiteness (i.e., *The Bachelor*) from its Other (i.e., The "Ghetto" Bachelor, *Flavor of Love*).

Flavor's Newfound Political Inoffensiveness

Flavor is portrayed on the show not only as the very opposite of desirable masculinity, but also as the parodic antithesis of his politicized persona which made him famous in the 1980s. Such explicit depoliticizing of Flavor underlines the role of reality television in gradually transforming him, over two decades, from an index of the Brutal Buck (i.e., Public Enemy) into the embodiment of the Sambo. Flavor's persona, thus, can be seen as the cultural battlefield on which white anxieties about blackness are being played out. From a member of the high profile rap group supportive of Black Panther ideology, Flavor becomes a public character to be only enjoyed for his entertainment potential. For example, Flavor's colorful and, at times, flamboyant wardrobe stands in stark contrast to the conservative, sober attire of the men on *The Bachelor*. Wearing a king's robe or a helmet with horns makes Flavor very entertaining to watch, but drained of any political commentary, reinforcing the notion that he is not to be taken seriously. His attire and presentation of self harkens back to the Sambo image from the minstrel era, reinforcing the idea that his main purpose is to entertain audiences, not promote critical consciousness as he did as part of PE.

That Flavor's embodiment is supposed to be a source of humor, with no resemblance to his former politicized identity, becomes particularly clear during the ceremonies. After the bachelor has determined for whom he has the greatest affinity, he announces publicly who will remain and who will leave the program during the much anticipated rose ceremony. He asks, "Will you accept this rose?" Those who do not receive roses go home immediately. Similarly, at the end of each program on *Flavor of Love*, Flavor reveals who will remain. A parodic allusion to both the rose ceremony and to Flavor's PE persona emerges when, instead of giving the women roses and asking them if they will accept the rose, Flavor provides the women with clock necklaces that have the chosen woman's photograph inside the face of the clock. As he gives the chosen woman the clock, Flavor states, "you know what time it is."

During the ceremonies Flavor appropriates his own trademark statements ("you know what time it is") and visual cues (clock necklaces) from his rap career with PE, redeploying them on the program. On *Flavor of Love*, however, Flavor uses of the expression "you know what time it is" to indicate that a contestant has received his approval and is not being eliminated. In the context of Flavor's work in PE, it carried a revolutionary political message: that it is time for radical social change. In the song, "Timebomb," Flavor and Chuck D rapped about the need to resist the temptation of drugs and alcohol, to recognize racial inequalities and fight against them, to have a healthy suspicion of the government, and to be proud of being black.

Attracted to this celeb-reality show by Flavor's celebrity as a PE rapper, audiences know about these meanings, and some contestants even communicate this knowledge explicitly and with admiration. One illustrative example of how Flavor's PE symbols are recognized as political, yet are depoliticized on the show, is episode two of the third season, entitled "In Flav We Trust." Here, Flavor is interviewing the contestants during the first evening together and contestant Rayna takes the opportunity to confess her admiration for him. She states emphatically that she has been following Flav since his days with Public Enemy and she knows that "the clock was a representation that it was time for us to take a look at ourselves as black people and show white America what we really were talking about." Flavor, though, rejects her political interpretation as wrong and replaces it with a general overused message about time: "the reason why I wear the clock is because time is the most important element in our lives and we can't afford to waste none of it." This exchange shows that Flavor's fans are aware of the political symbolism embedded in Flavor's previous PE performances, while the show actively works, sometimes co-opting Flavor himself, toward resignifying the protagonist as an entertaining figure alone. Such co-option functions to reinforce the "realness" of Flavor as a mindless entertainer: he not only acts as such; he also thinks of himself as just an entertainer whose most profound messages are clichéd life lessons, rather than radical political messages targeted at African Americans. While the clock and his catch phrase used to be and are still seen by fans as reminders of PE's messages of social change, on *Flavor of Love*, they are entirely drained of their political meaning. The expression is used as a compliment, to indicate that the women are receiving his affirmation and are staying on the show. When faced with an interpretation of the clock outside of this ceremonial use, Flavor denies PE's entrenched meaning of the clock as a visual reminder that it is "time for radical change," thus "perfecting" the depoliticization of his persona on this show.

Once a member of a powerful and politically relevant rap group that came under fire for its socially conscious lyrics, Flavor has been turned into an avidly clownish character, undermining his insurrectionist persona and the influence of PE's messages. Ultimately, Flavor himself is bereft of his previous relevancy and authority as his symbolism is given a new, harmless connotation in the context of the program and he steers clear of discussing any race related issues, or any important social issues at all. Drained of his former political significance, and posited as a harmless buffoon, it is interesting how popular Flavor has become and how easily he is digested by the mainstream.

Sealing and "Real"ing the Neo-Minstrel Box

So far, we have followed those elements in Flavor's general performance that distance him from both his former public persona and the stereotypical standards of desirable masculinity, and bring him close to the image of a buffoonish, entertaining, and slow-minded Sambo. In the remaining paragraphs of our analysis we illustrate the ways in which the show builds its Sambo caricature through examples of specific socially inept behaviors in which Flavor engages. Most of these behaviors take place during another central generic element in the dating show — the dates.

Both *Flavor of Love* and *The Bachelor* present the eligible bachelors going on dates with the female contestants. In *The Bachelor*, Dr. Stork picks up one group of women in helicopters to take them on a tour of France's Champagne region. Other dates include a cruise down the Seine River, a tour of Paris, and a stay on a yacht on the French Riviera. The dates are posited as inventive, fun, and in some cases extravagant.

In *The Flavor of Love*, however, Flavor takes his ladies to church with his mother, to the roller skating rink, and to such dining venues as Red Lobster. In the program "A Friend of Flav's is a Friend of Mine," Flavor tells contestant Sweetie regarding the dinner at Red Lobster: "I'm going to take you to my most favorite romantic spots to eat at." Because Flavor has indicated that he is taking her to his favorite spot and he is a celebrity, Sweetie states, "I'm absolutely sure it is going to be one of the most Hollywood of the Hollywood, only A-list people can get in." When they arrive at Red Lobster, Sweetie remarks, "I thought maybe we were going to walk behind it or whatever, like it was a joke." It is no joke to Flavor, who believes this date is something special for Sweetie, calling Red Lobster an "elegant place before it got too popular" and stating, "This is one of the first places that I was really trying to get romantic in. And it's a very good surprise for her." A combination of disappointment and distaste move across Sweetie's face as she watches Flavor suck the meat out of a lobster shell and shove pieces of zucchini in his mouth after he generously salts each piece. During the dinner, Flavor's main priority is his food, but he takes the time to provide rhymes such as, "I'm starvin' like Marvin. Give me the turkey, I'm carvin.'" Flavor's antics are meant to generate humor for the audience at Flavor's expense, as neither the location of the dinner, nor his behavior at dinner are what one would expect on a romantic date in general or with a celebrity in particular. His childlike nature and fun loving behavior are presented as a mirthful spectacle. However, he is not presented as an idealized mate, as are the men on *The Bachelor*. The influence of the writers and directors of the program are minimized in this instance as they are throughout the program, as Flavor's actions are presented as emanating organically from his personality, rather than from a host of industrial and commercial interests.

Food-related scenes are used in the show not only to portray Flavor as a socially inept and clownish Sambo, but to index him as a minstrel figure more generally. Diawara explains that "whites used to malign black people as watermelon and chicken thieves," (par 4) chicken being particularly used in minstrel imagery.[17] In *Flavor of Love*, fried chicken occupies a central, albeit unusual place. Thus, in episode four, we see Flavor preparing for a marathon-dating evening with the ladies. In order to ready himself for the first date, he has candles burning around the room and a nice fire in the fireplace, he pours champagne, prepares a plate of strawberries, and ... fried chicken. In his words: "Your man, Flavor Flav. I had it goin' on, you know what I'm sayin'? Had couple of bottles of champagne, you know what I'm sayin'? Strawberries, [emphatically] two big buckets of chicken!" The presence of fried chicken during an evening of romantic dates is meant to draw attention to the stereotype that African Americans display their allegedly inherent love for chicken even in the most unusual circumstances. Furthermore, the show deepens this minstrel originating representation of African Americans when Flavor challenges his dates to cook fried chicken for him and his mother. In the same episode, Flavor informs the contestants: "I love food! And even though I ain't no bigger than a bottle of ketchup, I do eat a lot. So I really do need me a girl that's kinda' good around the kitchen." He immediately spells out the challenge: cooking fried chicken. There is no explanation of why he has chosen fried chicken for the cooking challenge, of what are his favorite foods and why. The viewers are left to infer that this is the natural choice for Flavor, that there is a natural connection between who he is and his culinary choices.

Cooking is not the only challenge that Flavor opens for contestants. He frequently puts the ladies on the spot, assessing their skills in areas that he deems are important to being a girlfriend or wife. For example, he makes them think they are going on dates, but instead he drops them off at a children's party and a nursing home to assess their ability to take care of children and the elderly. While the men on *The Bachelor* always accompany the ladies on the dates, in the aforementioned instance, Flavor leaves the women to fend for themselves as he watches their performance on video from his limousine. Flavor also tests the contestants' capacity to be lucky, corresponding with the Sambo character's valorization of superstition over logic, by flying them to Las Vegas and assessing their ability to be successful on the roulette table. Perhaps the hardest evaluation is the lie detector test given by his former girlfriend, Brigitte Nielsen, who asks the women such private questions that all but one feel the need to lie.

Intermittently, Flavor provides the audience with his personal commentary on the contestants and dates. As he does so, he speaks directly into the camera to the audience at home, giving us his secret perspective on the women as if we are his confidants and friends. The process of sharing his thoughts about the contestants functions to reinforce the "realness" of the situation, as does his frequent comment: "We all know that Flav likes his ladies to keep it real." This comment is meant to suggest that Flavor favors those contestants who are authentic; those who do not pretend to be something that they are not. This statement combined with his conversations with the audience function to subtly cultivate the idea that there is a degree of authenticity to this program, and to his performance. Of course, a major draw of the celeb-reality genre is the opportunity to get a sense of what these stars are like behind the scenes and therefore some fans come to the program already with the expectation that the performances have a degree of fidelity to the person who exhibits them.

As these examples suggest, Flavor's dating situations are different from those shown on *The Bachelor* and the images of whiteness and blackness dovetail together to underscore exaggerated, stereotyped differences, with Flavor emerging as a neo-minstrel product offered up for consumption by contemporary audiences. Whereas the men on *The Bachelor* take the women to expensive locations, which of course are selected and paid for by the studio, Flavor takes his dates to Red Lobster, or to his back garden, insinuating his lack of maturity and sophistication, although these locations also have been selected and approved by his respective studio. The representation of Flavor's antics on the dates serves to reinforce this difference and when coupled with strategies that work to heighten the reality of the program, it is suggested that Flavor's situations and performances emerge organically from Flavor, rather than being the product of commercial forces that function to commodify African American masculinity for popular consumption.

Inside and Outside of the Neo-Minstrelsy Box

Women and minorities struggle for productive and respectable images in U.S. popular culture, recognizing the deleterious effects stereotypes impose on people who have been marginalized and maligned in American history. In order to combat such representations, Coleman suggests analyzing the ways images of whiteness and blackness are juxtaposed in mediated contexts (33). Examining the ways in which white masculinity and black masculinity take on similar roles but are portrayed in different lights, such as on *Flavor of Love* and *The Bachelor*, enables one to identify and "fracture hyper-racialized images" (33). Compared as he is generically and based on allusion to *The Bachelor*, Flavor on *Flavor of Love*, and black masculinity by extension, emerge as the deviant Other to an idealized white masculinity. The potency of whiteness is buttressed by Flavor's representation as a clownish bachelor. His self-reflexive references function to reinforce the realness of this reality television representation, rather than testify to its fiction. Ultimately, the image of Flavor on this program may eschew notions of violent black masculinity but it functions to reify the *status quo* by invigorating stereotypical representations of black masculinity that date back to minstrelsy, particularly the image of the Sambo caricature.

Our analysis has demonstrated that, while Flavor's performance distances whiteness from blackness and centers the former, it does so by parodying not white, but black masculinity. If the casts of the two shows were both white, the simple comparison would have been sufficient to conclude that one parodies the other. A white cast in *Flavor of Love* would even be a progressive cultural product, in Judith Butler's terms, as it would have destabilized, through parody, hegemonic standards of white masculinity and femininity, exposing the constructedness of social identities and their normalization only through consistent repetition. *Flavor of Love*, however, has a predominantly black cast, and the leading figure is a black man. While the comparison with *The Bachelor* is necessary, by itself it is insufficient in understanding the cultural work done by this text. Our analysis, therefore, has placed Flavor's performance in the show also against two diachronic moments: the artist's Public Enemy persona and the minstrel show tradition. This layered analysis illustrated how Flavor parodies not white masculinity, but his former Public Enemy persona and the image of respectable and desirable black masculinity more generally. His parody thus ghettoizes black masculinity, making it seem different and exaggeratedly distanced from the white standard, placing it in its own separate box, and rendering it unable to undermine, through parody, normative white masculinity. Because of this crucial difference in cast, Flavor's buffooneries can only parody progressive black masculinities like Flavor's PE persona, or those featured on black-fatherhood reality shows.[18]

Furthermore, Flavor's parodic expressions mirror the performance of the Sambo minstrel character. Flavor's portrayal on *Flavor of Love* represents, thus, a commodification of black masculinity in the form of neo-minstrelsy, a longstanding cultural product that continues to undermine African American political and cultural relevance. The mainstream's embrace of Flavor on this vapid program suggests a recurring and troubling ambivalence towards black masculinity on U.S. reality television. That is — with two notable exceptions[19] — images of African American men tend to be embraced when they portray black men as irrelevant jesters who do little to unsettle the *status quo*, but are vilified when they raise troubling questions about social structures and attempt to attain political significance. The scene of reality television appears, thusly, as a form of neo-minstrelsy.

Current public discourses may indicate that white anxieties toward black men are being played out onto the Sambo or the Brutal Buck dichotomy not just on reality television, but within the U.S. culture at large. Such binary representational dynamics can be noted, for example, in the presidential election campaign featuring, for the first time in the U.S. history, an African American candidate. The political right's attempts to cast Senator Barack Obama as either a dangerous terrorist or black extremist feed off of the Brutal Buck character.[20] And if the media only arguably has managed to cast Obama as a Brutal Buck for portions of the electorate, the public scandal around the figure of Reverend Wright indicates that the media fully evoked that image in their portrayal of Wright as a black man yearning for revenge and violence.

The damaging effects of this binary framework can be further seen in African American evaluations of Obama as not black enough, where blackness is defined along the stereotypical contours of the Brutal Buck.[21] Negative representations not only influence perceptions of the African American community and political leaders among the broader public, but they also have a harmful effect on black subjectivity. Coleman maintains that a split image can result in African American subjectivity when "culpable image makers, their conduit, the media, and an accepting society" converge to create and sustain "marred African American representations (the exterior image)" which function to "devastate Blackness, the interior self" (32). Similarly, Hooks argues that "there has never been a time in the history of the United States when black folks, particularly black men, have not been enraged by the dominant culture's stereotypical, fantastical representations of black masculinity" (89). At the same time, however, "contemporary black men have been shaped by these representations" (89). Rejecting representations that devastate black subjectivity and creating images that fracture ideologies of domination should be the charge of everyone committed to opposing racism and its manifestation in everyday life. Our analysis is part of the project of decolonizing our minds from the aesthetics of domination so prevalent in U.S. popular culture, and of demanding progressive representations that reflect and expand the complexity of our humanity.

Notes

1. The authors thank Robin Means Coleman for her insightful advice and feedback on an earlier version of this essay.

2. For a sampling, see Andrejevic, "Kinder" 251–270: Andrejevic, "Interactive" 230–248; Andrejevic; Doyle; Dubrofsky 39–56; Friedman; Hill; Holmes and Jermyn; Murray and Ouelette.

3. We are referring to the October 2008 special issue on race and reality television by *Critical Studies in Media Communication*, which contains two articles that focus on African American masculinity by Smith 393–412, and Dubrofsky and Hardy 373–392.

4. Orbe 32–47, Orbe and Hopson 219–226, Orbe, Warren, and Cornwell 107–134.

5. "Celeb-reality" is the name given to reality programs that feature celebrities. Traditional reality television programs have focused on the lives of everyday people. *Flavor of Love* is a hybrid subgenre: a celeb-reality because it features rap artist Flavor Flav and also an elimination dating show made after *The Bachelor*. For more details on subgenres of reality television, see Palmer-Mehta and Haliliuc 159–78.

6. Flavor's comeback commenced with *Surreal Life 3* and continued in the program, *Strange Love*, which documented his relationship with Brigitte Nielsen that began on *Surreal Life 3*.

7. At the time of this writing, two seasons of a spin-off entitled *I Love New York* and one season of *New York Goes to Hollywood* were produced, which center on Tiffany Patterson, one of the contestants from *The Flavor of Love*. Another spin-off, *Flavor of Love Girls: Charm School* (2007), featuring contestants from *Flavor of Love*, was produced.

8. Public Enemy's debut album, *Yo! Bum Rush the Show*, was released in 1987. It did not receive the attention or chart ratings that the group's two subsequent releases (*It Takes a Nation of Millions to Hold Us Down* and *Fear of a Black Planet*) enjoyed.

9. "Don't Believe the Hype" is a song off of PE's 1988 album, *It Takes a Nation of Millions to Hold Us Back*.

10. "Burn Hollywood Burn" is from PE's 1990 album, *Fear of a Black Planet*.

11. Some might argue that there was no break in the minstrel tradition, per se. For

example, *The Amos and Andy Show*, which had a presence in radio, television, and film between the 1920s and 1950s, was informed by the minstrel tradition.

12. According to Debra C. Smith, *Run's House* is coproduced by Simmons. Snoop is executive director of his show and his own Snoopadelic Films coproduces *Snoop Dogg*. Therefore, both men have some degree of influence over how black fatherhood is represented.

13. A grill is a removable chunk of metal (usually gold or silver, some are diamond encrusted) that is worn on the teeth. One might think of it as jewelry for one's teeth.

14. At the time of the first season of the *Flavor of Love*, Flavor had six children. However, it was revealed after the second season that Flavor's girlfriend was pregnant with his seventh child.

15. Cronin also is the creator, writer, executive producer of *Strange Love* and executive producer for *Surreal Life*.

16. XXL Magazine. "*Flavor of Love* Finale Breaks VH1 Ratings Records." *XXL Magazine*. Retrieved May 30, 2006 from http://xxlmag.com/online/?p=514. *XXL Magazine* was selected as a site for this study because it is the world's top selling hip-hop magazine with a circulation of 315,000. We selected the message board associated with the article listed because it was published at the pinnacle of the show's interest (the finale) and at a time when viewers would have had the opportunity to see all the episodes.

17. According to Lemons 102–116 and Epp 18–35.

18. See Smith 393–412.

19. Again, referring to Smith 393–412.

20. For a scholarly treatment of Obama's racialization through his relations with Jeremiah Wright, Bill Ayers, and Michelle Obama, see Aimee Carrillo Rowe.

21. For example, see Coates, "Is Obama Black Enough?"

Bibliography

Andrejevic, Mark. "The Kinder, Gentler Gaze of Big Brother." *New Media and Society* 4 (2002): 251–270.
_____. *Reality TV: The Work of Being Watched*. Lanham, MD: Rowman & Littlefield, 2004.
_____. "The Work of Being Watched: Interactive Media and the Exploitation of Self-Disclosure." *Critical Studies in Media Communication* 19 (2002): 230–248.
Bachelor. Episode Guide. The Bachelor Paris. 2006. 21 June 2006 from <http://abc.go.com/primetime/bachelor/episodes/2005-06/1.html>
Bogle, Donald. *Tom, Coons, Mulattoes, Mammies and Bucks*. 3rd ed. New York: Continuum International, 1994.
Boskin, Joseph. *Sambo: The Rise and Demise of an American Jester*. New York: Oxford University Press, 1986.
Butler, Judith. *Gender Trouble: Feminism and the Subversion of Identity*. New York: Routledge, 1990.
Carlson, Keri. "To Hell with Politics, Let's Get It On." *The Minnesota Daily* 24 May 2006. 24 May 2006 <www.mndaily.com/articles/2006/05/24/68410>
Carrillo Rowe, Aimee. "For the Love of Obama: Nation, Race, and the Politics of Relation." The Obama Effect Conference, Minneapolis, MN. October 23–25, 2008.
Coates, Ta-Nehisi Paul. "Is Obama Black Enough?" *Time Magazine* February 1, 2007. 25 October 2008 <http://www.time.com/time/nation/article/0,8599,1584736,00.html>.
Coleman, Robin Means. *African American Viewers and the Black Situation Comedy: Situating Racial Humor*. New York: Garland, 2000.

Derosia, Margaret. "The Court of Last Resort: Making Race, Crime and Nation on America's Most Wanted." In *Reality Squared: Televisual Discourse on the Real*. Ed. James Friedman. New Brunswick, NJ: Rutgers University Press, 2002. 236–258.

Diawara, Manthia. "The Blackface Stereotype." *Blackface*. Ed. David Levinthal. Santa Fe, NM: Arena, 1999. 7–17.

Dickinson, Greg, and Karrin Vasby Anderson. "Fallen: O.J. Simpson, Hillary Rodham Clinton, and the Re-Centering of White Patriarchy." *Communication and Critical/Cultural Studies* 1 (2004): 271–296.

Doyle, Aaron. *Arresting Images*. Toronto: University of Toronto Press, 2004.

Dubrofsky, Rachel. "The Bachelor: Whiteness in the Harem." In *Critical Studies in Media Communication* 23 (2006): 39–56.

Dubrofsky, Rachel E., and Antoine Hardy. "Performing Race in 'Flavor of Love' and 'the Bachelor.'" *Critical Studies in Media Communication* 25.4 (2008): 373–392.

English, James. *Comic Transactions: Literature, Humor, and Politics of Community in Twentieth-Century Britain*. Ithaca, NY: Cornell University Press, 1994.

Epp, Michael H. "Raising Minstrelsy: Humor, Satire and the Stereotype in 'The Birth of a Nation' and 'Bamboozled.'" *Canadian Review of American Studies* 33 (2003): 18–35.

Friedman, James. *Reality Squared: Televisual Discourse on the Real*. New Brunswick, NJ: Rutgers University Press, 2002.

Hill, Annette. *Reality TV: Audiences and Popular Factual Television*. New York: Routledge, 2005.

Holmes, Su, and Deborah Jermyn, eds. *Understanding Reality Television*. London: Routledge, 2004.

hooks, bell. *Black Looks: Race and Representation*. Cambridge, MA: South End, 1992.

Kraszewski, J. "Country Hicks and Urban Clicks: Mediating Race, Reality, and Liberalism on MTV's the Real World." In *Reality TV: Remaking Television Culture*. Ed. Susan Murray and Laurie Ouelette. New York: New York University Press, 2004. 179–196.

Lemons, J. Stanley. "Black Stereotypes as Reflected in Popular Culture, 1880–1920." *American Quarterly* 29 (1977): 102–116.

Lhamon, Jr., W. T. *Raising Cain: Blackface Performance from Jim Crow to Hip Hop*. Cambridge: Harvard University Press, 1998.

Lott, Eric. "Blackface and Blackness: The Minstrel show in American Culture." *Inside the Minstrel Mask: Readings in Nineteenth-Century Blackface Minstrelsy*. Ed. Annemarie Bean, James Hatch, and Brooks McNamara. Hanover: Wesleyan University Press, 1996. 3–34.

_____. *Love and Theft: Blackface Minstrelsy and the American Working Class*. New York: Oxford University Press, 1993.

Mercer, Kobena. *Welcome to the Jungle: New Positions in Black Cultural Studies*. New York: Routledge, 1994.

Murray, Susan, and Laurie Ouelette, eds. *Reality TV: Remaking Television Culture*. New York: New York University Press, 2004.

Nakayama, Thomas. "The Significance of "Race" and Masculinities." *Critical Studies in Media Communication* 17 (2000): 111–113.

Ollison, Rashod. "Public Enemy Made Music of Biting Truth." *The Baltimore Sun* 11 March 2007, 1(E).

Orbe, Mark. "Constructions of Reality on MTV's 'the Real World': An Analysis of Restrictive Coding of Black Masculinity." *Southern Communication Journal* 64 (1998): 32–47.

Orbe, Mark, and M. C. Hopson. "Looking at the Front Door: Exploring Images of the Black Male on MTV's 'the Real World.'" In *Readings in Intercultural Communication: Experiences and Contexts*. Ed. J. N. Martin, R. K. Nakayama, and Lisa A. Flores. Boston: McGraw-Hill, 2002. 219–226.

Orbe, Mark, K. Warren, and N. Cornwell. "Negotiating Societal Stereotypes: Analyzing

'Real World' Discourse by and about African American Men." *International and Intercultural Communication Annual* 23 (2001): 107–134.

Palmer-Mehta, Valerie, and Alina Haliliuc. "Reality Television: The Business of Mediating (Extra)Ordinary Life." In *The Business of Entertainment: Television.* Ed. Robert Sickels. Westport, CT: Praeger, 2008. 159–178.

Reality, Joe. "Flavor of Love Finale was VH-1's Highest Rated Show Ever." *Reality TV Magazine* 14 March 2006. 30 May 2006 <http://www.realitytvmagazine.com/blog/2006/03/flavor_of_love__1.html>

_____. "Flavor of Love Offers Up First Reality TV Vomit of the Year." Reality TV Magazine 2 January 2006. 30 May 2006 <http://www.realitytvmagazine.com/blog/2006/01/flavor_of_love_.html>

Rose, Tricia. *Black Noise: Rap Music and Black Culture in Contemporary America.* Hanover, NH: Wesleyan University Press, 1994.

Smith, Debra C. "Critiquing Reality-Based Televisual Black Fatherhood: A Critical Analysis of 'Run's House' and 'Snoop Dogg's Father Hood.'" *Critical Studies in Media Communication* 25.4 (2008): 393–412.

6

Jungle Fever: Bold, Beautiful and Unnecessarily Maligned

Daryl A. Carter

One of the most interesting activities of the last fifty years has been the growing number of interracial relationships; especially unions involving black men and white females. Indeed, the specter of miscegenation has been a part of the American experience since the first slaves stepped off the slave ships onto the shores of Jamestown. While there have always been such pairings, the numbers of black men and white women unions recorded have been relatively minimal. Moreover, in many states, prior to the mid–1960s, it was considered illegal for people of different races to be married. The Richard and Mildred Loving case was one such situation. This case centered on a white male/black female couple who were taken out of their home in the middle of the night, arrested and placed in prison for violating Virginia's anti-miscegenation laws. In 1967, their case went all the way to the U.S. Supreme Court where they reigned victorious.[1] Anti-miscegenation laws were implemented by white men who harbored a vehement fear of black men engaging in sexual liaisons with white women. The very notion of such romantic entanglements was considered taboo.

Despite such contraposition, black men involved in sexual relationships with white women has become more mainstream and commonplace since the mid 1970s. In no other area has this become more apparent than in the medium of television. Since Sidney Poitier played a young professional black man coming to dinner with a young, wealthy white woman in the Oscar nominated movie *Guess Who's Coming to Dinner* (1967), white Americans have generally recoiled at the thought of their young daughters bringing young, strapping, black men home to meet them. Television has shown these relationships either through rose colored spectacles or more commonly, a myopic and bigoted lens. Black men have been depicted as dangerous, shiftless, wanton sexual predators lusting after beautiful, chaste young white girls and women in an effort to corrupt the historically held image of pristine virtue that supposedly epitomized white womanhood. In fact, the deranged portrayals of such relationships have become so sophisticated and obscured the often blatant racism and sexism involved is hardly noticed by the viewer.

These relationships while repugnant and unthinkable to many whites and even some blacks, are the natural reaction to physical and emotional attractions that have drawn these groups together since the beginning of America. There are many historic reasons why black men and white women have found love, friendship, and comfort in one another's arms. However, Hollywood and much of the mainstream media promotes a less than flattering image of such couples. Such a sinister effort must be seen for what it is and stopped. As America faces an era unprecedented level of angst, division, and palpable hatreds, it must also come to grips with and see these relationships in the sympathetic, respectable, or even indifferent manner that accompanies relations between people from the North and people from the South. Black male/white female relationships should not be viewed as intolerable or disgusting but rather as beautiful and refreshing. Black men in these United States have a difficult time as it is living in a society where virtually everyone is despising or doubting them as well as dealing with the retrograde perception of the larger public that they "ain't worth shit." Due to such foolishness it is time to dispel such nonsense once and for all.

Despite the consistent level of innovation that frequently emerges from Hollywood, the industry still strikes a one trick pony note in its portrayal of African Americans. As journalist and public commentator Sylvester Monroe stated "studio executives seem to think that hard-core inner-city life is the only slice of black life there is."[2] Black Americans are more than often portrayed as dangerous, shiftless, opportunistic and lazy sub-human beings. We are seen as representing all that is wrong, deviant, immoral or amoral with America. In essence, blacks have not changed much in the minds of a majority of white Americans over the period of the last two centuries. Further, if one peruses through television channels with a remote control, they are likely to be bombarded with stereotypes of a different stripe: Black men and women depicted mainly as clowns, shuffling, jiving, sassing and cooning about for all to see. Ignorant cutups and loud-mouthed buffoons are in abundance.[3] Considering the long history and sordid legacy of discrimination in this country, it is unlikely that such degrading images will change anytime soon.

Due to this skewed view of African Americans and black men in particular, it is no wonder that so many falsehoods that have been embedded in the minds of white Americans. Such misguided viewpoints have not been solely confined to whites. Indeed, more than a few upscale blacks, whether wittingly or unwittingly, have bought into the negative notions about black men in this country. The media has adamantly displayed black men in the role of gang-bangers, criminals, unemployed biological fathers to several illegitimate children, etc. However, it seldom depicts honest, hardworking black men trying to do right by their families or striving to take part in the American Dream in a manner similar to that of supposedly decent, law-abiding white Americans. Such feelings greatly affect the way black men are treated in the workplace and the society writ large.

How does this portend to the current and future treatment of black men in regards to interracial relationships? It creates a situation in which whites are forever viewing blacks in a condescending manner. It turns black men into garish, explicit circus acts to be perversely viewed in special confines by voyeuristic, carnal minded whites only to be summarily dismissed after the audience has satisfied its inner beast. Another problem with this attitude is that it fosters an attitude and environment where a number of young white people believe that what I call slumming — the process of seeking interracial relationships during adolescence or adulthood and then disavowing of the relationship in order to take or resume their rightful place in white society — is acceptable. Such behavior is nothing new.

The relationships of founding father Thomas Jefferson and his mistress Sally Hemmings in the eighteenth century as well as many other whites during the Harlem Renaissance demonstrate such a fact. White and black sexual relations in America are as common as apple pie. The misguided belief and practice was that black women are less than human. They are oversexed, big breasted, animalistic creatures who have an uncontained sexual appetite (much like their fellow black males) and are pre-conditioned to enjoy sex. Part of the function of black women (particularly in the South) was to serve the sexual needs and desires of white men.

On the contrary, relationships between black men and white women are not easily accepted and are (in the minds of many people) scorned.

A notable example of this was the 1961 presidential inauguration of John Fitzgerald Kennedy. Then Sen. Kennedy had maintained a close social relationship with the legendary Rat Pack — Frank Sinatra, Peter Lawford, Dean Martin, Joey Bishop, and Sammy Davis, Jr. The Rat Pack was supposed to be the major entertainment in the nation's capital on the evening of January 20, 1961. However, Sammy Davis, Jr. had married Swedish actress May Britt, a white woman, shortly before the 1960 presidential campaign. That relationship combined with the supposed audacity of the couple to openly marry offended the tender sensibilities of the Kennedy family and entourage. He [Davis] was quickly uninvited because the Kennedy's did not want to be seen as supporting interracial relationships and marriage. Journalist Ted Schwartz argues that "Together they were a dangerous liability for Jack [Kennedy].[4] Legend has it that Joseph Kennedy who was known to be racially bigoted, sexist and anti–Semitic was so upset by Sammy Davis' actions that he ordered that Davis be dropped from the program despite the fact the entertainer had worked tirelessly to encourage and persuade African Americans to vote for Kennedy. This example demonstrates that the very idea of interracial contact of a romantic nature was so reprehensible to many white Americans that they could not imagine such a spectacle. It is also important to remember that during this time period, in many areas of the country, it was not only illegal, but perilous to engage in such dalliances.

The aforementioned story shows what could often have happened in the well-bred, well-fed, upscale high society. In other situations of a less highbrow nature the ramifications of such activity could be downright horrific. As author Jenifer Harris argues, "The history of lynching black men in response to unfounded charges of the rape of a White woman" is a perfect example of the visceral reaction to the thought of black/white sex as well as the white man regaining control of his virility that was thought to be largely emasculated by black male sexuality.[5] All of this demonstrates what Cornel West argued: that white Americans fear black sexuality, "white Americans are obsessed with sex and fearful of black sexuality."[6]

Another famous example of white America's fear of black men and their supposed sexual prowess is the case of early twentieth century famed prize fighter Jack Johnson. Johnson's brazen public display of parading white women in public and across state lines enraged more than a few white men and placed fear in the hearts of many blacks who feared public retaliation from white society. Many historians have argued that the 1911 Mann Act was ratified into law partly due to the behavior of Jack Johnson. Academics John D'Emilio and Estelle Freedmen remarked "His second wife had been white, and he had numerous affairs with others," including a prostitute originally from Minneapolis and working in Chicago named Lucille Cameron with whom he quickly engaged in sexual intercourse.[7] Her mother pursued charges against Johnson despite her daughter's refusal to comply with the prosecution. He was acquitted. The ending to this very public case did not eradicate the harsh feelings and vitriolic statements that a large segment of the media of that era reserved for such relationships.

Prior to the days of television, it was in some ways easier to malign the image of black men than it is today. The pre–TV days of print media allowed powerful whites, editors, reporters, and others to present an image of black men similar to that of an animal with no fear of reprisal or accountability. In addition, blacks had little or any recourse to contradict the racist orthodoxy presented in the newspapers and newsreels shown before movies in theaters. Even in more recent cases we have seen the hatchet jobs performed on black males that are eerily reminiscent to the media during the first half of the twentieth century.

Probably the most famous or infamous example — depending on your outlook — is the trial of O.J. Simpson. In 1994 Simpson was charged with two counts of first degree murder in the deaths of ex-wife Nicole Brown Simpson and her friend Ronald Goldman, a Los Angeles restaurant waiter. The case spawned a television station, Court TV, and a cottage industry of legal analysts acting as commentators on cases before the various courts in the land. Almost instantly the predominately white media and population condemned the former football star, while the black community rallied to the defense of Simpson. It goes without question that the case would never have received the attention it did if Simpson had slain his first wife, a black woman named Marguerite Simpson. Further, the media quickly took to the offensive to show that Simpson was an out-of-control, abusive, user of white women. *Time* magazine went so far as to put Simpson's mug shot on the cover of its magazine and darkened the man's skin tone. Understandably, such a callous act caused a big brouhaha within the black community and speculation of to the motives of *Time*.[8]

The lesson here is that when O.J. was simply playing football, leaping suitcases in airports, and providing commentary on Sunday afternoon football games he was a media darling. However, when his predilection towards white women and his violent treatment of them became widely known, Simpson became a pariah in the public mindset. The majority of public opinion, particularly white public opinion, was that he was being ostracized and deservedly so for much of his conduct, not just committing murder but for having the audacity to cohort with white women.

In more general ways, bawdy television talk shows such as *The Maury Povich Show*, and *Jerry Springer*, among others, always seem to depict black men as low-class, sex obsessed purveyors of white women. Furthermore, network and cable news network consistently show black males in various situations of difficulty that belie the truth. In addition, the media generally only shows those stories when it comes to interracial relationships that put black men in a negative light. For instance, how often does local or national media show loving, functional, and successful interracial relationships? The answer is almost never. Why do we not see more representations of these relationships on television?

The answer is quite simple: profit. Just like rap, hip hop, and gangster rap appeals to middle and upper class whites in the suburbs, visual displays of interracial sex also piques the interests of whites. A primary development in this area is that of pornography. Once thought to be disgusting and inconvenient due to the fact that one had to leave their home and venture downtown to the blue light district or other seedy sides of town to purchase or watch graphic movies or other arguably demented activities, porn has now become prominently mainstream due to the arrival of the Internet, DVD players, VCRs, and discreet mailing services. One of the most popular genres of pornography is that of interracial hardcore. I submit that the growing white viewership of such material reflects hidden desires on the part of white males that at once both titillates and reinforces racist feelings. Cultural critic Gail Dines argues "The black men are often described as thugs, pimps, hustlers, hip-hoppers, mofos, and bros who live in the hood and drive pimp-mobiles.[9] All too often the black men shown in these films are young, thuggish, low-rent, uncouth caricatures with oversized penises. Dines further argues: "To ignore the racist codings of black men in pornography in favor of a simplistic, decontextualized reading of the pornographic text as subversive is to operate in a world of white privilege where being the "fucker" is a status symbol with no real world burden."[10] Interestingly, it is here where Dines is misguided. Nothing could be further from the truth. The fact is that pornography helps to serve the interests of an industry that revels in the degradation and malicious stereotyping of African American men.

While the appearance of African Americans on television has dramatically increased over the period of the last quarter of a century, the sophistication and exploitation has also grown. Today, viewers are likely to see African American men in roles that are far more diverse than ever before. Such roles have only served to enhance stereotypes while disingenuously convincing the viewing public that *race* no longer plays a vital role in our society. This is one of the most dangerous and patently false assumptions ever projected onto the American landscape. As Cornel West so eloquently discussed in his groundbreaking 1993 book, *Race Matters,* "Black people in the United States differ from all other modern people owing to the unprecedented levels of unregulated and unrestrained violence directed at them."[11]

What television has done over the past fifty years has been to mollify, pacify and disengage the American public. While television was instrumental in helping to expose the inherent evil of the Jim Crow South, it has also coerced millions of Americans to surrender their intellectual capabilities and to accept what they see as fact with ne'er a peep. As noted by Al Gore in his brilliant attack on the current state of contemporary culture, *The Assault on Reason,* Americans watch some *"four hours and thirty-five minutes every day—* ninety minutes more than the world average," which can only have a negative impact of the psyche of the American mind.[12] Furthermore, with most Americans "staring at flickering images on a screen for more than thirty hours each week," it is no wonder such primitive and racist views persist in our society.[13] Indeed, try considering how much television you watch and then think about how often you are able to response to what you are seeing. Almost never, as Al Gore states, are television viewers able to respond to what they see. While the former vice president and recent academy award and Nobel Peace Prize winner was putting this analysis in the context of representative democracy, citizen participation, and the best interest of the republic, it also has deep implications for race relations and perceptions of interracial relationships.

As a black man who is the product of an interracial marriage and involved in a mixed marriage, I can attest to the lingering, often debilitating effects of racism and prejudice towards those in such relationships. I have dated black women in the past; however, I have usually been more attracted to white women. Neither is necessarily better but for me those relationships with white women have been far more productive and fruitful. All too often black men like me are criticized for choosing to date and marry white women. It has been said that we [black men] only seek out such relationships to show our social mobility, to take or steal the white man's property, or to reject black women who have stood by us since before the slave ships arrived from Africa. However, despite such narrow, idiotic thoughts, most black men engage in such relationships not because of some nefarious plot but because they genuinely fall in love with the other person. The same can be said for white women. This is not to say that there are not a minority of people out there, who do engage in these relationships for improper reasons. The same can be said of all human relationships. The powers that be, mainly white America, have consistently sought to devalue, dehumanize, and destroy — especially after the vestiges of legal slavery were stripped away — the dignity of black people in this country. By stripping any level of legitimacy and respectability from these couples, they are trying to say that these people are wanton and illegitimate. It is not only the white power structure that plays a major role in this issue; a number of fellow blacks do so as well.

Black women in particular, along with militant, pro-black everything males, are often contemptuous of such relationships. For many black women it is as if these relationships are a direct attack on their femininity, as if they alone are entitled to the companionship of black men. I cannot tell you how many times I have heard black women complaining about white women stealing "our men." The simple fact of the matter is that opposites attract and there are some longstanding ties that bind the black man and white woman. Some of those commonalities include shared misery. Both have been long considered either chattel property or second-class citizens in the United States. Furthermore, each group has been forced to struggle through obstacles such as glass ceilings in the workplace, retrograde politics, and a society that would make most people cringe at the very thought of trading places with them. black men who have decided to engage in such relationships have been thought of sexual predators, deviants, or worse. Likewise, white women have been thought of as traitors to their race, tramps, racially gullible in that white Guilt manner of which some speak, or prone to debasing themselves and losing their respective place in society for the venal pleasures of the flesh. Media has played a key role in the dissemination of such thoughts. These racial problems have a long and complex history that continues to plague the United States well into the twenty-first century. As noted in the landmark Report of National Advisory Commission on Civil Disorders in 1968, "the news media have failed to analyze and report adequately on racial problems in the United States and, as a related manner, to meet the Negro's legitimate expectations in journalism."[14] While the Kerner Commission was discussing the social upheaval of the late 1960s and the historic and contemporary plight of African Americans, it remains true today that the American media remains racially biased.

The media continues to promote images of African Americans which contradict reality. Moreover, they continue to present images which portray African Americans as dangerous to the well-being of whites and society in general. This is done by darkening the hue of peoples skin, using racial codes words and issues, like affirmative action, welfare, etc., and often putting the least educated, most ghetto elements of the African American on display for the world to see. While it can be said that this is also done to some extent across the board to other ethnic groups as well, the emphasis is both not as intense nor as damning in its impact. Finally, media perpetuates images that are acceptable to the mainstream viewing audience. By reinforcing negative images of African American they are helping to create an unyielding situation in which fear, resentment, and lunacy trumps logic and reason.

Despite the personal, visceral reactions to blacks that color the media's coverage, there is another powerful entity that also affects the coverage: money. Media coverage is dominated by special interests. As Pamela Newkirk notes in discussing NBC's decision to broadcast Bryant Gumbel from Africa in 1992, "$2 million cost of the critically acclaimed series had been money well spent, the project lost the all-important ratings war during the lucrative sweeps period."[15] She further argued "Nor is profitability the only challenge to fairer coverage: Black journalists must also confront the unwillingness of their white editors to tackle racial issues."[16] This is particularly true when one is discussing the coverage given to interracial relationships where the male is black and the woman is white. Are they portrayed as loving, wholesome relationships with children, stability, and comfort? More often than not, no! They are seen as illegitimate and perverse. Even the slightest hint of interracial interaction is still considered taboo and until recently such venable news networks as CNN didn't show very many black male/white woman on air pairings.

The most common image of black men that many see when they view or read media is that of a dangerous and scary fellow who cannot be trusted. Television has begun, under heavy political pressure and criticism in recent years, to put more blacks on the tube. However, the images they are currently presenting, if not of a felon, welfare queen, or moral degenerate, is that of a comical, hapless person which fails to arouse the sense of fear and dread in its white audience. In reality, today's television is a high-tech, sophisticated minstrel show that continues to manipulate the minds not only of whites but blacks as well. If one were to look at D.W. Griffith's 1915 horrendously racist film, "The Birth of a Nation," there is, in many ways, little difference.

The People v. O.J. Simpson is a perfect example of such negative and slanted coverage of black male/white female relationships. Simpson, a Hall-of-Fame football star and Heisman trophy winner, demonstrated the incessant need of the media to paint black men in a very negative manner. Nicole Brown Simpson and Ronald Goldman were brutally slaughtered in cold blood and soon afterwards Simpson was vilified throughout America. On the contrary, legendary NBC sports broadcaster Marv Albert was discovered to have brutalized an African American woman, Vanessa Perhach, during a conjugal visit which resulted in her being chewed with cannibalistic relish. Allegations of threesomes, group sex, bisexuality and other forms of non-traditional sexual activity became public knowledge as well. Eventually, Albert pleaded guilty to a misdemeanor charge of assault and battery and given a one year suspended sentence.[17] The reaction of a large segment of the public was immediate disgust, but there was also a strange and morbid curiosity about the Albert case that resulted in weeks of late-night jokes. In the eyes of many in the mainstream media, Albert was merely relegated to the status of a dysfunctional pervert. Why was Marv Albert not considered to be a threat to society, a beast, a sociopath like Simpson? Why not? Could it have been that he was a white man?

Another source of consternation is the image of black homosexuals in the media. While they may not be engaging in sexual relations with white women, many times they are engaging in sexual activities with white men. Even here it seems that blacks also have to play the role of the deviant villain, a theme that has been increasingly commonplace on network and syndicated television. An example of this is the wisecracking, flamboyant, assertive short order restaurant cook Lafayette Reynolds in the HBO series *True Blood* played by actor Nelsan Ellis and produced by Alan Ball, the director/producer of the 1999 Academy Award winning movie *American Beauty*. Lafayette is the epitome of the confrontational, talk trash, potentially violent, take no shit type of black man who works the diner as if he is the owner much of the time. During his off time, he sleeps around and services a number of white men. Some of them are vampires, others are prominent citizens in the community, most notably a well-respected Louisiana State senator.

Another HBO series produced by Ball was the Emmy award winning series *Six Feet Under* which ran on the network from 2001 to 2005. In this program, another black gay man, Keith Charles, was played by actor Michael St. Patrick. Keith personified long held stereotypes about black men being uptight, domineering, angry and to a large degree, paranoid in regards to the world around him. His attitude toward his white male partner David became so hostile that he (David) walked out of the relationship for a brief time. The fact that Alan Ball, an openly gay man himself, has decided to portray the only two black male characters in his series as gay makes one wonder what his motives are.

Another example of such deviancy was one notable episode of the NBC television program *Law & Order*, in which a black assistant district attorney in New York becomes involved, "on the down-low," with a white male colleague. Consequently, he gives him HIV and then proceeds to murder the man after he develops feelings for him. If that were not enough, he transmits the disease to his loving wife and children. While such situations often do take place in real life, it does nothing but reinforce negative feelings about black men and their sexuality. This may be one area in which whites and blacks hold similar opinions or at least disdain for homosexuals. Due to the very conservative leanings of the black community, based in large part on religion, homosexuality has been driven underground in many areas of black America.

The issue of same sex love is one of those rare instances where the condemnation of the alternative lifestyle has been universal between the races. Until recently homosexuality had been thought of as a psychological abnormality not just in the theological profession but by the medical profession as well. In 1974, the American Medical Association no longer declared it a disease. In fact, many people in the black community have considered such activity a white man's thing. The main reason seems to be that only whites denigrated themselves so willingly and with such joy.

White conservatives and evangelicals have believed that the homosexual community has been in direct opposition to the teachings of God and a part of the communistic, agnostic, or atheistic sector of society that has always been a threat to the sanctity of the American values and marriage. As one sexuality scholar has described the plight of gays and lesbians in the early years of the cold war, "although the meagerness of evidence to sustain the charge that homosexuals and lesbians threatened national security makes the preoccupation with sexual perversion appear in retrospect bizarre and irrational, the incorporation of gay women and men into the demonology of the McCarthy era required little effort."[18] The images distributed by the media of such relationships is that of either limp-wristed, high pitched, effeminate men engaging in various perversions or hyper-masculine men determined to hide their depravity.

Personal Recollections

Race is a funny thing. It is a social construct of which society says that one race is better than another. It is something that permeates American life so thoroughly that it appears to be an indelible part of the nation's landscape. Most children do not understand the nuances of race between the ages of two and ten. Furthermore, race to them is not all that important. I can still recall my earliest memories of how much race was a part of the American experience. My family moved around a lot because of my father's government job. Originally from Sacramento, California, we eventually moved to San Francisco, to Los Angeles, to Chicago, to Stockton, California, and other areas like Asheville, North Carolina, and Johnson City, Tennessee. Despite the upheaval of moving every two to four years, some things did not change.

I never thought of my parents as an interracial couple; mom is white and dad is black. Furthermore, I really did not understand the uniqueness of such a marital arrangement until I began noticing the other kids' parents. They were almost always white. This was more of a product of where we lived as opposed to any intentional design by my family. Unless one comes from such an environment, it is almost indescribable to understand the looks, whispers, and general surprise that came over the faces of most white people when one discovered that your family is interracial. This was particularly true in the 1980s and early 1990s. At best there is nonchalance, live and let live attitude that envelopes some of them, but all too often it is something far worse. It is unfathomable to some why a white woman would give up "her rightful place in society," to marry a man who less than 130 years before would have been an illiterate slave in the South. Love draws people together in a way that defies logic, reason, and societal mores. To this I say Thank God!

My parents came from different parts of the country; my father from Southern Georgia and my mother from Sacramento. They met at an Air Force Base in California's Central Valley during the early 1970s. Dad was an enlisted soldier returning from Vietnam, while mom worked in a bowling alley on post. Although neither one of them could have known it then, it was the beginning of a love affair that has survived for more than thirty-five years; thirty-three years of those years in the bonds of marriage. From the outset such a union was a challenge. Embarking on a new life in which there were so few black-white relationships their presence really stood out. This led to occasional dirty comments, ugly glances, and loss of friends but it also led to great friendships and family relations that survive to this day. On one occasion, when my mother was a police officer, she actually received an application to join the Ku Klux Klan in the female locker room. Unbeknownst to the recruiter, she was married to a black man.

One notable incident occurred in the late 1980s when I was just a little boy living with my family outside of Los Angeles. My mother was acquainted with a neighbor who was doing some work on his house and she allowed me to earn some spending money by helping the construction worker who was hired to do the work. Everything was going fine, then I asked him about a particular task to which he told me how to complete it. Then, almost under his breath, he told me to go along ahead and do it "like a good nigger." I immediately questioned him and he denied saying anything. Naturally, I was shocked by this display of blatant racism. However, despite the fact that my parents had duly informed me about the racism in American society, this was arguably the first real experience with it. In the grand scheme of things it didn't mean much, but I was personally wounded by such a vile comment. My parents were never told of the incident and everything ended up just fine. The fact that I was seven or eight years old, from California, and never an object of such direct hatred was certainly an upsetting situation. I guess I never told my parents, partly because I was embarrassed by the incident; but it would not be the last time that I was witness to or object of racial animus.

Later on my family moved again, this time to Stockton, California. I was in middle school at the time. At that age most kids are discovering the opposite sex and are curious about dating. I was no different. There was a little girl who was very attractive that I was interested in and wanted to ask out. However, when I told her, in a joking manner that she would "certainly want to be with me," she quickly informed me that she "only dated white boys." This was the first time that I had experienced the hatred and rejection associated with interracial dating from a personal perspective. Of course I had witnessed it in relation to my parent's marriage but never had it been so personal. I suppose one of the reasons for this is the fact that my parents never really made a big deal out of the racism they experienced. For me, however, the incident was terribly embarrassing and humiliating for it was done, not in private, but in front of a class of other kids during recess. I knew from that moment forward the difficulties that could arise from pursuing such relationships outside of "my race."

A few years later, we moved to Asheville, North Carolina, which was a little place in the western side of state, known for art, culture, hillbillies, and skiing. Highly mountainous and certainly remote, Asheville in the early 1990s was an economically bipolar community with half its residents being very poor, rural, and undereducated while the other half was high class, liberal and artsy. I was enrolled in a county high school about twenty minutes from our home. Moving around so much creates a situation where one is able to acclimate quickly to almost any new situation and to acquire friends more easily than others. Making new friends was relatively easy for me and soon I had several other kids with which I could play. This was the first time that I had lived in the South; albeit the Upper South. Furthermore, I was not astute to the racial dynamics of the area, so I had to navigate my way through the situation. The majority of teenagers of my generation were entering high school back then and looking forward to getting our driver's permits and more freedom that only comes with age. There was a girl in one of my classes, whom I will call "Julie" and another girl I will call "Jean." "Julie" was very attractive but she was also white. The school in which I was enrolled was only two or three percent black at best. We began to date soon after but little did we know that there would be such a visceral reaction to our companionship. "Jean" the mutual friend of ours was almost despondent at the notion of us dating. She was a racist in the most disturbing way. She pretended to be my friend and it took this situation to get the real "Jean" to expose her true feelings. Many other so called "friends" made fun of us and tried to make life difficult. Eventually, the relationship deteriorated due to the outside strain being placed on it. Furthermore, "Julie" struggled with her feelings as well as those of her racist family. Although she herself was accepting, she struggled to reconcile herself with what she had been taught since childhood. It was another painful lesson among many that would come. I have to admit that I did take perverse pride in the fact that shortly before my family moved to Tennessee "Jean" became pregnant at age 14 and subsequently became a high school dropout. Forgive me my pettiness!

Tennessee was much different than North Carolina. Asheville was a mountainous region and playground for extremists, eccentrics and the ultra-rich alike. Johnson City, Tennessee, was in the valley and much more connected to the outside world. Many people, then and now, moved into the greater Johnson City area to retire and sometimes just to relocate. However, I was quick to learn that the racism that was so blatant in North Carolina could also manifest itself in other more nefarious, subtle ways.

Johnson City from the outset was different than the other places in which I had lived. It was a university town that was a major part of the local economy. It had a large, thriving medical profession, and it was a place with few minorities but enough to not only notice the black population but to be fearful of it. Little did I know then but Johnson City would become my home during my formative and young adult years. I graduated from the local high school, earned my undergraduate and post-baccalaureate degrees and met my wife. Today, after spending a few years working on my Ph.D. in history at the University of Memphis, my family and I have returned to Johnson City. I accepted a full-time, tenure-track assistant professorship at my beloved alma mater. This is still our home.

This Appalachian town of fifty-five thousand can best be described as stratified. Interracial dating, although somewhat common among the teeny boppers today, is still taboo. I realized this early as I embarked on my personal life. Interestingly, the same racist sentiment that pervaded the white community was prominent in the black community as well. I realized for the first time the complexities of race in a way in which I had never known before. For instance, I quickly realized the differences between the sexes as it relates to interracial relationships. There was a significant divide between white men and women on the topic. White women seemed to be more willing to accept the unions of black men and white women more so than white men. Black women appeared to resent and sometimes even detest such relationships. For example, one middle aged black female administrator at the local university openly espoused her disgust at such unions. Moreover, she would not hesitate to share her feelings with students. I found this to be most peculiar. Upon further observation, countless conversations and personal experiences, I discovered that the sexes differed due to long standing, historical differences that have tied Black men and white women together throughout American history. Black women have historically been thought of as less than feminine; to put it mildly. Secondly, they have frequently been the object of unwanted white, male sexual aggression. Moreover, black women have been the glue that has all too often held together the often tenuous union known as the black family. Finally, they have also been marginalized by the larger society in comparison to black men and white people in general.

White women have suffered as well not just from sexism but from the notion that they were property as well, whether it is sexual or economic in nature, at once set on a pedestal while concurrently being reviled as being whores, tramps, sluts, etc. The supposed commercial/property nature of the white female experience draws distinct similarities to the black man in the United States. Can anyone really say that white women have had it that much better than black men in the universal sense? I would answer no. When that white woman engages in a sexual liaison with a black man, she in some very real ways becomes less than white, at least in the public's mind. She is seen in many ways as a traitor to her race. These ideas of racial inferiority create a most vexing situation for those of us engaged in such relationships.

I met my wife in the fall of 1999 in a political science class at East Tennessee State University. We struck up a conversation about the wisdom of women boxers entering the ring with male boxers; it is a disagreement that continues to this day. By February of 2000, we were an item. It certainly was not the first interracial relationship I had been involved in, but it was the first serious one she had taken part of. She quickly became aware of the menacing glances she would receive from other people when we were out and about. Many of these hostile reactions came from white men and black women. I chose to believe that this comes from the false notion that white women belong to white men and black men belong to black women. Furthermore, it is painfully obvious that the feelings on this issue espoused by those racists and naysayers were in part shaped by the various media representations of such relationships. The media has taught America that only black athletes, entertainers, and others who experience financial comeuppance choose white women for sexual partners. In addition, they do it to display their success as if those women are trophies to be mounted (no pun intended) on a wall. I find this supposition to be disturbing. If that were not enough, it is believed that black men are generally so self loathing and predatory in nature that they would chose the ugliest, most unattractive white women over any black women available. Although I cannot dispute the fact that there are some brothers out there who truly feel that way, the fact of the matter is that most of the time these relationships occur because serious and genuine romantic interest between the two parties exists. The television news, comedy shows, *Jerry Springer*, *Maury Povich*, and other media perpetuate this sick myth of black male/white female dysfunction.

Even our political campaigns help distort these relationships. A prime example of this is the 2006 United States Senate race in Tennessee. Then Congressman Harold Ford, Jr. of Memphis, an African American who was known to have dated white women in the past, was running against former Chattanooga Mayor Bob Corker. When the race really got tight in the fall, the Republican National Committee authorized and produced a political ad dubbed the "Call me, Harold," ad. In the commercial a blond, white woman longingly looks into the camera and asks Rep. Ford to call her. There was no question as to the intent of the ad: it was to warn white Tennessee voters that if they elected Ford, their lily white daughters would be in danger from manipulative, smooth, and predatory black men like Ford. The Corker campaign disavowed the ad but the damage was already done. Ford ended up losing the race by a mere fifty thousand votes. Any intellectually honest person would be hard pressed to deny that such a loss had nothing to do with race.

My wife and I watched the ensuing political race recoiling in horror at the prevailing power of race in American life. For me, it brought back bad memories from the 1988 presidential campaign between George Herbert Walker Bush and Michael Dukakis, when Lee Atwater, the late GOP antithetical race-baiting political operative, and the Republicans released an ad featuring a convict by the name of Willie Horton. Horton was on a weekend furlough from the Massachusetts State Prison when he raped and murdered a white woman and her husband. The message was clear: elect Dukakis and he will unleash oversexed black felons who would subsequently rape and murder America's lovely, delicate white daughters. However, the use of menacing looking, supposedly dangerous black men on the prowl for white women is really nothing new or unique to just political campaigns. I am a confessed news junkie who now actually resorts to praying that, when news media runs a story on a heinous crime, that it is not a black man who is the prime suspect. Needless to say, I am not the only one.

One may ask, "How does this really affect you and/or your family?" Well the answer is simple: every media story on this subject reinforces the notion that black men prey on white women and are therefore, menaces to society. Furthermore, those stories strongly suggest that not only am I and every other black man fiendish and venal but also that such relationships are illegitimate. No one questions the motives, aspirations, or plans of same race couples in this mean-spirited way. Yes, we may question whether or not a man is with a woman because of her money or vice versa but American society never displays the absolutely visceral reactions to those unions as it does to interracial relationships. I argue that the product is intentional. White, mainstream America, along with a significant portion of black America views such relationships as illegitimate, perilous, and wrong. It is a rare occasion when I turn on my television or open my newspaper and see a positive portrayal of interracial relationships. For black men it not only questions the relationship but devalues, humiliates, and emasculates them in a way that would never be tolerated by the white majority. How could this be? What is it that keeps this perverted notion an ever present part of our national life? I believe, despite the arguments to the contrary, that it reflects how truly racist America remains today. In addition, I argue that the debate over whether or not America's problem is race or class is simply subterfuge and disingenuous at best. As W.E.B. Dubois said at the beginning of the twentieth century, and still applies today, the problem of the twentieth century is the problem of the color line.[19] Arguments about class merely obscure the real problem because class almost becomes code for race so racists don't sound as bad in public. Further, with proper training and education, most people can disguise their meager beginnings but there is no way that I or most people can hide the dark hue of their skin. Only a few tokens can "pass."

My wife and I have a daughter that is seven years old and a nine month old son who, due to their mother's whiteness and my biracial background, appear white rather than mixed or black. It is often funny, yet sad when people first realize that she is the product of an interracial relationship. We have to instruct her, (as does every other biracial family), of the racist nature of the society of which she is a part. It is difficult to comprehend the anxiety one feels when one is out in public and receives menacing glances from both white men and black women. As if the relationship and the child are not good enough or somewhat illegitimate. At this time I would like to point out that even here in the South, not all white men and black women are of the same opinion on such matters. My family and I do have plenty of friends and acquaintances who see nothing wrong with our relationship. They are a godsend and are deeply appreciated. However, they certainly do not represent the majority.

Today, our family is loving, strong, and committed; as it should be. But the fact of the matter is that we will always have to deal with the bigotry that permeates American society. We will always have to deal with the vicious stereotypes from beyond the pale that caricature black men and their relationships with white women. We will continue to have to deal with the subject as we watch television that says, "White is right and Black is whack." We will continue to endure programming that portrays black men as buffoons and white women so inclined to participate in such relationships as traitors, whores, and degenerates.

Possible Solutions

There are many ways in which America can face up to the ugly truth about her history and the disturbing reality of its present. First, America needs to have a plethora of discussions across the nation about race. By this I do not mean that we need a national conversation per se. I mean we need to have community discussions in every region in the United States. Obviously, the racial problems of the North, South, Midwest, Interior West, and West are not identical. Solutions in Washington State will probably not work in the South. This means blacks and whites need to openly talk about the feelings each group has about each other. Such personal discussions will provide the catalyst for a new understanding of one another that can move the country forward collectively. It will also dispel myths, stereotypes, and deeply embedded untruths about one another that will show how interdependent and similar we all are.

Secondly, we need to address the issue of social inequality in American society. For example, in the city I used to live in, Memphis, many residents of the white race have a misguided idea that if there were only stronger gun laws, prison sentences, and legislative action, crime would decrease and everyone [whites] would be safer and happy. This is a fool's errand. Locking people up will not solve the underlining issues that created the unfortunately dangerous atmosphere many Americans encounter in their neighborhoods and cities. We know that poverty breeds crime yet we do nothing to foster an environment where economic progress touches the people on the lowest economic rungs. America tends to wall off its poor in the hopes that it will protect them from the social ills that are all too present in the ghetto and barrios of America. Poor people have every right to be angry and when hard times come (and they will, like the current mess left by President George W. Bush) supposedly well intentioned ideas about economic progress/growth and safety will not protect those in the middle class from the explosion of anger and violence from America's poor. Revolutions may not begin in the poor areas of society but it is the poor who will exact their vengeance upon those who have forsaken them. God talked about how the poor and meek with inherit the earth but man has forgotten that important lesson. After all, the problems present today are the result of man made decisions about the lives of these people. To stigmatize the poor, particularly black men, is to live by a sword that will eventually slit their own throats.

It is imperative that we address the proliferation and commercialization of media, including rap music that further denigrates black men. Such media portrayals are false and harmful to not just black America but also America at large. Most progressive Americans and thoughtful African Americans realize that the media portrayals of black men and interracial dating are false yet we laugh, enjoy, and support such stereotypes. I believe that this suggests that we really are one, apathetic about our national life, and two, still unable to deal with the remaining vestiges of slavery, Jim Crow, and the formal barriers between the races. Hollywood and the news media in all its forms create and shape opinions but also respond to the desires of the American citizenry. No financially conscious media outlet is going to use offensive stories if the result is going to be a loss of viewership, circulation, and revenue.

Conclusion

Race permeates every aspect of American society. While the issue of personal, romantic relationships may be more of a sub-issue, it reflects the larger, more complex nature of American society. It shows the inherent bigotry that maintains the separation between the races. Sexuality and its problematic nature demonstrate the uniqueness of America's racial plight. This is no more clearly seen than in the media, where caricaturing individuals, groups of people, the sexes, and the races is considered to be not only sport but entertainment as well. Furthermore, such unconscionable behavior only serves to denigrate, humiliate and dehumanize decent people; not to mention the specific impact it has on African American men and white women.

The commercialization and selling of the myth of black sexual prowess and white female submissiveness/looseness serves only to further marginalize two of the most important groups of people in the United States. Besides the obvious need for procreation to promulgate the species, one can scarcely imagine a United States without black men and white women. They are indispensable. For those out there whom will inevitably take umbrage at such a statement, I caution you to understand the focus of this chapter is not the importance of black women or white men per se, but the two aforementioned groups of whom this article has been written about. Finally, the most important issue here is that the media has distorted these relationships in a way that is most unflattering and disturbing. Black men are not dangerous, devious, and vile human beings that prey on the flesh and the pleasures of white women. In addition, white women are not the race traitors or victims of unwanted sexual advances that the media has portrayed them as.

Finally, we as Americans need to seriously contemplate ourselves, our history, our country, and how it all fits together. This arguably would be one of the most important things we can do to heal our contemporary and historic wounds. Furthermore, the larger issues of which we have been discussing, the media portrayal of black/white relationships, would benefit from such introspective analysis. Maybe then we could finally see that race truly is a social construct that separates Americans. There is an old saying which goes, "at night when two people get between the sheets, no one really notices the color of the other person." Such a notion aptly applies here. Such images must be aggressively nullified.

Notes

1. 388 U.S. (1967)
2. Sylvester Monroe, "Hollywood: The Dark Side-Condition of African Americas in the TV and Movie Industry," *Essence*, 1994.
3. *Ibid.*
4. Ted Schwarz, *Joseph P. Kennedy: The Mogul, the Mob, the Statesman, and the Making of an American Myth* (Hoboken, NJ: John Wiley & Sons, 2003), 390.

5. Jennifer Harris, "Worshipping at the Alter of Barry White: Ally McBeal and Racial and Sexual Politics in Crises," in *Searching the Soul of Ally McBeal: Critical Essays,* ed. Elwood Watson (Jefferson, NC: McFarland, 2006), 163.
6. Cornel West, *Race Matters* (New York: Vintage, 1993), 119.
7. John D'Emilio and Estelle B. Freedman, *Intimate Matters: A History of Sexuality In America* (Chicago: University of Chicago Press, 1988), 202.
8. *Time Magazine,* June 28, 1994.
9. Gail Dines, "The White Man's Burden: Gonzo Pornography and the Construction of Black Masculinity." *Yale Journal of Law and Feminism* 18 (2006): 292.
10. *Ibid.,* 297.
11. West, xiii.
12. Al Gore, *The Assault on Reason* (New York: Penguin Press, 2007), 6.
13. *Ibid.,* 7.
14. The National Advisory Commission on Civil Disorders, Final Report.
15. Pamela Newkirk, "Whitewash in the Newsroom: Thirty Years After Kerner, the Media Still Reflect the Biases of White America," *The Nation,* March 16, 1998, 22.
16. *Ibid.,* 23.
17. Albert receives 12 month suspended sentence. *Court TV online,* October 24, 1998.
18. John D'Emilio, *Sexual Politics, Sexual Communities: The Making of a Homosexual Minority in the United States, 1940–1970,* 2nd ed. (Chicago: University of Chicago Press, 1998), 48.
19. W.E.B. DuBois, *The Souls of Black Folk* (Chicago: McClure, 1903).

Bibliography

D'Emilio, John. *Sexual Politics, Sexual Communities: The Making of a Homosexual Minority in the United States, 1949-1970,* 2nd ed. Chicago: University of Chicago Press, 1998.
_____, and Estelle B. Freeman. *Intimate Matters: A History of Sexuality in America.* Chicago: University of Chicago Press, 1988.
Dines, Gail. "The White Man's Burden: Gonzo Pornography and the Construction of Black Masculinity." *Yale Journal of Law and Feminism* 18 (2006).
Gore, Al. *The Assault on Reason.* New York: Penguin, 2007.
Harris, Jennifer. "Worshipping at the Altar of Barry White: Ally McBeal and Racial and Sexual Politics in Crises." In *Searching the Soul of Ally McBeal: Critical Essays,* ed. Elwood Watson. Jefferson, NC: McFarland, 2006.
Kerner Commission, *Report of the National Advisory Commission on Civil Disorders.* Washington: U.S. Government Printing Office, 1968.
Newkirk, Pamela. "Whitewash in the Newsroom: Thirty Years After Kerner, the Media Still Reflect the Biases of White America." *The Nation,* March 16, 1998.
Schwarz, Ted. *Joseph P. Kennedy: The Mogul, the Mob, the Statesman, and the Making of an American Myth.* Hoboken, NJ: John Wiley & Sons, 2003.
Monroe, Sylvester, "Hollywood: The Dark-Side Condition of African Americans in the TV and Movie Industry." *Essence Magazine,* 1994.
Time. June 28, 1994.
West, Cornel. *Race Matters.* New York: Vintage, 1993.

7

Celebrity Culture and Racial Masculinities: The Case of Will Smith

David Magill

Film stars embody anxious resolutions; they seemingly reconcile the contradictions inherent in identity and culture as a means of assuaging our doubts about such collective identifications. As a result, we can examine stars as a means of tracing the anxieties obsessing U.S. culture and the fantasies that allay those fears. Of particular interest in this regard is the African American film star, a figure that embodies both American fantasies and fears of blackness. As Michele Wallace notes, "This problem of how the procedures of celebrity are used to disenfranchise us all is not unknown in other communities and sectors of cultural production.... But it seems particularly unexamined and uncritiqued in African American cultural and intellectual production" ("Masculinity" 301). This essay unpacks the disenfranchising mechanisms of celebrity culture by examining one star of particular interest in this regard: Will Smith.

Often described as "the 'safest image' of black masculinity available to the film industry" (Cruz), Smith raises for many viewers the question, is he a sellout? That is to say, does he undercut progressive black politics through his film and music career, capitulating to white audiences and their notions of blackness as he rises to stardom? Of course, we might respond that the question itself is flawed in its assumption of representivity by the black individual. After all, we don't ask whether Bruce Willis undercuts white politics in his performances. But if we consider this issue within the historical context of Hollywood's racial imaginary, then the questions becomes deceptively complex. Similar to Paul Robeson, Will Smith's star image takes on different meanings when read through different lenses (black and white).[1] And those differences do not easily map to black = sell out and white = achievement. Different U.S. racial discourses make varied sense of Will Smith as a phenomenon of black masculine stardom, even as those discourses might be adopted individually across racial lines. Will Smith's star characteristics, then, are valued differently across cultural groups, even as his celebrated traits remain constant.

Will Smith's "star identity" presents a unique border figure for observing the color line's intricate and racially contradictory logics. The #1 black actor in terms of salary demanded and film income generated, Smith presents a fantasy of black identity that ambivalently challenges the color line through a liberally racial vision of black masculinity that calms white cultural fears. In this manner, Smith is similar to previous black celebrity incarnations; as Manthia Diawara notes, black characters such as the ones seen in Eddie Murphy's early cinematic performances appear threatening before becoming "deterritorialised from a black milieu and transferred to a predominantly white world" (71). Smith's star persona, as evidenced through his films, music, and interviews, presents white anxieties over black manhood and assuages them through the fantastic resolution of America's racial contradictions while at the same time acknowledging black anxieties regarding whiteness and power. The combination redraws the color line in more palatable fashion through the U.S. cultural imaginary.

In other words, Smith's black manhood draws on a set of characteristics that map well onto both black and white anxieties about masculinity. Robyn Wiegman notes, "In his relation of sameness to the masculine and in his threatening difference to the primacy of white racial supremacy, the African American male is stranded between the competing — and at times overdetermining — logics of race and gender" (160). But Smith's persona works to defuse the racial threat so as to claim a safer masculinity that still "keeps it real." As Maurice Wallace notes, "The high profile of race in the West has created out of the black male body a walking palimpsest of the fears and fascinations possessing our cultural imagination" (Wallace, *Constructing* 2). The black star figure provides a cultural space to examine the construction and maintenance of such palimpsests in order to expose the ways in which racial discourses replicate within and through celebrity culture. Smith's career will be traced to understand his particular configuration of black masculinity, to map its constituent qualities, and to consider the implications of such a configuration.

The Fresh Prince's Star Qualities

Will Smith defines his star persona from the start of his career as the "Fresh Prince"; in this sitcom, we immediately see the characteristics that mark him as a star, albeit in embryonic form: nice, fun-loving, and at this point child-like. Reviewers describe him as "affably off-center"; "Hollywood's Mr. Clean"; "more choirboy than bad boy"; "hard-working and driven."[2] The Fresh Prince persona that defines the start of Will Smith's career, a persona crafted through his music and TV career, distinguishes him from the typical black stereotypes of lazy, angry, and hypersexual. "The Fresh Prince of Bel-Air" labels Smith as fun-loving and, most importantly, sexually non-aggressive. Tom Carson notes, "His favorite gambit is to make like an overgrown child" (86). Though he is heterosexual on the show, with jokes about his female conquests a means of demonstrating his potential, the early relationships are defined as adolescent hormone-induced desires with no maturity save for the occasional "Emmy episode" common to most sitcoms. As a result, the Prince can still be charming.

Made in America, his first major movie, follows the same trajectory: Smith plays Tea Cake, a funny, wisecracking teenager with a heart of gold.[3] He's sensitive to female needs, with his only hint of sexuality coming during a masturbation scene at a local sperm bank. That scene both suggests black manhood's hypersexual nature — Smith must ask for a "second cup"— and contains it by making it masturbatory. In a film about the anxieties of cross-racial procreation, the copulative threat of the black boy/man is neutralized. His next early film, *Six Degrees of Separation*, is perhaps where he plays his most non-masculine character. Yet even in that role, he plays the trickster, masquerading as upper class and claiming access to the legacy of black film star Sidney Poitier; also, he interestingly defuses the film's biggest potential threat by refusing to kiss Anthony Michael Hall — a double was inserted to protect Smith's rap and film career from claims of homosexuality.[4] Thus, Smith evacuates challenges to his manhood while simultaneously portraying another young, non-procreative male.

The early films thus contain the seeds of Smith's star persona, but these seeds flower with his next film. Will Smith's status as a "star" arises with the 1996 release of *Independence Day (ID4)*. Smith's portrayal of Captain Stephen Hiller contains many of the characteristics I listed above: wisecracking jokester and affable young man. But *ID4* adds and contains a few new features. First of all, Will Smith becomes a sexual being — indeed, our first look at him is when he is in bed with his girlfriend (Vivica A. Fox), although they are sleeping instead of making love. But the implications are clear. Thus, Smith leaves behind the boy persona of the Fresh Prince, as he notes: "My everyday life now is drastically different from that of the Fresh Prince" (Taubin 64–5). Markedly heterosexual yet devotedly monogamous (not hypersexual), hard-working (an Air Force pilot who is the best of the best), and honorable (he wants to marry a stripper with a child, thus redeeming her in the viewer's eyes), Hiller becomes a character used by the film to assuage anxieties about the Other. *ID4* thus marks Smith's rise to stardom as well as the beginning of a pattern to which his blockbusters return time and time again: the interracial buddy film. Yet it's a twist on the genre, as we shall see.

ID4 presents a basic plot structure common to many Will Smith movies: he teams up with a white man to defeat a menacing villain. Wesley Morris notes, "The typical Will Smith movie has an incongruous innocence. It stars a semi-tough, big-eared, endlessly charismatic rapping matinee idol who can be relied upon to avenge the nation's capital or save the universe with sarcasm, irony, and corniness." Smith grafts the childish innocence and fun-loving personality of the Fresh Prince onto the hard armored body of a patriotic national hero. In *ID4*, however, Smith is not the only hero — Bill Pullman's President and Jeff Goldblum's Jewish computer whiz as well as Randy Quaid's eccentric pilot also deal decisive blows to the alien armada. As Amy Taubin writes, "*ID4* is a feel-good movie about how the end of the world is averted by good men who put aside their racial and ethnic difference." In this light, Vivica Fox's comment that "the film is not black or white — it's universal" reveals the ways in which *ID4* presents a multicultural fantasy that tames Will Smith's blackness through a secure, wholesome masculinity subordinated to the nation writ large. The otherness of blackness is seemingly subsumed into the racially demarcated hierarchical structure of American manhood itself bent on the destruction of a greater Other: the evil alien. Thus, Smith is the one to capture an alien prisoner (with a punch and a wisecrack — "Welcome to Earth" — that marks him as representative "human") and flies the ship that allows the Jewish computer expert to plant a virus in the alien starship's computer system. His heroics in the service of humanity, completed with the assistance of other racial and ethnic minorities, erase his specificity against the larger alien menace. So, while Smith stands out as a star, the film recodes black hipness as accessible for mainstream whiteness such that one critic can claim that Smith's "dynamism marginalizes objections" of stereotyping and jingoism.

Big Willie Style

Smith's future starring vehicles remove the ensemble of heroes in favor of a strict two-man buddy system, yet they maintain the containment structure of black hipness coded onto normative white standards of masculinity. Importantly, however, each film also produces a surface discourse of racial identity, a hip black manhood, meant to counteract racial claims while it supports that rejuvenated white masculinity. *Men in Black*, for example, cemented

Will Smith's national star status. Critics dubbed July 4 "King Willie week-end," linking him to the spectacle surrounding the nation's founding by not-ing, "He doesn't raise hell and best of all, he's staunchly patriotic." ("Mister Smith"). Yet the film produces the same star image for Smith: a wisecrack-ing, rebellious, charismatic black man who devotes his physicality and sex-ual potency to defending white women and the nation against alien incursion. Will Smith's blackness gets elided within a larger discourse of masculine nationhood *even as* the film marks blackness as hip and cool. The film has it both ways, ceding his hipness while linking it to a universal identity. For exam-ple, consider the speech Zed, the leader of the Men in Black, gives as they indoctrinate James Edwards (Will Smith) into their collective as Agent J:

> You'll dress only in attire specially sanctioned by MIB special services. You'll confirm to the identity we give you. Eat where we tell you. Live where we tell you. From now on, you'll have no identifying marks of any kind. You'll not stand out in any way. Your entire image is crafted to leave no lasting mem-ory with anyone you encounter. You are a rumor, recognizable only as déjà vu and dismissed just as quickly. You don't exist. You were never even born. Anonymity is your name, silence your native tongue. You are no longer part of the system. You are above the system, over it, beyond it. We're them. We're they. We are the Men in Black.

Zed's speech overwrites the visual scene of Will Smith's blackness. As Zed speaks of "identifying marks," we see Smith's fingerprints burned off in a close-up on his black skin. Zed's speech bears marked similarity to that other individual known only by his initials: IM, from Ralph Ellison's *Invisi-ble Man*.

J, in effect, becomes an invisible man and does so willingly, giving up his name and identity to join the anonymous hierarchical collective of the Men in Black. In so doing, he joins a "greater" cause — defeating the alien other and maintaining the nation/world against encroachment. As such, he falls under the purview of K (Tommy Lee Jones). An older white man who provides tutelage for J, K is the agent with superior knowledge and firepower. K hands J a small gun (a joke at the expense of black hypersexuality and phys-ical enhancement) and then admonishes him not to discharge his weapon in public. K provides the brains to defeat the bug menace, while J provides the muscle and the speed. Yet J has one advantage — as he proclaims, "I make this look good." Thus, while J can claim a cool pose, he also adds potency to the white male, or as Robyn Wiegman has argued, rescuing white masculinity from its peripheral positioning in multicultural discourse. Further, because J is constantly under K's supervision, Will Smith's persona becomes contained within that larger discourse. Taubin relates, "Will Smith is probably the only African American actor in Hollywood guaranteed to be non-threatening to a white middle class audience." In fact, his star persona is built on diffusing that threat while joking about the racial issues to maintain his hip blackness.

Yet within the film, Will Smith cracks wise about the racial disparities he faces. When he lands on a bus while chasing an alien, he comments, "It just be raining black men in New York," in response to white shock at his arrival. Similarly, when distracting the villainous alien bug by killing cockroaches, Smith's wisecrack is similarly racial: "That must be your uncle — you know you all look alike." Such comments suggest Smith's connection to a racial trickster identity even as other sections of the film disavow that identity. Thus, audiences can choose to respond to Smith in alternate fashions. Smith can have his blackness and avoid its ramifications in MIB's individualism, while K dispatches the bug and saves J. This trend continues in his other multi-racial buddy films: *Enemy of the State*, *Wild Wild West*, and *Men in Black II*. In each movie, Will Smith cracks jokes and fights for truth and justice while a white man takes the position of guidance and/or superiority. In *Enemy of the State*, it's Gene Hackman who helps Will Smith turn the tables on the government in a tale that Stuart Klavens describes succinctly: "This, then, is the subtext of *Enemy of the State*: Will Smith, having become deracinated by a life in Georgetown, gets in touch with his Negro self and becomes Eddie Murphy." Of course, the "Negrofication" of Will Smith, which (coincidentally or not) begins at the point in the movie where he is shopping for lingerie modeled by white women, is turned around by the movie's end thanks to a white man who, in the film's denouement, is revealed to still be watching over Smith. And importantly, Smith's star figure lets us know that even as he dresses "black" (in the film's imaginary) to blend in and gain invisibility, he's still Will Smith. Thus, again Will Smith can both be black and disavow its negative associations through the intervention of a white man.

Wild Wild West asserts this pattern once more through Smith's portrayal of James West, a sheriff hero who uses violence to solve his issues until shown the error of his ways by a kindler, gentler smarter Kevin Kline. The film's director Barry Sonnenfeld, noting that Will Smith's race altered the remake of the old television show significantly, commented, "We deal with the fact that he's black," a comment that both recognizes and dismisses Smith's racial identity. And the film deals with race mostly through jokes that note the racist stereotypes while misdirecting us from the movie's liberally racist portrayals. For example, the opening sequence features a naked Smith falling from a water tower into a room of ne'er-do-wells. Yet he gets the jump on them because they are immobilized by his nakedness; presumably, the stereotypical black physique transfixes them in a parody of white envy for black genitalia. At another crucial point, James West faces a lynching for "playing the bongos on a white woman's ta-tas." That the lynching is engineered by Kline's white character as a diversion and averted by his last minute rescue of West suggests where the true power lies. Smith cannot rescue himself despite his own racial jokes about "redneck" as a powerful term that, of course, suggests he thinks otherwise. Once again, Smith plays a national hero — working directly for the President — who provides the firepower and one-liners to support the white character's heroism and growth. His characterization attacks an overtly undesirable white masculine supremacy while supporting a covert claim to authority and power.

Men in Black II further extends this trend. J can joke that his car "came with a black dude [as driver] but it kept getting pulled over," describe himself as "new hotness" against K's "old and busted," and respond to the suggestion that he "go get coffee while I handle this" with the retort, "You want it black, with a couple cubes of kiss my ass." But he can also wholeheartedly adhere to the movie's final comment: "You are who you are," a statement that trumpets individualism over a recognition of the dominant racially hierarchical power structures as a pretext for convincing K to return and save the universe with his knowledge. *I, Robot*, Will Smith's recent sci-fi blockbuster, follows in this vein by allowing the muscular Smith to save a race of robots from extinction and create a new world order. That the robots are translucent white seems to suggest their race-lessness, yet they are a new race and Will Smith is their savior. Individualism trumps race again.[5]

Hitch signals Smith's foray into romantic comedy, yet this film also signifies on the buddy-film concept I have been discussing as central to Will Smith's star construction. In particular, *Hitch* relies on stereotypes of black male sexuality as a means of creating its comedic vision. Smith plays Alex "Hitch" Hitchens, a "date doctor" who spends his time instructing other men in the art of romance. Smith's clientele are mostly white and obviously less accomplished than Smith, signaling to the audience that Smith is the film's dominant masculine figure. As such, the film becomes an extended set of interactions where Smith offers his sexual potency to white men in order to land women for them. The film's central plot involves Hitch assisting Albert Brennaman (Kevin James) in his pursuit of Allegra Cole (Natasha Henstridge). But the film evacuates any threat to white womanhood in three ways: first, it makes clear the object is romance and marriage (Hitch turns down the one sexual predator he meets); second, Albert's final success with Allegra Cole arises not from Hitch's advice but in spite of it; and third, Smith himself pursues happiness with a Hispanic woman, played by Eva Mendes. Interestingly, as Omarya Cruz notes, Mendes was cast precisely to avoid American audience issues with black-white romances, creating a vision of interracial love that is exotic and titillating yet not dangerous to mainstream American audiences. Thus, Smith's hip blackness can be safely taught to white men without the fear of racial taint or miscegenation. The film's only true acknowl-edgements of his blackness come either in the form of stereotypes (teaching Albert how to dance because white men can't dance and black men have rhythm, for example) or, in one curious scene, in the form of overt racism as Hitch cannot hail a cab in New York City. But these incidents are anom-alies in the film, and their effect is muted by the character's otherwise race-less life.

Will Smith's star figure, then, is built on a complex set of significations that offers his blackness *as* hipness but that simultaneously offers a withdrawal of race from his characters so as to allow white audiences to revere him. Smith even stated, "Hollywood is not racist," a statement at odds with many other black figures' comments. Bob Ivy claims, "Smith's screen persona has moved beyond skin color. They've been black heroes, but more important, they've been heroes who just happened to be black." But I would suggest that his screen persona is quite aware of his race when it needs a touch of style to liven up those dreary white boys. Thus, *The Legend of Bagger Vance* becomes another movie in this line, one that many critics reacted to with disgust. Smith passed on *Bamboozled,* Spike Lee's satire of racial stereotyping, to take on this role, another in the long line of magical black men who return white men to their phallic strengths and identities. Smith commented that the role fit the movie's Jazz Age setting, a statement that suggests a sense of history similar to my students, for it ignores the powerful figures of W.E.B. DuBois and Booker T. Washington, the poetic ideals of Langston Hughes and Claude McKay, and even the cinematic antecedents of Paul Robeson to return black manhood to uncritical minstrelsy.

Contradictions, or Contractual Obligations?

I have been defending a coherent vision of Will Smith's cinematic por-trayals; however, three films seemingly diverge significantly from the pattern I have delineated: *Ali, The Pursuit of Happyness,* and the *Bad Boys* films. *Ali* certainly is Smith's most racially aware movie, depicting Ali against a back-drop of civil rights and the murders of Malcolm X and Martin Luther King. Further, most reviews comment on the fact that Will Smith subsumes him-self completely into Muhammed Ali's persona. He does not "act like Will Smith"; however, our perceptions of Will Smith dominate our understand-ing of Ali. So even as Ali refuses to fight in Vietnam in a courageous chal-lenge, it's Will Smith, patriotic American, who makes it doubly acceptable and Will Smith who makes Ali's lack of work in the civil rights battles (within the film) also acceptable. So the portrait allows Smith to maintain his distance from the most dangerous aspects of black manhood that Muhammed Ali represented, confining that danger to the ring.

The Pursuit of Happyness shares with *Ali* a biographical focus in its treatment of the real-life rags to riches saga of homeless father cum stockbroker millionaire Chris Gardner. But it also shares a rejection of race as a determinant either in economic or cultural terms. The film opens with a pan shot over the Declaration of Independence, a text that Smith references during a key voiceover in the film. Smith (as Gardner) examines the figure of Jefferson on a nickel, then comments that Jefferson's declaration only promises the *pursuit* of happiness, not happiness itself. Gardner's character does not question the racialized historical construction of "men" that undergirded Jefferson's vision of access to such pursuits, and his contemporary interpretation of Jefferson's promise evacuates any racial conflict, seeing it only as the individual. As such, *The Pursuit of Happyness* accepts uncritically the ideological narrative of equal opportunity without considering the more complex inferential manifestations of racism that Stuart Hall has identified as perniciously undermining social progress.[6] Thus, Will Smith as Chris Gardner invites a doubled acceptance of individual achievement, referencing Gardner's competitively landing a prestigious stockbroker position and Will Smith's competitively attaining star status in the Hollywood system as uninflected by racial issues.

I'd like to say that the *Bad Boys* films, as black buddy films, depart from this stereotype. Yet in contributing to Will Smith's star power, they also work to assuage white audiences. While his character Mike Lowrey is single, stylish, sexually potent, and rich, the movie centers him by placing him against a villain who, while white skinned, is foreign (German) and who heads a gang of hybrid criminals selling out to South American drug interests. By substituting one villainized racial minority for another, the politics can remain the same. Further, Lowrey is a cop with a heart of gold, such that one woman says, "If I'm in trouble, the only one I would go to is Mike Lowrey." So when white female victim Julie Nott needs help, Lowrey defends her. Thus, Smith is placed on the side of the law and in the role of protecting the Southern white woman, traditionally white positions. In addition, the movie ends by letting everyone know Will Smith is not a typical violent black male. Faced with his friend's murderer, Lowrey refuses to shoot him without provocation, demonstrating he is not a brutal killer. Yet then the bad guy pulls a gun, enabling Lowrey to empty his clip and gain revenge. He kills, but he is not a killer. Thus, Will Smith's persona both claims blackness and denies it simultaneously through careful positioning of his character.

Bad Boys II plays the same racial games. In the opening scene, Will Smith arrives on screen in fantastic fashion; arising from beneath a white hood comes his muscled, armed figure, shot from below in slow motion to accentuate his body and make him seem larger than life, like a star (the same trick used in John Wayne films). The symbolic import of dropping his white covering imputes his blackness to the audience. But his first line is "Blue power, motherfucker. Miami PD." His claim is not to race but to the law, even as his partner Burnett says sarcastically, "Oh damn, it's the nigras." Importantly, the satire of white supremacy, combined with the visual portrayal of Klan members as stereotypically redneck, poor, and unkempt — just as in *Wild Wild West* — seems to mock white supremacy as a crazy man's belief held by only a few disenfranchised souls. Thus, mainstream whites can side with Lowrey against prejudice and feel good. The viewer can then participate with Lowrey as he ogles female nightclub dancers erotically, has sex with his therapist in a scene that reminds us of his sexual potency, and does whatever it takes to bring down the Cuban and Haitian drug lords infesting Miami. We are asked to identify with him. That the movie implicitly seeks to remove these nationalities from our shore by marking them as drug lords damaging the body politic is clear when the villain threatens, "You're in my house," and Lowrey responds, "You're in my country." Smith's loyalties to nation over race are juxtaposed clearly against the villain's profit motive. His victory over the drug cartel and its hypersexual leader is, then, a victory over unsavory racial elements and a re-constitution of black power into the white imaginary.

Keepin' It Real

Smith's star persona, then, is much more complicated than a simple sell-out vs. keeping it real dichotomy, a debate that occurs regarding his rap music as well. Rather, Smith's star figure constitutes a negotiation of his racial identity so as to claim a safe masculinity through racial jokes made in good fun. His onscreen version of black manhood echoes the family-centered, strong persona of his life, but he too claims an individualism that allows people to see him as without race. So it's vexing — there's lots of positive attributes to Will Smith, but his film career uses these positives to e-race his celluloid persona for consumption. Against the vagaries of discrimination and the advancements of civil rights, Will Smith constructs a star figure that makes black masculinity look good.

Notes

1. For more on Paul Robeson, see Richard Dyer's influential reading in *Stars*.
2. See Syson, Damon. "Actions Speak Louder Than Words: Will Smith is Hollywood's Mr. Clean." *The Independent*. October 6, 2003: 2; Carson, Tom, "Invincible Man," *Esquire*

August 1999 (132.2): 52; and Taubin, Amy, 'Playing It Straight: R.E.M. Meets a Post-Rodney King World in Independence Day," *Sight and Sound* 6.8 (1996): 6.

3. Smith's character name obviously echoes Zora Neale Hurston's character in *Their Eyes Were Watching God*, an intertextual reference that signifies masculine agency and sexual desire yet mutes it through the antics of Will Smith.

4. Sidney Poitier offers us another intertexual and interracial reference with his critical role in *Guess Who's Coming to Dinner?* But while Poitier's character offers a challenge to racial hegemony through the positive portrayal of interracial romance, Smith's character defuses the challenge of interracial sex because the desire is homosexual. Once again, cross-racial procreation is contained.

5. This essay was written before the release of Will Smith's most recent films, *I Am Legend* and *Hancock*. Both films participate in the trajectory I am tracing, as I will trace in a later essay.

6. For more on inferential racism, see Stuart Hall's "The Whites of Their Eyes: Racist Ideologies and the Media," 36–37, and Michael Omi's "In Living Color: Race and American Culture."

Bibliography

Blount, Marcellus, and George P. Cunningham, eds. *Representing Black Men.* London: Routledge, 1996.

Carson, Tom. "Invincible Man." *Esquire* August 1999 (132.2): 52.

Cruz, Omayra Zaragosa. "Easy Lover: Calculating the Upside of Eva Mendes." *Popmatters.com*, April 6, 2005. *http://www.popmatters.com/columns/cruz/050406.shtml.* May 30, 2007.

Diawara, Manthia. "Black Spectatorship: Problems of Identification and Resistance." *Screen* 29.4 (1988): 71.

Dyer, Richard. *Heavenly Bodies.* New York: St. Martin's, 1986.

_____. *Stars.* London: BFI, 1998.

Gabbard, Krin. *Black Magic: White Hollywood and African American Culture.* New Brunswick, NJ: Rutgers University Press, 2004.

Gardiner, Judith Kegan, ed. *Masculinity Studies and Feminist Theory: New Directions.* New York: Columbia University Press, 2002.

Guerrero, Ed. "The Black Man on Our Screens and the Empty Space in Representation." *Callaloo* 18.2 (1995): 395–400.

Hall, Stuart. "The Whites of Their Eyes: Racist Ideologies and the Media." In *Silver Linings.* Ed. George Bridges and Rosalind Brunt. London: Lawrence and Wishart, 1981.

Harper, Phillip Brian. *Are We Not Men? Masculine Anxiety and the Problem of African-American Identity.* New York: Oxford University Press, 1996.

hooks, bell. *We Real Cool: Black Men and Masculinity.* New York: Routledge, 2004.

Ivry, Bob. "Bamboozled by Bagger: Old Hollywood Stereotype Gets an Offensive Update." *The Record.* November 19, 2000. Y10.

Klawans, Stuart. Rev. of *Enemy of the State. The Nation* December 14, 1998. 267(20). 42.

LaSalle, Mick. "Will Smith — The Next Ronald Reagan?" *San Francisco Chronicle* June 29, 1997. 32.

Longsdorf, Amy. "A Different Kind of Wise Guy." *The Record* November 1, 2000. Y1.

"Mister Smith Goes to Stardom." *People Weekly* July 22, 1996. 46.4. 64–71.

Morris, Wesley. Rev. of *Men in Black II. The Boston Globe* July 3, 2002. C1.

Syson, Damon. "Actions Speak Louder Than Words: Will Smith Is Hollywood's Mr. Clean." *The Independent* October 6, 2003. 2–3.

Taubin, Amy. "Playing It Straight: R.E.M. Meets a Post-Rodney King World in *Independence Day.*" *Sight and Sound* 6.8 (1996): 6–8.

Wallace, Maurice O. *Constructing the Black Masculine: Identity and Ideality in African American Men's Literature and Culture.* Durham, NC: Duke University Press, 2002.

Wallace, Michele. "Masculinity in Black Popular Culture: Could It Be that Political Correctness is the Problem?" In *Constructing Masculinity.* Ed. Maurice Berger, Brian Wallis, and Simon Watson. New York: Routledge, 1995.

Wiegman, Robyn. *American Anatomies: Theorizing Race and Gender.* Durham, NC: Duke University Press, 1998.

PART II

Contemporary Mediated
Performance and the Cultural
Politics of Masculinity

8

Constructions of
Mathematical Masculinities
in Popular Culture

Marie-Pierre Moreau, Heather Mendick,
and Debbie Epstein

Popular representations of scientists have a long history in the mass media (going back at least as far as Mary Shelley's *Frankenstein*). However, mathematics and mathematicians have only relatively recently begun to take centre stage in contemporary, English-speaking, popular culture, as reflected in a number of books, films and television dramas (including fictions, documentaries and reality genres) featuring them. These include: *A Beautiful Mind* (a film; Goldsman 2001), to which the title of this contribution alludes, *Good Will Hunting* (a film; Affleck and Damon 1997), *Pi* (also a film; Aronofsky 1998), *Proof* (a film; Madden 2006), *Enigma* (a film; Apted 2001), *The Curious Incident of the Dog in the Night-time* (a book; Haddon 2003), *The Da Vinci Code* (a book and a film; Brown 2003; Howard 2006), *Numb3rs* (a TV series; Gansa 1997), *Fermat's Last Theorem* (a documentary; Singh and Lynch 1998), *21* (a film; Luketic 2008), *The Oxford Murders* (a film; de la Iglesia 2008) and *Gifted* (a book; Lalwani 2007). Parallel with this, there has been an explosion of the publication of mathematical and logical puzzles (for example, *sudoku*) in both print media and on-line as well as the growth of computing games (for example, *Runescape*) that require mathematical approaches to play them successfully.

In relation to these developments, this contribution focuses on constructions of "mathematical masculinities" in popular culture. Drawing specifically on two films, *A Beautiful Mind* and *Good Will Hunting*, and one television drama series, *Numb3rs*,[1] we reflect on how such representations are gendered, and how this intersects with class, race and sexuality. We argue that while mathematicians, as constructed in those fictional accounts, combine the attributes of dominant groups (as, generally, they are white, middle-class, heterosexual men), they are also constructed as other. The masculinities of these mathematicians are indeed associated with characteristics seen as undesirable, such as mental health problems — ranging from obsessional behavior to schizophrenic disorders, lack of social skills and sternness of lifestyle and personality. This leads us to question whether these texts, with their focus on faltering, extraordinary, or maybe simply alternative mathematical masculinities, challenge hegemonic masculinities (Connell 1995) and open new possibilities for men's gender identities.

Now we consider the context for analyzing constructions of mathematical masculinities in popular culture and our theoretical and methodological framework for doing this. We then pursue a more in-depth exploration of these constructions, concentrating on the three texts quoted earlier. The implications of such constructions are then discussed in relation to the emergence of alternative masculinities.

The Context

Over the recent years, there has been a noticeable decline in the numbers of students of mathematics beyond compulsory level. It has happened in England and Wales (Henry 2002; Kirkman 2002; MacLeod 2005; *Times Educational Supplement* 2003), with similar trends in other countries (Boaler 2008). While the influence of popular culture on subject choice has become a legitimate research question, more and more (male) mathematicians have become the prominent figures of films, books and television dramas (as illustrated by the many examples quoted earlier).

There is a strong gender dimension both to the study of mathematics and to the representations of mathematicians in popular culture. The literature has well evidenced that girls and women are less likely than boys and men to continue with mathematics. However, mathematics is becoming less popular with both boys and girls (Mendick forthcoming). Besides, those representations of mathematicians in popular culture are highly gendered, and are overwhelmingly of men mathematicians. This reflects the wider societal association between mathematics and masculinities (Mendick 2006). Indeed, mathematics, above all other disciplines, has been described as iconic of rationality, with the mathematician personifying the Enlightenment vision, and rationality itself being strongly associated with masculinity (Harding 1998; Lloyd 1993; Walkerdine 1988; Wertheim 1997). These popular culture constructions draw on a gendered binary framework, in which the rational opposes the emotional, with the former being associated with the masculine and the latter with the feminine.

Our argument draws on a project funded by the Economic and Social Research Council (ESRC: RES-000-23-1454), *Mathematical Images and Identities*, conducted between April 2006 and July 2007 (*www.londonmet.ac.uk/ mathsimages*; Mendick, Epstein and Moreau, 2008). Additional funding from the UK Resource Centre for Women in Science Engineering and Technology (UKRC) resulted in a four-month extension of the project focusing on gender issues, and allowed for more data analysis to be conducted between September and December 2007 (Mendick, Moreau and Hollingworth, 2008). The *Mathematical Images and Identities* project explores how pupils and undergraduates studying in a range of institutions in England and Wales position themselves in relation to popular representations of mathematics and mathematicians and how representations of mathematics and mathematicians in popular culture are deployed in their identity constructions. On the basis of answers to a questionnaire completed by 14–15 year old students and second and third year undergraduates (students of mathematics or media studies), popular culture texts featuring mathematics or mathematicians were identified and critically analyzed. While focus groups and interviews were also conducted with those groups, the focal point of this chapter consists in the critical analysis of those texts identified through the survey, with particular attention to *A Beautiful Mind, Numb3rs* and *Good Will Hunting*.

This chapter draws on a feminist, post-structuralist theoretical framework which recognizes the influence of gender on our lives (Connell 1987), the socially constructed differentiation of men and women, the masculine and the feminine, as well as the asymmetry and hierarchy between these categories (Delphy 1993; Héritier 1996, 2002). Men and women are not homogeneous categories, although they may be constructed as such, thus the need to talk about masculini*ties* and feminini*ties*. This allows us to acknowledge not only the differences between men and women, but also the differences across groups of men (and across groups of women), including between (and across) mathematical masculinities and non-mathematical masculinities.

Drawing on earlier post-structuralist works, we acknowledge the discursive construction of gender, and the real effects of discourse on our lives (Davies 1989; Weedon 1997). Within feminist, post-structuralist perspectives, the individual is constructed as a "post-structuralist subject of choice" (Hughes 2002), that is as both subject(ed) *to* and subject *of* discourse (Jones 1997). This subject is the critical viewer described in Buckingham and Bragg (2004) and other critical media studies research, that is s/he is not passively absorbing discourses transmitted by popular culture, but actively interpreting or reading them, both incorporating and resisting them (Hall 1973). The term reading captures the way that watching television, using the internet and so on is "an active process of decoding or interpretation, not simply a passive process of 'reception' or 'consumption' of messages" (Morley 1992: 76). As a result, we do not understand popular culture constructions of mathematicians as having a direct, causal, measurable effect on students' decisions to continue with mathematics, or on students' gendered identities, and we see our own readings of these texts as one among many.

Reading Mathematical Masculinities

We now turn to the analysis of three popular culture texts: *A Beautiful Mind*, *Good Will Hunting* and *Numb3rs*. These texts were retained as they all feature at least one mathematician central to the plot, as well as being mentioned by school students or undergraduates in the questionnaire survey when asked to recall particular examples of mathematics/mathematicians in popular culture. *A Beautiful Mind* and *Good Will Hunting*, in particular, were the most mentioned pieces of popular fiction. Although *Numb3rs* got less mentions, it was also retained for the purpose of this chapter as, like the former texts, it attracts a wide audience in a number of countries, and has also inspired the development of a mathematics education program based on the series (www.weallusematheveryday.com).

A Beautiful Mind (Goldsman 2001), a film based on Sylvia Nasar's biography (2001) of the same name, features the life of John Nash (played by Russell Crowe), from his time as a student at Princeton University through old age, when after being diagnosed with schizophrenia he wins the Nobel Prize for economics for his earlier work on game theory. *Good Will Hunting* (Affleck and Damon 1997) also focuses on the figure of a mathematical genius: Will Hunting (played by Matt Damon), a young working-class Irish-American who works as a janitor at the Massachusetts Institute of Technology (MIT), and whose huge mathematical abilities are discovered by MIT mathematics professor and Fields medal winner, Gerald Lambeau (Stellan Skarsgård). *Numb3rs* (Gansa 1997), an ongoing TV drama, which shows on TV in the UK as in many other countries, is centered on the collaboration between two brothers working together to solve criminal cases: Charlie Eppes (played by David Krumholtz), a young and brilliant professor of mathematics at the fictional California Institute of Science "CalSci," and Don Eppes (played by Rob Morrow), his older brother and a special agent at the Los Angeles office of the FBI.

POPULAR CULTURE, MATHEMATICIANS AND WHITE MIDDLE-CLASS HETEROSEXUAL MASCULINITIES

As in most pieces of popular culture featuring mathematicians, these three texts (*A Beautiful Mind, Numb3rs* and *Good Will Hunting*) propose images of mathematicians which are overwhelmingly male, thus producing, and reproducing, the traditional association between mathematics and masculinity. In contrast, women mathematicians are scarcely present in those accounts. Their invisibility is not a new phenomenon. A quick overview of biographical volumes on mathematicians (for example, Ashurst 1982; Bell 1986 [1937]; Morgan 1972; Turnbull 1962 [1929]) reveals their focus on "men of mathematics," as Bell puts it in his two volumes of the same name, and how the contributions of the likes of Sophie Germain and Hypatia are disappeared or downgraded (with the exception of those feminist-inspired books dealing specifically with women mathematicians, such as: Osen 1994 [1974]; Perl 1978).

Yet, this disappearing remains a topical issue to this day; in popular culture, mathematicians are very rarely women and those rare women mathematicians usually occupy a subordinated position. This subordination, which is multifaceted, does not only materialize in the side-lining of women in the plot, as they are very rarely central characters (with the exception of Catherine, in *Proof*).[2] It is also a generational subordination, as these women are often the descendants of a celebrated (male) mathematician. A striking example of this is Catherine (Gwyneth Paltrow), the daughter of a mathematical genius (Robert, played by Anthony Hopkins), in the film *Proof* (Madden 2006). This idea of mathematics as an heritage from the father is very much central to the film, as Catherine's struggle with her father's inheritance (his mathematical skills and his, possibly related, insanity) is integral to the storyline. This patrilinear transmission of the mathematical gift to daughters has no equivalent when it comes to men mathematicians, suggesting they do not need to owe their mathematical skills to a forefather to be good at mathematics. Indeed, in the three texts we retained for more in-depth analysis, none of the male central characters doing mathematics seem to have inherited it, as their social background suggests. The same cannot be said of the one woman mathematician given some form of importance in these three texts, that is Amita Ramanujan, whose name precisely suggests some kind of descent from Srinivasa Ramanujan, the self-taught Indian mathematician.

A second aspect of women mathematicians' subordination in those popular culture accounts rests with their student status. This is for example the case in *Numb3rs*, in which Amita is Charlie's doctoral student (although she switches supervisor and speciality at the end of season one in order to pursue the possibility of a romantic relationship with him). In a similar vein, in *A Beautiful Mind*, Alicia Larde, although a Physics graduate, is a student of John Nash, and later his wife. In relation to this multiple positioning (daughter/student/wife or girlfriend), these women are also often positioned as assistants to more senior mathematicians. As student/wife (Alicia Larde/Nash) or student/girlfriend (Amita Ramanujan), they provide all forms of support. This is apparent in *A Beautiful Mind*, where Alicia Nash goes to great lengths to support her husband through schizophrenia, as well as in *Numb3rs* where Amita is seen providing emotional, intellectual and domestic support to Charlie (for example, helping him to solve FBI cases). Although Will Hunting is supervised by Professor Lambeau, there is no symmetry whatsoever as Will vehemently challenges the authority of Prof. Lambeau (and finally breaks away from him), and as the film clearly sends the message that, despite his lack of formal education, Will's mathematical abilities are superior to Lambeau's. In a striking contrast to the relationship between Charlie and Amita, Will is never positioned as an assistant to Lambeau.

Simultaneous to the sidelining of women mathematicians is the sidelining of non heterosexual, non white, non middle-class, men mathematicians. As a result, mathematicians in popular culture are overwhelmingly constructed as white, middle-class, heterosexual men. There are however exceptions to this, for example Will Hunting, an Irish-American from a working-class background. Yet, *Good Will Hunting* is very much the story of his middle-classization, as, in becoming a mathematician, he is required to embrace the values of the middle-class and to leave his (working-class) neighborhood, friends and job behind.

Yet, although mathematicians, as constructed in popular culture, usually belong to dominant groups in relation to gender, race, class and sexuality, the figure of the mathematician is also often associated with characteristics which contribute to constructing them as other and which may not fit exactly with the traditional features of hegemonic masculinities. It is those characteristics that we discuss in the next section.

MATHEMATICAL MEN AS OTHERS?

A recurrent feature in these fictional accounts of men mathematicians is that are they are not just any mathematician, they are figures of genius. This is for example the case in *Numb3rs*, where much emphasis is put on Charlie's precocious ability to solve complicated mathematics problems, on the fact that he was five year ahead of his age at school, entered Princeton at 13, and got his first journal article published at 14. Again, *A Beautiful Mind* narrates the life of a mathematician of extraordinary ability who goes on to win a Nobel prize. Despite his lack of formal education, *Good Will Hunting*'s main character promptly solves a problem which Lambeau hoped to see his best MIT students solve by the end of term. When Lambeau, a winner of the Fields Medal, asks his students to tackle an even harder problem which took him and his team two years to resolve, Will settles it swiftly too.

This extraordinary gift for mathematics seems to come at a price. In particular, mathematical masculinities, as constructed in these fictional accounts, are closely associated with some sort of mental health issues, although at diverse degrees. These mathematicians often present symptoms of schizophrenia, paranoia, or some form of social anxiety disorder, such as Robert (Anthony Hopkins) in *Proof*, Maximillian Cohen, a mathematician and main character in *Pi* (Aronofsky 1998), or John Nash in *A Beautiful Mind*. There are also some suggestions of mental health issues in relation to Charlie Eppes and Will Hunting. Charlie reacts to events in a very emotional way with a suggested lack of control over his emotions, for example spending the last three months of his mother's life, while she is dying of cancer, working on a mathematical problem he knows to be unsolvable. These mathematical men are constructed as fragile, in sharp contrast with dominant masculinities, as other research related to white middle-class masculinities has evidenced (Williams, Jamieson, and Hollingworth 2007). However, this fragility does not express in the same way for different figures of mathematicians. With working-class Will Hunting, there is a scene when he loses control reacting with severe violence when he meets a man who abused him as a child. The element of physical violence in the way Will expresses his emotions contrasts with Charlie's (more middle-class) ways. This incident happens prior to Will entering the mathematical community, embarking on a course of therapy, and falling in love with a wealthy Harvard student, thus suggesting that the story of Will is also one of redemption through incorporation of middle-class practices.

Because of their suggested fragility, these mathematical men are often constructed as in need of being protected, rather than as being protective. In *A Beautiful Mind*, John Nash gets through schizophrenia thanks to a combination of marital support, medical care and benevolence from the Princeton academic community (although to some extent they also ostracize him). In *Numb3rs*, Charlie's brother and father are often seen worrying about his psychological and emotional state, and in *Good Will Hunting*, Will enrolling on a course of therapy is a condition for his avoiding prison. This need of protection, combined with a suggested lack of reliability as wage earners (as for example in *Numb3rs* when Charlie forgets about his teaching duties, or in *Good Will Hunting* when Will leaves MIT on impulse or sends friends in his place for job interviews) suggests they may not exactly fit with the image of the male main breadwinner, who brings in a steady income to support his dependents.

Another common feature of these mathematical men is their lack of social skills and geekiness. In *A Beautiful Mind*, John Nash is described as a loner with few friends. Will Hunting may have a small fixed group of friends, yet, he finds it difficult to manage the closeness that his relationship with girl-friend Skylar (played by Minnie Driver) involves. He initially denies his love for her and runs away when she asks him to follow her to Stanford where she has been accepted at Medical School. In *Numb3rs*, Charlie's best (and per-haps only) friend is a theoretical physicist at Princeton, Prof. Larry Fleinhardt (played by Peter MacNicol), who has in common with Charlie an obsession for mathematics and a certain level of awkwardness in social situations. This supposed lack of social skills is indeed often explicitly related to their obses-sion for mathematics, as is the case both in *A Beautiful Mind* and *Numb3rs*, where the main characters tend to see the world through the spectrum of mathematics and go to length to discuss and explain it, something which may slightly put off all those who don't belong to the mathematical genius cate-gory. An interesting example of this permanent obsession for mathematics combined with a lack of social skills, is symbolized by a scene when John Nash observes about the tie of another student: "There has to be a mathematical explanation for how bad that tie is." This obsession with mathematics inter-feres with relationships and makes difficult or impossible forming new rela-tionships, resulting in mathematicians' private lives being often constructed as inexistent or in conflict with and secondary to their mathematical iden-tity. A particular dramatic example of it can be found in *Pi*, when Max is seen drilling into his own head, metaphorically excising the mathematical ability from his brain, before he can go onto a happier and more relational future. The (happy) ending of *Good Will Hunting* provides another example of it, when Will leaves behind high-level mathematics to go see about a girl. In this respect, an underlying message may be that a life dedicated to high-level mathematics may be antithetic to a fulfilled private life and domestic happiness.

The exploration of some of the attributes allocated to these mathemati-cians also suggests that, in these fictional accounts, mathematicians' lives are read as if everything in their life, personality, practices and beliefs was sub-jugated to their mathematical self and was converging to them becoming great mathematicians. In a way, the discourse of popular culture on mathemati-cians does not only suggest that mathematics take over their life, it also sug-gests that it takes over their identity. Such accounts are also characteristic of biographies, which because of drawing officially on facts rather than fictions, can be very powerful in establishing regimes of truth. Sylvia Nasar's biography of John Nash (2001), or Andrew Hodges' of Alan Turing's (1983) are from this perspective very characteristic as they read small details in the lives of these men as evidence of their mathematical genius. This draws on a vision of the homogeneous, unified self which has been long questioned (Flax 1993), yet continues to function when it comes to these mediated accounts of mathematical identities. This is not to say that non-mathematicians have not been constructed as homogeneous selves, however, it is rarely in such a way that their selves seem to be totally subjugated to one thing.

MATHEMATICIANS AND THE COMPETING OF MASCULINITIES

In the previous section, we have argued that popular culture associates mathematical masculinities with a set of characteristics which contribute to their construction as other. In this section we discuss how these masculinities fit within the categories of masculinities conceptualized by Connell (1995). Connell distinguishes four types of masculinities: hegemonic, subordinate, complicit and marginalized. We begin by briefly outlining each of these and then discuss the positioning of mathematical man within this framework.

Hegemonic masculinity "embodies the currently accepted answer to the problem of the legitimacy of patriarchy, which guarantees (or is taken to guarantee) the dominant position of men and the subordination of women" (Connell, 1995: 77). This position is contextual and contested but is associated in its traditional form with physicality and violence. Connell exemplifies the category of subordinate masculinities by discussing gay masculinities and the ways that they are positioned at the bottom of a gender hierarchy of masculinities and are associated with femininity. Since only a minority of men practice the hegemonic patterns, complicit masculinities are "constructed in ways that realize the patriarchal dividend, without the tensions or risks of being the frontline troops of patriarchy" (79). Marginalized masculinities are those of men who are part of groups occupying dominated positions, mainly in relation to structures of race and social class.

These mathematical masculinities can hardly be described as marginalized because they are of white, middle-class, heterosexual men in successful careers. Even Will Hunting is marginalized only because he has not yet taken up a position as a mathematician and his story is one of becoming. However, these figures of the mathematical genius are seemingly constructed in sharp contrast with hegemonic masculinities as subordinate masculinities are. Indeed Connell includes nerds and geeks within this category. However, we would argue that this is problematic for two reasons. First, as Connell argues:

> Historically there has been an important division between forms of masculinity organized around direct domination (e.g., corporate management, military command) and forms organized around technical knowledge (e.g., professions, science). The latter have challenged the former for hegemony in the gender order of advanced capitalist societies, without complete success. They currently coexist as inflections or alternative emphases within hegemonic masculinity [165].

As we argued earlier, rationality, science and technology are central to the organization of the current gender order and: "Hegemonic masculinity establishes its hegemony partly by its claim to embody the power of reason, and thus represents the interests of the whole society; it is a mistake to identify hegemonic masculinity purely with physical aggression" (164). With the expansion of the internet and other technologies, the power of white middle-class masculinities based around rationality and their role in legitimating male power have increased since Connell wrote these words. Second, we would argue that, while the figure of the mathematical genius draws on specific tropes from the figure of the nerd, there are significant differences between them. The status given both to mathematicians and to geniuses allows them to escape the position of subordination occupied by the nerd. However, mathematical masculinities are also not easy to fit into the model of hegemonic masculinity, as men mathematicians are, more often than not, constructed in textual accounts as fragile, in need of protection, and geeky. It thus seems relevant to ask whether the figures of mathematicians in texts such as *A Beautiful Mind*, *Numb3rs* or *Good Will Hunting*, challenge the model of hegemonic masculinities contingent to Western, capitalist societies in which our study is based.

Since masculinities are relational, we do this by looking at the competing masculinities within these three texts. *Numb3rs* allows a controlled comparison: the two brothers are similar in family background, social class, sexuality, race and nationality. *A Beautiful Mind* allows a less controlled comparison between Nash and Hansen and the other mathematicians. In *Good Will Hunting* there is a wide range of competing masculinities, with comparisons between men who occupy a range of social class and work positionings.

Turning to *Numb3rs*, a system of binary oppositions organized around an atypical type of masculinity (the mathematical genius) and a more traditional, dominant type of masculinity (the non mathematician or those mathematicians of lower abilities) is apparent. Drawing on *Numb3rs* and its sibling rivalry, some binary oppositions are highlighted in the table on the following page.

These characteristics combine together to offer two different versions of

Table 1. Analysis of Systems of Binary
Oppositions in *Numb3rs'* Charlie and Don

Charlie Eppes	*Don Eppes*
Mathematician	FBI officer
Genius	Intellectually average
Likes theory	Likes action
Lack of control on emotions	Control of emotions
Fragile	Tough
In need of protection	Protector
Some visible involvement in domestic activity	No visible involvement in domestic activity
Non alcoholic drinks and wine	Beer
Exercising the mind	Exercising the body

(white, middle-class, heterosexual) masculinities, two embodiments of the discourses of masculinity: Charlie's alternative form of masculinity, in opposition with Don's more hegemonic type.

In *A Beautiful Mind*, John Nash's character is contrasted with that of Martin Hansen (played by Josh Lucas). Both men are extraordinary mathematicians. Yet, only John Nash incarnates the figure of the genius. As we highlighted earlier, this mathematical genius comes at a price, and the film goes to lengths to demonstrate some kind of relationship between John Nash's abilities, his mental health issues, lack of social skills and difficulties in building relationships. In contrast, Martin Hansen is a very popular figure, surrounded by friends and confident with women, who becomes the powerful head of the Princeton mathematics department, and is constructed as an economically and emotionally stable breadwinner.

In *Good Will Hunting*, Will's identity quest is symbolized by the opposition between Sean Maguire (played by Robin Williams) and Gerald Lambeau. Another overarching opposition in the film is that between Will's working-class friends and the academic men in the film (mainly Sean and Gerald). In contrast to *Numb3rs'* Charlie and *A Beautiful Mind's* John Nash, Will's self is not unified, nor does he want to subjugate all his life to his mathematical identity. This contrast is possibly related to the fact that Will is in a process of becoming a mathematician and is still struggling between different types of competing, classed masculinities, mathematical or not.

Although these figures clearly offer alternatives to the hegemonic positions, whether they can be read as constituting a radical critique of hegemonic masculinity needs to be questioned. A first point to be made is that, as we highlighted, in these mediated accounts, mathematical masculinities are always contrasted with more traditional and more dominant masculinities (such as Don in *Numb3rs*, or Martin Hansen in *A Beautiful Mind*), which are often constructed in a more positive light. There is no critique of these more hegemonic characters, or of the patriarchal system of gender relations they contribute to legitimating. Another point to be made is about how much this figure of the mathematical genius represents a rupture with hegemonic masculinities. In many ways, as discussed earlier, these mathematical men can be read as iconic of masculinity as they are associated with rationality and technical knowledge, and as mathematics is seen as a form of higher intelligence and is a strongly competitive field. The story of these extraordinary mathematicians is one of conquering and mastering, both of which are more often than not a masculine enterprise (Mendick 2004), which positions them in a powerful position. In some way, Connell's observations about the sports world could be paraphrased and applied to mathematics: "Only a tiny minority reach the top as professional athletes; yet the production of masculinity throughout the sports world is marked by the hierarchical, competitive structure of the institution" (36). As in sports, mathematics is marked by the race for excellence, with marks of distinction (such as the position, the prestige of the institution and department, awards — such as the Fields medal) being used to create a hierarchy of mathematicians. This suggests that the way mathematical masculinities collide with hegemonic masculinities is not clear-cut, and it may be that the emphasis in the constructing of the mathematical genius figure on "rationality and responsibility rather than pride and aggressiveness" (Connell, 1989: 296–297) represents a shift more than a rupture with hegemonic masculinities.

Mathematical masculinities may be closer to complicit masculinities. They are different from the hegemonic type, yet do not challenge the patriarchal system. An example of this is the competition arising between John Nash and Martin Hansen in *A Beautiful Mind* around a game of Go. Hansen successfully tempts him into playing by asking him "You scared?," Nash answers sarcastically with a sentence which tells us a lot about the competition between the two men (which in many ways can be seen as characteristic of hegemonic masculinities): "Terrified, mortified, petrified, stupefied by you." In an older example, *Straw Dogs* (Peckinpah 1971), when a group of villagers attacks the house where mathematician David Sumner (played by Dustin Hoffman) is taking sabbatical leave, he is able to protect his wife from the local laborers in conventional macho ways. In *Numb3rs*, Charlie may not embody the characteristics of dominant masculinity, yet he still benefits the societal association between masculinities and mathematics, and for example does not challenge the fact that Amita is positioned as an assistant to him.

Conclusions

As it has been argued, mathematicians in contemporary mediated accounts are, more often than not, white, middle-class, heterosexual men. Yet, their collusion with dominant groups do not protect them from being constructed as others, although theirs are not the subordinate or marginalized masculinities conceptualized by Connell. These are also men who do not necessarily fit with the hegemonic forms of masculinity. They are rather complicit as they may not embody hegemonic masculinity, yet benefit from the way the gender order is constructed. Their construction as other, simultaneous with their complicit masculinity, suggests, as Wetherell and Edley (1999) observe, that "we need to allow for the possibility that complicity and resistance can be mixed together" (352). We may also need to consider that these different types of masculinities are not embodied by particular figures, although some particular figures can be closer to particular types, as our analysis of Charlie's and Don's masculinities suggests. Rather they need to be read as competing discourses, as "labels to describe the effects of discursive strategies mobilized in contexts as opposed to labels for different types of men" (*ibid.*: 352). Overall, the texts analyzed cannot be read as radically critiquing of hegemonic masculinity as they do not challenge the patriarchal order, with the dominant position of (some) men and the subordination of women. Although they may disrupt some of these tropes, these texts simultaneously serve to reaffirm the limits within which masculinities can go astray.

Beyond this, and in regard of the link between learning mathematics and gendered identities, we need to question how these discursive constructions of mathematical men, with their complicit gender identities, and the discursive construction of women and non white, non middle-class or non heterosexual men deploy in students' discourses. This is beyond the remit of this chapter, yet, it is a question we are looking at in the rest of the project and a key one to explore if we want to understand how mediated accounts of mathematical masculinities and feminities influence students' relationship with the subject.

Acknowledgments

The authors would like to thank the following people and organization: the Economic and Social Research Council which funded the project on which this essay is based; the members of the project advisory group, particularly Helen Lucey, The Open University, and Jeff Evans, Middlesex University, who commented on an earlier version of this chapter; Teresa Carbajo-Garcia, the project administrator; the many school and university students who participated to the project; and the school and university staff who facilitated access to the fieldwork.

Notes

1. More specifically season one.
2. Women mathematicians are also somewhat sidelined in materials satellite to those fictions. For example, and as observed Silverberg (2006), only three characters in *Numb3rs* do not have a character profile on the CBS website, including the two women in the series (Amita Ramanujan and Megan Reeves). In the same vein, this official website of the TV channel never gets Amita's surname right, calling her Ramanjuan or Ramajuan.

Bibliography

Ashurst, F. G. *Founders of Modern Mathematics*. London: Frederick Muller, 1982.
A Beautiful Mind. Akiva Goldsman. Universal Pictures/Dreamworks Pictures/Imagine Entertainment, 2001.
Bell, E.T. *Men of Mathematics*. New York: Simon & Schuster, 1986 [1937].
Boaler, Jo. *The Maths Crisis*. London: Penguin, 2008.
Brown, Dan. *The Da Vinci Code*. Croydon, UK: Corgi, 2003.
Buckingham, David, and Sara Bragg. *Young People, Sex and the Media: The Facts of Life?* Basingstoke, Hampshire, UK: Palgrave Macmillan, 2004.
Connell, Robert W. *Gender and Power*. Cambridge: Polity Press, 1987.
Connell, Robert W. "Cool Guys, Swots and Wimps: The Interplay of Masculinity and Education." *Oxford Review of Education* 15, no. 3 (1989): 291–303.
_____. *Masculinities*. Cambridge: Polity, 1995.
The Da Vinci Code. R. Howard. Writer: A. Goldsman, Columbia Pictures. 2006.
Davies, Bronwyn. *Frogs and Snails and Feminist Tales: Preschool Children and Gender*. Sydney: Allen & Unwin, 1989.
Delphy, Christine. "Rethinking Sex and Gender." *Women's Studies International Forum* 16, no. 1 (1993): 1–9.
Enigma. Michael Apted. Writer: T. Stoppard, Jagged Films and Broadway Video for Senator Entertainment and Intermedia Films, 2001.
Fermat's Last Theorem. Horizon. Simon Singh and John Lynch. Writer: British Broadcasting Corporation, 1998.
Flax, Jane. *Disputed Subjects: Essays on Psychoanalysis, Politics and Philosophy*. London: Routledge, 1993.
Good Will Hunting. Ben Affleck and Matt Damon. Lawrence Bender Productions/Miramax, 1997.
Haddon, Mark. *The Curious Incident of the Dog in the Night-Time*. London: Jonathan Cape, 2003.
Hall, Stuart. *Encoding and Decoding in the Television Discourse*. Birmingham University, UK: Centre for Cultural Studies, 1973.
Harding, Sandra. *Is Science Multicultural? Postcolonialisms, Feminisms and Epistemologies*. Bloomington and Indianapolis: Indiana University Press, 1998.

Henry, Julie. "Pupils Shun Maths for 'Softer' Subjects." *Times Educational Supplement,* 9 August, 2002.
Héritier, Françoise. *Masculin, féminin. La pensée de la différence.* Paris: Odile Jacob, 1996.
_____. *Masculin/féminin ii: Dissoudre la hiérarchie.* Paris: Odile Jacob, 2002.
Hodges, Andrew. *Alan Turing: The Enigma of Intelligence.* London: Unwin, 1983.
Hughes, Christine. *Key Concepts in Feminist Theory and Research.* London: Sage, 2002.
Jones, Alison. "Teaching Post-Structuralist Feminist Theory in Education: Student Resistances." *Gender and Education* 9, no. 3 (1997): 261–269.
Kirkman, Susannah. "A-Level Battlefield." *Times Educational Supplement,* 4 October. 2002.
Lalwani, Nikita. *Gifted.* London: Viking. 2007.
Lloyd, Genevieve. *The Man of Reason: "Male" and "Female" in Western Philosophy.* London: Routledge, 1993.
21. Robert Luketic. Writers: P. Steinfeld, A. Loeb GH Tree and B. Mezrich/Michael de Luca Productions/Relativity Media/Trigger Street Productions, 2008.
MacLeod, Donald. "Course Closures Creating Maths 'Wasteland.'" *Guardian,* 11 February, 2005.
Mendick, Heather. *Masculinities in Mathematics.* Maidenhead, Berkshire (UK): Open University Press (McGraw-Hill Education), 2006.
_____. "A Mathematician Goes to the Movies." *Proceedings of the British Society for Research into Learning Mathematics* 24, no. 1 (2004): 43–48.
_____. "Subtracting Difference: Troubling Transitions from GCSE to A-Level Mathematics. *British Educational Research Journal,* December, 2008.
Mendick, Heather, Debbie Epstein, and Marie-Pierre Moreau. *End of Award Report: Mathematical Images and Identities: Education, Entertainment, Social Justice.* Swindon: Economic and Social Research Council, 2008.
Mendick, Heather, Marie-Pierre Moreau, and Sumi Hollingworth. *Mathematical Images and Gender Identities: A Report on the Gendering of Representations of Mathematics and Mathematicians in Popular Culture and Their Influences on Learners.* London, IPSE, London Metropolitan University, 2008.
Morgan, Bryan. *Men and Discoveries in Mathematics.* London: John Murray, 1972.
Morley, David. *Television, Audiences and Cultural Studies.* London: Routledge, 1992.
Nasar, Sylvia. *A Beautiful Mind.* London: Faber and Faber, 2001.
Numb3rs. Alex Gansa. CBS, 1997.
Osen, Lynn. *Women in Mathematics.* Cambridge, MA: MIT Press, 1994 [1974].
The Oxford Murders. Álex de la Iglesia. Writers: J. Guerricaechevarría, A. de la Iglesia, and G. Martinez. Eurimages/La Fabrique de Films/Telecinco Cinema/Tornasol Films S.A., 2008.
Straw Dogs. Sam Peckinpah. 1971.
Perl, Teri. *Math Equals: Biographies of Women Mathematicians + Related Activities.* Menlo Park: Addison-Wesley, 1978.
Pi. Darren Aronofsky. Harvest Filmworks/Plantain Films/Protozoa Films/Truth and Soul, 1998.
Proof. John Madden. Writer: D. Auburn, Miramax Films, 2006.
Silverberg, Alice. "Alice in Numb3rland." *Focus* 26, no. 8 (2006): 12–13.
Times Educational Supplement. "Fewer Undergraduates Opt for Maths." 17 January, 2003.
Turnbull, H.W. *The Great Mathematicians.* London: Methuen, 1962 [1929].
Walkerdine, Valerie. *The Mastery of Reason: Cognitive Development and the Production of Rationality.* London: Routledge. 1988.
Weedon, Chris. *Feminist Practice and Poststructuralist Theory.* Oxford, UK: Basil Blackwell. 1997.
Wertheim, Margaret. *Pythagoras' Trousers: God, Physics and the Gender Wars.* London: Fourth Estate, 1997.

Wetherell, Margaret, and Nigel Edley. "Negotiating Hegemonic Masculinity: Imaginary Positions and Psycho-Discursive Practices." *Feminism & Psychology* 9 (1999): 335–356.
Williams, Katya, Fiona Jamieson, and Sumi Hollingworth. "'He Was a Bit of a Delicate Thing': White Middle Class Boys, Gender, School Choice and Parental Anxiety." In *Gender and Education Conference*. Trinity College of Dublin, 2007.

9

Killing Off White Hegemonic Masculinity in *Indian Killer*

Jane E. Rose

As the historical record documents, because of European colonization of the Americas, the various nations and tribes of American Indians, indigenous populations that once spanned the continent, have experienced domination, exploitation, extermination, assimilation, displacement, and marginalization. Sherman Alexie, a Spokane/Coeur d'Alene Indian, addresses these issues from a contemporary perspective in his 1996 novel *Indian Killer*. As Alexie remarks in an interview with Tomson Highway, "It's also a novel about, not just physical murder, but the spiritual, cultural and physical murder of Indians. The title, *Indian Killer*, is a palindrome, really. It's 'Indians who kill' and it's also 'people who kill Indians.' It's about how the dominant culture is killing the First Nations people of this country to this day, still."[1] Alexie critiques the hegemonic forces of white masculinity and superiority through his depiction of several male characters whose identity and psyche suffer from the effects of white hegemony: John Smith, an Indian adopted by a white couple; Reggie Polatkin, who is of mixed race; and Jack Wilson, who claims to be Indian but whose heritage is questionable. Marie Polatkin, the only major Indian female character in the novel, is torn between her ethnic identity and assimilation into white culture. The greatest challenges to contemporary Indians who have escaped extermination are assimilation, marginalization, and displacement. These challenges force them to question who they are and where they can belong. Struggling with their identity in the urban setting of Seattle, Washington, these characters become suspects in a series of murders of white males. The murder of white males, I argue, represents symbolically the killing off of hegemonic white masculinity.

Providing a complete historical survey of the cultural definitions and stereotypes of hegemonic masculinity is beyond the scope of this essay; therefore, I will define it from a contemporary perspective. According to Tim Carrigan, Bob Connell, and John Lee, hegemonic masculinity refers to "how particular groups of men inhabit positions of power and wealth, and how they legitimate and reproduce the social relationships that generate their dominance."[2] Historically, European and Euro-American males have benefited from dominance and privilege at the expense of both women and marginalized males who hold subordinate positions. In Alexie's novel, hegemonic masculinity is associated with sexism; racial superiority and dominance; contamination and corruption of Indian culture; and the inevitable transformation of Indian masculinity. Killing off these elements of white hegemonic masculinity is a step in mediating a new masculine identity for the males negotiating their existence in urban Seattle as they deal with their own conflicted feelings about their identity and the anger they feel toward whites for the destruction and oppression of all Indians.

These urban Indians are torn between maintaining authentic identity and accepting white influence by assimilating white values, customs, and traditions. As a result, they must attempt to mediate between two identities to form a new masculine identity in contemporary America. Achieving authentic Indian identity may be impossible. A consideration of the construct of authentic Indian identity is helpful in understanding the complexity of the situation urban Indians in *Indian Killer* face. As Paige Raibmon explains, in the late 1800s and early 1900s, colonizers in devising policies and anthropologists in studying Indians relied on a definition of Indian authenticity and inauthenticity in terms of what is white versus what is Indian. Indians were viewed as "traditional, uncivilized, cultural, impoverished, feminine, static, part of nature and of the past" while whites were defined as "modern, civilized, political, prosperous, masculine, dynamic, part of society and of the future."[3] As she further explains, "Aboriginal people inevitably deviated from their prescribed cultural set, because no culture conforms to an unchanging set of itemized traits, a fact that goes uncontested when the culture in question is the dominant one."[4] To survive economically, Aboriginal people struggled between maintaining tribal customs and becoming modern through assimilation of white practices. According to Raibmon, many Aboriginals "made good use of stereotypes; they 'played Indian' for white audiences by performing dances and selling curios."[5] In *Indian Killer* urban Indians either participate in or observe fancy dancers at powwows despite the elders' disapproval: "It [fancy dancing] was too modern, too white, the dance of children who refused to grow up."[6] Euro-Americans often define American Indians by nineteenth-century stereotypes such as the noble savage and the vanishing Indian. This stereotyping complicates the understanding and acceptance of Indians in modern urban America, such as the Seattle setting of the novel.

Viewing ethnic identity as a social product, Joane Nagel asserts that ethnic identity is a matter of choice. In her study of American Indian ethnic identity, Nagel researched United States census reports from 1960 through 1990 and found that during this time period the American Indian population increased threefold. This increase was not caused by biological circumstances; that is, more births and fewer deaths, but by "ethnic switching," which is switching from non–Indian in a past census to Indian in a current census. She labels this occurrence "ethnic renewal," a process that may occur both individually and collectively. As Nagel explains, "*Individual ethnic renewal* occurs when an individual acquires or asserts a new ethnic identity by reclaiming a discarded identity, replacing or amending an identity in an existing ethnic repertoire, or filling a personal ethnic void" while "[c]*ollective ethnic renewal* involves the reconstruction of an ethnic community by current or new community members who build or rebuild institutions, culture, history, and traditions."[7] Furthermore, she claims "that ethnic renewal among the American Indian population has been brought about by three political forces: (1) federal Indian policy, (2) American ethnic politics, and (3) American Indian political activisim."[8] In brief, after World War II, American Indians living on reservations were encouraged to relocate to urban areas, including Seattle, for job training in order to further assimilation. In some cities Indian centers not only offered services but also a place for tribal members to meet, thus helping to establish a collective tribal identity.[9] The civil rights movement in the 1960s prompted a renascence in Indian ethnic pride and a stronger willingness to identify as Indian particularly to acquire land and preferential treatment for jobs and college scholarships.[10] Red Power activism rose in the 1960s and 1970s as more and more younger Indians contested white hegemony.[11] Thus these influences resulted in an increase in Indian identification: "Americans of varying degrees of Indian ancestry who formerly reported a non–Indian race, but who changed their race to 'Indian'" and "'wannabes,' non–Indian individuals who want to be American Indian and thus identify themselves as such."[12] I provide this information from Nagel's study because the main characters of *Indian Killer*, specifically Reggie and Marie Polatkin, want to deny their Indian identity for reasons to be discussed, and at other times, they assert it as they become activists in Indian rights and confront and expose wannabe Indians like Clarence Mather and Jack Wilson. Of the major characters, it is John Smith who wants to achieve a genuinely authentic Indian identity, both individual and collective.

However, as a result of white hegemony, John Smith's Indian identity is conflicted for many reasons, and because it is, he appears to be the most likely suspect in the murder of white males. One reason is that he is a displaced Indian who has no idea what his tribal affiliation is. All he knows is that in the late 1960s he was born to an unwed fourteen-year-old Indian girl at the Indian Health Services Hospital. She could be Navajo, Lakota, Apache — any Indian girl, thus implying a kind of universal experience yet reinforcing the fact that Indian identity is not monolithic.[13] Because his biological father is unknown, he could be either full blood or mixed blood.

John's adoption by a white couple, Daniel and Olivia Smith, adds to his inner conflict. They adopt an Indian baby because they are unable to conceive a child of their own, because they do not want to adopt a special needs child; that is, one with "Down's syndrome," "missing arms and legs," or "mentally retarded," and because they are too impatient to wait for a white baby to be available.[14] The adoption agent tells the Smiths, "The best place for this baby is with a white family. This child will be saved a lot of pain by growing up in a white family. It's the best thing really."[15] Despite their good intentions to raise an Indian baby, the non–Indian Smiths are not equipped to nurture him, their cultural and ethnic incompatibility symbolized by Olivia's dry white breast.

Ironically, Daniel and Olivia name the baby John Smith, reminding one of the legendary seventeenth-century explorer John Smith whose exaggerated accounts of fighting off Indians and meeting Pocahontas historians have questioned for their authenticity.[16] The name has also been a common name for white males, suggesting a kind of generic whiteness or white everyman and thus extinguishing John's Indian ethnicity. Chippewa Indian Gail Guthrie Valaskakis discusses the importance of naming in Native traditions for linking individuals to community, to storied memory, to the land, and to spirituality.[17] John Smith's name holds no spiritual power because it does not connect him to any tribe and land. It also reinforces and foreshadows the struggle John Smith faces growing up in a white family and white-dominant society, knowing that his true heritage is Indian but being deprived of his tribal affiliation. Lack of knowledge about his biological parents and tribe, because of the sealing of adoption records, haunts him and forces him to create a tribal connection:

> His adopted parents had never told him what kind of Indian he was. They did not know. They never told him anything at all about his natural parents, other than his birth mother's age, which was fourteen. John only knew that he was Indian in the most generic sense. Black hair, brown skin and eyes, high cheekbones, the prominent nose. Tall and muscular, he looked like some cinematic warrior and constantly intimidated people with his presence. When asked by white people he said he was Sioux, because that was what they wanted him to be. When asked by Indian people, he said he was Navajo, because that was what he wanted to be.[18]

And so he is both a generic white man and generic Indian with no true sense of who he really is. To compensate for this lack of knowledge and to achieve a non-generic identity, John Smith creates myths or stories about his Indian family on the reservation including a mother who is proud of him and a large extended family who "play Scrabble using the tribal language." He envisions himself as a four-year-old grass dancer at a powwow. At sixteen he tells stories with his family. One uncle was a World War II army veteran. Another was a salmon fisherman and yet another a builder of skyscrapers.[19] These stories give him the role of story teller so important in transmitting Indian oral history and allow him to navigate and be included in both white and Indian cultures.

Through his depiction of John Smith, Alexie indicts the practice of white families adopting Indian babies which was allowed before the passing of the Indian Child Welfare Act in 1978 stopped the adoption of Indian children by non–Indian families. The Congressional declaration of policy states:

> The Congress hereby declares that it is the policy of this Nation to protect the best interests of Indian children and to promote the stability and security of Indian tribes and families by the establishment of minimum Federal standards for the removal of Indian children from their families and the placement of such children in foster or adoptive homes which will reflect the unique values of Indian culture, and by providing for assistance to Indian tribes in the operation of child and family service programs.[20]

This act serves to protect Indian children from the dilution and extinction of Indian identity by not placing Indian children in white homes. Alexie's own cousin was adopted by a non–Indian family. Alexie says that these Indians became lost birds often becoming suicidal and alcohol or drug dependent.[21] That's exactly what happens to John Smith; he becomes a lost bird or soul.

John Smith's identity conflict is heightened by the fact that his white parents expect him to assimilate despite their efforts to educate him in Indian customs and traditions. This attempt to meld two different cultures in his upbringing consequently leads to a schizophrenic existence as an adult, literally and figuratively — a contesting double identity. Figuratively John is caught between two worlds which he tries to understand and to fit in, especially since he has been denied his Indian culture and will never be a part of its history. Literally, he suffers from paranoid schizophrenia hearing voices and having delusions.

The process of assimilation starts with religion and education. As a child, John is baptized by Father Duncan, a Spokane Indian Jesuit, who represents a combination of Christian and Indian religious traditions. Father Duncan holds John in his arms and sings both Spokane Indian songs and Catholic hymns. In blending religious rituals, Father Duncan brings together Euro-American and American Indian cultures, but this practice has not resulted in a successful melding or coexistence of the two identities. As John matures, his influence on him is rather traumatizing as Duncan adds to John's confusion about identity and distrust of white people by telling him about non-natives killing off most of the Indians but Indians not having the heart to kill all the white people.[22] At various times throughout the novel, John experiences hallucinations and visions about Father Duncan. As Stuart Christie explains, "On the surface, Father Duncan presents Alexie's desire to ironize white liberal assumptions about innate American Indian authenticity and holiness.... An 'irony,' Duncan embodies what, for the adult John, will amount to irresolvable contradictions between 'split' Indian and white selves, as well as the pitfalls associated with oppositional cross-cultural inheritances."[23]

John is further indoctrinated in Catholicism at St. Francis School where he is the only Indian and where his adolescent years are indeed awkward. His experience at St. Francis is reminiscent of the practices of the Indian boarding school movement. His hair is cut short, and he wears polished topsiders. He has conformed to look like the white boys at the school. Like the advocates of the boarding school movement, St. Francis School officials see John Smith as a trophy — proof of "a successfully integrated Indian boy."[24] Alexie is critiquing a practice of white hegemonic influence that occurred in the eighteenth and nineteenth centuries. This was the attempt, promoted by Catholic missionaries and boarding schools for Indian children, to "kill the Indian and save the man," a slogan attributed to army officer Richard Henry Pratt, founder of The Carlisle Indian School in Carlisle, Pennsylvania. The goal was to extinguish Indian customs, languages, and identity, especially to eliminate the influence of tribalism. Many children were forced to go to boarding schools by federal mandate; others chose to go out of curiosity and eagerness to learn. Indian children were taught Catholicism, English, and Euro-American manners and customs. For boys, assimilation into white culture meant transforming one's masculinity to meet the expectations of white maleness. Boys were expected to learn an industrial trade or the practice of farming.[25]

Adolescence is an important time for self-identification, especially in the development of males from boys to men, but John is hindered by his split identities. While John makes friends with white boys, awkward sexual encounters with white girls begin to make him feel out of place. As the narrator points out, "John felt insignificant at those times and retreated into a small place inside of himself, until the girls confused his painful silence with rapt interest."[26] His attempts to date are futile: white girls break up with him and their fathers are uncomfortable with him. This awkwardness with girls confuses him and makes him question his masculinity. In addition, some people question his identity while others stereotype him as alcoholic, poor, and irreligious. Fighting off anger, he wants to run and hide. This feeling intensifies, and he becomes increasingly angry.[27]

Even when John is among a lot of Indians at an all-Indian basketball tournament, he still does not really fit in and feels alienated.[28] Deeply fascinated with them, he notices their similarities but focuses on their differences:

> So many Indians, so many tribes, many sharing similar features, but also differing in slight and important ways. The Makahs different than the Quinaults, the Lummi different from the Puyallup. There were Indians with dark skin and jet-black hair. There were Indians with brown hair and paler skin. Green-eyed Indians. Indians with black blood. Indians with Mexican blood. Indians with white blood. Indians with Asian blood. All of them laughing and carrying on. Many Indians barely paying attention to the game. They were talking, telling jokes, and laughing loudly. So much laughter. John wanted to own that laughter, never realizing that their laughter was a ceremony used to drive away personal and collective demons. The Indians who were watching the game reacted mightily to each basket or defensive stop. They moaned and groaned as if each mistake were fatal, as if each field goal meant the second coming of Christ. But always, they were laughing. John had never seen so many happy people. He did not share their happiness.[29]

Perhaps those demons pertain to a mixed cultural and ethnic identity resulting from miscegenation, which dilutes the bloodlines of nations and tribes and thus causes racial impurity, thereby preventing the possibility of living as a truly authentic American Indian. As Stuart Christie argues, "Alexie's novel solidifies racial purity as the guarantor of authentic Indian existence,"[30] but as I have shown, hegemonic forces and the inevitability of modernization preclude racially pure Indians from living authentically. What John sees as their contentment and sense of belonging, however, reinforces his own displacement, unhappiness, and confusion about his identity. He does not "recognize these Indians. They are nothing like the Indians he had read about."[31] Obviously, John has his own view or ideal of Indians that white culture may have created based on its definition of authentic versus inauthentic Indian identity, false expectations which may be impossible to meet.

As an adult in the urban environment of Seattle, John's sense of alienation increases. After high school graduation, he rejects college, despite good grades and his parents' wishes, and opts for construction work building skyscrapers. His choice comes from reading about Mohawk Indian steel workers who helped construct the World Trade Center buildings, for "he figured it was the Indian thing to do."[32] As James Doyle points out, "few jobs are as dangerous as heavy construction and few heavy construction jobs are as dangerous as 'high steel' construction. For over a hundred years now, a single group of men has been associated with high steel construction, the Kahnawake (or Caughnawaga) Mohawks."[33] The Kahnawakes have earned a living through steel construction since 1886 when they built bridges and buildings in eastern Canada and the eastern United States.[34] Anthropologist David Blanchard has discovered "three important symbolic aspects of high steel work for the Kahnawake man, namely, ironwork as a rite of passage from youth to adulthood, as a link with one's Mohawk traditions and past heritage, and as a ritual defining one's gender role."[35] Among Kahnawake Mohawks ironwork is considered to be "real work," which they define as physically demanding, hard, and dangerous. One must be able to climb and balance skillfully atop dangerously high places.[36] Thus modeling his father, a young Kahnawake enters a "rite of passage into manhood" when he takes his first real job as an ironworker.[37] In addition, Mohawk tradition has progressed from the days of trapping and fur trading to the contemporary excitement of steel construction as young Mohawks leave the reservation and go from city to city to build high rises. Also in keeping with the tradition of separating males and females in times of sexual activity and fertility to avoid mixing the sexual powers of men and women, ironwork necessitates men leave women to work with fellow steel workers. A sense of manliness is enhanced through real work requiring physical strength. As Doyle explains, "Traveling to distant job sites and staying with other Kahnawake men provide the kind of all-male group that reinforces a sense of manhood distant from the supportive role they provide their womenfolk on the reservation."[38] Adapting to colonization, assimilation, and modernism, the Mohawks as a collective group negotiated a new masculinity through steel construction and urban living that John Smith must attempt to do on his own. Like them, he is trying to bridge the chasm between the ancient and the modern.

It is interesting to note Mohawk Indians' involvement in the World Trade Center. Before its destruction in the terrorist attack on the United States on September 11, 2001, the World Trade Center, often referred to as the Twin Towers, was viewed as the epitome of American inventiveness, since for a while the towers were the tallest buildings in the world, of U.S. dominance in capitalistic venture, and of corporate greed and success, especially after private companies linked to Wall Street moved in in the 1980s. In light of years of European colonization and expansion, the World Trade Center symbolizes the pinnacle of success in displacing indigenous populations from their land in the United States' quest to be the leader in world trade. The Mohawks' participation in the construction of these super tall buildings indicates assimilation into and adaptation to white culture at the same time as they reinforce their manhood. Smith is attracted to the fearlessness required of working at such heights. The Mohawk steel workers are the new urban warriors. More importantly, they have been entered into the oral tradition of Native American myth making. The Mohawk construction workers "had passed from ordinary story to outright myth."[39]

> They were crazy bastards, walking across girders without safety harnesses, jumping from floor to floor like they were Spiderman's bastard sons. There were three or four generations of Mohawk steel workers. Old Mohawk grandfathers sat around Brooklyn brownstones and talked stories about working on the Empire State Building. They scared children with tales of relatives, buried alive in building foundations, who come back to haunt all of the white office workers.[40]

Wearing his black hair long tucked under his hard hat and standing over six feet tall, John is often called chief by his foreman and like the Mohawk steel workers climbs up the sides of buildings. But unlike the Mohawks, he has left no reservation, is following no elders' footsteps, and has no group of fellow Indian steelworkers with whom to form camaraderie. Nor does John have a woman waiting for him on a reservation. To mediate his identity and to develop manhood, John Smith chooses to enter the occupation, history, and myth of the Mohawk steel workers.

However, as an Indian outside Mohawk affiliation but inside the brotherhood of white steel workers, John is forced to make choices that go against the grain of hegemonic white male expectations. Remaining a loner, John refuses to take part in the sexist mindset of macho construction workers and declines drinking with them after work: "Somewhere inside himself, John knew they just wanted him to be a part of the team. He understood what it meant to be a teammate. But he did not want to deal with complications, the constant need to reassert his masculinity, the graphic talk about women. John could no longer stand such talk about women."[41] He wants to avoid having to hear about the "horrible things they might do" to any beautiful woman, white or Indian, who attracts their gaze. Such talk John had also heard from his white classmates in high school and from his father's rich white friends at parties.[42] Even John's adopted mother Olivia, very beautiful with "clear pale skin and blue, blue eyes," had been the target of the male gaze and sexist objectification. His high school classmates enraged him with comments like "Your mom is a babe" and "If she was my mom, I would never have quit breastfeeding." They even went so far as to suggest that John himself could have sex with his mother since he is adopted, especially since according to the movies, "Indians always want to fuck white women."[43] This blatant sexism, specifically the objectification, victimization, and domination of women, which I believe Alexie attributes to white hegemonic masculinity, repulses John Smith. He recognizes and rejects the male need to assert masculinity by disparaging and sexually conquering women, thereby demonstrating a position of power and superiority.

This view of women is a stark departure from the treatment of women in American Indian societies. Native women have been respected as life-giving forces, as nurturers, and as healers. Their ability to menstruate and bear children is considered as great and powerful as the power attributed to warriors.[44] Native women have held positions of farmer and tribal leader like Wilma Mankiller who served as chief of the Cherokees.[45] Although various tribes may designate gender roles differently, native women have been valued for their skills in fulfilling domestic duties essential to the family and producing goods like baskets, food, clothing, and pottery. They have been treated as equals and honored for their accomplishments.[46] Noting the power and intelligence of Native women, Paula Gunn Allen acknowledges their policy-making roles in the Iroquois Confederacy and traces the origins of white feminism to tribal women like the Iroquois Clan matrons.[47] Euro-American women, although having the appearance of being respected, have struggled to gain equality with men and to break gender boundaries.

John also avoids falling into the trap of alcohol addiction to which many Indians fell victim after Europeans introduced alcohol to the natives of eastern North America in the sixteenth century to entice them into trading furs. In regard to drinking, he does not trust his co-workers: "John knew his co-workers wanted to poison him with their alcohol and mean words. They wanted to get him drunk and helpless. John had never taken a drink in his whole life and he was not about to start now. He knew what alcohol did to Indians. Real Indians did not drink."[48] John's choice to abstain from drinking brings attention to the plight of many Indians. Peter Mancall cites startling statistics regarding the problem of alcohol in contemporary Indian communities: high death rates ("four times higher for Indians than for the general population"); cases of fetal alcohol syndrome; and high incidences of alcohol-related diseases, suicides and homicides.[49]

John avoids alcohol addiction, but he must cope with his mental illness. Despite his parents' protests, he refuses to take medication for his schizophrenia, white men's medicine: "Vitamins, cough drops, and other circles, brighter and smaller, that quieted the voices in his head for a little while. But John knew those pills slowly poisoned him, too. He could take the pills and die young, or ignore the pills and live forever with the music in his head."[50] Is John Smith a schizophrenic? Or are the voices and music in his head coming from the spirits of ancestors trying to communicate with him? Does he experience delusions and hallucinations, symptoms of the disease, or spiritual visions? Because of his assimilation and parenting by whites ignorant of American Indian culture and spirituality, has he been misjudged? Certainly the stress of his environment, one cause of schizophrenia, could have triggered his illness.[51] But as a displaced Indian male not raised by a tribe, it is also possible that he is experiencing spiritual visions, but he is not able to comprehend what they mean.

John's confused identity, mental illness, and discontent with aspects of dominant white male culture triggers an epiphany. Working on the fortieth floor, John starts hearing voices in his head again and soon realizes that he must kill a white man. But he must determine which one he should kill — rich or poor?[52] He "believe[s] that both the richest and poorest white men in the country [live] in Seattle."[53] The richest white man, probably named Bob or Ted or Dan, owns the largest toy company in the world and exploits thousands of Indians as workers. But, he rationalizes, if he kills the wealthiest white man in the world, then the next wealthiest one will take his place. So then he contemplates killing the poorest white man who survives by stealing "aluminum cans from John's garbage" to sell them for booze.[54] But killing poor white men would be futile because "they were already dead. They were zombies." John struggles to make the right decision, the most important one in his life. He considers which white men had committed the most horrible acts on Indians and recalls priests cutting off Indians' tongues to prevent them from speaking their own languages.[55] Furthermore, he rationalizes: "White people no longer feared Indians. Somehow, near the end of the twentieth century, Indians had become invisible, docile. John wanted to change that. He wanted to see fear in every pair of blue eyes."[56] Interestingly, according to the National Institute of Mental Health, schizophrenics "are not especially prone to violence," making John a less likely suspect of murders of white men.[57] However, if not a schizophrenic, John is motivated by other reasons tied to his Indian identity. He feels compelled to seek revenge on the colonizers and exploiters in the name of justice.

Although Smith is viewed as the principal suspect in the murder of males, Alexie interweaves more commentary regarding white hegemonic culture and the struggle to achieve Indian identity through other possible suspects in the murder of white males, including the mixed blood Reggie Polatkin, his cousin Marie Polatkin, and wannabe Indian Jack Wilson. Like John Smith, these characters strive to belong to a community. As marginalized Others, John, Reggie, and Marie struggle to be comfortable in white society and yet be connected to the community of urban Indians while Jack Wilson wants to be accepted into the urban Indian community. All three males, Smith, Polatkin, and Wilson are so psychically damaged and insecure about their identity and masculinity that they cannot find fulfilling relationships with women.

Urban Indian, Reggie Polatkin, has a problem with Dr. Clarence Mather, a white professor, for his role in misrepresenting, co-opting, or contaminating Indian culture, history, and traditions. He prevents Mather from profiting from the tapes of Pacific Northwest elders that he discovered in a university storage room. Dr. Mather wants to publicize them and write an article about them. But Reggie would rather destroy them than let the stories on those tapes be possessed, corrupted, and misunderstood by Mather as representative of white hegemonic culture.[58] Like Alexie, Vine Deloria, Jr. is concerned about the ethics of non–Indian scholars benefiting from research about American Indians, especially when that research is based on irresponsible practices and questionable sources. He proposes forming a system of proved "Master Scholars" of various Indian tribes. These scholars should be better equipped to conduct credible research and should establish a relationship with the tribes that is mutually beneficial, especially in regard to the funding of research projects.[59]

Before their major disagreements, Polatkin and Mather had been friends bound by the fact that Mather wanted to be "completely Indian" and Reggie wanted to be "completely white" or at least "to earn the respect of white men." Friendship with Reggie had allowed Mather entrance into the social circles of urban Indians.[60] Reggie was kicked out of college because of his confrontation with Mather. His expulsion and Mather's exploitation of Indian artifacts for his own gain give Reggie motive for killing white males.

As does his cousin Marie Polatkin, Reggie, "a very handsome man, with a strong nose, clear brown skin, and startling blue eyes that instantly revealed his half-breed status," suffers from an identity crisis.[61] His Spokane Indian mother Martha married Bird Lawrence, a white man, in order to leave the reservation and live a more comfortable life. Lawrence teaches his son to respect helpful Indians like Red Cloud and to devalue hostile ones like Crazy Horse. In Lawrence's view, hostile Indians received their just reward when they died of the small pox; in fact, it was "God's revenge."[62] Through abuse, he teaches Reggie about events and people in Indian history and tries to turn him into the Indian he wants him to be, often calling him a "stupid, dirty Indian." Lawrence presents a version of history of Anglo-European and Indian relations that revisionists have had to correct. This upbringing almost extinguishes Reggie's Indian identity: "Over the years, Reggie had come to believe that he was successful because of his father's white blood, and that his Indian mother's blood was to blame for his failures. Throughout high school, he'd spent all of his time with white kids. He'd ignored his mother, Martha. He hadn't gone to local powwows. He hadn't danced or sang. He'd pretended to be white, and had thought his white friends accepted him as such. He'd buried his Indian identity so successfully that he'd become invisible."[63]

And yet when he hears an insult against Indians, Reggie Polatkin lashes out. When he was a senior in high school and on a date with his white girlfriend, a drunken Indian passed out in the pizza restaurant. His girlfriend confesses to hating Indians but not him because "[he's] not like those other

Indians." Reggie angrily acts out by having rough sex with his virgin white girlfriend. He has sex with her for a week hoping to get her pregnant: "He wanted her to give birth to a brown baby. He'd wanted to dilute his Indian blood. He'd wanted some kind of revenge. He'd wanted some place to spill his pain."[64] As an adult, Reggie avoids serious relationships and uses white women, Indian groupies, for one-night stands, for he likes the power of such domination.

Through Reggie's cousin, Marie Polatkin, Alexie extends his commentary on the contamination and co-optation of Indian history and culture by white academics. Indian activist and twenty-three-year-old English major at the University of Washington, Marie Polatkin, like John Smith, struggles to find a community since she lives off the reservation. She is losing her Spokane Indian identity because her Indian parents raised her to assimilate into white society. On the reservation, she was often ridiculed for her studiousness and non-participation in the Spokane Indian culture, including not learning the language. Marie even tried to remove her Indian identity by scrubbing away her brown skin tone but eventually became reconciled to her Indianness:

> She looked in the rearview mirror of the van and saw what anyone would see reflected, an Indian woman. Dark eyes and hair, brown skin. She could not be white if she wanted to be white. And she had wanted to be white more than once. When she was nine years old, sitting on the front porch, she had rubbed her face with a piece of her dad's sand paper, trying to get rid of her color. Her skin was raw and bloody when she quit, still Indian. Now she was proud of being Indian, but it wasn't a simple feeling. In the eyes of the white world, any Indian woman was the same as all the other Indian women. Only white people got to be individuals. They could be anybody they wanted to be. White people, especially those with the most minute amount of tribal blood, thought they became Indian just by saying they were Indian. A number of those pretend Indians called themselves mixed-bloods and wrote books about the pain of living in both the Indian and white worlds. Those mixed-blood writers never admitted their pale skin was a luxury. After all, Marie couldn't dress up like a white woman when she went to job interviews. But a mixed-blood writer could put on a buckskin jacket, a few turquoise rings, braid his hair, and he'd suddenly be an Indian. Those mixed-bloods could choose to be Indian or white, depending on the social or business situation. Marie never had the opportunity to make that choice. She was a brown baby at birth, born to a brown mother and brown father.[65]

As a full blood, Marie clearly understands and resents the privileges that come from lighter skin, particularly being able to pass for white or Indian as needed.

In time Marie became completely estranged from the reservation and its culture: "Through her intelligence and dedication, Marie had found a way to escape the reservation. Now she was so afraid the reservation would pull her back and drown her in its rivers that she only ventured home for surprise visits to her parents usually arriving in the middle of the night. Even then, she felt like a stranger and would sometimes leave before her parents knew she was there."[66] When one thinks of Nagel's study of Indian identity renewal, Marie is an example of an Indian who relocates from the reservation to the city to assimilate but who eventually re-identifies with her Indian heritage.

As an urban Indian, Marie empathizes with the plight of homeless Indians, and as the sandwich lady, she helps to feed the homeless Indians who wander the streets of Seattle. But her activism does not stop there. Alexie uses her as a spokesperson for his views regarding non–Indians teaching Native American Studies — literature, history, and culture. Specifically, Marie attacks Dr. Clarence Mather, a white professor, for misrepresenting American Indians through a reading list of questionable, indeed fraudulent, texts, such as *The Education of Little Tree*, which "was supposedly written by a Cherokee Indian named Forrest Carter" but "was actually the pseudonym for a former Grand Wizard of the Ku Klux Klan."[67] Other books included "three anthologies of traditional Indian stories edited by white men, two nonfiction studies of Indian spirituality written by white women, a book of traditional Indian poetry translations edited by a Polish-American Jewish man, and an Indian murder mystery written by some local white writer named Jack Wilson, who claimed he was a Shilshomish Indian."[68] Marie researched Wilson's background to find that he is not Indian, and she questions why Mather does not include on his syllabus "real Indians ... writing real Indian books" like Simon Ortiz, Roberta Whiteman, and Luci Tapahonso.[69] Marie constantly challenges Mather's authority, and frustrated with him, "she want[s] Dr. Mather to disappear. She want[s] every white man to disappear. She want[s] to burn them all down to ash and feast on their smoke."[70] She too could be the Indian killer.

Another potential suspect is Jack Wilson, a former police officer and Wannabe Indian, turned Indian writer. Jack Wilson, orphaned as a child, desired to be Indian and studied American Indian culture. Impressed with the fact that the rearing of Native children was a communal effort, he sought to achieve some kind of tribal link to the eleven foster families who raised him.[71] Moving from family to family, Wilson was so traumatized as a foster child that he wet the bed. Blond haired and blue eyed, he boasts of his ancestral ties to a Shilshomish Indian. Wilson tries to be Indian by dancing to pow-wow music in his apartment, and he hangs out at an Indian bar. But still he does not understand that Indians do not live by social hierarchies such as class distinctions. The rich mix with the poor. However, they do follow tribal distinctions: "The rich and poor Spokanes may hang out together, but that doesn't necessarily mean the Spokanes are friendly with the Lakota or the

Navajo or any other tribe."[72] Most importantly, however, Wilson is ignorant of the fact that "the white people who pretend to be Indian are greatly teased, ignored, plainly ridiculed or beaten, depending on their degree of whiteness."[73] The Indians call him Casper the Friendly Ghost.

Through his depiction of Jack Wilson, Alexie critiques non–Indians who profit by claiming to be Indian and writing about Indians. Wilson writes books about Aristotle Little Hawk, the last Shilshomish Indian, "a practicing medicine man and private detective in Seattle."[74] Wilson uses his contacts at the police station to obtain information about the Indian killer for his latest book. Obviously more white than Indian, he is burdened by the white guilt he feels concerning the discrimination against homeless and displaced Indians that he witnessed while on the police force. The memory of his discovery of the body of Beautiful Mary, a homeless Indian prostitute, who had been "raped, then stabbed repeatedly with a broken bottle," haunts him.[75] Nobody cared about her death and finding her killer, but they care about who is killing off white males. Eventually, a white homeless man is arrested for Mary's murder.

As a homicide detective, Wilson witnessed the worst elements of white male culture namely that of violence:

> Working homicide, he quickly learned that monsters are real. He also knew that most of the monsters were white men. Plain, quiet men who raped and murdered children. Plain, quiet men who cut women into pieces. Ted Bundy, the Green River Killer, the I-5 Killer. Famous killers, obscure killers. The white man who grabbed his infant son by the ankles and smashed his head against the wall. The white man who doused his sleeping girlfriend with gasoline and then dropped a lit match on her face. While black and brown men were at war with each other, their automatic gunfire filling the urban night, the white men were hunting their own mothers, lovers, daughters.... While the other detectives had families and outside interests, Wilson had only his tribe of monsters."[76]

After leaving the force, Wilson, living alone without a wife and children, misses his monsters and so he turns to writing about them. But one must question who the real monsters are — white males as colonizers, dominators, and exploiters or the Indians who resist them?

By setting up the profile and motive for each possible suspect, Alexie has laid the groundwork for the killing of white males, but more significant, I argue, is what the white male victims represent in terms of Alexie's critique of white hegemonic masculinity. The first victim is Justin Summers, a white blue-eyed college student, whom John Smith bumps into on the University of Washington campus and who responds to John with "Watch your step, Chief."[77] Noting that John seems to be disoriented, Summers inquires whether he is okay to which John replies, "You're not as smart as you think you are ...

not even close.... I'm older than the hills," thereby referring to generations of Indians who existed before the coming of European colonizers.[78] Summers ends the strange meeting by flashing the peace sign. This brief encounter represents the clash between Indians and whites — the ongoing struggle to reach peaceful coexistence.

The killer considers men in gray suits who could be viewed as conquerors, colonizers, capitalists. Like a warrior of old, the killer, feeling "powerful" and "invincible" because of the special knife, "a custom-made bowie with three small turquoise gems," he or she carries,[79] selects Summers as the first victim because of his perceived arrogance, confidence, self-absorption, rudeness, and apparent white upper-class privilege evident from his being able to afford to attend college and to wear expensive clothing like a leather jacket.

Noting the fear in Summers' blue eyes, the killer stabs him in the stomach, cuts off his scalp to keep as a souvenir, and becoming more enraged, thrusts the knife again and again into his chest. Finally, "with hands curved into talons [like an owl's] the killer tore the white man's eyes from his face and swallowed them whole."[80] The killer has killed off Euro-American dominance and supremacy signified by white males with blue eyes. Having taken coup, the killer leaves behind two white feathers of the owl, the harbinger of evil and death.

In seeking revenge on white hegemony, the killer subscribes to a masculinity of old — that of the warrior — and to the rituals of warfare practiced by certain tribes — scalping, counting coup, and cannibalism. The killer is a lone warrior and shifts shapes by taking on the being of the owl. Shape-shifting is the American Indian idea that human beings can magically turn into "another living creature — for example, the shamanistic idea of the Lakota Sioux warriors shape-shifting into buffalo or wolves to enhance hunting skill and to honor the animal hunted."[81] The question of whether the Europeans or Indians initiated the practice of scalping in the New World has sparked debate and misinformation. Prior to the 1960s and the Red Power movement, the view that scalping was a warfare tactic of Indians prevailed. In the 1960s, the Red Power and other anti-establishment movements promoted the idea that Indians never scalped but were instructed and persuaded to engage in it, and they were offered rewards to attack the colonists' adversaries.[82] Marie Polatkin argues about this issue with her white classmates. Acting as an Indian authority, Marie follows the rhetoric of the Red Power movement when she corrects her classmates who claim "Indians started that whole scalping business": "You've got it all wrong.... The French were the first to scalp people in this country. Indians just copied them."[83] However, according to James Axtell, there is "abundant evidence that scalping took place in Native America well before Europeans arrived," and it was noted among the eastern Indians.[84] Furthermore, as Axtell explains, "Men grew scalplocks to symbolize their soul or personhood; these were never touched without grave insult, because their loss was tantamount to social death, even if physical death did not occur. Young males earned status by taking the scalp of an enemy, which then could be adopted by a family, like a living captive, to replace a dead member or to avenge the dead person's restless spirit."[85] As the warriors of earlier times did, the killer takes the scalp as a trophy.

Cannibalism, as a ritual of war, was practiced by Indian tribes of New England, the Great Lakes, the Plains, and the Southwest, including the Mohawks, Delawares, Tuscaroras, Chippewas, Miamis, Ottawas, Chickasaws, Commanches, Tonkawa, and Karankawa. Indian captivity narratives often describe instances of cannibalism. For instance, Father Isaac Jogues witnessed the Mohawks dismember the feet, hands, and heart of a slain Huron. It is believed that every object has a spirit so to eat a thing meant absorbing its spirit and along with it its power.[86] Thus the killer's eating the eyes and heart of his victim is a means of empowering the self. Interestingly, John Smith, if he is the killer, identifies the most with the Mohawks, whose name means man eater.

The killer decides the next victim should be "perfect and beautiful" and goes hunting for that person. At the park the killer notices black, Latina, and white nannies attending children: "Every morning, those brown women left their children behind and traveled to better neighborhoods to take care of their employers' children. Brown women spent more time with the white children than their own parents did. Brown children were left behind." Becoming angrier, the killer thinks of "those rich, white children holding their arms out to strangers, not mothers, and about brown children holding their arms out to air."[87] The killer wonders where the fathers are. Again the killer seems deeply disturbed by the privileges or rewards of being white and upper class at the expense of others. A little blond blue-eyed boy, six-year-old Mark Jones, catches the killer's eye. Will this perfect child grow up to be a monster? And if so, should the monster be killed before it has time to do harm? That evening the killer kidnaps Mark from his bedroom after witnessing him at home with his mother who appears lonely.[88] Mark's father is conspicuously absent. Holding the child hostage for a time, the killer contemplates the power of sacrificing "the first-born son of a white family" and the message the act would send to the world. The sacrifice is never made, for eventually the killer returns Mark Jones to his mother. This time killing is not necessary perhaps because the boy is still innocent, is not yet corrupted by hegemonic influences. And the killer had put fear into people: "The killer had counted coup, had won the battle without drawing blood."[89]

The tribes of the Great Plains practiced counting coup ("blows"), "war honors that emphasized bravery, cunning, and stealth over the actual killing of an enemy."[90] As Tom Holm reports, "According to some tribal elders the best coup was touching an enemy in the heat of battle and thus leaving him alive to wallow in shame and self-reproach. In effect, the warrior had captured the enemy's spirit."[91] This time the killer takes great pride in winning without killing.

The third victim is not so lucky. To the killer, Edward Letterman is living the American Dream. He appears to be a happily married white man and successful businessman. He has a lovely wife and children, yet he corrupts his marriage vows and desecrates his family life by turning to the sex industry to gratify prurient desires viewed as aberrant in the killer's mind. At a porn shop, Letterman watches a movie showing a white man and brown-skinned woman having sex, "doing her from behind like a dog would."[92] The killer is repulsed by what he or she sees on the film and by the sex items available for sale. The killer follows Letterman to his car where Letterman tries to barter for his life by holding up pictures of his wife and sons and by trying to buy off the killer but to no avail, for he is stabbed savagely and scalped. The killer eats his heart.[93] This victim represents both the greed and lust of hegemonic white masculinity — corruption of the American dream, mockery of marriage and family, and absence of morals.

All in all, in killing off white hegemonic masculinity, the killer has adopted and adapted various rituals perhaps to practice what is known as "'mourning'" warfare — a highly ritualized form of blood vengeance or spiritual indemnification." Holm explains the practice: "When a kinsman or kinswoman died or was killed in battle, some groups believed, the clan's, tribe's, or nation's collective spiritual power was diminished directly in proportion to that of the slain person. Retaliatory raiding took place to take captives and/or kill a certain number of enemy warriors. In numerous cases, captives were adopted as replacements for deceased relatives. Killing an enemy or torturing a captive to death was intended to repair the metaphysical imbalance caused by a death." Moreover, according to Holm, mourning warfare kept populations relatively stable, promoted group cohesion, and reaffirmed the tribal sense of superiority."[94] Thus the killer has not simply committed random acts of violence but has sought to achieve spiritual rejuvenation after years of Indian genocide by killing off symbols of white male dominance.

But has the killer achieved justice and spiritual rejuvenation for American Indians? The murder of white males has provoked retaliatory crimes against Indian men as white males seek their own justice. They are encouraged by a Rush Limbaugh-type character named Truck Schultz who uses his radio show to incite violence and hatred between whites and Indians by deliberately giving misinformation about the Indian killer. And so the cycle of violence continues as Marie Polatkin predicts after insisting that John Smith is not the killer and as the last chapter, a creation story about the killer dancing forever, suggests.

Male characters in the story continue to deal with the violence as they attempt to reconcile their ethnic identity and manhood in white dominant society. Having coped by channeling his anger about racial injustice by beating up white men, Reggie Polatkin will not surrender as did Captain Jack, the great Modoc fighter. Leaving the urban scene of Seattle, Reggie will keep running, hiding, and fighting, "though he knew every city was a city of white men."[95] Clearly, for mixed blood Reggie Polatkin, authentic Indian identity is impossible, for he will never be able to escape the hegemonic forces of white masculinity.

Wannabe Indian Jack Wilson will continue to strive to be accepted as Indian. Atop the last skyscraper in Seattle, he becomes a victim when he is held captive by John Smith, who many believe to be the Indian killer. Claiming his Indianness, Wilson pleads for his life as Smith contemplates how he will kill him and dispose his body.[96] When Wilson asks what John wants from him, he replies, "Let me, let us have our own pain."[97] John recognizes that a white man is co-opting the Indian identity. He makes a final attempt to reclaim Indian culture and history — this time from a white man who wants to be Indian. Smith spares Wilson's life but symbolically cuts his face "from just above his right eye, down through the eye and cheekbone, past the shelf of the chin, and a few inches down his neck" to mark him to others. John wants everyone to know what Wilson did, and he says to him, "You're not innocent."[98] In Smith's eyes, Wilson too is a representative of white hegemonic masculinity, claiming and exploiting Indian identity for his personal gain, which he continues to do after John releases him. Wilson writes a book about Smith as the Indian killer.

John Smith steps off the last skyscraper in Seattle. But this is not a schizophrenic-induced suicide. John attempts to reach spiritual transcendence by flying up to the Indian spiritual world, the only way he can escape white hegemony. Through spiritual transcendence, he will be able to meet an Indian father and mother he never knew. More importantly, he can finally achieve authentic Indian identity and manhood, for "she [his mother] could know John's real name."[99]

Sherman Alexie's *Indian Killer* is more than a murder mystery about a serial killer. It is an emotionally charged critique of hegemonic white masculinity and its devastating effects on Indian culture and identity. Alexie strategically uses his characters, urban Indians struggling to bridge the divide between Indian and white cultures, as spokespersons for his critique. They bring attention to the difficulty many Indians experience trying to achieve authentic identity because of assimilation into white culture and separation from their tribal roots and culture, and they voice the desire to write Indians into history on their own terms. Lastly, as I have shown, the symbolic killing of white males represents the attempt to avenge the extermination and corruption of Indian cultural values and traditions and to eradicate white hegemonic masculinity.

Notes

1. Tomson Highway, "Spokane Words: Tomson Highway raps with Sherman Alexie," *Aboriginal Voices* (January-March 1997), http://www.fallsapart.com/art-av.html (accessed April 4, 2000).

2. Tim Carrigan, Bob Connell, and John Lee, "Toward a New Sociology of Masculinity," in *The Masculinity Studies Reader*, ed. Rachel Adams and David Savran (Malden, MA: Blackwell, 2002), 112.

3. Paige Raibmon, *Authentic Indians: Episodes of Encounter from the Late-Nineteenth-Century Northwest Coast* (Durham, NC: Duke University Press, 2005), 7.

4. *Ibid.*, 9

5. *Ibid.*, 8.

6. Sherman Alexie, *Indian Killer* (New York: Warner, 1996), 36.

7. Joane Nagel, "American Indian Ethnic Renewal: Politics and the Resurgence of Identity," in *American Nations: Encounters in Indian Country, 1850 to the Present*, ed. Frederick E. Hoxie, Peter C. Mancall, and James H. Merrell (New York: Routledge, 2001), 331.

8. *Ibid.*, 332.

9. *Ibid.*, 338–339.

10. *Ibid.*, 340, 341.

11. *Ibid.*, 342.

12. *Ibid.*, 335.

13. *Indian Killer*, 4.

14. *Ibid.*, 9–10.

15. *Ibid.*, 10.

16. Camilla Townsend, *Pocahontas and the Powhatan Dilemma* (New York: Hill and Wang, 2004), 52–56, 58.

17. Gail Guthrie Valaskakis, *Indian Country: Essays on Contemporary Native Culture* (Waterloo, Ontario, Canada: Wilfrid Laurier University Press, 2005), 116–118.

18. *Indian Killer*, 31–32.

19. *Ibid.*, 44, 45, 48.

20. Indian Child Welfare Act of 1978, Tribal Court Clearinghouse (Tribal Law and Policy Institute, n.d.), http://www.tribal-institute.org/lists/chapter21_icwa.htm (accessed February 14, 2006).

21. "Spokane Words."

22. *Indian Killer*, 14.

23. Stuart Christie, "Renaissance Man: The Tribal 'Schizophrenic' in Sherman Alexie's *Indian Killer*," *American Indian Culture and Research Journal* 25, no. 4 (2001): 9.

24. *Indian Killer*, 19.

25. For histories of missionary and boarding schools, see Eds. Margaret L. Archuleta, Brenda J. Child, and K. Tsianina Lomawaima, *Away from Home: American Indian Board-*

ing School Experiences, 1879–2000 (Phoenix: Heard Museum, 2000); David Wallace Adams, *Education for Extinction: American Indians and the Boarding School Experience 1875–1928* (Lawrence, KS: University Press of Kansas, 1995); Michael C. Coleman, *American Indian Children at School, 1850–1930* (Jackson, MS: University Press of Mississippi, 1993).

26. *Indian Killer*, 17.

27. *Ibid.*, 18, 19.

28. Though not as significant in *Indian Killer*, the game of basketball often figures prominently in Native American fiction, including Alexie's novel *Reservation Blues* and collection of short stories *The Lone Ranger and Tonto Fistfight in Heaven*. As Peter Donahue reports, Alexie's characters claim that basketball was invented by Indians and not by James Naismith as many believe. Researcher Joseph Oxendine has found that several aboriginal games, including one requiring a hoop and pole, may have been precursors to the contemporary game of basketball. This historical information is important in that it again points to the cooptation of American Indian custom by white hegemonic culture. See Peter Donahue, "New Warriors, New Legends: Basketball in Three Native American Works of Fiction," *American Indian Culture and Research Journal* 21, no. 2 (1997): 45–46.

29. *Indian Killer*, 21.

30. "Renaissance Man," 2.

31. *Indian Killer*, 22.

32. *Ibid.*

33. James A. Doyle, *The Male Experience*, 3rd ed. (Boston: McGraw Hill, 1995), 254.

34. *Indian Country*, 51.

35. *Male Experience*, 254.

36. *Ibid.*

37. *Ibid.*, 255.

38. *Male Experience*, 256.

39. *Indian Killer*, 132.

40. *Ibid.*, 132–33.

41. *Ibid.*, 131.

42. *Ibid.*

43. *Ibid.*, 76, 77.

44. *The Woman's Way* (Alexandria, VA: Time-Life, 1995), 23, 26.

45. *Ibid.*, 36, 38, 165.

46. *Ibid.*, 72.

47. Paula Gunn Allen, "Who Is Your Mother? Red Roots of White Feminism," in *The Longman Anthology of Women's Literature*, ed. Mary K. DeShazer (New York: Longman, 2001), 892, 896–97.

48. *Indian Killer*, 131–32.

49. Peter Mancall, *Deadly Medicine: Indians and Alcohol in Early America* (Ithaca, NY: Cornell University Press, 1995), 6.

50. *Indian Killer*, 74.

51. "Schizophrenia," National Institute of Mental Health, (24 January, 2007), http://www.nimh.nih.gov/healthinformation/schizophreniamenu.cfm (accessed May 26, 2007).

52. *Indian Killer*, 25, 27.

53. *Ibid.*, 27.

54. *Ibid.*, 28.

55. *Ibid.*, 29.

56. *Ibid.*, 30.

57. "Schizophrenia," National Institute of Mental Health, (24 January, 2007), http://www.nimh.nih.gov/healthinformation/schizophreniamenu.cfm. (accessed May 26, 2007).

58. *Indian Killer*, 136–139.

59. Vine Deloria, Jr., "Research, Redskins, and Reality," in *American Nations: Encounters in Indian Country, 1850 to the Present*, ed. Frederick E. Hoxie, Peter C. Mancall, and James H. Merrell (New York: Routledge, 2001), 459–60, 463–64.

60. *Indian Killer*, 136.

61. *Ibid.*, 90.

62. *Ibid.*, 91.

63. *Ibid.*, 94.

64. *Ibid.*, 183.

65. *Ibid.*, 232.

66. *Ibid.*, 34.

67. Alexie is emphatic about exposing frauds and plagiarists. He discovered that a writer named Nasdijj, who claimed to be mixed blood, his mother being Navajo, had stolen ideas from one of his published short stories. Nasdijj's real name was discovered to be Timothy Barrus, and he may not be Indian at all. See Sherman Alexie, "When the Story Stolen Is Your Own," *Time*, 6 February 2006, 72.

68. *Indian Killer*, 58–59.

69. *Ibid.*, 67.

70. *Ibid.*, 85.

71. *Ibid.*, 157.

72. *Ibid.*, 179.

73. *Ibid.*

74. *Ibid.*, 162.

75. *Ibid.*, 159.

76. *Ibid.*, 161.

77. *Ibid.*, 41.

78. *Ibid.*, 41, 42.

79. *Ibid.*, 49.

80. *Ibid.*, 54.

81. Andrew Macdonald, Gina Macdonald, and Mary Ann Sheridan, *Shape-Shifting: Images of Native Americans in Recent Popular Fiction* (Westport, CT: Greenwood, 2000), xiv–xv.

82. James Axtell, "Scalps and Scalping," in *Encyclopedia of North American Indians*, ed. Frederick E. Hoxie (Boston: Houghton Mifflin, 1996), 570.

83. *Indian Killer*, 57.

84. "Scalps and Scalping," 571.

85. *Ibid.*

86. Richard Vanderbeets, "The Indian Captivity as Ritual," *American Literature* 43, no. 4 (January 1972): 550.

87. *Indian Killer*, 150.

88. *Ibid.*, 153.

89. *Ibid.*, 300.

90. Tom Holm, "Warriors and Warfare," in *Encyclopedia of North American Indians*, ed. Frederick E. Hoxie (Boston: Houghton Mifflin, 1996), 667.

91. *Ibid.*

92. *Indian Killer*, 326.

93. *Ibid.*, 328.

94. "Warriors and Warfare," 667.

95. *Indian Killer*, 408, 409.

96. *Ibid.*, 403–405.

97. *Ibid.*, 411.

98. *Ibid.*

99. *Ibid.*, 413.

Bibliography

Adams, David Wallace. *Education for Extinction: American Indians and the Boarding School Experience 1875–1928.* Lawrence: University Press of Kansas, 1995.

Alexie, Sherman. *Indian Killer.* New York: Warner, 1996.

_____. "When the Story Stolen Is Your Own." *Time,* 6 February 2006, 72.

Allen, Paula Gunn. "Who Is Your Mother? Red Roots of White Feminism." In *The Longman Anthology of Women's Literature,* ed. Mary K. DeShazer, New York: Longman, 2001, 889–98.

Archuleta, Margaret L., Brenda J. Child, and K. Tsianina Lomawaima. *Away from Home: American Indian Boarding School Experiences, 1879–2000.* Phoenix: Heard Museum, 2000.

Axtell, James. "Scalps and Scalping." In *Encyclopedia of North American Indians,* ed. Frederick E. Hoxie, Boston: Houghton Mifflin, 1996, 570–72.

Carrigan, Tim, Bob Connell, and John Lee. "Toward a New Sociology of Masculinity." In *The Masculinity Studies Reader,* ed. Rachel Adams and David Savran. Malden, MA: Blackwell, 2002, 99–118.

Christie, Stuart. "Renaissance Man: The Tribal 'Schizophrenic' in Sherman Alexie's *Indian Killer." American Indian Culture and Research Journal* 25, no. 4 (2001): 1–19.

Coleman, Michael C. *American Indian Children at School, 1850–1930.* Jackson: University Press of Mississippi, 1993.

Deloria, Vine, Jr. "Research, Redskins, and Reality." In *American Nations: Encounters in Indian Country, 1850 to the Present,* ed. Frederick E. Hoxie, Peter C. Mancall, and James H. Merrell, 459–67. New York: Routledge, 2001.

Donahue, Peter. "New Warriors, New Legends: Basketball in Three Native American Works of Fiction." *American Indian Culture and Research Journal* 21, no. 2 (1997): 43–60.

Doyle, James A. *The Male Experience.* 3rd ed. Boston: McGraw Hill, 1995.

Highway, Tomson. "Spokane Words: Tomson Highway raps with Sherman Alexie." *Aboriginal Voices* (January–March 1997). http://www.fallsapart.com/art-av.htm (accessed April 4, 2000).

Holm, Tom. "Warriors and Warfare." In *Encyclopedia of North American Indians,* ed. Frederick E. Hoxie. Boston: Houghton Mifflin, 1996, 666–68.

Indian Child Welfare Act of 1978. Tribal Court Clearinghouse. Tribal Law and Policy Institute: n.d. http://www.tribal-institute.org/lists/chapter21_icwa.htm (accessed February 14, 2006).

Macdonald, Andrew, Gina Macdonald, and Mary Sheridan. *Shape-Shifting: Images of Native Americans in Recent Popular Fiction.* Westport, CT: Greenwood, 2000.

Mancall, Peter. *Deadly Medicine: Indians and Alcohol in Early America.* Ithaca, NY: Cornell University Press, 1995.

Nagel, Joane. "American Indian Ethnic Renewal: Politics and the Resurgence of Identity." In *American Nations: Encounters in Indian Country, 1850 to the Present,* ed. Frederick E. Hoxie, Peter C. Mancall, and James H. Merrell. New York: Routledge, 2001, 331–53.

Raibmon, Paige. *Authentic Indians: Episodes of Encounter from the Late-Nineteenth-Century Northwest Coast.* Durham, NC: Duke University Press, 2005.

"Schizophrenia." National Institute of Mental Health (24 January 2007). http://www.nimh.nih.gov/publicat/schizoph.cfm (accessed May 26, 2007).

Townsend, Camilla. *Pocahontas and the Powhatan Dilemma.* New York: Hill and Wang, 2004.

Valaskakis, Gail Guthrie. *Indian Country: Essays on Contemporary Native Culture.* Waterloo, Ontario, Canada: Wilfrid Laurier University Press, 2005.

Vanderbeets, Richard. "The Indian Captivity Narrative as Ritual." *American Literature* 43, no. 4 (January 1972): 548–62.

The Woman's Way. Alexandria, VA: Time-Life, 1995.

10

Narrative's Role in Constructing Masculinities in *We Were Soldiers*

Bradley Smith

Since the Vietnam War, there have been efforts to reestablish cultural models of masculinity that were at the center of American narratives during World War II. As Susan Jeffords puts it, the process might best be termed "the remasculinization of American culture" (*Remasculinization of America* 168). In the cultural realm of American society, Vietnam is still being fought through efforts to overcome what some have called a "crisis in masculinity." Yet "crisis" is a misleading term, as Bryce Traister has noted, a term that masks the forms of male power that the field of masculinity studies is designed to interrogate (qtd. in Breu 4). Instead of a "crisis" of masculinity, it may be productive to discuss a system of competing models of masculinity, in which one (or more) of many different models is always in crisis. In this system different cultural narratives and their proponents compete for dominance so that one model or a hybrid of models controls discourse in a culture. In his history of masculinity, titled *From Chivalry to Terrorism: War and the Changing Nature of Masculinity*, Leo Braudy outlines some of the major forms of masculinity that have been used in cultures around the world for the last 2,000 years. Braudy characterizes the world today as one where the "ability to know (or think we know)" is a large factor in a world more interconnected than it has ever been before (520). Braudy continues, "But for all this 'knowledge,' whether in ancient societies or our own, stereotyped beliefs about what is masculine or feminine survive long after the original need or reason for them has gone because they purport to be fundamental and unchanging, the bedrock of history rather than an expression of it" (520). Thus, the urge to define masculinity is constantly permeated by the nostalgia for older forms, forms that have become the "bedrock" of our history. Braudy characterizes this tension as one where the social and cultural changes that shape masculine identity "collide or must make peace with a strong countertide of honor and nostalgia" (Braudy, 179).

The masculinity that is portrayed in the film *We Were Soldiers*, then, is made up of multiple layers of masculinities, through an intersection of newer forms and a nostalgia for older ones. The layers intermingle and settle, like sediment on a river bottom, so that if analyzed in one particular context, they appear at first glance to be a whole. Yet when examined in detail, it is clear that masculinity in a given context is a conglomerate of older forms — a piece of shale or limestone where smaller particles form layers and clumps. We must remember that this seemingly geologic process is taking place when we examine a text for forms of masculinity.

The most prevalent materials that formulate the construction of masculinity in *We Were Soldiers* are the forms of masculinity that grow out of nineteenth-century Europe and America. There are of course older forms that we could examine as well as emerging narratives of masculinity that are reshaping the way we speak about the concept. However, I have chosen to focus on nineteenth-century forms of masculinity because these forms dominate the discourse of the film's narrative. Furthermore, the nostalgia the movie creates for these forms controls the way we presently talk about masculinity in American society. The narratives of science, technology, and Manifest Destiny (or the narrative of the frontier) govern the construction of these forms. However, on closer examination, one can see forms of masculinity that have been in place for ages — the warrior as hero, the knight-errant, the crusader, etc.

We Were Soldiers, starring Mel Gibson as Lt. Col. Hal Moore, tells the story of 395 American Air Cavalry soldiers in a battle against 2,000 North Vietnamese regular troops. As the film points out, the North Vietnamese troops are highly trained, highly motivated, know the terrain on which they are fighting, and have been fighting wars for the last 20–30 years — first against the Japanese in World War II, then the French in the First Indochina War, and finally the South Vietnamese and the Americans in the Vietnam War. Surrounded for three days, the first division of the Seventh Air Cavalry fought off the North Vietnamese and controlled the battlefield after the fighting ended; however, I am reluctant to say they were victorious. Both sides had different conceptions of the word, and in this fight both sides could claim victory for different reasons. Seventy-nine Americans lost their lives in the battle and hundreds of Vietnamese lost theirs. In the way that the battle was subsequently shaped by historical and personal accounts and by the creators of *We Were Soldiers*, a narrative emerges that places the battle squarely in the realm of American mythology. This narrative emerges out of these accounts as a reenactment of Custer's Last Stand — a space that rewrites the story, allowing "Custer" to win. Through this reliance on American mythology for the movie's structure, the narrative creates a context in which the Vietnam War soldier undergoes a process of remasculinization by comparing actions of Vietnam War soldiers to models of masculinity from America's World War II era.

This work occurs in the way that soldiers are characterized in the movie. War and warriors in American culture are inextricably bound through a metonymic relationship. Through this relationship, the concept of war is mapped onto the soldier, bringing with it a set of attributes and associations that are usually applied to the concept of war. In other words, in the minds of Americans, war is embodied in the soldier. Jeffords alights on this idea when she discusses how soldiers are characterized as mechanized in Vietnam War narratives. Jeffords cites instances of American soldiers being portrayed as the "green machine" as evidence of this phenomenon (11). This mechanization of the soldier is only shown in narratives about Vietnam for its display, or as Jeffords terms it, the technology of the war becomes spectacle (9). Soldiers, when conceptualized in these terms, become cinematic fetishisms and thus contribute to the formation of the subject/spectator. Kaja Silverman in *The Acoustic Mirror: The Female Voice in Psychoanalysis and Cinema* discusses the process through which spectation drives the formation of the subject. Silverman writes: "The history of the subject who rediscovers him- or herself within cinema unfolds through a series of 'splittings' or divisions, many of which turn on the object. Indeed, the case can be even more forcefully stated: These splittings or divisions produce both subject and object, constituting the one in opposition to the other (Silverman 6). In this theory the subject splits off from the object, defining its boundaries through its residence in the symbolic order and in relation to the object.

Another characterization of soldiers is equally true in narratives about the Vietnam War: these narratives show the human side of the soldier. The soldier as the technology of war remains present in these narratives but is secondary to the narrative's primary focus — to show the human qualities of the soldier. The film's characters, then, are also "split" into (at least) two forms: the soldier as mechanism of war and the soldier as human. Thus, the two conceptualizations of the soldier create two different subjectivities soldiers can occupy. Braudy writes that stereotypes of masculinity began to split the masculine body into these two categories during World War I (402). Furthermore, this trend has continued in narratives of masculinity to the present day, so that "Since the end of the Vietnam War, American films have been filled with characters in whom the line between human and the technological is ambiguous," e.g., Robocop, or the Terminator (Braudy 550).

In narratives featuring soldiers, the soldier's ability to kill, enhanced through mechanization, is used only as a backdrop against which his or her humanness can be revealed. The soldier is simultaneously part of the technology of war and part of a tradition of Western humanized "man." This split between soldier as "Man" and soldier as fighting machine allows for the reproduction of militant masculinity in America because the film's soldiers are simultaneously fetishisms that distract the spectator from the absence of the real and "speaking subjects" that protect the masculine subject against the knowledge of his discursive insufficiency and with whom the subject is encouraged to identify (Silverman 30).

Remember that the soldier is a metonym for war. The result of this metonymic pairing is that criticisms of war are automatically a criticism of the soldier. Yet criticisms of the actions of soldiers are taboo in American culture (I would add mainly because of the protests during Vietnam). As Lt. Col. Moore puts it in a documentary about the making of *We Were Soldiers*, America should "hate war, love the American warrior." (*We Were Soldiers: Getting It Right*). However, since the soldier stands in metonymically for war, this statement asks the American public to simultaneously hate the American soldier and love the American soldier. This occurs because Americans are asked to "hate" the mechanisms of war — the spectacle of the soldier — and love the warrior — the soldier-as-human. Through this contradiction, militant masculinity is allowed to perpetuate in American society because the contradiction makes it difficult to effectively critique military action.

The Role of Realism and the "Realistic" in Constructing Cultural Narratives

According to Silverman, film can be defined by its distance from the phenomenal (3). In fact as Hugo Munsterberg argues, the phenomenal world and the cinematic image are in binary opposition — that is the viewer must be "distinctly conscious of the unreality of the artistic production" and that film "must be kept absolutely separated from the real things and men" (qtd in Silverman 2). What happens, then, when the phenomenal world is narrativized in cinematic form, when the film is billed as being "based on real events" or "based on a true story?" How does this sleight of hand affect its viewers? I would argue that in such cases the film becomes more emotionally engaging. American audiences have shown a preference for "real" stories. As Christopher Breu, author of *Hard-Boiled Masculinities*, states, the "realness" of a story "represented one of the major evaluative criteria that readers used in their letters to editors of magazines like *Black Mask* and *Clues*" (Breu 11). The result, according to Breu, was an intentional blurring of fiction with everyday life where meanings from one form would shape and reformulate those from the other and vice versa (11). This process created a cultural fantasy of the "realness" of hard-boiled masculinity that, "in eliding its very status as fantasy, encouraged a conflation of the forms of masculinity imagined in fiction with those enacted in daily life" (11).

Certainly viewers realize that the images and sounds they see are not the noumenal world. However, the narrative in such instances often withstands this critique. That is, when a narrative makes a "truth claim" it becomes the noumenal in the minds of viewers. In such instances, the narrative creates an "impression of reality." We have already seen that these stereotypes are mistakenly believed to form the "bedrock of history," and so their presence in narratives that claim to be based on real events goes unnoticed and in some cases contributes to the "impression of reality" that the narrative creates. This process occurs through the spectator's identification with the speaking subject. In the context of *We Were Soldiers*, the speaking subject is also the humanist subject, an individual who is established as the narrative's "hero." This identification creates an emotional bond between the spectator and the speaking subject enhanced by the idea that this is a real person somewhere in the real world. That is, the spectator comes to the awareness of how much the speaking subject is like him or her. This bond, paired with the perception that the movie's story is True, creates the "impression of reality."

What makes these stories "real" to its audience, then, are the aesthetic elements borrowed and co-opted from nineteenth-century realist art. As Linda Nochlin writes in her book *Realism*, the realist art movement and subsequent art that worked to capture the realist aesthetic was driven by what she calls the "Religion of Humanity" (53). And Robert Stam points out in *Subversive Pleasures: Bakhtin, Cultural Criticism and Film* that the realist aesthetic has continued to present day in the form of movies, "the aesthetic and narrative heir to the nineteenth-century mimetic novel and the 'well-made play' " (10). For the realists, humanism takes center stage, and what becomes important is the story of one person who can encapsulate all of human experience — the humanist subject. As we well know, the idea that one person can encapsulate all of human experience is actively exclusionary. Linda Hutcheon points out the problems inherent in the humanist subject in *A Poetics of the Postmodern*, where she writes that Irigaray has shown that theories of the subject are really theories of the masculine, more specifically theories of bourgeois, white, individual, western "Man" (159).

According to Nochlin, the nineteenth century is also when scientific objectivism became the dominant discourse governing narratives so that "contemporary ideology came to equate belief in the facts with the total content of belief itself" (45). Even today, we are still dealing with this notion that the objective facts create the entire truth. These two notions, the Religion of Humanity and scientific objectivism are the two main cultural forces at work in *We Were Soldiers*. Together, they work to reestablish the Vietnam soldier as a heroic masculine figure, who is meant to encapsulate all of human experience.

Ultimately, these two ideological constructs — the Religion of Humanity and scientific objectivism — manifest themselves as part of the film's narrative structure. They both help organize the story, turning the movie into a historiography. Because of this, the movie shares a common element with history and fiction. That is, the meaning and shape of the movie is "not *in the events,* but *in the systems* which make those past 'events' into present historical 'facts.'" (Hutcheon 89). The real events that occurred in the past are now only known to us through the social lens of its retelling. As Hutcheon writes, "The past really did exist, but we can 'know' that past today only through its texts, and therein lies its connection to the literary" (128). Likewise, those in the field of history have noticed the linkage between literature and history. The most noteworthy of these is perhaps Hayden White, who writes in *The Content of the Form* that the production of meaning is a performance, because a set of real events can be emplotted in a number of ways to form any number of different kinds of stories (44). Also worth mentioning in this discussion is F. R. Ankersmit's *Historical Representation: Cultural Memory in the Present.*

Critiquing "Realism = Right" in the Context of We Were Soldiers

Like other texts about the Vietnam War, *We Were Soldiers* is an attempt to capture the "essence" of Vietnam; it is an attempt to capture the "truth" about the war. In the documentary about the movie titled *We Were Soldiers: Getting It Right*—the title of which alone speaks volumes — director and screenwriter Randall Wallace discusses his goals for the movie: "I opened the book *We Were Soldiers Once* [*And Young*], and I almost immediately came upon the words, 'Hollywood has gotten the story of the Vietnam veteran wrong every damn time,' and I knew then that I had to be a part of getting this story right." According to Lt. Col. Moore in that same documentary, what other movies about the war were missing was the concept of the brotherhood of soldiers. Moore says, "I have not seen a movie on Vietnam yet that captures that basic truth of the love of the American soldiers for one another" (*We Were Soldiers: Getting It Right*). Yet this element, the connection between soldiers, is exactly what Jeffords finds in *most* Vietnam War narratives. Furthermore, that bond excludes the feminine: "Although Vietnam narratives show the bonding of soldiers from diverse and often antagonistic backgrounds, those bonds are always and already masculine" (Jeffords 59). This homosocial bond is one that reaches beyond narratives about the Vietnam War. In fact, it is one of the driving forces in defining American masculinity. Sedgwick summarizes Heidi Hartmann's definition of patriarchy saying that the making of power relationships between men and women are dependent on power relationships between men and men. Sedgwick continues, "We can go further than that, to say that in any male-dominated society, there is a special relationship between male homosocial (*including* homosexual) desire and the structures for maintaining and transmitting patriarchal power: a relationship founded on an inherent and potentially active structural congruence" (25).

The chief objective of this movie, then, was to make the experience of the Vietnam War soldier as "real" as possible. And by "real" the film's creators meant that it had to feature a group of individuals who come together as a brotherhood of fighting men through the exclusion of the feminine, and it had to tell the objective facts of the battle. In re-creating this "reality" the creators of *We Were Soldiers* are actually fitting the movie into a long tradition of Vietnam War stories, a tradition that works to reestablish the masculinity, the heroism, and the humanity of the American soldier.

Where this film is different from others is the aesthetics it uses to achieve these ends. Whereas most texts about the Vietnam War have been categorized as postmodern (and I think falsely so), *We Were Soldiers* fits into a realist aesthetic. Jim Neilson in *Warring Fictions: Cultural Politics and the Vietnam War Narrative* writes that Vietnam War novels and autobiographies were composed in the midst of the postmodern/poststructuralist movements:

> Vietnam War authors describe a world that is fragmented and illogical, a world where the distinctions between past and present, fact and fiction, true and false, reality and hallucination collapse. Their experiences during and after the war seem to fit the defamiliarizing aesthetics, skeptical conceits, and alleged radicalism of postmodernism and the surreal subjectivity of New Journalism [53].

Yet oftentimes Vietnam War authors saw their experiences in Vietnam as *being* fragmented and illogical, a mixture of truth and falsity, reality and hallucination. Their narratives fit more logically in a modernist tradition of attempting to capture the essence of the moment through form. Rather than a *de*-familiarizing aesthetic, the fragmentation featured in so many Vietnam War narratives is an attempt at translating the environment formally. It is an attempt at *familiarizing* and capturing the events of the war in a logic that fits with the aesthetic of the war itself.

We Were Soldiers, on the other hand, with its agenda of capturing the love of the American soldiers for one another, is not about how crazy, fragmented, and illogical Vietnam was but how sane and competent American soldiers were in the face of adversity. The movie is about the heroism of the American soldiers in Vietnam. And for these goals, the fragmented framework that accompanies most Vietnam War narratives is inadequate. What does fit is a more traditional narrative framework, one used in the presentation of World War II narratives. The effect of this connection, and the goal, was to instill in the Vietnam soldier the same masculinity awarded the soldiers of World War II. In "Fathers, Sons, and Vietnam: Masculinity and Betrayal in the Life Narratives of Vietnam Veterans with Post Traumatic Stress Disorder," Tracy Karner points out that many Vietnam-era soldiers entered service and volunteered for combat duty in an attempt to deal with the legacy of their fathers, many of whom were veterans of World War II. The rejection of the Vietnam soldier by American society led many Vietnam soldiers to believe that "The implicit social covenant that their country made with them to honor their sacrifice remained uncompleted" (Karner 73). To receive the kind of heroism Vietnam War soldiers sought meant coming to some sort of parity with the soldiers of their father's generation and in many cases their fathers. Thus the narrative aesthetics through which that parity could be achieved were the same ones that characterized the feats of their fathers.

Vietnam War soldiers were in search of ontological acceptance by American society. They wanted to be called heroes. They wanted their deeds to be seen as honorable and valorous. Without this verbal recognition they could not come to parity with their fathers' generation, to which such words had been applied liberally. Braudy writes that the idea of the military hero "infects the tangled nexus of war, masculine honor, and sexuality as well," especially in the period after World War II (546). According to Braudy, there was a basic paradox in modern warfare: as the technology of war evolved and the prevalence of weapons of mass destruction increased, "so also did the emphasis on the individual soldier, the ordinary hero" (477).

The tradition of the "military hero" dates back to Greece in Western culture and is an idea that has long been used to valorize the actions of warriors. According to the *Oxford English Dictionary*, "hero" originally referred to "men of superhuman strength, courage, or ability, favoured by the gods." Around 1586, the word took on the additional meaning of: "A man distinguished by extraordinary valour and martial achievements; one who does brave or noble deeds; an illustrious warrior." The word further generalized around 1667 to mean: "A man who exhibits extraordinary bravery, firmness, fortitude, or greatness of soul, in any course of action, or in connexion with any pursuit, work, or enterprise." Through these definitions, we can see that the idea of who can be defined as a hero has generalized over time. First, heroes were a select few who had the favors of the gods. Then the word could be applied to a larger group: illustrious warriors. Eventually, it could be applied to men outside the scope of the military, so that a man who showed bravery in any pursuit could be deemed a hero. This formulation of the hero is one of the main reasons why people are willing to fight and die in military conflict: the idea of being a hero is at the center of masculine identity.

This issue bubbled to the surface during Vietnam. Men who were trying to define themselves in terms of American discourses of masculinity were denied that ontological category. Spitting on soldiers when they returned from Vietnam and calling them baby killers shook the military to its core. It countered the one argument that kept most soldiers fighting, that they were heroes protecting their country from enemies foreign and domestic. Poignantly, one Vietnam veteran came to the realization that he might not be a hero when he remembered what he had learned about the Revolutionary War in school. He thought about Americans fighting for freedom against the British, and he realized that in the context of the Vietnam War, he was one of the Red Coats (*Vietnam: A Television History*). After that realization the soldier could no longer support the idea that he was a hero. Upon reaching that conclusion, he thought about deserting. This distinction is one where the soldier came to realize a distinction identified by Braudy, that he was not a soldier fighting for his home but a soldier fighting for an army (Braudy 306).

In addition to this effort to establish the brotherhood of fighting men and the individual soldier, the creators of the movie also worked hard to objectively portray the events that occurred before, during, and after the battle. In doing so, the creators of the film went out of their way to avoid things that audience members might construe as "subjective," or outside the "objective facts of the battle, for instance, any political leaning the film might take. This can be seen in what was deleted from the movie.

The one scene that touched indirectly on the mainstream politics of the war was purposefully deleted by director Randall Wallace. The scene was a debriefing of Moore by Secretary of Defense Robert McNamara and the general in charge of operations in Vietnam, General Westmoreland. In the scene, Moore tries to curb the over-abundant optimism of the two men over his victory. He tries to tell them that the war will not be as easy a victory as they think. In response to Westmoreland's opinion that the American military will "run the little bastards back home," Moore's character tells the men, "We won. Hell, we slaughtered them. But they didn't see it that way. We won't run the little bastards back home, sir. They are home" (*We Were Soldiers*). The scene could be taken as a conservative look at the futility of the Vietnam War, even as early as the first major battle fought completely by American troops. Despite its affirmation of victory, despite its overlooking of the loss of human life, the scene implies that McNamara and Westmoreland are not part of the brotherhood of soldiers — they don't know what it is like on the battlefield. It gives the perception that the people running the war might not have the ability to do so. Furthermore, it implies that Hal Moore, having won the victory, *does* have that ability. Even though the scene upholds the discourses of masculinity underwriting the rest of the movie, its mild critique could be perceived as being political. And while the movie is already political, the politics remain hidden in the movie's narrative "reality." This scene brings politics into the foreground. In the director's commentary, Wallace gives his reasons for cutting the scene:

> In the end I felt that we needed to cut this scene because the movie is not about politics. I didn't want to raise an intellectual issue at the end. I wanted this movie to say ultimately that soldiers are human beings, no matter what we thought about the Vietnam War, no matter how it divided us. Those arguments over politics ultimately obscure for us a much more immediate reality, which was the men who died on both sides of the conflict are human beings: somebody's father, somebody's husband, somebody's son, somebody's brother. And that's what I wanted to come through. And I felt this scene in some ways took us away from that moment and that the end that we had gave us that moment, that reality, that truth [*We Were Soldiers*].

Wallace's statement that the movie is not about politics does not make the movie apolitical. It merely *hides* the politics inherent in his argument. The movie only partially portrays the Vietnam War soldier as somebody's father and somebody's husband. It portrays the soldier as a hero and human being separated from the idea of the soldier as the technology of war. In such a system, where the soldier is simultaneously both human and mechanized, only one possibility can dominate during a given moment. If the movie shows the humanity of the soldiers, it can simultaneously show them as agents of war but only secondarily to their humanity. Therefore, the movie takes that second half of the binary and uses it to describe the North Vietnamese troops. Instead of predominantly showing the North Vietnamese soldiers as human beings, the fiction shows them as the agents and technology of war. As I have mentioned, the movie points out that the soldiers Moore's division has engaged are highly trained, highly motivated to fight, and have been fighting wars their whole lives. As Moore says in the deleted scene with McNamara and Westmoreland "Sir, they pushed 2,000 men through artillery and napalm, and they came willingly" (*We Were Soldiers*). The statement sums up the motivation, training, and discipline of the North Vietnamese soldiers, part of the North Vietnamese war machine.

The characterization of the American and North Vietnamese soldiers in these ways leads to a reclamation of the masculinity of the American Vietnam War soldier. The ways in which the two sides are represented allows for the movie to abstract the American soldiers from the violence they are committing and allows the spectator to identify with the American soldiers, especially Mel Gibson's character. Therefore, the American soldiers are perceived not in terms of their military actions but as "somebody's father, somebody's husband, somebody's son, somebody's brother." As such, the critiques of the sixties and seventies weighed against the Vietnam War disappear in this movie. Without those critiques, the masculinity of the Vietnam War soldier becomes the movie's unifying factor. Once the men become separated from the violence they are committing, they lose the villainous status associated with that violence and move into the position of war hero. Furthermore, the partial objectification of the North Vietnamese soldiers contributes to this process. Through the movie's efforts to show the North Vietnamese as a capable and worthy opponent, the North Vietnamese are objectified as mechanisms of war. Though the movie strives to show one North Vietnamese soldier as being somebody's husband, ultimately all of the soldiers become canon fodder against which the prowess of the American soldiers can be measured.

The Re-narration of Custer's Last Stand and the Re-masculinization of the Vietnam War Soldier

Like other American narratives of masculinity, *We Were Soldiers* relies heavily on the Western for its cultural basis. In *Gunfighter Nation: The Myth of the Frontier in Twentieth Century America*, Richard Slotkin posits the discourse began with the writing of James Fenimore Cooper and evolved into a broad-reaching myth of manifest destiny to justify the American expansion of empire into the "frontier." This myth was reworked for the specific historical and ideological context of the Vietnam War. For example, before the end of the twentieth century, search-and-destroy missions in Vietnam were coined "playing cowboys and Indians," and Vietnam itself was being called "Indian country."

Slotkin writes that the frontier myth developed so that in order to "settle" land, the proprietors of the myth created a cycle of action that he terms regeneration through violence. Through this cycle, the myth of a savage war is blamed on Native Americans and later, all groups onto which is projected the status of Otherness. A prime example of this cycle was the Battle of Little Bighorn. Braudy writes that President Ulysses S. Grant, General Phil Sheridan, and members of Grant's cabinet used Custer's "sacrifice" as a justification for further war (306). As the myth goes, savage heroes — men with intimate knowledge of Indians but with a firmly entrenched hatred of Indians — were needed to protect the settlers from the Indians who began these savage wars.

Through the work of these heroes, the Indians would be exterminated or pushed out of the land, making it safe for farmers. But, because of his own savagery, the hero is not fit to live in the settled land. He must once again push out to the frontier.

Most important, this hero is of Anglo-Saxon heritage. According to Slotkin, Theodore Roosevelt's writings had a lot to do with the establishment of the frontier myth. And in these writings, Roosevelt stretches the western myth backward to include the Teutonic barbarians' overthrow of the Roman Empire and then the conquering of Britain. In this myth, the Anglo and Saxon tribes were always on the edge of the wilderness and civilization. Consequently, "Roosevelt ignores the racial and ethnic diversity that actually characterized cowboys during this era and represents the whole class as essentially Anglo-Saxon" (Slotkin 39).

In this movie, the story of Custer's Last Stand controls the narrative of the plot. Hal Moore is introduced to the audience as a leader in an experimental branch of the American military, the Air Cavalry. Over the course of the movie Moore's character becomes obsessed with a massacre of French soldiers during the first Indochina War in the Ia Drang Valley — the same valley where the battle in which he participates will eventually take place. He keeps flipping back to a book that pictures the Vietnamese soldiers standing over the bodies of the dead French. This comparison solidifies the Otherness of the Vietnamese soldiers in the face of "whiteness" as represented by both the American and the French soldiers. When he learns that his regiment is going to be deployed, Moore also learns that the units are being renumbered. Moore becomes the commanding officer of the first division of the seventh cavalry, the same regiment as Custer's. After this renumbering, the movie adds a book that pictures all of the soldiers in Custer's unit dead while Indians ride over them next to the book on Moore's desk picturing the massacre of the French soldiers. The two pictures are set side by side in the frame. The movie cuts back and forth between the books and Moore looking even more worried. What we have in *We Were Soldiers* is the overlapping of this nostalgia for the honor of the cavalry and the technology of modern war. The use of "Custer's Last Stand" as a frame for this narrative highlights the heroism of Moore and his men. Braudy writes, "Yet, so far as national psychology and propaganda were concerned, there was nothing more honorable than a useless cavalry charge against an enemy with greater firepower" (Braudy 280). He continues later to say that heroes are made greater in the eyes of their society through death in a lost cause (284).

At the beginning of the battle, Moore finds himself and his troops outnumbered, surrounded, and cut off, generally in the same predicament as Custer. If it is clear that Moore and his regiment represent Custer, then it is equally clear that the North Vietnamese Army represents the "Indians." They become, despite what I believe to be the best intentions of Wallace, the same fighting machines that Native Americans became to the tellers of the myth of Custer's Last Stand, separated from their humanness.

After being overrun and barely fighting off the North Vietnamese — establishing the battle as a "lost cause"— Moore asks Sergeant Major Plumley (Sam Elliott), "I wonder what was going through Custer's mind when he realized he had led his men into a slaughter" (*We Were Soldiers*). Here the tide starts to turn. The myth is rewritten. "Sir," the Sergeant Major replies, "Custer was a pussy. You ain't." In feminizing Custer, Plumley is rejecting Custer from the brotherhood of fighting men and removing his hero status. Instead, he places those qualities on Hal Moore. This scene also has the effect of individualizing the battle. The success or defeat of the American troops is placed solely on Moore's shoulders. This mirrors what Braudy has said took place in narratives about the Battle of Little Bighorn (307). Braudy writes that the battle's memory is built on individual moments, rather than grand military schemes. Likewise *We Were Soldiers* individualizes the soldiers so that it becomes a group of ones against an army. At the center of that group of ones is Mel Gibson's character Lt. Col. Hal Moore, on whose shoulders rest the fate of his men. After that discussion, Moore's belief in himself is restored. He is able to plan the final attack against the North Vietnamese. In it, he leads a full-frontal assault on the North Vietnamese position. With the help of a helicopter, the American troops wipe out the North Vietnamese soldiers holding the position. For the scope of the movie, the battle turns Custer's Last Stand and the Vietnam War into an American masculine victory. In limiting the presentation of the war to this one battle, one in which American troops fought well and defeated their opponent, the rest of the war that followed and all of its controversy is erased. All that is remembered by the movie is this military victory. The rest is forgotten. The figure of the emasculated Vietnam soldier is replaced by a remasculinized soldier.

As the battle closes, Sergeant Major Plumley turns to Moore, who is looking up at the mountain where a major of the North Vietnamese Army has been planning the battle strategy and tells him, "You were wondering how Custer felt, sir. You ought to ask him" (*We Were Soldiers*). The roles have been reversed. The narrative takes Moore, who is doomed by his associations with Custer and turns him into the Western hero — the man who is able to drive off the Indians and do his part in "protecting America from all enemies, foreign and domestic."

Furthermore, it takes the perceived *failure* of Custer and places it on the major in the North Vietnamese Army. In the end, the movie gives the impression that Moore has overcome his fate and is now stronger than the myth that controls him. In defeating the North Vietnamese, Moore has proven that he and his men in Vietnam will not suffer the same fate as Custer.

The power of the historiography and the realist aesthetic can be seen in the playing out of this myth. Someone who wished to discredit this critique might say that Custer's myth is not part of the *narrative* of the battle, but a real, historical, documentable fact. Moore's division *was* the same division as Custer's. Furthermore, as Neil Sheehan points out in *A Bright Shining Lie*, the "unlucky" division assignment was noted by members of the regiment at the time. The *second* division of the Seventh Cavalry took over patrolling the Ia Drang Valley after Moore's division left. In an ambush that happened two miles from the original landing zone of the battle, the third company of the second division engaged in a fight where 151 Americans were killed, 121 were injured and four were missing in action (Sheehan 579). Sheehan writes, "On November 17, 1965, 'history repeated itself,' one of the survivors of the third company said" (579). Through this comparison to another account, we can see how the narrative was formed from the historical events. National myths like Custer's Last Stand find their way into history through collective memory, helping to give it order. The discourses of masculinity embedded in the myth — the heroism and the humanity/individualism of the soldier — help to form connections across time and between events so that the two become intertwined, forming a narrative that furthers the myth.

Furthermore, the myth begins to control the retelling of history. The movie plays up the fact that Moore's men are surrounded and cut off. It also plays up the large advantage the North Vietnamese had in manpower. As the movie portrays it, the North Vietnamese had a nearly five to one advantage of men on the ground at the time of the battle. But the movie does not take into account when counting men the nearly 300 sorties Navy and Air Force planes provided in air support (Sheehan 577), nor does it count the men in charge of the artillery batteries four miles away who joined the battle by shelling coordinates called out by soldiers at the battle scene (Sheehan 577), nor does it account for the helicopter pilots who flew in troops and provided air support for the troops on the ground — even though the aid provided from these sources were major factors in winning the battle. If not for the manpower and technology from these other branches of the military, Moore's troops would surely have been overrun. Moore's troops may have been surrounded, but he was not cut off from the rest of the military. The ratio of five to one was probably something more like three to one or two to one, when all military personnel involved in the battle are counted. Furthermore, the technology possessed by the American military gave them a decided advantage. In the four days of fighting in the Ia Drang Valley, 230 American soldiers were killed. The North Vietnamese took what they termed "acceptable losses" before they retreated. But there was no massacre. The only similarity between Moore's battle and Custer's was the number of their regiment. The rest was the perception and imagination of those rewriting/retelling the story.

The Vietnam War and the peace demonstrations that went with it are perceived by many in this country as a "festering wound" in the body of American history (*We Were Soldiers: Getting It Right*). The way much of the country reacted to the war was perceived to be atypical and abnormal. Wallace gives his thoughts on the issue: "The soldiers who came back from Vietnam were never given the gratitude and the respect that their country owed to them. We give that to them, and we've all moved toward being whole. My hope is that the American family can heal wounds that have been there since Vietnam" (*We Were Soldiers: Getting It Right*). This idea that there needs to be healing after the political debates about Vietnam shows a desire to return to the cultural consensus of the pre–Vietnam era. The healing Wallace wants to occur is really the remasculinization of America and the reestablishment of the soldier as hero. This series of events shows, as do others in American history, that the violent criticism of a cultural norm can lead to a further dependency on the ideologies that are being challenged. The reactions of the remasculinization of America and the reestablishment of the soldier as hero have happened to some extent. One only needs to look at the Persian Gulf War to see that once again soldiers arrive home as heroes. In fact, the reaction to the troops arriving home after the Persian Gulf War shows a stronger reaction in the opposite direction than before the Vietnam War. Because of the negative reaction to the troops arriving home during the Vietnam War, there was a conscious effort during the Persian Gulf War to reestablish good will between the troops and the public. The outpouring of public support manifested itself as numerous yellow ribbons tied to trees, and in the turnout to welcome home the troops. Such an outpouring of support was an attempt to "heal" the wounds of the Vietnam War. Yet such "healing" is not the direction in which the American public should move. The successes of the Vietnam era are slowly being eaten away because of their violent beginnings. The healing that Wallace is looking for will only lead us to repeat the mistakes that were made during the Vietnam War and will lead us into conflict over the same ideological issues that were central to the political debates of the sixties and seventies.

Bibliography

Ankersmit, F. R. *Historical Representation: Cultural Memory in the Present.* Stanford, CA: Stanford University Press, 2001.

Braudy, Leo. *From Chivalry to Terrorism: War and the Changing Nature of Masculinity*. New York: Alfred A. Knopf, 2003.

Breu, Christopher. *Hard-Boiled Masculinities*. Minneapolis: Minnesota University Press, 2005.

Jeffords, Susan. *The Remasculinization of America: Gender and the Vietnam War*. Bloomington: Indiana University Press, 1989.

"Hero." *Oxford English Dictionary*. Oxford: Oxford University Press, 2005. 20 January 2006 <http://dictionary.oed.com.proxy.lib.ilstu.edu:2048/cgi/entry/50105289?query _type=word&queryword=hero&first=1&max_to_show=10&sort_type=alpha&result_ place=1&search_id=CwxU-IMjzPU-6899&hilite=50105289>

Hutcheon, Linda. *A Poetics of Postmodernism*. New York: Routledge, 1988.

Karner, Tracy. "Fathers, Sons, and Vietnam: Masculinity and Betrayal in the Life Narratives of Vietnam Veterans with Post Traumatic Stress Disorder." *American Studies* 37 (1996): 63–94.

Neilson, Jim. *Warring Fictions: American Literary Culture and the Vietnam War Narrative*. Jackson: University Press of Mississippi, 1998.

Nochlin, Linda. *Realism*. Harmondsworth: Penguin, 1971.

Sedgwick, Eve Kosofsky. *Between Men: English Literature and Male Homosocial Desire*. New York: Columbia University Press, 1985.

Silverman, Kaja. *The Acoustic Mirror: The Female Voice in Psychoanalysis and Cinema*. Bloomington: Indiana University Press, 1988.

Slotkin, Richard. *Gunfighter Nation: The Myth of the Frontier in Twentieth Century America*. New York: HarperCollins, 1992.

Sheehan, Neil. *A Bright Shining Lie: John Paul Vann and America in Vietnam*. New York: Vintage, 1988.

Stam, Robert. *Subversive Pleasures: Bakhtin, Cultural Criticism, and Film*. Baltimore: Johns Hopkins University Press, 1989.

Vietnam: A Television History. Written and produced by Judith Vecchione. Narrated by William Lyman. Videocassette. WGBH Boston, 1983.

We Were Soldiers. Screenplay by Randall Wallace. Based on the book *We Were Soldiers Once ... And Young* by Lt. Gen. Hal Moore (Ret.) and Joseph L. Galloway. Dir. Randall Wallace. Perf. Mel Gibson, Barry Pepper, and Sam Eliot. DVD. Paramount Pictures, 2002.

We Were Soldiers: Getting It Right. Ed. Benjamin Epps. Wheelhouse, 2002. With *We Were Soldiers* Dir. Randall Wallace. DVD Paramount Pictures, 2002.

White, Hayden. *The Content of the Form: Narrative Discourse and Historical Representation*. Baltimore: Johns Hopkins University Press, 1987.

11

Masculinity and Domesticity in *A Home at the End of the World* and *Househusband*

Helena Wahlstrom

> A housewife is a woman ... the role of housewife is a family role, it is a feminine role.... A man cannot be a housewife ... [such] a claim rings of absurdity, or deviation. It runs counter to the social customs of our culture.
>
> Ann Oakley, *Housewife*

> It is a curious fact that the word home, in its derivations, signifies to enclose. A home is an enclosure, a secret, separate place — a place shut in from, and guarded against, the whole world outside.
>
> John Ware qtd. in Shamir, "Divided Plots"

The recent phenomenon of the househusband, and of fictional representations of the househusband in U.S. literature and film, raises questions concerning meanings of domesticity as this relates to masculinity. This study addresses such meanings by investigating representations of men as homemakers/housewives/househusbands in two contemporary American novels. It will also briefly address the relationship between househusband fictions and the housewife novels of the 1970s. If there is general consensus today that gender relations and family formations are shifting in the post–postmodern era, there is no consensus on the significance — or value — of these shifts. An important question is whether such changes affect the supposed feminization of domesticity and domestic spaces. Also, it is of interest to explore the ways that such shifts are imaginatively envisioned in fictional texts, and if fictional representations offer new ways of engendering domesticity.[1]

In literary studies specifically, domesticity in women's writing — in terms of themes, genre, and literary style, has received a fair amount of critical attention in the past three decades; there, domesticity has typically been linked to definitions of femininity (e.g., Armstrong 1987; Cooperman 1999; Matthews 1987; Ogden 1986; Shamir 1996).[2] Meanwhile, links between masculinity and domesticity remain largely unexplored, partly as a result of the power of the American family ideal, which distorts and renders invisible "deviation" (Andersen 1991). Indeed, in (male-authored, canonical) literature, literary and cultural studies, and more particularly in masculinity studies, white American manhood has typically been defined in terms of an escape from home and family (Twain 1886; Kerouac 1957; Fiedler 1966; Coveney 1966; Kimmel 1996).

However, the following analysis investigates the ways that contemporary white masculinity is constructed — and conflicted — precisely *at home* in two novels; Michael Cunningham's *A Home at the End of the World* (1990) and Ad Hudler's *Househusband* (2002). The analysis focuses on the two protagonists — Cunningham's Bobby Morrow, a sexually ambiguous member of "alternative" or non-nuclear families, and Hudler's Linc Menner, a full time homemaker and heterosexual husband and father. In the novels, these fictional figures both illustrate and problematize men's domesticity, and although they belong in different novelistic genres — Cunningham's book is perhaps a domestic tragedy, Hudler's a domestic comedy — they share some central concerns. This study explores the ways that housework is represented as influencing the protagonists' sense of identity, and how gender is represented as having impact upon how housework, or homemaking, is done and perceived.

In critical and fictional texts, the term domesticity has been variously used to denote a range of attitudes and practices, including docility, love of home and family, as well as involvement in the practical work of housekeeping.[3] For the purposes of this study, I take domesticity to mean both an attitudinal orientation towards home life, and a practically enacted responsibility for housework (Cooperman 1999).[4] In this sense, Cunningham's housewife figure Bobby Morrow and Hudler's expert homemaker Linc Menner are both domestic figures. Due to the culturally specific link between domesticity and femininity in U.S. culture, however, the protagonists' domesticity affects their gendered identities in sometimes problematical ways.

From Housewives to Househusbands

The meaning and ideological power of housewife differs significantly across (for example) nations and classes, and also across historical time; this is likely to be true also of the term "househusband." In 1970 Anne Oakley discussed the hopelessly low status of the housewife, and suggested not only the abolition of housewives, but also of nuclear families, a family form that she believed would continue to hold women captive in the housewife role.[5] Many critics after Oakley have also focused on the general devaluation of housework and domesticity. Others have attempted to raise the status of housework. Some by mystifying domesticity, claiming that housework is a route for women to spiritual experience, a way to experience "holiness" (Cooperman 1999 4). Others again have taken a pragmatic stance, defining housework as necessary and therefore important work that must be performed in order for families, relationships and reproduction to exist. Importantly however, housework has also figured as oppositional/detrimental to the liberated female self. As critics have observed, the feminist movement of the 1970s used the housewife as an ideological springboard — women would have to leave the housewife behind in order to become liberated subjects (Johnson and Lloyd 2004). Thus feminist theory has often viewed the housewife, and domesticity, with scepticism and with a distance that has been perceived as necessary for selfhood. This idea also found artistic representation in women's liberation novels of the 1970s, or housewife fictions, which often described the female protagonist's (attempted) journey away from home, marriage, and housewifehood (Wahlstrom 1997; Whelehan 2005).

Hence, while women's special connection to domesticity has been both refuted and celebrated by feminist thinkers, explained now by biological factors, now by socialization processes, it is above all significant that domesticity has been viewed, also by feminist critics, as entirely feminine, and links between men and domesticity, when mentioned at all, have been refuted in rather absolute ways.[6] Despite resistance — both patriarchal and feminist — to links between men and domesticity, there have of course historically existed examples of men who have been oriented towards home and family (Tosh 1999; McCall 1998) and who have also performed housework in practical terms (Beer 1983; Smith 1998; Johansen 2001). However, cultural representations have continuously, at least throughout much of the twentieth century, signaled that for men to do housework is wrong — for example, men's housework has historically often been represented as an absurdity in media images and commercial advertising (Johnson and Lloyd 2004). I contend that looking at domesticity as multiply gendered instead of as strictly feminine may lead to new readings of fictional representations of men and at-home-ness.[7]

While women still perform the major part of housework in the U.S. (as elsewhere), there is a slight trend towards an increasing number of men who actively choose to stay at home full time while their female spouses work, and who identify themselves as househusbands. This is a "new man" figure in U.S. culture, one who is constructed against the authoritative yet absent husband of the American family ideal. As with the term housewife, the definition of househusband is not consistent — at times, "househusband" is used to denote a man who does any housework at all — but according to one study, in 1996 as many as 8 percent of the men in the group "married men between 25 and 54 with children under 18 living at home" were ready to call themselves full time househusbands, and had taken this role because their wife earned more money than they did.[8] Hence, researchers note: "there is a small but growing core of men who have decided to stay at home with their children while their wives work" (Wentworth and Chell 641). Importantly, the househusband breaks the conventional gendering of housework as feminine and claims space for men inside the home, thereby also challenging the well known private/public gender dichotomy.[9]

In recent fictions, too, men's housework is given space, and voice. It is worth repeating that this does not mean that there is no history of men doing housework, nor indeed that there are no previous examples of fictions where men do housework. It is of course important that contemporary househusband narratives are created within a historical context where the social possibility of men's housekeeping is *perhaps* shifting. Most crucial however is the fact that white househusband narratives present these men as pioneers, as the first to do this kind of work. This is a sign of the invisibility of (other) men's domestic histories, but also an active erasure of such histories; a "real" white man is always a pioneer. Such an emphasis also supposedly caters to perceived conventions of a masculine self-image. Unlike housewife novels of the 1970s in which female protagonists tried to escape the conventions of home and motherhood, and where the "naturalness" of women's reproductive work was questioned, househusband fictions — which also are at least ostensibly interested in breaking gender conventions — make claims for men *entering* the home space, and sometimes legitimize the entry by emphasizing expertise and uniqueness.

Critical texts in the 1980s and 1990s that address men's housework demonstrate clearly that men's domesticity involves a gendered tightrope act. One example is William Beer, who writes in 1983:

> Men can be good at housework, and the experience can often be a source of great personal and emotional satisfaction. At the same time, being involved in housework is not necessarily contradictory to manhood; a man does not have to become feminine to adapt. My own feeling is that doing housework makes me more of a man, because it is an adventure like others, with its tribulations and rewards. One of my hobbies is mountain climbing, and I have climbed all forty-six peaks over four thousand feet in the White Mountains of New Hampshire, as well as some peaks in the Rockies. A day of cooking, cleaning, childcare and household management is not unlike climbing a mountain.... *Housework may not be Everest, but it is an adventure that awaits*

any man who wants to forge ahead and meet the challenges of unexplored terri-
tory [Beer 1983, emphases added].

Beer's presentation, although filled with ambivalence, is clearly intent on constructing housework as a real man's job, and as something no man has ever done before. The househusband to Beer is thus a pioneer and an adventurer who via domesticity becomes more of a man. On the other hand, although this will not necessarily happen, there is always the risk that he will become feminine in the process.

A similar kind of tightrope act is also envisioned in Ad Hudler's novel *Househusband* (2002), where the protagonist Linc Menner actively chooses to stay at home while his wife works. Linc is a heterosexual suburban husband, a landscape artist turned primary homemaker, who runs a household and cares for a three-year-old daughter while his wife, the president of a hospital, is the family's often absent breadwinner. The househusband here, then, is constructed as the symmetrical other half of a heterosexual couple, and the Menners differ from their neighbors only in that they have reversed familial gender conventions. In this narrative, domesticity becomes something men may do even better than women, for housewives in the novel are typically represented as comparatively lazy and uninvolved next to the househusband's engaged thoroughness. However, the male protagonist's status as homemaking expert is not uncomplicated. While Linc breaks gender conventions by choosing housework over professional work, his insistent claims of domestic skill, exemplified by detailed lists of chores and the insertion of cooking recipes in the narrative, as well as his references to himself as someone who mothers, are elements that underscore his ambivalence about masculinity and housework. Importantly, the child Violet is a prerequisite for Linc's staying at home; for him as for most protagonists of contemporary househusband fictions, life as househusband also involves more or less full-time parenting.[10]

But not in all fictions. Bobby Morrow, one of the central characters in Cunningham's *A Home at the End of the World* (1990), is a bisexual whose existence focuses on home and acts of caring and nurture, but not within a nuclear family context, and not necessarily in connection with fatherhood. As a teenager, Bobby gradually loses his birth family, and becomes the almost-adoptive brother of his friend and lover Jonathan Glover. After Jonathan, an only child, leaves home for college, Bobby lives with the Glovers and learns housekeeping skills from Jonathan's mother Alice. In his late twenties he moves to New York City to stay with Jonathan, who is now openly homosexual, and heterosexual Clare. With them Bobby forms an alternative family of three that eventually moves to upstate New York to rear their baby girl and care for each other. In both of these family contexts, Bobby has the role of homemaker. Although Bobby is less constrained by heteronormativity than Linc, he nevertheless realizes that his unusual life choice of at-home-ness renders him a deviation in U.S. society.

Familial Disorder 1: A Home at the End of the World and Non–Nuclear Domesticity

Michael Cunningham's breakthrough novel, *A Home at the End of the World* (1990) describes the shift from a strict heterosexual nuclear family in the 1960s to a "post-nuclear"— Cunningham's own term — and more sexually diverse family in the 1990s. The central characters in the novel are Jonathan, who is homosexual, and Bobby, who is bisexual or possibly asexual, Jonathan's heterosexual mother Alice and Bobby and Jonathan's heterosexual roommate Clare.

As in his other novels Cunningham employs as a central character the cultural icon of the cold war era suburban housewife, here in the figure of Alice, who lives with her husband Ned and son Jonathan in a suburban home in Cleveland Ohio.[11] Alice is clearly marked by a (white middleclass) Great American Housewife ideal (Ogden 1986), which in turn is defined by the American family ideal.[12] The qualities and experiences typical of the Cunningham housewife also characterize Alice Glover. Firmly placed within the confines of her nuclear family and its stereotypically gendered demands, Alice feels imprisoned in her life and isolated from the outside world. Because of her positioning she lives in close contact with her child Jonathan, and has full responsibility for running things, but experiences ambivalence about the worth of the work she performs, for which she receives little recognition from her family. She also experiences her husband, who belongs to the world outside as an alien presence when he is at home. To him, she thinks, "Whatever took place in his absence became a domestic comedy of sorts, a pleasant little movie playing to a sparse house across town" (*A Home* 57). In addition, she experiences sexual frustration because marital sex follows a strict script of passive female and active male behavior.

The second housewife figure in Cunningham's novel is Bobby Morrow, a character whose experience partly parallels Alice's, but also makes some radical departures, above all in that he has no connection to the nuclear norm within which the housewife (ideal) typically has been constructed. Bobby enters into Alice's family — the Glovers — as a teenage friend and secret lover of her son Jonathan. The boy, who at this point is motherless, is more or less adopted into the Glover home. In a central scene Bobby enters the kitchen at night, supposedly on the hunt for something to drink, and finds Alice in the kitchen in the process of rolling out pie crusts. After this initial domestic encounter, Alice begins to teach Bobby how to bake.[13] Some years pass, and when Bobby's father dies he moves in permanently with the Glovers.

Bobby learns cooking and baking, and after his small restaurant fails, he works as a baker for several years, cooking dinner for Alice and Ned in the evenings. Interestingly, then, Alice's frustrated yet energetic housewifehood is displaced onto Bobby, for whom there is no set housewife script to follow, but for whom domesticity becomes equally central. Observing Bobby, Alice reflects: "[w]hen his work came successfully out of the oven, fatly golden and steaming, he contemplated it with frank, unmitigated wonder.... He seemed to believe that from such humble, inert elements as flour, shortening, and little envelopes of yeast, life itself could be produced" (*A Home* 97). Food is central to Bobby's idea of building "home" and familial relations. Like Alice, Bobby prefers home spaces, and he nurtures and cares for the members of his extended family without any clear reward in view. Like her, too, he is sexually frustrated and ambivalent.

The novel does not foreground a search for stable identity in individual terms, but rather emphasizes fluidity of identity, and the importance of family — in whatever form — as a context that can provide safety and connection; the "home" of the novel's title is what Bobby longs for and strives to establish. Bobby's masculine identity is anti-macho, but he is not perceived as feminine by himself or others. On the contrary, he has "hunk" status and attracts both women and men. Cunningham makes a clear point of juxtaposing Bobby's strong and attractive exterior with his searching and sensitive interior, and emphasizes his desire to achieve connection with others via housekeeping and caring work.

But housework also has its ambivalences in Cunningham's text, where the different pulls of desire and desperation are ever present. Bobby is a baker, and similar to housewifing in general, baking is tedious but safe. Summarizing eight years of his life, Bobby reflects: "For eight years I squeezed roses onto birthday cakes and thought of what I'd make for dinner. Each day was an identical package, and the gorgeousness of them was their perfect resemblance, each to the other. Like a drug, repetition changes the size of things. A day when my cinnamon rolls came out just right and the sky clicked over from rain to snow felt full and complete" (127). Like Bobby, Alice recognizes housework as offering a hiding place: "[I had] disappeared into marriage, let myself be carried along by the simple, ceaseless comfort of domestic particulars" (*A Home* 292). In other words, both Alice and Bobby recognize the shelter that domesticity offers, as well as its isolating and numbing effects. A point comes, however, when Bobby realizes he has to give up his role in the

Glover family: "We were in the kitchen, and I could see myself reflected in the window glass. At that moment I looked gigantic, like a geek from a carnival, with a head the size of a football helmet and arms that hung inches above the floor. It was strange, because I'd always thought of myself as small and boy-like, the next best thing to invisible.... I understood that my supply of this particular drug — these red-checked towels and this crock of wooden spoons — was about to run out" (128). The mixed metaphors used to describe Bobby's realization that his interior and exterior selves do not cohere present him both as a large child and a sample from a freak show, which clearly suggests a distance from adult masculinity as well as normativity/normalcy; furthermore, housework as a drug signals the sedative effects of domesticity mentioned previously.

Thus, while Cunningham envisions a possibility of male housewifehood, he also foregrounds its inherent impossibility. Bobby's reflection in the window functions as a painful confrontation with the particular incompatibility of men and domesticity. Male domesticity is not glorified, but marked by the same mix of tedium, longing, and comfort as its female counterpart. In Oakley's words, "the modern concept of work, as the expenditure of energy for financial gains, defines housework as the most inferior and marginal work of all" (Oakley 1970 4). Instead of raising the status of housework, Bobby's gender compounds its aspect of "invisibility." As Calvin Smith points out in an article on househusbands, men find it hard to voice their domestic experiences, which therefore typically go unnoticed and unspoken, simply because "men don't do this sort of thing" (Smith 1998 1). Indeed, for Bobby his contentment with routine tasks is his "embarrassing secret" (*A Home* 157), and domesticity overall is marked for him by a certain guilt about his inappropriate lack of ambition.

After leaving the Glovers, Bobby moves in with Jonathan and Clare who are roommates in New York City. In this post-nuclear family, which eventually will undergo even further shifts, Bobby continues to embrace domesticity; he cooks, he cares for the family, he is content to stay at home, he holds a no-status job and is financially dependent on the others. Indeed, later when Clare and Bobby become lovers, Jonathan reflects that Bobby is like the young bride in an arranged marriage, where Clare is "the husband" (*A Home* 251). However, while Jonathan is stuck in a grid of gendered definitions where dominant equals husband and uninitiated and domestically oriented equals wife, Bobby never signals any such divisions.

When the family moves to an old house near Woodstock, Bobby retains his domestic position, performing tasks that are conventionally seen as women's work. Such taking over by men of conventionally feminine responsibilities in the household and family has been defined as "masculine domesticity" (Marsh 1990). However, in the house Bobby also holds a position as handyman that has been defined as "domestic masculinity" (Gelber 2001). Cunningham's text offers a version of masculinity and domesticity that encompasses both these concepts, but that seems to go beyond them also. While previous scholarship explores the (expansion of) chores or tasks performed by men in their homes and families at certain points in history, it does not question the basic assumption that domesticity, like domestic space, is primarily coded feminine. With Bobby, Cunningham questions this conventional assumption. Bobby nurtures and cooks, cares for the family, mends and maintains the house, but he is also marked by a devotion to the very idea of home and family.

A central space where domesticity is played out is the kitchen. Unlike the other male characters in the novel, Bobby refuses marginalization or alienation in the home spaces he inhabits as an adult.[14] Instead, with the Glovers, he claims the central kitchen space — the heart of the home — that has been Alice's domain. In New York City with Jonathan and Clare, he does the same. In the near-nuclear context of his life in the Glovers' home, food was a field of professional expertise that also served to gather family members. Now, with Clare and Jonathan, shared meals are significant signs that define family relations. Food in Cunningham's text thus becomes a central trope for the work of caring, and for nurturing others in a familial context, echoing the words of one critic, who observes about non-heterosexual families that "[t]he work of preparing and sharing meals creates family. Many lesbigay families point to the continuous preparation of daily meals and/or the occasional preparation of elaborate meals as evidence of their status as families" (Carrington 1999). Hence, the kitchen is an important space for creating, or constructing family through domestic work.

But nor is the kitchen space unambiguously positively charged. Standing in the tiny Manhattan kitchen one evening, in hiding from Clare and Jonathan, Bobby thinks that "[a] move from life to death might resemble my stepping into the kitchen — into its soft nowhere quality and foggy hum" (*A Home* 152). The sinister aspect of the kitchen in this passage suggests that the home space where life is maintained is also one where life may be (susp)ended.

Importantly however, Bobby also brings domesticity to work when he and Jonathan open The Home Café. According to Cooperman: "housework — traditionally conceived as private-sphere activity — is more accurately an art and science of the boundaries. Boundaries between public and private, boundaries of home and family ... Housework sweeps thresholds, opens passages to the outside world" (Cooperman 1999 9). Clearly, by repositioning Bobby's domesticity as professional work — as well as Alice's, who when she is widowed starts a catering business — Cunningham disturbs the idea that "house-wife" is a position completely resistant to change or locked in the past, and shakes the gender dichotomy of private versus public.

In the case of Bobby, "housewife" clearly has limits as a meaningful defi-nition, because of its links to marriage, heterosexuality, parenthood, and the nuclear family norm. Also, while for Alice motherhood and marriage are inte-gral to her position as housewife, Bobby's position is not defined in terms of a socially sanctioned or legally binding relationship, nor is parenthood a strong identity for him. While he fathers a child with Clare in the biological sense, this is a less central issue than the general idea of building a familial context that may "contain multitudes."[15] On finding out that there is going to be a baby, he tells Clare and Jonathan: "We can have it. We can all three have it" (*A Home* 254). For Bobby, home and family are flexible notions, and can exist independently of children.

Cunningham's novel thus moves beyond the nuclear norm to envision domesticity as closely linked to masculinity while revising both concepts in non-conventional terms.[16] A sign of this rejection of convention is that Bobby is never called either housewife or househusband in the narrative. Although Bobby himself does not seem to mourn the indecisiveness and unconvention-ality of his family life, to Jonathan their lives describe a domestic tragedy. In the final chapters of the novel Clare leaves with the baby girl, rejecting her "strange" family. Left behind are Bobby, Jonathan, and the latter's ex-lover Eric, who is dying of aids. Together they form yet another family in the old house, but one that will not reproduce, and whose domestic future seems rather bleak. A different envisioning is offered by Ad Hudler, whose novel *Househusband* presents us with a clearly heterosexual and nuclear-minded male protagonist, whose domestic accomplishments are empowering yet ambiguous.

Familial Disorder 2: Househusband and Nuclear Domesticity

Linc is a 30-something landscaping artist who moves with his wife Jo and their 3-year-old daughter Violet from California to Rochester New York where Jo has a new job as the director of a hospital. Linc gives up his busi-ness because of the move, but initially sees himself as at-home only temporar-ily. Gradually he realizes that his family needs him to stay at home much more than they need for him to get a new job outside the home. Unlike Cun-ningham's text, which focused on non-normativity and fluidity of identity, Hudler's novel describes a gendered "role reversal" within the framework of an affluent white heterosexual family, where the man takes the place of the conventional housewife of the family ideal.

What is evident in Linc's narrative is that he feels strongly that he violates a norm by choosing domesticity, and that others regard his choice as suspect. However, he also feels that his choice is appropriate and that he is accomplished as housekeeper and parent. This creates an ambivalence in Linc's self-perception, and as a result he needs to find ways to legitimize his full time presence at home. Legitimacy is achieved above all by thinking about life at home in terms of work, and by working hard to make visible his own efforts. He reflects upon the impulse to achieve legitimacy thus:

> The bottom line here is guilt. I do not deserve to have hired help because I am not working and bringing in money. This is my job, and I have to do it well, and I have to do it by myself, and because the job creates nothing tangible (Translation: *Money!*), I go out of my way to let Jo know how hard I am working. The only time I order takeout is when Jo isn't home for dinner. It is important that when she gets home I am clattering about in the kitchen, sweating and fretting, because I have to show her that my work here is as consuming and demanding as hers. Even if I've had a good day I most likely will not tell Jo because I don't want her to think that my life at home is enjoyable and fulfilling, not even for the seven percent of the time that it truly is. She cannot work harder than I do at home, because if she does I'll feel like a slacker, guilty, guilty, guilty.... I am earning my keep.... I'm sure this is why I bitch so much to Jo about all my responsibilities. I am convincing her — perhaps myself as well — of my worth to this household [*Househusband* 52].

The desire to prove his worth creates a situation where Linc can never relax. His domestic life is marked by severe needs to control his space and those in it. For example, he does not spend time with his daughter because it is nice and emotionally gratifying, but to be able to control and monitor her development with expertise — when they visit an upscale café, it is not to enjoy the pastries, but to practice good table manners. Importantly, his various fields of expertise: housecleaning, laundry, home improvement, gardening, child rearing/education, discipline, and not least cooking, serve to legitimize his own position in the home, but also elevate him into a superman position *visavis* others. This clearly sets him apart from the protagonist of earlier housewife fictions, who were often marked by not feeling at home in domestic work at all. For example, he perceives himself as a better mother and housewife than his female neighbors, because he takes the job more seriously than they do. Also, while Bobby learns domestic skills from Alice but has no male role model, Linc has not learned his domestic skills from anyone, woman or man, and describes his own mother as hopelessly messy; thereby he also embodies the "self-made-ness" of the American Adam.[17]

Although Linc presents himself as a superior domestic expert, he must repeatedly reinforce this position via inclusions of for example lists of chores and must remember items that illustrate his ability for tangential thinking and his extraordinary multitasking skills; his cooking skills are confirmed not only by the exquisite and nutritious meals he prepares, but also by the inclusion of actual recipes at the end of several chapters. There is a kind of hyper-realism or overload in the amassing of detailed descriptions of the hard work and grime that the everyday contains. Whereas this can be read as making housework visible in a general sense, in the narrative it serves rather to underpin Linc's homemaking superman identity. Not least, housework as expertise helps Linc to distance himself from women, whom he sees as less serious housekeepers.

Yet, male identification is also problematical. Linc is superior to other men, who are threatening, negligent, degrading or even physically violent, and generally represented as problems in the novel. On one occasion Linc speaks with a group of male neighbors, and inwardly reflects: "I wanted to tell [the men] that the reason they get hounded by their women is that they truly care about the world we live in, that they're the dispensers of the details that keep us human" (*Househusband*, 250). Paradoxically, here he protagonist, unlike other men, is able to see and appreciate the work that women do in their homes and families. Most importantly, not only is Linc different from other men, an exception and a pioneer; in the narrative there is no tendency towards including domesticity in masculinity. Instead Linc suggests that; "I'm a minority, part man, part woman" (59). Late in the narrative, he repeats: "woman and man, I am both of these now" (281). The suggestion that he is only "part man" is perhaps partly grounded in a recognition of the transgressive element in his care for his daughter in a culture where adult men in the company of small children are typically viewed with suspicion. However, it also illustrates a mode of thought where domesticity cannot escape its feminine engendering.

And there is more gender trouble for Linc. Seemingly reaffirming his masculinity he repeatedly voices disclaimers of the housewifely role: "I'm not a housewife, Jo. Don't expect the Ozzie and Harriet show here" (*Househusband* 21). However, he never defines himself in masculine terms, for example by the word "father"; instead he uses feminine labels: mother, housewife, and indeed woman, a practice which is also reinforced by those around him. His neighbor Marilyn quips: "Sexy man moves into the neighbourhood as a mom" (108), and his wife Jo reassures him: "You're a wonderful mother, Lincoln. I've never seen better" (173). When, in a reverse movement, Jo lovingly bolsters his masculinity in an intimate moment by saying he is "far from being a woman," Linc secretly thinks: "What do you mean I'm far from being a

woman? I'm just like they are. I can do what they do, I can do it even better!" (211). To Linc, then, housework and domestic life, as well as parenthood,
are strongly feminized and feminizing.

The desire to be acknowledged as a real housewife and mother also surfaces when Linc has made a sophisticated lunch for the housewives in the
neighborhood, who nevertheless view him as an "other" and refuse to let him
into their female loop. He envisions his secret revenge: "as this food, laced
with my cells, found its way into their bloodstream, *I would become part of
these women*, their livers and kidneys, their hair, their skin, and though their
conscious minds would tell them to avoid me, *the very molecular structure of
their bodies would recognize me as kin*" (*Househusband* 149, emphases added).
While at times he wishes to be included in "womanhood," he nevertheless
views the women around him as lazy good-for-nothings who are unable to
control both their offspring and their own lives.[18]

While socially closed off from the loop of the neighborhood housewives,
Linc also has all of nature against him. His attitude reinforces a natural connection between women and children, one that he never can (or never wants
to) achieve. For example, he notes that: "When Jo puts Violet to bed, she
walks into the kitchen afterward looking dreamily sedate and emotionally
overwhelmed" (*Househusband* 128). He also notes his own "inability — unwill-
ingness? — to emotionally intertwine with a child's personality as [he has] seen
only women do" (44). As a consequence of the gendered distribution of "natural connection," while Linc has a functional relationship with his daughter
Violet, he will never be able to "lose himself" in parenthood the way women
can: "I cannot expect to satisfyingly lose myself in motherhood,.... Conversely,
a mother and her child remind me of a grafting of two fruit trees, genes and
tissue infused into one another until there is one body, and over time neither
can distinguish one from the other, they become a new creation, sacrificing
personal identity to create anew.... I love Violet. She is my job. I do my job
very well (196). It seems evident that Linc must distance himself from strong
emotional parenthood, by claiming that Violet is his "job" — his field of expertise — rather than an emotional concern in order to distance himself from femininity. Strong emotional parenthood equals motherhood in Linc's universe,
and "losing oneself" in fatherhood is not a conceivable option.

The centrality of the notion of legitimacy in Hudler's representation of
the househusband echoes sociological studies of men's housework. More than
a decade after Beer's description of housekeeping as equal to mountaineer-
ing, Calvin Smith observes that "[t]he myths of the natural connection of
women with the traits that were said to be definitional of good mothering
(nurture, intuition, low ambition for anything else) have been challenged ...
but there is still the fact that motherhood is a 'career' option for women; that

is, *full-time motherhood is still a status available only to women.* The consequence of the naturalization of gender is that men do not have legitimately
available to them the status of full-time child career and housekeeper" (Smith
1998 140, emphases added). Linc's perception of gender difference echoes
exactly the myth that Smith names. What is most striking about Smith's comment however is that just as domesticity conventionally is perceived as singly
gendered, so is parenthood; to denote full time parenthood for both men and
women, Smith — like Hudler's protagonist — employs "motherhood."

Yet this engendering also opens up possibilities for Linc. As we have
seen, he defines himself in feminine terms. If he is a mother (not a father)
this should mean that strong emotional parenthood is available to him, also.
However, he continuously displaces strong emotional attachment onto women.
Hence, a number of ambiguities and paradoxes are harbored in the protagonist, the most profound one being the impossibility for Linc to reconcile his
identity as parent, nurturer and homemaker with a masculine identity.

Hudler has claimed that unlike other role reversal comedies,

> *Househusband* takes a more serious look at the emotions surrounding a pri-
> mary caregiver's life. The other big difference is that my character, Linc Men-
> ner, is never a bumbling, stumbling idiot at home. Indeed, he succeeds at the
> task immediately. He's also more in touch with his female side, as many men
> are today. If *Mrs. Doubtfire* or *Mr. Mom* were filmed today, I think the char-
> acters would be more androgynous simply because society has evolved, and
> men have become more comfortable in nurturing roles [Hudler 2007].

As I hope to have demonstrated, the claim that Linc is in touch with his
female side, whatever this signifies, is highly problematical. Clearly, he is not
particularly at ease with his nurturing role. His narrative describes a trajectory from manic housekeeping marred by frustration and gradual deterioration, as evidenced by his inattention to personal hygiene and physical exercise
and his lack of a sex life, which later is turned around into gradual improvement after he receives clear acknowledgement of his efforts from his wife Jo.
By book's end, the family expects another baby and Linc decides to stay home
indefinitely.

At this point, he solves his gender ambivalence by figuring as a kind of
godlike creature in relation to his female family members. This fantasy is
exemplified earlier, when he enters the neighbor women's bodies via the food
he has cooked for them. Now he describes the same physical mixing of his
self with Jo and Violet, but at the same time he stands above them, controlling and gazing upon them. Incidentally, now it is he who eats them: "It is I
who cleans up their piss and blood, vomit, shit and hair, the very droppings
of their humanity, which make their way under my fingernails and probably
into the sandwich I will eat for lunch. I know when they hurt, why they hurt,

how they hurt, because I am standing above, not only watching, but directing, prodding, restraining" (*Househusband* 287).

This exploration of two examples of representations of masculinity and domesticity in contemporary fiction reveals that, while the novels are very different, notions like gender transgression, familial responsibility, and domestic legitimacy — both the legitimacy of men in domestic spaces and domestic work as legitimate work — are central concerns for both Cunningham and Hudler, albeit in varying ways.

Conclusion

Househusband texts explore possibilities for masculinity and domesticity to merge, and often describe the considerable effort such merging involves. They suggest what social scientists have also found about househusbands in social reality: "most [find] little societal support for their role" (Wentworth and Chell 2001 642). Unlike housewife fictions of the 1970s, these texts are concerned with the possibility to enter, and claim space within, the home and the family. The gendered struggle, then, is a reversed movement from that in housewife fictions. Like the earlier genre, househusband texts are confessional narratives that bring the reader close to the everyday that constitutes domesticity, and often describe limited possibilities for breaking gender conventions. Also like the housewife in 1970s fiction, the househusband may be frustrated by his confinement in the home and his lack of adult interaction. However, unlike the housewife, by staying at home the househusband does not comply with a gendered script, but instead apparently transgresses one. This transgression is filled with gendered tensions. While both Bobby Morrow and Linc Menner recognize that choosing the domestic position can result in relinquishment of full masculine status, Linc counters this effect by balancing his domestic skills with an element of machismo, whereas Bobby rejects the hierarchical thinking and misogyny of machismo completely. Also unlike housewife fictions, in househusband narratives men's domestic legitimacy is a major concern. Even when — as in the case of Cunningham — the nuclear family is rejected, the notion of male legitimacy in the home space and in domestic work is central.

What seems significant is that Bobby embraces domesticity only in familial contexts that are non-nuclear, first his "adoptive" family the Glovers, and then his own post-nuclear, or queer, family. Thus, Cunningham inserts a male character into the heart of homemaking and nurturing practices while this character also comes to symbolize a disruption of the idea that such practices necessarily are gendered feminine and take place within a nuclear fam ily context. This seems to suggest that re-gendering domesticity from "feminine only" to "masculine also," entails a move away from the nuclear family — domesticity and masculinity are envisioned as intersecting in a character who is placed in a post-nuclear familial context — and in the future, too — this is utopia. That Bobby is a utopian figure in the novel is signaled already by his last name Morrow. The domestic man is a queer subject and a utopian subject, and as such has visionary significance but ultimately does not figure as a "realistic" representation.

In *Househusband* male housekeeping and full-time parenting, which at first looked like a transgression of a gendered norm, becomes instead a conservative reaffirmation of norms. First, the norm of male supremacy and authority. Linc's last name suggests that while some husbands are men, this househusband is even "menner." Linc the puppeteer who watches, directs, prods, and restrains female family members is clearly in a position of mastery, and his misogyny surfaces throughout the text. Second, the novel embraces the norm of the heterosexual family that closes itself off to the world, and gendered shifts occur only within that norm. The strong connection between domesticity and femininity is maintained throughout the text, even as it simultaneously, and paradoxically, presents a refashioning of domesticity in terms of masculine control.

Hence, although both novels deal with white middle class characters who explore issues of kinship, caring, and the performance of housework on an everyday level, the texts approach these matters in very different ways. *A Home at the End of the World* is a novel that jars and expands conventional boundaries of domesticity and kinship, moving into the possibility of what Kath Weston has termed "families we choose" (Weston 1997). As domestic man, Bobby Morrow is a kind of utopia that destabilizes heteronormative and nuclear norms. *Househusband*, meanwhile, embraces heteronormativity and seems more interested in claiming the legitimacy of the white heterosexual father as homemaker by suggesting that it is possible to do housework and still be a "real man." Nevertheless, both novels in interesting ways critique the limits of both masculinity and domesticity at a certain point in American history. They demonstrate clearly that violation of gendered family norms creates anxieties and irreconciliabilities that are difficult to resolve within the framework of a heterosexual and patriarchal U.S. context.

Notes

1. Although my constructionist critical perspective differs from his psychoanalytic one, I take inspiration from Berthold Schoene Harwood's study *Writing Men*, where he notes the importance of continuing to speak of "patriarchal masculinity" and "the insidu-

ous impact its inherent conceptual contradictions and inconsistencies continue to exert on the individuation and self-formation of both men and their other" (Schoene Harwood 2000, xi). When I speak of the husband of the family ideal, it is such "patriarchal masculinity" I refer to.

2. The focus of the present study in no way suggests that the subject of women and domesticity has been emptied out. However, see also Laura McCall's "Not So Wild a Dream," which investigates male and female nineteenth century writers' preoccupation with domestic matters. Although such matters were typically placed within "womanhood" by authors of both sexes, McCall finds that domesticity was much more present in much fiction written by men than the domophobia/escape theme usually highlighted in American literary history (McCall 1998).

3. According to the *OED*, "domesticity" denotes being a servant, home or family life, devotion to home, and homeliness — thus, linguistically speaking, "domesticity" blends spatial and occupational denotations, familial and work-life associations, actions and emotions, as well as references to being homely, which in turn denotes plainness, simplicity, and absence of beauty (obsolete meanings of homeliness are familiarity, intimacy, and kindness).

4. As literary scholar Jeanette Batz Cooperman points out, domesticity carries "the emotional and psychological dimension of devotion to home" and is thus different from, and more than, "mere housekeeping" (2).

5. Interestingly, Oakley brings up two examples from 1960s England of "deviations" that ran into trouble: the first is the husband who claimed "housewife benefits" since he did all the housework while his wife was the family's "breadwinner"— the second is the example of two women who were married while fully aware that the husband was a woman.

6. An example is Cooperman, who observes that "It seems unfair to give biology the final say and assume that men's consciousness cannot also be shaped by domesticity. What the collective result would be, it is far too early to say; we will need to embed a sense of domestic responsibility in the male psyche and let it germinate for a century of two before the comparison [with women] is fair. But just as we cannot understand the past if we ignore its patriarchal context, we cannot look forward if we give women proprietary, biological rights to domesticity" (Cooperman, 1999, 9). Whereas Cooperman seems sympathetic to the idea of domesticity as unbound by biology, she nevertheless casts women ("we") as those who must embed domesticity in men, who simply do not have it.

7. According to literary scholar Milette Shamir, "the current tendency to equate women's novels with domestic fiction is inaccurate. Since the term 'domestic,' unlike 'romance' or 'sentimentalism' does not refer to aesthetic or formal conventions that can be easily pinpointed but ... to the theme of 'the interior of households,' it might be fruitful to use the term widely and to read Hawthorne and Stowe, Melville and Hale, as responding to the same phenomenon: the increasing importance of the regime of the home in middle-class antebellum culture." Shamir continues: "Domestic fiction often ... help[ed] implement a vision of the home as a sharply divided realm, and interrogat[ed] the implications of the splitting of the domestic interior on psychic and gender identity" (Shamir 1996, 431).

8. Numbers have gone up from approximately 2 percent in the mid–1970s to approximately 8 percent in the mid–1990s. Men's place in households has been studied recently, especially in historical and sociological research. One example is Margaret Marsh's study on men's housework in the nineteenth century, another Steven Gelber's work on the DIY man of the 1950s (Marsh 1990, Gelber 2001). Work focusing specifically on househusbands includes Beer's American study and Smith's Australian one, as well as Christopher Carrington's study on "lesbigay" families *No Place Like Home* (Beer 1983, Carrington 1999, Smith 1998). A small number of critical articles are also available on the topic of househusbands, for example Wentworth and Chell who note that "Only recently has the male

version of housewife, labeled househusband, come into existence as an alternative for men (Wentworth and Chell 2001, 641)." Wentworth and Chell observe that: "Hayghe (1990) cited Bureau of Labor statistics that reveal a slight increase over a 13-year period in married couples with children (under 18 years old) with only the mother in the labor force. These statistics show that is 1975, 1.6 percent of families fit that model. By 1988, it had increased to 2.2 percent." Tang (1999), using more recent Bureau of Labor statistics, reported that there has been an ... increase in men aged 25 to 54 years who did not work or look for work due to home responsibilities, when the numbers from 1991 (4.6 percent) were compared with those from 1996 (8.4 percent) (Wentworth and Chell 2001, 641). Notably, Wentworth and Chell look only at "married couples with children (under 18 years old) with only the mother in the labor force"— that is, at heterosexual two-parent families. From a slightly different angle, see Fassinger's investigation of housework among divorced fathers and mothers in the U.S. (Fassinger 1993).

9. For a comprehensive overview of feminist challenges to the public/private dichotomy, see Davidson and Hatcher, *No More Separate Spheres!* (2002).

10. This is also true, for example, in Joseph Oberle's book *Diary of a Mad Househusband,* and in the films *Mr. Mom* and *Mrs. Doubtfire.*

11. *Flesh and Blood* (1995) and *The Hours* (1999). Cunningham's most recent title *Specimen Days* (2005) does not work with the housewife figure to the extent of his previous fictions, but is consistent with his earlier work in its positioning of family relations as a central concern.

12. Notably, critics use the term housewife variously to refer to women who do housework besides their paid employment (e.g,. Ogden 1986), or women who engage in full-time housewifehood (e.g., Mathews 1987, Oakley 1970). Margaret Anderson helpfully delineates the American family ideal — the family of breadwinner-father, homemaker-wife, and children — as made up of three sets of criteria: first, the family is placed exclusively in the private sphere, second, family is a site for harmonious and companionate interaction and nurture, and third, the family is nuclear and heterosexual, and follows a prescribed sexual division of labor. Importantly, the family ideal "not only departs considerably from the actual realities of contemporary families, but it also distorts family experiences of the past" (Andersen 239). It is clear that the housewife ideal builds on the very qualities Anderson outlines: it is the housewife who will provide the nurture and harmony the family needs, who will be positioned almost exclusively in the private sphere, and whose portion of the sexually differentiated labor will be done inside the home, above all in the kitchen space. For while "housewife" connotes family and marriage, it also connotes certain kinds of work termed housework, especially in the working and middle classes.

13. For Alice, food is a means of communication with her family but one that backfires: Jonathan complains to Bobby that all his mother ever speaks to him about is what they will have for dinner. Food is also her own field of expertise. A picture in the local paper shows the Glover family cutting into one of Alice's casseroles — at this point her cooking has become "renowned." The tedium of housework, the failing communication with her husband and son, and the loneliness Alice experiences at home stand in stark contrast to the newspaper image that glorifies the nuclear family and stresses harmoniousness, neatness, and home as a place for accomplishment. Once the son leaves home for college, Alice gives baking classes in the evenings, but only once she has broken her domestic isolation by taking a job as a secretary. As long as her nuclear family remains intact, Alice's attempts at transgressing the housewife script — whether bonding with the teenage boys, or taking on a new sexual persona with her husband — are typically stunted.

14. While Bobby's mother reigns supreme in the upper regions of his childhood home, especially the kitchen, his father builds a big wooden clock in the basement, a DYI project that only emphasizes his marginal place in the house. Steven Gelber discusses the basement specifically as a "masculine space" within the home (Gelber 2001, 277).

15. Cunningham's representation of Bobby seems to me to foreshadow the central presence of Walt Whitman and his utopian text *Leaves of Grass* in the latest novel, *Specimen Days* (2005).

16. And here, importantly, Cunningham departs from the narrow definition of domesticity (meaning marriage and children) that Shamir and McCall investigate in nineteenth century fiction.

17. Nina Baym writes about the Adamic myth from a feminist perspective in *Feminism and American Literary History* (1992).

18. In an interview Ad Hudler claims that his novel takes sides with women. In the process, however, positions all women as housewives, and all men (excepting himself and his fictional protagonist) as non-domestic beings:

> Q: What do you hope women take away from reading this?
> A: I want women — mothers especially — to feel good about what they do, to realize that at least one man out there "gets it" and appreciates all that they do. I wanted Linc Menner to validate their emotions and frustrations.
> Q: What do you want men to take from it?
> A: I'm not sure. I didn't write the book for men [Hudler 2007].

Bibliography

Anderson, Margaret. "Feminism and the American Family Ideal." *Journal of Comparative Family Studies*. Vol. XXII: 2 (Summer 1991): 235–46.

Armstrong, Nancy. *Desire and Domestic Fiction: A Political History of the Novel*. New York: Oxford University Press, 1987.

Baym, Nina. *Feminism and American Literary History*. New Brunswick, NJ: Rutgers, 1992.

Carrington, Christopher. *No Place Like Home: Relationships and Family Life Among Lesbians and Gay Men*. Chicago: University of Chicago Press, 1999.

Cooperman, Jeanette Batz. *The Broom Closet: Secret Meanings of Domesticity in Postfeminist Novels by Louise Erdrich, Mary Gordon, Toni Morrison, Marge Piercy, Jane Smiley, and Amy Tan*. New York: Peter Lang, 1999.

Coveney, Peter. "Introduction" *The Adventures of Huckleberry Finn* by Mark Twain. London: Penguin, 1966.

Cunningham, Michael. *A Home at the End of the World*. New York: Farrar, Straus and Giroux, 1990.

_____. *Flesh and Blood*. London: Hamish Hamilton, 1995.

_____. *The Hours*. New York: Farrar, Straus, Giroux, 1999.

_____. *Specimen Days*. New York: Farrar, Straus, Giroux, 2005.

Davidson, Cathy N., and Jessamyn Hatcher, Eds. *No More Separate Spheres! A Next Wave American Studies Reader*. Durham, NC: Duke University Press, 2002.

Fassinger, Polly A. "Meanings of Housework for Single Fathers and Mothers: Insights into Gender Inequality." In *Men, Work, and Families*. Ed. Jane C. Hood. Newbury Park: Sage, 1993. 195–216.

Fiedler, Leslie. *Love and Death in the American Novel*. New York. Stein and Day, 1966.

Gelber, Steven M. "Do-It-Yourself: Constructing, Repairing, and Maintaining Domestic Masculinity." In *Family and Society in American History*. Eds. Joseph M. Hawes and Elizabeth I. Nybakken. Urbana: University of Illinois Press. 2001. 68–303.

Hudler, Ad. *Househusband*. New York: Random House, 2002.

_____. "Interview." www.adhudler.com May 30, 2007.

Johansen, Shawn. *Family Men: Middle-Class Fatherhood in Early Industrializing America*. New York: Routledge, 2001.

Johnson, Lesley, and Justine Lloyd. *Sentenced to Everyday Life: Feminism and the House-wife*. Oxford: Berg, 2004.
Kerouac, Jack. *On the Road*. New York: Viking, 1957.
Kimmel, Michael. *Manhood in America: A Cultural History*. New York: Free Press, 1996.
Marsh, Margaret. *Suburban Lives*. New Brunswick: Rutgers University Press, 1990.
Matthews, Glenna. *"Just a Housewife": The Rise and Fall of Domesticity in America*. New York: Oxford University Press, 1987.
McCall, Laura. "'Not So Wild a Dream': The Domestic Fantasies of Literary Men and Women, 1820–1860." In *A Shared Experience: Men, Women, and the History of Gender*. Eds. Laura McCall and Donald Yacovone. New York: New York University Press, 1998. 176–194.
Mr. Mom. Dir. Stan Dragoti. 1983.
Mrs. Doubtfire. Dir. Chris Columbus. 1993.
Oakley, Ann. *Housewife*. London: Allen Lane, 1974.
Oberle, Joseph. *Diary of a Mad Househusband*. Fridley, MN: Kimm, 1996.
Ogden, Annegret S. *The Great American Housewife: From Helpmate to Wage Earner, 1776–1986*. Westport CN: Greenwood, 1986.
OED online. "domesticity"; "homeliness"; "housewife"; "househusband."
Shamir, Milette. "Divided Plots: Interior Space and Gender Difference in Domestic Fiction." *Genre* XXIX (Winter 1996): 429–72.
Smith, Calvin D. "Men Don't Do This Sort of Thing: A Case Study of the Social Isolation of Househusbands." *Men and Masculinities*, vol. 1: 2 (October 1998): 138–172.
Tosh, John. *A Man's Place: Masculinity and the Middle-Class Home in Victorian England*. New Haven: Yale University Press, 1999.
Twain, Mark. *The Adventures of Huckleberry Finn*. 1886.
Wahlstrom, Helena. *Husbands, Lovers, and Dreamlovers: Masculinity and Female Desire in Women's Novels of the 1970s*. Uppsala: Acta Universitatis Upsaliensis (Doctoral Diss., as H. Eriksson), 1997.
Wentworth, Diane Kayser, and Robert M. Chell. "The Role of Househusband and Housewife as Perceived by a College Population." *Journal of Psychology*, 2001, 135 (6): 639–650.
Weston, Kath. *Families We Choose: Gays, Lesbians, Kinship*. New York: Columbia University Press, 1991.
Whelehan, Imelda. *The Feminist Bestseller*. New York: Palgrave Macmillan, 2005.

12

Anxious Male Domesticity and Gender Troubled *Corrections*

Kristin Jacobson

> Am I a social novelist, or am I sort of an old-fashioned domestic novelist?
> — Jonathan Franzen, quoted in Lorraine Adams'
> "Literary Life Without Oprah"[1]

Reviewers of Jonathan Franzen's *The Corrections* (2001) characterized it as a "hybrid novel" that combined the feminine sentiment associated with the domestic novel and the masculine satiric edge associated with the social novel. Benjamin Svetkey in *Entertainment Weekly*, for example, not only described *The Corrections* as a "domestic drama" but also "a big, ambitious, unwieldy hybrid of a book."[2] Jesse Berrett, writing about *The Corrections* for *The Village Voice*, characterized Franzen as "half brainiac hipster, half traditionalist."[3] Such celebratory reviews could have marked a turn in American literature and culture, a movement characterized at least in part by its challenging of the gendered dualism that has traditionally set 'high' masculine intellect against 'low' feminine sentiment. However, the endorsement of this coupling between the social and domestic dramas did not last long. The 'Franzen Affair,' the public spectacle tipped off by the author's snide remarks about the Oprah Book Club that led to his novel being pulled from the club, reestablished strict gendered boundaries.[4] The case and its aftermath highlight white heterosexual American masculinity's fraught mediation of domesticity.

The Franzen-Oprah miff is a Zeitgeist matter, particularly for understanding the status of white masculinity, American authorship, and canon formation. Close cultural and textual analysis of the Affair and related cultural texts demonstrates how Franzen's gender, race, and literary class performance roles require or at least encourage him to speak out against Oprah's Book Club;

the frequent attempts by American critics and the author to distance male authorship from the taint of the feminine and domestic suggest that to appear on Oprah would make Franzen less of a writer of serious (e.g. masculine and good) fiction. Thus, Franzen's failure to circulate in the American public sphere as a hybrid author — both domestic and masculine, popular and serious — reminds us that the proliferation of mediated masculinities in the public and literary spheres does not necessarily mean patriarchy's deep structures have or are undergoing radical change. Rather, as Fredric Jameson points out in regard to postmodernism's revolutionary potential, the case furthers the argument that such mediated identities more often advance "a much narrower class-cultural operation serving white and male-dominated elites."[5] Franzen, in this case, profits monetarily and culturally for writing the type of book that could appear on Oprah while he will not. He maintains his masculinity and artistic sophistication, in other words, by resisting domestication.

In the discussion that follows I consciously employ fairly typical characterizations of masculinity and femininity even as I plumb notions of hybridity that challenge such dichotomies. These conventional descriptions are not endorsements of essentialized or stereotypical notions of gender difference. Rather, they reflect widely accepted or understood notions of the distinctive cultural and literary features that define American masculinity (e.g., wit, anti-domestic) and femininity (e.g., sentiment, domestic). As Judith Halberstam does in *Female Masculinity*, I aim to employ, if not flaunt, such stereotypical notions of gender in order to explain and, when necessary, explode them.

Significantly, these conventional and frequently stereotypical constructions influence both the American novel's gendered framing and authors' gendered performances. These literary classifications and hierarchies, in turn, shed light on American masculinity more generally. Ultimately, the Franzen case emphasizes white heterosexual masculinity's continued investment and success in resisting hybridization with low, mass, or otherwise feminine cultures (even as it produces hybrid texts). In other words, this case emphasizes that exploring or celebrating postmodern hybridity alone is not enough; we must also consider how hybridities like *The Corrections'* 'domestic masculinity' circulate in the public sphere.

The concept of hybridity plays a key role in my analysis of American masculinity and authorship. Hybridity in contemporary American culture has been understood both negatively — due to its pseudoscientific application in miscegenation laws — and positively — due to the way it challenges binary divisions such as femininity and masculinity. Here my use of hybridity explores its counter-hegemonic potential, following what Linda McDowell calls "the coincidence between post-colonial cultural studies and feminist scholarship."[6] As Homi K. Bhabha explains in "Signs Taken for Wonders," hybridity represents "that ambivalent 'turn' of the discriminated subject into the terrifying, exorbitant object of paranoid classification — a disturbing questioning of the images and presences of authority."[7] Like Bhabha, I am interested in how this "terrifying" hybridity — particularly in the form of domestic masculinity — gets classified in twenty-first-century American culture.

The hybrid concept of domestic masculinity refers not only to men's particular relationships with the domestic sphere or feminized, domestic practices but also to the generic blending of the social and domestic novels. Generically, longstanding gendered distinctions have been made between the masculine social novel and the feminine domestic novel. Milette Shamir describes this split in nineteenth-century fiction in terms of "divided plots." Shamir argues, "The example of the domestic division plot shows the romance and sentimental traditions to be competing over the same space [the home], albeit from different angles and perspectives."[8] The Franzen case emphasizes how gendered genres continue to help produce literary and social hierarchies that often exclude or degrade women and femininity. These patriarchal hierarchies reproduce gender distinctions that differentiate the so-called niche category of women's fiction from the more 'universal,' well-respected, and frequently more masculine genres. Cases of domestic masculinity, therefore, "trouble" — in the Judith Butler sense — gender stability and, by extension, the patriarchy that depends on such stability.[9]

Jonathan Franzen's Gender Troubled Corrections

As a novel with characteristically feminine and masculine tropes connecting it to both domestic and social fictions, Franzen's hybrid novel "trouble[s] the gender categories that support gender hierarchy and compulsory heterosexuality."[10] While a full analysis of The Corrections' gender troubling is beyond the scope of this essay, let me briefly outline the novel's hybrid characteristics by looking at one of its key characters. Chip, the middle Lambert child, epitomizes the novel's hybrid, domestic masculinity. The Corrections— through Chip's character — revises what Nina Baym calls the narrative of "beset manhood."[11] This foundational masculine and anti-domestic story imagines women as "entrappers and domesticators" and presents the domestic sphere as an impediment to male development and comfort.[12] Peggy Cooper Davis and Carol Gilligan, building on the work of Nancy F. Cott, clarify that such "flights from relationship are grounded in what we call the logic of patriarchy."[13] Patriarchal logic discourages relational and egalitarian interactions in favor of competition, dominance, and hierarchy. Much twentieth-century suburban fiction, such as John Updike's Rabbit series, continues to engage this anti-domestic narrative.

Unlike Mark Twain's Huckleberry Finn or John Updike's Rabbit Ang-
strom, Chip does not successfully resist domestication. Chip's character arch
maps a movement from the anti- to the pro-domestic. In a clear rejection of
the home, Chip's character trajectory begins with labeling his parents "killers"
and concludes with the prodigal son returning and reconciling himself to
family, home, and responsibility.[14] Chip is introduced, in fact, in a section
called "The Failure." When he returns home, Chip initially moves into his
parents' house to help care for his father who suffers from Parkinson's disease,
and the established bachelor eventually marries. His response and changed
demeanor after a near-death experience in Lithuania provide additional evidence of the novel's use of domestic sentiment — materialized in Chip's recognition of the Lambert home's spiritual geography. When Chip returns to St.
Jude for Christmas, he notes how the family house is "saturated with an aura
of belonging to the family. The house felt more like a body — softer, more
mortal and organic — than like a building."[15] In short, Chip turns his selfish,
anti-domestic life around, becoming a responsible caretaker. Like many of
the nineteenth-century heroines of American domestic fiction, Chip becomes
domesticated and establishes a home after a series of trials.

Likewise, artwork such as *Ron Ironing, Dallas, Texas, 1996* by Clarissa
Sligh, 'serious' novels such as Michael Cunningham's *A Home at the End of
the World* (1990), and 'popular' fiction such Michael Nava's mystery *Rag and
Bone* (2001) produce texts that explore domestic masculinity and challenge
the conventional gender dichotomies.[16] Domestic masculinity in these artistic forms especially heightens an awareness of "the 'unnatural' [that] might
lead to the denaturalization of gender as such" because conventional gender
roles consider masculinity already outside, unnatural, or foreign to domesticity.[17] Like these other transgressive texts, *The Corrections'* hybrid domestic
masculinity troubles or otherwise 'queers' conventional gender roles, spaces,
and readings, particularly as they relate to men and homemaking. The novel's
interrogation of heterosexual, white masculinity and high profile status as an
Oprah pick, furthermore, enhances the stakes. As the author of this transgressive novel, Franzen appears to be stuck between choosing a feminized
popularity or a masculine respect for both himself and his novel. He cannot
seem to carve out a successful hybrid identity.

Franzen's troubles in part emerge out of established cultural norms
invested in maintaining distinctions between masculinity and domesticity. For
example, emphasizing masculinity's aversions to domesticity, the derisive term
"cotquean," according to *The Oxford English Dictionary Online*, refers to "A
man that acts the housewife, that busies himself unduly or meddles with matters belonging to the housewife's province."[18] This term exists on a continuum with more vulgar slurs that insult masculinity through an association

with femininity (e.g., mama's boy, girlie-man, pussy, and sissy). The reverse frequently holds true as well: "we still believe that masculinity in girls and women is abhorrent and pathological."[19] Without a doubt, patriarchy depends on these terms and imbues them with gravity as a means to solidify gender hierarchy. The Franzen Affair demonstrates the remarkable power gender hierarchy maintains in twenty-first-century American culture. These instantiated anxieties of the feminine present one of the greatest challenges to any politics or text that seek to trouble gender hierarchies in the worlds within and beyond American fiction.

As I have begun to suggest, the Franzen Affair's public spectacle ironically reorders the textual, gendered boundaries that *The Corrections* blurs. While Franzen mixes gendered genres in *The Corrections*, his own and his critics' public remarks circulating around the Affair suggest the author and the public are less than comfortable with domestic masculinity. As Eva Illouz points out in regard to Oprah's Book Club, "The cultural objects that irritate taste and habits are the very ones that shed the brightest light on the hidden moral assumptions of the guardians of taste. Such cultural objects make explicit the tacit divisions and boundaries through which culture is classified and thrown into either the trash bin or the treasure chest."[20] In this case, feminine culture as represented in the *Oprah* show remains "trash."

Just what did Franzen say or imply that led Winfrey to call off her invitation and reporters and writers across genres and publishers to spill untold amounts of ink over the riff? One comment, told to *The Oregonian* and published on October 12, 2001, stated Franzen's displeasure over the Oprah book club logo: "I see this as my book, my creation, and I didn't want that logo of corporate ownership on it."[21] Franzen remarked three days later on the National Public Radio show "Fresh Air" "that 'more than one reader' had confided to him that they were 'put off by the fact that it is an Oprah pick.' In a typical backhanded compliment, he [Franzen] said of Oprah: 'She's picked some good books, but she's picked enough schmaltzy, one-dimensional ones that I cringe, myself."[22] Shortly after these remarks Oprah canceled Franzen's appearance. Winfrey disinvited Franzen on October 22, 2001.[23]

Newsweek caught up with Franzen shortly after the cancellation. Franzen explained his controversial remarks by positioning himself as a writer detached from mass culture: "'The Oprah Show,' like almost everything on TV, is not really quite real to me because I don't see it,' he said [referring to the fact that he does not own a television set]. 'I think if it had been more real to me I would have realized, 'Hey, watch what you're saying.'"[24] Franzen's explanation does not suggest he did not mean what he said about Oprah's Book Club, only that he did not realize he should have been more careful about what he said in public. By emphasizing that he does not own a television set, furthermore, Franzen distances himself from mass and popular American culture. Franzen's post-miff essay "Meet Me in St. Louis" (published in *The New Yorker* in December 2001) also attempted to diffuse and explain his criticism of *Oprah*.[25] The essay begins by emphasizing his Midwestern compulsion to please and the "so fundamentally bogus" filming he was required to participate in as part of the *Oprah* appearance.[26]

However, Franzen's 1996 *Harper's* essay, "Perchance to Dream" — which he revised and re-titled "Why Bother?" for his 2002 collection, *How to Be Alone* — provides the context for many reviewers' remarks and persistent questions about *The Corrections'* place within American literary history and culture. Franzen writes in the introduction to *How to Be Alone* that after the publication of *The Corrections*, "My interviewers were particularly interested in what they referred to as 'the *Harper's* essay.' ... Interviews typically began with the question: 'In your *Harper's* essay in 1996, you promised that your third book would be a big social novel that would engage with mainstream culture and rejuvenate American literature; do you think you've kept that promise with *The Corrections?*'"[27] The *Harper's* essay did set up *The Corrections* within the masculine tradition of the postmodern social novel that engages both high and low cultures, epitomized in works by authors such as Don DeLillo. Nevertheless, for his essay collection Franzen decided to revise the *Harper's* essay because he thought its argument was not clear and because he no longer agreed with the "very angry and theory-minded person" who wrote the essay "from this place of anger and despair, in a tone of high theoretical dudgeon that made me cringe a little now."[28]

What was once an ivory tower of escape from mass culture now is now a trap in the form of a "high theoretical dudgeon." Significantly, both his pretentious *Harper's* essay and his *Oprah* invitation made Franzen "cringe." Franzen's double-consciousness of high and low and masculine and feminine puts him at war with himself. His critics tend to agree. As Joanna Smith Rakoff points out in her profile of Franzen, "he embodies both the humble charm and earnestness of the Midwesterner and the haughty superiority of the New Yorker. And, I suppose, it's no surprise that such oppositions — which clearly coexist in Franzen himself— are at the heart of *The Corrections*."[29] Written prior to Franzen's selection as an Oprah book, Rakoff presents these contradictions as producing interesting tensions — both within the author himself and his work. After the *Oprah* blow-up, however, both Franzen and his critics cannot seem to envision his work or the author as both sentimental and intellectual. As I will explore in more detail shortly, Franzen's specific concerns arise not only out of an anxiety about the confusing of high and low cultures, but also from the ways Oprahfication specifically genders and races that blurring.

The fact that Franzen's snobbery played so large in the press indicates many do worry about what popular, feminized commercial success can do for and against a writer's long-term reputation, especially when that writer is white, heterosexual, and male.[30] They worry, in other words, about the impact of being domesticated. The critical response to the Franzen Affair demonstrates that Franzen's anxieties by no means represent an isolated or individual artistic quirk. For example, *Entertainment Weekly* writer Ty Burr reproduces distinctions between art and women's fiction in his commentary: "If some of Oprah's book choices tend to fall out of art and into earnest, womanly fiction, is it enough that she's getting people ready?"[31] According to Burr, "womanly fiction" is not "art" — however "earnest." Presumably, Oprah's Book Club may only prepare — get people ready — for more serious, manly fiction that can only exist outside *Oprah*'s sphere.

Even when writing for a popular magazine such as *Entertainment Weekly* critics like Burr constitute an old guard invested in maintaining high (masculine) and low (feminine) distinctions. While John Seabrook suggests "culture and marketing" merge at a zero point called "nobrow," he also recognizes that the publishing industry houses a last guard of "genteel tastemakers" who remain invested in the "old High-Low" hierarchy.[32] Seabrook also points out in relation to *The New Yorker* that we increasingly live in an age where what is popular is what constitutes what is good; consequently, these "genteel tastemakers" confront a new dilemma: "How do you let the Buzz into the place, in order to keep it vibrant and solvent, without undermining the institution's moral authority, which was at least partly based on keeping the Buzz out?"[33] What happens, in other words, when good literature turns popular?

Rather than reconciling popularity and quality, much literary and cultural criticism has responded by continuing to invest itself in their separation. If "quality, once the exclusive property of the few, has slowly and inexorably become available to the many," how do readers' determine a novel's literary worth?[34] Rather than developing new strategies or methods of evaluation, a vocal contingent responding to the Franzen case continues to suggest that the old means of determining literary worth are still the best. According to this formula, Winfrey and her ilk cannot read serious fiction. Where a novel may blur high/low and masculine/feminine and be praised for its postmodern blending, the trained critic/reader continues to examine sales as a key means to distinguish literature's genuine article from a cheap knock-off. If a lot of people are reading it (and especially if those readers are women), then the novel simply cannot be that good — or those readers certainly will not get the story's importance. These attitudes about *The Corrections'* selection as an *Oprah* book suggest little has changed since Nathaniel Hawthorne complained about "that damned mob of scribbling women," many of whom wrote popular domestic fiction in the nineteenth-century.[35]

Winfrey's debatable influence on an author or novel's cultural currency is further complicated by her impact on an author's hard currency. Oprah's Book Club economics stagger the mind. According to Jeff Jacoby, reporter for the *Boston Globe*, the *Oprah* endorsement "prompted Farrar, Straus & Giroux to increase their print run from 65,000 to 600,000.... The added sales, it is said, will swell Jonathan Franzen's royalties by more than $1.5 million."[36] *Entertainment Weekly* reported the *Oprah* announcement increased the print run from 90,000 to 800,000.[37] Whatever the exact numbers, an Oprah Book Club selection is a financial jackpot for writers and publishers.

Several commentaries on the Franzen affair considered this dilemma between high art status and a popular, commercially successful readership.[38] David Mehegan in the *Boston Globe* characterized Franzen's problem as something "many fiction writers, past and present" have grappled with: "He wants to be famous and sell a lot of books, but he also wants to be honored in his tribe. And he's not sure he can be both."[39] "Tribe" is an especially curious and apt word choice. "Tribe" implies elite white male writers without requiring Mehegan to spell out the specific gender and racial paradigm for his readers. Mehegan may also be subtly referring to Franzen's *Harper's* essay, "Perchance to Dream," where Franzen describes straight white men as a "tribe" "much more susceptible to technological addictions than women are."[40]

Thus we can begin to see that while much American postmodern fiction by white males may blur the boundaries between high and low cultures, the evaluation process remains invested in solidifying the separation between these classes and their gendered implications. For example, novelist Allan Gurganus goes so far as to suggest Franzen's selection as a National Book Award finalist would have been impacted if Winfrey had selected *The Corrections* earlier: "because you are not nominated for certain prizes if you have had huge critical success. It's not an unmixed blessing."[41] Joseph Epstein concurred in *Commentary*, taking the joining of high art and obscurity to the next level. Epstein praises Richard Russo's *Empire Falls* (2001) because, unlike Franzen's novel, neither Winfrey nor the National Book Award singled it out.[42]

The possibility of Oprahfication, thus, engenders a triple whammy: high sales, a the feminine domestic reader, and the possibility that the novel could be read not as story engaged in questioning the status quo (vis-à-vis the critique offered by the social novel) but as yet another *Oprah* novel (or sentimental woman's fiction) providing "Medicine for a Happier and Healthier World."[43] The conscious and unconscious acts by Franzen and various critics emphasize, as John Seabrook observes, how "people become more obsessed than ever with status" when "the old High-Low hierarchy" becomes blurred or absent.[44]

In the contemporary American fiction world, Oprah's Book Club emphasizes a text's feminine qualities, both in terms of content and readership. These
connotations are almost universally negative. For example, Philip Hensher,
writer for *The Spectator*, characterizes typical *Oprah* selections and the divi-
sive attitude toward her club: "[*Oprah* selections are] heartrending tales of
love prevailing over circumstances, kitch guff about the human spirit, epics
about hoeing in Wyoming and smutty reconstructions of the lives of strong
women during the American Civil War."[45] Eva Illouz's more positive analysis of Oprah's Book Club also emphasizes the club's feminine choices: "the
genre of novels chosen by Oprah is its [the detective novel's] feminine and
therapeutic counterpart."[46] These chick books, women's fiction, or, broadly
defined, domestic fictions, must be defined *against* not *with* Franzen's *The
Corrections*, lest the novel risk being taken outside the realm of serious (masculine) fiction.

Franzen's defenders also frequently emphasize that their critique of
Oprah's Book Club stems from the way books are read on the show, or Winfrey's emotional reading rubric. Janice Radway disagrees with this critique,
"She's criticized by high-art critics or even cultural-studies scholars, because
they say when she picks a book like *Beloved*, she's not looking at its aesthetic
complexity — she's making it sentimental, confessional. That seems like a
pointless criticism to me. When you write a book and put it out, that book
can be read in many ways by many different people."[47] Radway emphasizes
that Winfrey's method is one of many. Critics following a Frankfurt School
mentality emphasize the combination of Winfrey's popularity and power
makes her dangerous to literary studies — a threat that stems in part from her
popularization and possible dumbing down of literary critique. In this vein,
Thomas R. Edwards writing in the *Raritan* goes so far as to hint the book
club is a sham: "Oprah, or her panel of referees, pricked up their ears at the
sound of this one [*The Corrections*] even before they read it, assuming they
did."[48] He goes on to characterize the club's "prevailing taste" as "schmaltzy,"
"female," and "one-dimensional or at best middlebrow."[49] According to
Edwards, Winfrey's sentimental reading may be one of many but it is clearly
one of the worst. Significantly, Cecilia Konchar Farr argues in *Reading Oprah:
How Oprah's Book Club Changed the Way America Reads* that Winfrey's emotional reading rubric has been over-emphasized and over-simplified in the criticism. Countering such selective analysis of the Book Club's reading methods,
Farr demonstrates how Winfrey leads her readers through "all three modes —
reflective, empathic, and inspirational."[50] However, reviewers and critics rarely
address this point.

The harsh critiques of Winfrey's reading rubric and book club selections
help contextualize the "unseemly tinge" the *Oprah* logo represents to Franzen

and general readers who may feel uncomfortable reading or liking an *Oprah* pick, at least in the (masculine) public sphere. As John Young suggests, "The 'Oprah' editions are thus less 'authentic,' in Walter Benjamin's terms, than the first editions."[51] The *Oprah* sticker, like a movie-version book cover, produces texts less genuinely *Literature*. As a result, to retain status some readers may avoid *Oprah* picks or explain how they read a novel *before* it was an *Oprah* selection. Scott Stossel reports, "Several people I know refuse to read an Oprah-selected book — or if they do read it, they decline to read it in public — not out of principled objection to what Oprah is doing or what she represents (in fact, each of these people say, as Franzen did, that they admire and support what she does), but because they feel embarrassed to be publicly associated with an Oprah-selected book."[52] In fact, some readers went so far as to request editions of *The Corrections* without the *Oprah* sticker. Farr clarifies in *Reading Oprah*, "So when Farrar, Strauss put the Oprah seal into the cover art of Franzen's *The Corrections*, it became a different book. It became a mass-produced, popular choice rather than a marker of distinction and taste. And elite readers began to insist on unmarked covers."[53] Kathleen Rooney also reports in her study *Reading with Oprah: The Book Club That Changed America* how some readers went even further by establishing anti–*Oprah* book clubs.[54]

Why does this elitism expressed by the author, critics, and some of *The Corrections'* readers exist when Nobel Prize winning author Toni Morrison has appeared on the show several times? Farr reminds us, "For Americans, artistic standards come trailing shrouds of an aristocratic Western cultural tradition, where real art is supposed to be underappreciated, reserved for a discriminating few."[55] In this light, Franzen — unlike Toni Morrison — may be perceived to be "selling out" if he appears on *Oprah* because white male writers have not "historically been excluded from both the market and the canon."[56] Nevertheless, Franzen claims after his fallout with Winfrey that he did not have "any preconceptions about what kind of reader makes a good reader for my work,"[57] and he was hesitant to claim "the work I'm doing is simply better than [Michael] Crichton's."[58]

Tellingly, Franzen does not cite Toni Morrison in his remarks that attempt to reconcile himself with Winfrey and her supporters. While Michael Crichton has never appeared on Oprah's Book Club, Crichton seems to represent the club's supposed lowbrow popular taste. Interestingly, like the club's supposed reductive reading rubric, this low or middlebrow reputation persists despite the club's emphasis on "the transforming possibilities of serious fiction."[59] Moreover, Crichton's novels are not associated with women's fiction, a feminized readership, or an analysis of oppression — three commonly cited hallmarks of Winfrey's picks.[60] Franzen plays it safe and tries to deflect the racial and gendered implications by comparing his work with that of another white male author — at most Crichton and Franzen occupy distinctive literary class positions.

The Crichton comparison underscores Franzen's lack of confidence in Winfrey's ability to read his novel and his distress about what Cecilia Konchar Farr emphasizes as the club's social justice imperative — what Franzen disparages in "Why Bother?" as "The therapeutic optimism now raging in English literature departments [that] insists that novels be sorted into two boxes: Symptoms of Disease (canonical work from the Dark Ages before 1950) and medicine for a Happier and Healthier World (the work of women and of people from nonwhite or nonhetero cultures)."[61] Franzen suggests here that great literature is not political — at least in the social justice sense. As Farr points out, social justice novels "by and large, run counter to the traditional Western literary mainstream."[62] Franzen further emphasizes this aspect in his *Harper's* essay when he compares the lack of serious writing by white male writers to white flight. In this vision, "black, Hispanic, Asian, Native American, Gay, and women's communities" have moved into "the depressed inner city of serious works" left empty by the fled heterosexual white male writers.[63] Franzen's urban metaphor maintains strict cultural boundaries and reveals a nostalgia for a 'lost city' where white men primarily formed its vital core: "Little wonder that despite his yearning for novels to matter, Franzen couldn't see when they did, because a lively, inventive cultural center looked like a gutted inner city to his shortsighted gaze."[64] Franzen's *Harper's* essay, his initial remarks about the Oprah's Book Club, and his later backpedaling reveal more than mere idiosyncratic anxieties about race and gender. The critics, Franzen, and even many general readers seem to be saying that Franzen's novel should not be read within an African American and feminized context.

While not every critic unequivocally embraces Winfrey's productions or her unqualified model minority status, her body of work, nevertheless, connects *Oprah* and the Book Club to an African American heritage.[65] Winfrey's celebrity is associated with, as Sherryl Wilson points out, "an African American tradition of thought:" "by this I am referring to her mediation of African American cultural material through the promotion of black women writers in her book club, her key performances in the film versions of Alice Walker's *The Color Purple* and Toni Morrison's *Beloved*, Harpo's TV production of Gloria Naylor's *Women of Brewster Place* and her relationship with Maya Angelou who has referred to Winfrey as her 'prodigy.'"[66] To this list we can also add Harpo's TV 2005 production of Zora Neale Hurston's *Their Eyes Were Watching God* and the Oprah Winfrey Presents musical version of *The Color Purple*.[67] Wilson explains, "black feminism and African American thought in which self is constructed in relation to community and significant others" constitutes one of the show's important traditions.[68] R. Mark Hall also notes the book club's emphasis on literacy as a significant practice to achieve cultural uplift.[69] Winfrey, thus, blurs categories by her careful cultivation of "her success, wealth and celebrity — with all of the connotations of consumption and commercialism — whilst being simultaneously considered 'down home.'"[70] To insert Franzen into this context would mean that he would be out of his 'natural' cultural element — forced to participate in a discourse associated with both feminized consumer culture and African American rhetorical and cultural traditions. Rather than embrace this opportunity to cross or blur boundaries, Franzen balks and then Winfrey forecloses the possibility by canceling his appearance on the show.

Franzen eventually does clarify that he and Winfrey are on the same team: "Both Oprah and I want the same thing and believe the same thing, that the distinction between high and low is meaningless."[71] Franzen also did not turn up his nose at selling the film option for *The Corrections* and later appeared as a guest on the *Today Show*'s book club.[72] However, he does not go so far as to say that the distinction between masculine and feminine modes of reading are meaningless. His gestures after Winfrey's revoking of the invitation to appear on the show do not seriously address what made him different from any other author who has appeared. Examining the novel's marketing provides further insights into how masculinity circulates and why Franzen distanced himself from Oprah's Book Club.

Marketing Masculine Domesticity: Gendered Genres, Authors, and Audiences

Marketing plays a key role in a novel's status and gender identity as well as an author's own celebrity and status. Good writers, notably, rarely fight for the label of women's fiction — despite the fact that women comprise the largest market share of book buyers.[73] As our examination of the reviews has shown, authors and readers who covet women's fiction are read as commercial rather than serious writers/readers. The critics' remarks demonstrate that part of the politics of literary greatness is what gets labeled and read as women's fiction. Authors seemingly trade seriousness for popularity in the marketplace. Publishers make conscious marketing decisions to assure serious and popular fictions find their respective audiences.

How books are marketed logically plays a significant role in the author and text's reception by both critics and the general public. Connie Lauerman's article "He Reads, She Reads" explores the role book marketing, including book jackets, play in the gendering of genres.[74] From her and other's research we can begin to see how gendered genres and gendered readerships result from a combination of marketing, literary tradition, and cultural notions about gender identity and behavior. For example, Janet Maslin's "Moms Read with Heart, Dads with a Firm Jaw" also underscores the relationship between book marketing and gender by examining the stereotypically gendered releases for Mother's and Father's Day.[75] Jessica Jernigan's "Slingbacks and Arrows: Chick Lit Comes of Age" explains that self-consciously "girlie-fiction" uses cover art to identify itself to its readership: "the retro cover iconography is a playful nod to such girly classics as *Gentlemen Prefer Blonds* and *Valley of the Dolls*."[76] The release dates and use of cover art help shape who reads particular books and how books are read.

Cover art may be the most powerful extra-literary shaper of a text's gendered identity. One women's genre, what Deborah Phillips calls the "aga-saga," uses prudently chosen cover art to signify to its readers that this is, indeed, chick lit: "The Aga-Saga can be immediately known by its cover: invariably white, with a tasteful watercolour illustration of the kind recognizable from greeting cards. These usually depict a domestic still life, a kitchen empty of people apart from a carefully strewn hat, bouquet or vase of flowers. Sometimes a lone woman is part of the scene, wrapped in a novel or a shawl, or she may be located out of doors, gazing at a picturesque landscape."[77] Both Philips and Jernigan's essays suggest that novels that wish to appeal to women or announce their femininity frequently do so by reproducing stereotypical feminine iconography. Their analysis also suggestions that these books help others perform their femininity through the consumption of these texts. These books tend to affirm a fairly limited notion of femininity — whether the reader consumes them straight or as a queer guilty pleasure.

Given the above graphic signifiers of chick lit, we can turn to Franzen's cover to investigate the extent to which it draws from these publishing industry standards and techniques for marking and marketing women's fiction. The publishing industry carefully announces *The Corrections'* domestic masculinity in the novel's cover art. Notably, there are very few changes between the cover art for the *Oprah* and regular editions and between the soft and hard cover editions of *The Corrections*. The *Oprah* cover has a small "Oprah's Book Club" logo while the others do not. All editions anticipate or use Franzen's name recognition by prominently placing his name in large letters at the top, taking nearly half of the cover space. Even when the cover alters to include information regarding the novel's National Book Award, Franzen's name remains the prominent aspect of the cover art and design. Franzen's name size and position signifies his literary promise if not prominence: this is a name to know.

The cover's lower half includes a picture of a 1950-ish white, upper-middle class family dinner scene, with a small blonde boy featured in the left corner. At the beautifully set table we see a woman's hands presenting a perfectly cooked turkey and an older brother in a bright red jacket. The younger brother's petulant look provides the ironic commentary on the otherwise idyllic scene of the carefully presented table. The prominence of Franzen's name and the prudently featured petulant boy in the picture deftly signify the author's status as a writer and the text's use of the anti-domestic tradition. The family scene also seems to hail — through the use of the stereotypical symbols of family and food — the women who like to purchase and read chick lit. The cover art presents a shrewd combination of domestic and masculine codes.

The cover art for *The Corrections* is especially interesting given that even a cursory survey of the literature written during and after the Franzen Affair suggests hybrid domestic novels, particularly ones written by men, must pass as masculine to be accepted as high art. *New York Times Book Review* writer Margo Jefferson goes so far as to suggest Franzen "was worried that Oprah's audience would alienate male readers."[78] Referencing Ann Douglas's argument about the "feminization of American culture," Jefferson suggests the corollary to Douglas' argument "is the notion that any man who wants his work recognized, and marketed as the Great American Novel, must shun the taint of the feminine."[79] Jefferson agrees here with Nina Baym and Judith Fetterley's respective critiques of "beset manhood" and the construction of the American literary canon.[80] While many writers, critics, and reviewers comment on the elitism embedded in the Franzen Affair, few connect this hierarchy to sexism. Jefferson characterizes the Affair as a "fable about the literary class system today, with all its anxiety-ridden contradictions."[81] She implies but never directly deploys the term sexism and its relation to the "literary class system." However, clearly there is more at work than a simple division between high and low cultures. These cultures remain distinctly gendered entities, particularly in the literary canon.

A recent study of *The New York Times Book Review* conducted by Paula Caplan and Mary Ann Palko provides more compelling evidence of the continued gender bias within American literary hierarchy. Cynthia Cotts of *The Village Voice* reports the Brown University study examined *The New York Times Book Review* for a one year period (from 2002 to 2003) and found "72 percent of all books reviewed in the *NYTBR* were written by men, and 66 percent of all reviews also carried a male byline. In other words, the most influential venue in the publishing world showcases male authors and reviewers by an average of two to one."[82] Like Franzen's remarks, the *NYTBR*'s bias is not idiosyncratic but rather revealing of an institutionalized sexism. While more representation by women authors and reviewers would not necessarily solve institutional sexism, it would help address a literary hierarchy already biased toward men.

Femininity and the Oprahfication of the publishing industry is also apparently not just a dilemma for white male fiction writers like Franzen. William C. Dowling's article, "Saving Scholarly Publishing in the Age of Oprah: The Glastonbury Project" laments "the drying up of resources for 'intensive studies of small but worthwhile subjects' in favour of trend-driven publishing, today even by some leading university presses, on subjects formerly associated with punk rock lyrics, supermarket tabloids, or the Oprah Winfrey show."[83] Erica Rand's *Barbie's Queer Accessories* epitomizes Dowling's critique of the popular cultural turn in monograph publishing. Dowling's choice to examine the recently "expanded section on Gender and Cultural Studies" during a trip to "Micawber Books, our most dependable local purveyor of 'serious' titles" results in the discovery of Rand's book.[84] According to Dowling, *Barbie's Queer Accessories* sounds the death-knell of the "traditional scholarly monograph:" such books are "driving out of existence a more 'traditional' sort of scholarly publication."[85] Thus, an Oprahfication or the "quasi-autobiographical mode that has become the trademark of so much writing in cultural studies" and a turn toward the popular (gender, queer studies) rather than the traditional (serious scholarship) threatens scholarly publishing and writing as well as fiction writing.[86] Once again topics associated with femininity and social justice get disparaged and distinguished from more so-called serious topics and approaches.

Such anxious eruptions about Oprahfication cross scholarly, popular, and literary divides, providing examples and reminders of how American masculinity frequently depends upon the violent repression of the feminine and the personal. Franzen and the critics' rhetorical violations of Winfrey's intellectual integrity comprise another part of this patriarchal logic. In this case, Winfrey's race, her gender, and her status as a popular (i.e., not intellectual) television host make her a prime target for Franzen and his supporters to reassert a (white) patriarchal hierarchy for literary taste and a highly conservative and conventional understanding of American masculinity.

While not directly related to Winfrey, Arnold Schwarzenegger's remarks at the 2004 Republican National Convention further remind us that when the stakes are high, the call goes out for a man's man and not a girlie-man. We allegedly want someone hard not soft or sensitive — girlie — to run our country, especially when that person must deal with terrorists and war. In the public sphere, sensitivity and sentiment apparently code the opposite of strength and authority. In the frank words of Katha Pollitt, columnist for *The Nation*, "Republicans are real men. Democrats are gay. President Bush is a resolute he-man who will keep us safe from terrorists; Sen. John Kerry is a flip-flopper who wants to take a more 'sensitive' approach to the war on terror and who, as Vice President Dick Cheney, sneered, seems to think, 'Al Qaeda will be impressed with our softer side.'"[87] Pollitt goes on to say, "At this rate, we won't have a woman president until 3000, and she'll have to be a five-star general."[88] While literary critics have certainly elected a broader range of authors and texts to its exclusive literary prizes and the canon, the Franzen case reminds us of the continued strong presence of gender hierarchies (not to mention race and high/low class gradations) within American culture. The overlap between contemporary American political and literary cultures underscores the diffuse and deeply embedded patriarchal understanding of American masculinity.

In Franzen's case, re-establishing his authorial masculinity — correcting his novel's status as a book that would *not* appear on *Oprah*— stabilizes cultural norms about the difference between high and low art forms as well as masculine and feminine aesthetics and taste. Franzen's case underscores "gender is an identity tenuously constituted in time, instituted in an exterior space through a stylized repetition of acts" and that these "tenuous acts" carry significant stabilizing power.[89] The case also preserves Franzen's white (heterosexual) masculinity from any taint of (African American) feminization. As querying American masculinity seemingly demands queering it, Franzen must assume a tough guise against popularity or feminine culture to straighten out his place in the literary canon. Thus, even as fictions break apart gendered binaries, real authors and critics frequently correct any confusion and re-establish clear gender differences. As William P. Murphy, an anthropology and African studies professor at Northwestern University, laments, "Missing in our political culture is a broader language recognizing the ideals, efforts, and quieter forms of heroism."[90] The Franzen-Oprah case, especially within the context of American masculinity, demonstrates that such failures are not the exclusive problems of the national political sphere; we still frequently fail to attain this goal in our literary and cultural analysis of texts with consistency. In the aftermath of the scandal, for example, Franzen ponders whether he is a "social novelist" or "an old-fashioned domestic novelist" rather than framing his role along gender-bending terms. Likewise, we frequently continue to evaluate novels, to construct American literary history, and even elect our Presidents along strictly constructed notions of masculinity.

The Aftermath: American Masculinity and the Oprahfication of Literary Greatness

The conclusions drawn thus far seem to affirm that the more white masculinity changes vis-à-vis postmodernism and the blurring of genders and genres, the more it remains the same. While some postmodern literary and cultural criticism presumes the death of the author, the Franzen-Oprah case provides a telling moment where the author is very much alive and gender and racial identities become solidified — reterritorialized in the Deluzian sense — rather than sliding across a scale of more fluid possibilities.[91] As Halberstam remarks, "the battered white male boxer [in America cinema] ... is not unlike the structure of white male masculinity, which seems impervious to criticism or attack and maintains hegemonic sway despite all challenges to its power."[92] American literary and political cultures ultimately suggest American masculinity has successfully resisted hybridization.

The Corrections performs domestic masculinity; however, it circulates generically within a much stricter classification system. In order to maintain literary and cultural hierarchies still largely defined according to gender difference, The Corrections' mixed genres or domestic masculinity must be firmly re-contained or repositioned within (white) masculinity — especially, perhaps, where a white male author and a popular audience of predominately female readers are concerned. A failure to do so would threaten the author's (and novel's) capacity for literary greatness, a category still conservatively defined via an aesthetic and content associated with an elite white male experience. As a result, rather than suggest a post-gender or post-feminist world, Franzen's particular "gender trouble" with his novel The Corrections provides a case study in the complicated etiquette required for negotiating and maintaining patriarchal structures, especially as they relate to gender difference and conceptions of masculinity, within American communities where gender and status matters.[93] Furthermore, these strictures not only continue to define literary greatness but the very leadership qualities necessary for political success in the twenty-first century.

The Franzen Affair helps us understand why American white male authorship — particularly when faced with the highly charged feminine spectacle of Oprahfication — does not permit textual hybridity to continue unchecked. Franzen's critique of Oprah's "corporate logo" and his disquiet about the wide range of texts canonized by Winfrey serve, at least in part, to locate his literary talent in high art, allegedly beyond or outside corporate sponsorship. Franzen emphasizes, "I feel as if I'm not the first writer to have experienced some minor discomfort over the selection. I'm just the first one who was unwise and insensitive enough to mention some of that discomfort in public."[94] Franzen's and his critics' rhetorical gymnastics reveal the gender and race performance cues that demand Franzen speak out to distance himself and his novel from Winfrey's brand of chick lit.

While such living legends as Maya Angelou and Nobel prize winning author Toni Morrison appeared on Oprah several times, their appearances did not challenge the literary and gendered hierarchies in the same ways that Franzen's selection threatened to do. In the words of Henry Louis Gates in *Loose Canons*, "Thomas Pynchon. Now there was someone you never saw on 'Oprah Winfrey.'"[95] While the reclusive Pynchon is not seen anywhere, let alone on *Oprah*, we can extend Gates' joke to encompass great white male authors generally.[96] As a 2001 interview in *Poets & Writers* points out, Franzen initially cultivated this isolation and modeled his author identity on DeLillo, Pynchon, and Gaddis.[97] These authors remain above, outside, or beyond the fray. After the Affair Franzen reinvents this author identity and, according to James Wolcott, accomplishes "a symbol act of parricide."[98] In a 2002 *New Yorker* article about William Gaddis' fiction, "Mr. Difficult," Franzen distances himself from this elite group. In fact, he describes himself as "paralyzed" because he wishes to write books that are both excellent and good reads.[99] Whether we see Franzen as "a pious opportunist" or a truly reformed elitist, his struggle between difficulty and a good read has larger symbolic significance for contemporary American masculinity and authorship.[100]

Significantly, the Book Club also changed shortly after the Affair. Winfrey took a break from the Book Club not long after her problems with Franzen. The original Oprah Book Club began in 1996 and ran through 2002. The Book Club returned in February 2003 but with a change: the club now features 'great' works of literature. When Winfrey brought the book club back after the hiatus, she began selecting literary masterpieces like John Steinbeck's *East of Eden*, Alan Paton's *Cry, The Beloved Country*, and Gabriel García Márquez's *One Hundred Years of Solitude*; the summer 2005 reading was a trilogy of Faulkner novels. The book club's shift to greatness took author appearances out of the show's format, affirming established notions that great writers — authors of *Literature* — do not appear on television. Now literary critics assist Winfrey with leading readers/viewers through these great works. As a result, not only does Winfrey no longer have to deal with temperamental authors, but she may also be building her own literary credibility, if only in the popular sphere, through such classic and more frequently male-authored texts. Notably, from 1996 to 2002 only ten out of forty-three authors were men. Since the turn to great works, men wrote eight out of the ten club picks between 2003 and April of 2007. Winfrey's selections now follow the same male dominated trends seen in the *New York Times Book Review*.

We may understand Winfrey's reterritorialization of great literature as an effect and response to the Franzen Affair. While the redesigned club does not necessarily challenge what constitutes the literary canon, it does continue to transfer the power of cultural and literary analysis beyond the control of high (academic, elite) culture — effectively mixing high art with what generally gets characterized as a low forum for literary analysis. Like John Ersk-

ine's great books curriculum at Columbia during the 1920s, Winfrey's rein-
vented book club opens great works and access to literary critics to the masses,
which produces paradoxical effects.[101] That is, the redesigned club both challenges and affirms the cultural elitism upon which conventional American
masculinity depends.

Joan Shelley Rubin explanation of Erskine's "recasting of the classics"
speaks directly to the book club's redesigned format:

> His recasting of the classics as recent publications fed the very "cult of the
> contemporary" he intended his advocacy of tradition to combat; the conno-
> tations of "great" undermined his attack on the proclivity of the modern
> magazine to be "a medium not for literature but for advertising," buying "rep-
> utations rather than writings." He also deplored the "journalistic tendency"
> in current books. Yet, despite his intentions, the headline introducing Ersk-
> ine's *Delineator* articles revealed how susceptible his stance was to a radical
> revaluation of the nature and object of reading the classics. The banner pro-
> claimed "There's Fun in Famous Books." This was a kind of literary "inva-
> sion of the body snatchers," in which the spirit of consumer culture
> appropriated the soul of the Arnoldian aesthetic, leaving only its outward
> form intact.[102]

Oprah's Book Club does not share Erskine's anxiety about consumer
culture — to the contrary, the club embraces consumer culture. Nevertheless,
Erskine's banner proclaiming the "fun" in classic books works just as well for
Winfrey's reincarnated book club.

Winfrey's great books project also tempts the same dangerous elitism and
conservatism frequently associated with middlebrow politics: "Erskine's innovation signaled a return to a less egalitarian policy: a fixed syllabus, handed
down by the faculty and recommended for everyone regardless of aptitude,
background, or vocational plans — to say nothing of gender, race, class, or
ethnicity."[103] With the current emphasis on male writers Winfrey's reading
list also arguably reproduces a "fixed syllabus" of literary greatness; however,
Kathleen Rooney points out that the club's "catholic taste, its ability to look
beyond the automatically accepted 'classic' of the Western canon, and its willingness to distribute critical authority among all its participants" sets the club
apart from other great works projects.[104]

Whether or not the Oprahfication of literary greatness will alter the core
of American masculinity that depends on, as Stephen Ducat argues in his book
*The Wimp Factor: Gender Gaps, Holy Wars, and the Politics of Anxious Masculin-
ity*, a deeply flawed notion of masculinity remains to be seen.[105] As we watch
and even participate in the next *Oprah* effect, we would do well to keep Jane
Elliott's words of caution in mind: "but if the tide is really turning, it may
soon be possible to borrow that form [domestic fiction] but leave its baggage
behind. If gendered literary standards persist, the family-saga novel may be

reborn as a highbrow form, while the women's literary culture that developed it remains as stigmatized as ever."[106] The Franzen Affair and its aftermath underscore that in order to address women's, nonwhite, and homosexual stigmatization within American culture we need to reinvent conventional American masculinity in ways that better incorporate and value domesticity as well as other traditionally feminine practices and forms. Novels such as *The Corrections* are engaged in crafting alternative narratives to American masculinity's conventional "melodramas of beset manhood."[107] Significantly, however, art does not mirror life in this case. The Franzen Affair's high-profile public mediation of masculinity, domesticity, and authorship combined with the author's resulting gender and status troubled anxieties suggest that 'real' white, heterosexual masculinity, arguably the dominant model for American masculinity, remains unchanged at its core. In practice, patriarchal masculinity predominantly persists uncorrected.

Notes

1. Lorraine Adams, "Literary Life Without Oprah," *The Washington Post*, 19 November 2002, sec. C, p. 1.
2. Benjamin Svetkey, "Domestic Drama," *Entertainment Weekly*, 14 September 2001, 85.
3. Jesse Berrett, "Family Man," *The Village Voice* 46, no. 38, 25 September 2001, 72.
4. *Publisher's Weekly* referred to the flap as "Oprahgate."
5. Fredric Jameson, *Postmodernism, or, The Cultural Logic of Late Capitalism* (London: Verso, 1991), 318.
6. Linda McDowell, "Spatializing Feminism," in *BodySpace: Destabilizing Geographies of Gender and Sexuality*, ed. Nancy Duncan (New York: Routledge, 1996), 41.
7. Homi K. Bhaba, "Signs Taken for Wonders: Questions of Ambivalence and Authority Under a Tree Outside Delhi, May 1817," in *"Race," Writing, and Difference*, ed. Henry Louis Gates Jr. and Anthony Appiah (Chicago: University of Chicago Press, 1986), 174.
8. Milette Shamir, "Divided Plots: Interior Space and Gender Difference in Domestic Fiction," *Genre* 29, no. 4 (Winter 1996): 431.
9. Butler defines "trouble" as "inevitable, and the task, how best to make it, what best way to be in it." Judith Butler, *Gender Trouble* (New York: Routledge, 1990), vii.
10. *Ibid.*, viii.
11. Nina Baym, "Melodramas of Beset Manhood: How Theories of American Fiction Exclude Women Authors," *American Quarterly* 33, no. 2 (Summer 1981): 123–139.
12. *Ibid.*, 133.
13. Peggy Cooper Davis and Carol Gilligan, "Reconstructing Law and Marriage," *The Good Society* 11, no. 3 (2002): 58.
14. Jonathan Franzen, *The Corrections* (New York: Farrar, Straus and Giroux, 2001), 15.
15. *Ibid.*, 541.
16. My larger project that examines late twentieth-century domestic fictions written

by and about both men and women, *Domestic Geographies*, analyzes these literary examples of domestic masculinity in greater detail.

C.f. Clarissa Sligh, *Ron Ironing, Dallas, Texas, 1996*; accessed 25 May 2004; available from http://www.clarissasligh.com/HTML/LW_THE%MEN_1.html; Michael Cunningham, *A Home at the End of the World* (New York: Picador USA, 1990); Michael Nava, *Rag and Bone* (2001. New York: Berkley Prime Crime, 2002).

17. Butler, 149.

18. "Cotquean," Def. 3, *The Oxford English Dictionary Online* 2nd ed. (1989, accessed 19 May 2004); available from http://dictionary.oed.com; Internet.

19. Judith Halberstam, *Female Masculinity* (Durham, NC: Duke University Press, 1998), 268.

20. Eva Illouz, *Oprah Winfrey and the Glamour of Misery* (New York: Columbia University Press, 2003), 4.

21. Franzen, qtd. in Jeff Baker, "Oprah's Stamp of Approval Rubs Writer in Conflicted Ways," *The Oregonian* 12 October 2001, sec. Arts and Leisure, p. 5.

22. Jeff Jacoby, "Too Good for Oprah," *Boston Globe*, 1 November 2001, sec. A, p. 19.

23. *The Complete Review*'s "A Book, an Author, and a Talk Show Host: Some Notes on the Oprah-Franzen Debacle" has a detailed outline of the unfolding events and links to publication materials: http://www.complete-review.com/quarterly/vol3/issue1/oprah.htm.

24. Franzen, qtd. in Jeff Giles, "Errors and 'Corrections,'" *Newsweek* 138, no. 19, 5 November 2001, 68.

25. Jonathan Franzen, "Meet Me in St. Louis," *The New Yorker* 77, no. 44 (December 24–31, 2001): 70.

26. *Ibid.*

27. Jonathan Franzen, *How to Be Alone* (New York: Farrar, Straus and Giroux, 2002), 3.

28. *Ibid.*, 4–5.

29. Joanna Smith Rakoff, "Making *The Corrections*: An Interview with Jonathan Franzen," *Poets & Writers* (September/October 2001): 27.

30. The chick lit community is very aware of its status and the Franzen Affair. (Thank you to April Kent at New Mexico Highlands University for making me aware of this fact.) For example, Candace Bushnell's *Trading Up* (New York: Hyperion, 2003) lampoons Franzen's snobbery through the character Craig Edgers, author of *The Embarrassments* (C.f. pages 187–188; 192; 202–204). Another popular chick lit author, Plum Sykes, takes a quick jab at Franzen in *Bergdorf Blondes* (New York: Hyperion, 2004) (C.f. page 208).

31. Ty Burr, "A Smart Writer's Dumb Move," *Entertainment Weekly*, 16 November 2001, 167.

32. John Seabrook, *Nobrow: The Culture of Marketing, the Marketing of Culture* (2000. New York: Vintage, 2001), 199.

33. *Ibid.*, 64.

34. *Ibid.*, 166.

35. Nathaniel Hawthorne, "To William D. Ticknor" (19 January 1855) In *The Centenary Edition of the Works of Nathaniel Hawthorne*, Vol. XVII, eds. William Charvat, Roy Harvey Pearce, and Claude M. Simpson (Columbus: Ohio State University Press, 1962), 304.

36. Jacoby, A19.

37. Burr, 167.

38. See James Wood, "It's Not Tolstoy, but It Does Belong to High Literature," *The Guardian*, 9 November 2001, 3, and David Mehegan, "Franzen Not Alone in Oprah Dilemma," *Boston Globe*, 10 November 2001, sec. F, p. 1.

39. Mehegan, sec. F, p. 1.

40. Jonathan Franzen, "Perchance to Dream: In the Age of Images, a Reason to Write Novels," *Harper's Magazine* 292, no. 1751 (April 1996): 52.

41. Gurganus, qtd. in Mehegan, sec. F, p. 1.

42. *Empire Falls* did win the Pulitzer Prize — an award granted after the publication of Epstein's article. Joseph Epstein, "Surfing the Novel" *Commentary* (January 2002): 37.

43. Jonathan Franzen, "Why Bother?" *How to Be Alone* (New York: Farrar, Straus and Giroux, 2002), 79.

44. Seabrook, 168.

45. Philip Hensher, "Writing Beyond His Means," *The Spectator* (24 November 2001): 44.

46. Illouz, 167.

47. Radway, qtd. in "A Novelist, a Talk-Show Host, and Literature High and Low," *The Chronicle of Higher Education*, 48, no. 14, 30 November 2001, sec. B, p. 4.

48. Thomas R. Edwards, "Oprah's Choice," *Raritan* 21, no. 4 (Spring 2002): 78.

49. *Ibid.*, 78.

50. Cecilia Konchar Farr, *Reading Oprah: How Oprah's Book Club Changed the Way America Reads* (Albany: State University of New York Press, 2005), 50.

51. John Young, "Toni Morrison, Oprah Winfrey, and Postmodern Popular Audiences," *African American Review*, no. 35.2 (2001): 182.

52. Scott Stossel, "Elitism for Everyone," *The Atlantic Online*; accessed 29 November 2001; available from http://www.theatlantic.com/unbound/polipro/pp2001-11-29htm; Internet.

53. Farr, 88.

54. Kathleen Rooney, *Reading with Oprah: The Book Club That Changed America* (Fayetteville: University of Arkansas Press, 2005). C.f. chapter two.

55. Farr, 80.

56. Young, 185.

57. Franzen, qtd. in Giles, 69.

58. Franzen, qtd. in Wood, 3

59. R. Mark Hall, "The 'Oprahfication' of Literacy: Reading 'Oprah's Book Club,'" *College English* 65, no. 6 (July 2003): 655.

60. My remarks should not imply that Crichton's novels are apolitical. His recent novel, *State of Fear*, for example, engages in the debate about global warming.

61. Franzen, "Why Bother?" 78–79.

62. Farr, 32.

63. Franzen, "Perchance to Dream," 39. A slightly revised vision appears in "Why Bother?" C.f. Franzen, "Why Bother?" 62.

64. Farr, 97.

65. R. Mark Hall, for example, suggests the Book Club "supports traditional female identities. In short, even as Winfrey frames reading in terms of female empowerment, 'Oprah's Book Club' depends upon fundamentally conservative forces in the history of literacy sponsorship for women in this country" (Hall 661). Paul Street's essay "The Full Blown 'Oprah' Effect: Reflections on Color, Class and New Age Racism" provides a representative analysis of Winfrey's celebrity and what it represents to black and white American communities. Paul Street, "The Full Blown 'Oprah' Effect: Reflections on Color, Class and New Age Racism," *The Black Commentator* 127; accessed 24 Feb 2005; available from http://www.blackcommentator.com/127/127_oprah.html; Internet.

66. Sherryl Wilson, *Oprah, Celebrity and Formations of Self* (New York: Palgrave, 2003), 180; 72.

67. The musical version of *The Color Purple* opened at the Broadway Theatre on December 1, 2005.

68. *Ibid.*, 94.

69. Hall, 655.

70. Wilson, 157.

71. Franzen, qtd. in Epstein, 34.

72. Producer Scott Rudin optioned *The Corrections* and screenwriter David Hare is writing the screenplay. Hare also wrote *The Hours'* screenplay for Rudin. See Karen Valby, "Correction Dept," *Entertainment Weekly*, 25 October 2002, 23.

73. Connie Lauerman explains "Ipsos BookTrends reports that a whopping 81% of books are purchased for women but cautions that this figure may be somewhat skewed because the household diaries it uses to gather data tend to be filled out by women." Connie Lauerman, "He Reads, She Reads: Do Choices Speak Volumes? What Men and Women Read Does Tend to Differ, But Some Readers and Writers Chafe at Labels Such as 'Women's Books,'" *The Los Angeles Times*, 26 Nov 2001, sec. E, p. 3.

74. Lauerman, E3.

75. Janet Maslin, "Moms Read with Heart, Dads with a Firm Jaw," *New York Times*, 7 May 2004, sec. E2, p. 33.

76. Jessica Jernigan's "Slingbacks and Arrows: Chick Lit Comes of Age," *Bitch* 25 (Summer 2004): 70.

77. Deborah Phillips, "Keeping the Home Fires Burning: The Myth of the Independent Woman in the Aga-Saga," *Women: A Cultural Review* 7, no. 1 (1996): 48.

78. Margo Jefferson, "There Goes the Neighborhood," *New York Times Book Review*, 25 November 2001, 35. Thomas R. Edwards makes the same inference. See Edwards, 78.

79. Jefferson, 35. C.f. Connie Lauerman's article "He Reads, She Reads: Do Choices Speak Volumes?"

80. C.f. Nina Baym's "Melodramas of Best Manhood: How Theories of American Fiction Exclude Women Authors" and Judith Fetterley's "'Not in the Least American': Nineteenth-Century Literary Regionalism," *College English* 56 (1994): 877–95.

81. Jefferson, 35.

82. Cynthia Cotts, "Boy, Girl, Boy: Sexism at *The NYT Book Review?*" *The Village Voice*, 7–13 January 2004, 25.

83. William C. Dowling, "Saving Scholarly Publishing in the Age of Oprah: The Glastonbury Project" *Journal of Scholarly Publishing* (April 1997): 115.

84. *Ibid.*, 116.

85. *Ibid.*, 118.

86. *Ibid.*, 116.

87. Katha Pollitt, "Girlie Vote," *Chicago Tribune*, 15 September 2004, 25.

88. *Ibid.*, 25. Various newspaper and magazine articles provide an analysis of the gender politics involved in Hillary Clinton's failed bid for the 2008 Democratic nomination that update Pollitt's 2004 analysis. One of the most prominent and controversial articles was Gloria Steinem's *New York Times* op-ed piece, "Women Are Never Front-Runners." Longer scholarly articles are certainly forthcoming.

89. Butler, 140.

90. William P. Murphy, "Worldview Takes a Verbal Beating in Political Rhetoric," *Chicago Tribune*, 19 September 2004, 5.

91. C.f. Gilles Deleuze and Félix Guattari, "What is a Minor Literature?" In *Kafka: Toward a Minor Literature*, Trans. Dana Polan (Minneapolis: University of Minnesota Press, 1986): 16–27.

92. Halberstam, 275.

93. By suggesting "gender matters" I am invoking Butler's work, *Bodies That Matter: On the Discursive Limits of "Sex"* (New York: Routledge, 1993).

94. Franzen qtd. in Giles, 68.

95. Gates, 15.

96. In the satirically lowbrow mystery Henry Louis Gates uses to introduce *Loose Canons*, Thomas Pynchon wants out — out of the mafia-like canon. And when Pynchon succeeds at the conclusion of Gates' introduction, he presumably could appear on the show — except now, of course, Oprah's Book Club is invested in the canon.

97. Rakoff, 28.

98. James Wolcott, "Advertisements for Himself," *The New Republic* 227, no. 23–24 (2–9 December 2002): 36–40.

99. Jonathan Franzen, "Mr. Difficult: William Gaddis and the Problem of Hard-to-Read Books," *The New Yorker* (30 September 2002): 100–11.

100. Wolcott, 36–40.

101. See Joan Shelley Rubin's *The Making of Middlebrow Culture* (Chapel Hill: University of North Carolina Press, 1992) for a discussion of Erskine.

102. *Ibid.*, 175–176.

103. *Ibid.*, 176.

104. Rooney, 200.

105. Stephen Ducat, *The Wimp Factor: Gender Gaps, Holy Wars, and the Politics of Anxious Masculinity* (Boston: Beacon, 2004).

106. Jane Elliott, "O Is for the Other Things She Gave Me: Jonathan Franzen's *The Corrections* and Contemporary Women's Fiction," *Bitch* 16 (Spring 2002), 74.

107. C.f. Baym, "Melodramas of Best Manhood: How Theories of American Fiction Exclude Women Authors." In addition to Franzen's *The Corrections*, Michael Nava's *Rag and Bone*, and Michael Cunningham's novels, other significant American novels engaged in the revaluing of American masculinity and domesticity include Change-rea Lee's *A Gesture Life* (1999) and Anne Tyler's *Saint Maybe* (1991).

Bibliography

Adams, Lorraine. "Literary Life Without Oprah." *The Washington Post* 19 November 2002, sec. C, p. 1.

Baker, Jeff. "Oprah's Stamp of Approval Rubs Writer in Conflicted Ways." *The Oregonian* 12 October 2001, sec. Arts and Leisure, p. 5.

Baym, Nina. "Melodramas of Beset Manhood: How Theories of American Fiction Exclude Women Authors." *American Quarterly* 33, no. 2 (Summer 1981): 123–139.

Berrett, Jesse. "Family Man." *The Village Voice* 46, no. 38, 25 September 2001, 72.

Bhabha, Homi K. "Signs Taken for Wonders: Questions of Ambivalence and Authority Under a Tree Outside Delhi, May 1817." In *"Race,"Writing, and Difference*, ed. Henry Louis Gates Jr. and Anthony Appiah, 163–184. Chicago: University of Chicago Press, 1986.

"A Book, an Author, and a Talk Show Host: Some Notes on the Oprah-Franzen Debacle" *The Complete Review: A Literary Saloon & Site of Review.* 3.1 (February 2002) accessed 18 August 2008; available from http://www.complete-review.com/quarterly/vol3/issue1/oprah.htm

Burr, Ty. "A Smart Writer's Dumb Move." *Entertainment Weekly*, 16 November 2001, 167.

Bushnell, Candace. *Trading Up*. New York: Hyperion, 2003.

Butler, Judith. *Bodies That Matter: On the Discursive Limits of "Sex."* New York: Routledge, 1993.

_____. *Gender Trouble*. New York: Routledge, 1990.

"Cotquean." Def. 3. *The Oxford English Dictionary Online* 2nd ed. 1989, accessed 19 May 2004; available from http://dictionary.oed.com

Cotts, Cynthia. "Boy, Girl, Boy: Sexism at *The NYT Book Review?*" *The Village Voice*, 7–13 January 2004, 25.

Cunningham, Michael. *A Home at the End of the World*. New York: Picador, 1990.

Davis, Peggy Cooper, and Carol Gilligan. "Reconstructing Law and Marriage." *The Good Society* 11, no. 3 (2002): 57–67.

Deleuze, Gilles, and Félix Guattari. "What Is a Minor Literature?" In *Kafka: Toward a Minor Literature*. Trans. Dana Polan. 16–27. Minneapolis: University of Minnesota Press, 1986.

Dowling, William C. "Saving Scholarly Publishing in the Age of Oprah: The Glastonbury Project." *Journal of Scholarly Publishing* (April 1997): 115–34.

Ducat, Stephen. *The Wimp Factor: Gender Gaps, Holy Wars, and the Politics of Anxious Masculinity*. Boston: Beacon, 2004.

Edwards, Thomas R. "Oprah's Choice." *Raritan* 21, no. 4 (Spring 2002): 75–86.

Elliott, Jane. "O Is for the Other Things She Gave Me: Jonathan Franzen's *The Corrections* and Contemporary Women's Fiction." *Bitch* 16 (Spring 2002): 70–74.

Epstein, Joseph. "Surfing the Novel," *Commentary* (January 2002): 32–37.

Farr, Cecilia Konchar. *Reading Oprah: How Oprah's Book Club Changed the Way America Reads*. Albany: State University of New York Press, 2005.

Fetterley, Judith. "'Not in the Least American': Nineteenth-Century Literary Regionalism." *College English* 56 (1994): 877–95.

Franzen, Jonathan. *The Corrections*. New York: Farrar, Straus and Giroux, 2001.

_____. *How to Be Alone*. New York: Farrar, Straus and Giroux, 2002.

_____. "Meet Me in St. Louis." *The New Yorker* 77, no. 44 (December 24–31, 2001): 70–5.

_____. "Mr. Difficult: William Gaddis and the Problem of Hard-to-Read Books." *The New Yorker* (30 September 2002): 100–11.

_____. "Perchance to Dream: In the Age of Images, a Reason to Write Novels." *Harper's Magazine* 292, no. 1751 (April 1996): 35–54.

Giles, Jeff. "Errors and 'Corrections,'" *Newsweek* 138, no.19, 5 November 2001, 68–69.

Halberstam, Judith. *Female Masculinity*. Durham, NC: Duke University Press, 1998.

Hall, R. Mark. "The 'Oprahfication' of Literacy: Reading 'Oprah's Book Club.'" *College English* 65, no. 6 (July 2003): 646–67.

Hawthorne, Nathaniel. "To William D. Ticknor" (19 January 1855). In *The Centenary Edition of the Works of Nathaniel Hawthorne*, Vol. XVII, eds. William Charvat, Roy Harvey Pearce, and Claude M. Simpson, 304. Columbus: Ohio State University Press, 1962.

Hensher, Philip. "Writing Beyond His Means." *The Spectator* (24 November 2001): 44–45.

Illouz, Eva. *Oprah Winfrey and the Glamour of Misery*. New York: Columbia University Press, 2003.

Jacoby, Jeff. "Too Good for Oprah." *Boston Globe*, 1 Nov. 2001, sec. A, p. 19.

Jameson, Fredric. *Postmodernism, or, The Cultural Logic of Late Capitalism*. London: Verso, 1991.

Jefferson, Margo. "There Goes the Neighborhood." *New York Times Book Review*, 25 November 2001, 35.

Jernigan, Jessica. "Slingbacks and Arrows: Chick Lit Comes of Age." *Bitch* 25 (Summer 2004): 68–75.

Lauerman, Connie. "He Reads, She Reads: Do Choices Speak Volumes? What Men and Women Read Does Tend to Differ, but Some Readers and Writers Chafe at Labels Such as 'Women's Books.'" *Los Angeles Times*, 26 November 2001, sec. E, p. 3

Maslin, Janet. "Moms Read with Heart, Dads with a Firm Jaw." *New York Times*, 7 May 2004, sec. E2, p. 33.

McDowell, Linda. "Spatializing Feminism." In *BodySpace: Destabilizing Geographies of Gender and Sexuality,* ed., Nancy Duncan, 28–44. New York: Routledge, 1996.

Mehegan, David. "Franzen Not Alone in Oprah Dilemma." *Boston Globe*, 10 November 2001, sec. F, p. 1.

Murphy, William P. "Worldview Takes a Verbal Beating in Political Rhetoric." *Chicago Tribune*, 19 September 2004, 5.

Nava, Michael. *Rag and Bone*. New York: Berkley Prime Crime, 2002.

"A Novelist, A Talk-Show Host, and Literature High and Low." *The Chronicle of Higher Education*, 48, no. 14, 30 November 2001, sec. B, p. 4.

Phillips, Deborah. "Keeping the Home Fires Burning: The Myth of the Independent Woman in the Aga-Saga." *Women: A Cultural Review* 7, no. 1 (1996): 48–54.

Pollitt, Katha. "Girlie Vote." *Chicago Tribune*, 15 September 2004, 25.

Shamir, Milette. "Divided Plots: Interior Space and Gender Difference in Domestic Fiction." *Genre* 29, no. 4 (Winter 1996): 429–72.

Sligh, Clarissa. *Ron Ironing, Dallas, Texas, 1996*; accessed 25 May 2004; available from http://www.clarissasligh.com/HTML/LW_THE%MEN_1.html

Steinem, Gloria. "Women Are Never Front-Runners." *New York Times* 8 Jan 2008, sec. A, p. 23.

Rakoff, Joanna Smith. "Making *The Corrections*: An Interview with Jonathan Franzen." *Poets & Writers* (September/October 2001): 27–33.

Rooney, Kathleen. *Reading with Oprah: The Book Club That Changed America*. Fayetteville: University of Arkansas Press, 2005.

Rubin, Joan Shelley. *The Making of Middlebrow Culture*. Chapel Hill: The University of North Carolina Press, 1992.

Seabrook, John. *Nobrow: The Culture of Marketing, the Marketing of Culture*. New York: Vintage, 2001.

Stossel, Scott. "Elitism for Everyone." *The Atlantic Online*; accessed 29 November 2001; available from http://www.theatlantic.com/unbound/polipro/pp2001-11-29htm

Street, Paul. "The Full Blown 'Oprah' Effect: Reflections on Color, Class and New Age Racism." *The Black Commentator* 127; accessed 24 February 2005; available from http://www.blackcommentator.com/127/127_oprah.html

Svetkey, Benjamin. "Domestic Drama." *Entertainment Weekly*, 14 September 2001, 85.

Sykes, Plum. *Bergdorf Blondes*. New York: Hyperion, 2004.

Valby, Karen. "Correction Dept." *Entertainment Weekly*, 25 October 2002, 23.

Wilson, Sherryl. *Oprah, Celebrity and Formations of Self*. New York: Palgrave, 2003.

Wolcott, James. "Advertisements for Himself." *The New Republic* 227, no. 23–24 (2–9 December 2002): 36–40.

Wood, James. "It's Not Tolstoy, But It Does Belong to High Literature." *The Guardian*, 9 November 2001, 3.

Young, John. "Toni Morrison, Oprah Winfrey, and Postmodern Popular Audiences." *African American Review*. 35.2 (2001): 181–204.

13

Neil LaBute's Bodies in Question
Marc Shaw

Sociologist R.W. Connell argues that in the views of popular ideology, "masculinity is fixed;" men are men, the result of the natural consequences of biology: "testosterone, big muscles, and the male brain."[1] Contrary to popular ideology, however, masculinity is indeed an active construction, a public demonstration that maleness is mediated by as many factors as there are men. Still, biology remains important in the presence of the male body as *site* (location) and *sight* (vision to others) of signification. As Connell points out, "through social institutions and processes, bodies are given meaning. Society has a range of body practices which address, sort and modify bodies." These body practices vary from "deportment and dress to sexuality, surgery, and sport."[2]

Theatre literally means *a place of seeing* (a *site* for *sight*), and in Neil LaBute's theatre we gaze upon male bodies as they define and perform their contemporary masculinities. Theatre can magnify various signs for an attentive audience, and the codes of performed gender are no exception. LaBute's plays examine male body practices and question how male bodies signify social, historical, and even religious processes. Sitting in the audience in the same room as these bodies-in-question, the audience can deconstruct the ideological monolith of a single, fixed masculinity.

John Lahr of *The New Yorker* branded Neil LaBute, "the best new playwright to emerge in the past decade."[3] LaBute burst to national prominence when he adapted one of his own plays, the appropriately-named *In the Company of Men*, winning the Filmmakers Trophy at the Sundance Festival in 1997.[4] In the film, two mid-level businessmen hatch a plot while traveling to a temporary assignment somewhere in Middle America. The pair agrees that during their weeks in the unnamed town, they will date the same naïve woman, pretend to fall in love with her, and then simultaneously jilt her when their work there ends. What follows is a study of diverging masculinities, social Darwinism, and misanthropy. And with that aggressive film debut, LaBute established his reputation as a writer who asks probing, thorny questions of how humans, both men and women, treat each other.

In two significant ways, a similar inquisitiveness injects itself into Neil LaBute's theatre. First, in his most popular and critically-acclaimed theatrical works — *Bash: Latterday Plays* (1999), *The Shape of Things* (2001), *The Mercy Seat* (2002), and *Fat Pig* (2004) — we witness male protagonists wrestle with specific definitions of masculinity within their respective bodies. In this analysis, I explore the specifics of those masculinities in conflict. Importantly, in order to fully understand LaBute's bodies-in-question, a suitable investigation presents LaBute's works as performance, not solely as words on the page. We must imagine ourselves in the theatre with LaBute's writing enacted by three-dimensional bodies that have been — as R. W. Connell states — addressed, sorted and modified.

Second, the inquisitive LaBute relishes the moment of theatrical performance. It allows him to investigate how to address, sort, and modify another body in question: his audience in the theatre. LaBute admits:

> [Theatre is] so unique: you have live performers, and you have a relationship with the audience that is quite malleable and constantly shifting, very quicksilver. I'm curious about that relationship, and I'm interested in manipulating it. I find that interesting both as a practitioner and as a viewer: when that happens to me as an audience member, I say, 'Oh, it didn't end how I thought it would; I like that; [...].' We feel fairly safe, collectively, together, sitting in those seats: people are up on the stage and they're lit, and we're not, and we're sitting in judgment as an audience. I like to remove the safety of that.[5]

Part of LaBute's handling of his audience is the deliberate shifting of their expectations about masculinity, troubling the audience's preconceived notions of masculine roles dictated by popular ideology. As site/sight, the bodies onstage perform and then re-form their gender. We will consider LaBute's plays within the context of masculine identity and that shifting presentation to his audience. Every one of the men in LaBute's plays explored below — the Young Man from *iphigenia in orem*, John from *a gaggle of saints*, Adam from *The Shape of Things*, Ben from *The Mercy Seat*, and Tom from *Fat Pig* — alters his masculinity at the same time that LaBute manipulates the audience's expectation of that same gender formation.

Latterday Masculinities: Troubling the Mormon Male in Bash

Bash: Latterday Plays contains three short one-acts, two of which explore a specific crisis in masculinity for the male Mormon (Latter-day Saint) characters presented.[6] First, to position Neil LaBute's personal history within his subject material, it is important to mention that LaBute graduated from the LDS Church-owned Brigham Young University, and he was converted to the faith during that time. LaBute never attacks the religion itself but utilizes the Mormon culture as a localizing force as he writes. Social forces shape our identities, and LaBute chooses a specific one, unique yet familiar to him. The word "latterday" in his title allows LaBute a dual reference to the religion and to the retelling of ancient myths in a contemporary setting. In the first of *Bash*'s three short plays, *iphigenia in orem*, a Mormon businessman from Orem, Utah, speaks to an unseen listener in a Las Vegas hotel room, recounting the circumstances of his baby daughter's death. LaBute adapts Euripides' tragedy, *Iphigenia in Aulis*, in which Agamemnon sacrifices his daughter so that the gods will let his ship sail off to war. In LaBute's revision there are no warriors or kings, only the nameless Young Man who excitedly admits that his office sales job is like "playing at 'war'" with "all the faxes coming in, people zipping around, emergency strategy sessions, all that."[7] Anyone familiar with the original Greek myth will deduce that this latter-day version ends with a chilling confession. While home one Friday evening, after being informed that he has been laid off from his sales job and, consequently, feeling desperate for sympathy from his employer, the Young Man traps his baby daughter, Emma, under heavy bed covers. He then exits the bedroom, leaving Emma alone to suffocate. Now racked with guilt some months later, the Young Man tries to convince himself it was "fate that took her," but the details of his confession belie that wish (28). There may not be a pantheon of gods as in Euripides' work, but God definitely exists in the Young Man's life, and his religious conditioning plays a huge role in his own sense of his masculinity and future damnation.

The Young Man takes his socially and religiously prescribed roles (the specific body practices) of breadwinner and patriarch seriously. LaBute does not set out to attack the LDS doctrinal admonition that men should work while women should stay in the home and raise the children. However, he does take the time to establish a Mormon cultural backdrop as he zooms in on an ideal gone terribly wrong in application. Every tragic figure miscalculates in some way, and the Young Man's *hamartia* (his flaw or, better, miscalculation) is that his pride never allows a reconsideration or reformation of his masculinity. Reformation comes too late for him; from the audience we see how he has changed *since* his crime. But that is too little, too late. The Young Man's entire sense of self-worth has been built into the roles of breadwinner and salesman. He must provide at any cost, even to the point of desperately considering his own baby daughter's death as an economic prospect:

I realized that's what this was [the baby under the covers]. An opportunity. And I wasn't going to waste it. [...] The point I wanna make, though see, is that it didn't have to happen that way. I took a risk, this calculated risk for my family that this whole episode would play out in our favor, give me that little edge at work and maybe things'd be okay, or they'd change their minds because of, you know... (27-28) [Clarification added].

Nothing justifies the Young Man's murderous actions, yet we still feel a simultaneous repulsion and sympathy toward him. Tragedy necessitates this mixed, dual sentiment: if the Young Man were merely thoroughly despicable, LaBute's work would not function with full tragic effect.

Paramount to *Bash*'s efficacy is LaBute's construction (and troubling) of the Young Man's masculine identity, but also the Young Man's relationship with the live theatre audience. As LaBute said himself, "I'm interested in manipulating" that audience relationship, and he does so by playing to the audience's preconceived notions of masculine roles. We first see the Young Man as the archetypal Mormon family man, then —*switch*— we must somehow append "killer" to his evolving identity near the end of the play. One dramatic device LaBute utilizes in constructing the character/audience dynamic is having the Young Man address an unseen guest. The Young Man has just met this person in the hotel lobby that evening. LaBute uses this invisible guest so the Young Man can face the audience and, in effect, build rapport through addressing us. We do not know of his crime at the beginning of the play, so there is no reason to distrust or dislike the Young Man, and there are no other characters to discredit him. The Young Man establishes that, as part of his religion, he does not drink alcohol, but he immediately asks his (apparently already drunk) guest if he or she wants more to drink. He needs the guest really drunk and forgetful by the time he gets to his confession about his baby daughter.

In a similar way, LaBute gets his audience "under the influence" before *we* hear the Young Man's confession. In buying time as the alcohol takes hold on the listener, we hear a red herring — a completely falsified account of baby Emma's death that establishes the Young Man as a quintessential family man. In the fake account, we hear of a distraught father finding the poor baby; the parents' grief; how he and his wife, Deb, hold each other and make love "in a moment when [their] entire universe had been changed" (21). In order for the audience to further fall under the Young Man's influence, LaBute provides plenty of leeway within the text so an experienced actor can embody an amiable character. Some likable attributes include the Young Man's excitement in talking to his new Las Vegas friend; or, from the text an actor might sense that the Young Man is slightly corny, a bit pathetic with, perhaps, a moustache and an infectious laugh. Overall, he comes off as a friendly, and even charming, man. But as the play ends and we determine the truth about what he did that evening, the audience's perception of him changes. We see his sweat, his untidy suit, his whole body wriggling in an old, Vegas-hotel chair, and we hear his laugh anew, attempting sincerity. Our view of him shifts as we feel a simultaneous disgust and sadness for him. Those corporeal details or quirks that might have been endearing before, might now feel sinister, sickening, or hollow.

One important component of the Young Man's constructed masculinity is his relationship with the two main women he mentions in his narrative: his wife and a female co-worker. His wife, Deb, is a homemaker whose enacted femininity complements and enables the Young Man's provider status. Throughout his story, the Young Man continuously positions her in her domestic duties, at Safeway buying milk, or talking to someone in the produce aisle. Unlike his female co-workers, his wife Deb's existence seems neither a positive nor a negative in the Young Man's life. Like any married couple, they have their silences, concerned chats, ups and downs. Most noteworthy, however, is that by the end of the monologue, the Young Man has distanced himself from his wife by taking a sales job "on the road." He is unable to confess the killing to Deb because, ironically, "it would kill her. Kill us as a family" (30). So although the Young Man sacrificed his daughter as the desperate act of a provider, his guilt now increasingly removes him from his wife and children at home. He remains a provider but no longer presides as a patriarchal presence in his home. He no longer feels at home there; he stays on the road where he can "drive and think" (30). Like an updated Willy Loman, LaBute's salesman heads to the road already spiritually dead.

The neutral tone with which the Young Man describes Deb stands in contrast to his most hated female co-worker. The Young Man seems to have a chauvinistic nostalgia for the old days. Unapologetically, he admits that "there's definitely an order to things in business," and that includes having "the old boys at the top" "the way it was supposed to be" (22-23). Clearly, the Young Man manifests a crisis of masculinity — he feels completely threatened by women as his professional equal. He resents "women with their MBAs and affirmative action nonsense" and wants the assertive females in his office "to get the boot" (23). In other words, the Young Man thinks his family's structure and *modus operandi* constitute an ideal, and the world would be a better place if it only everyone followed suit and lived like him. He describes his female co-worker in gendered terms: "I mean, talk about clichés and all that, she was a walking one ... the business suit and blunt cut hair thing going, can't remember ever even seeing her smile, you know what I'm saying"(24). The insinuation from the Young Man seems to be that his co-worker is an angry, empowered lesbian who never smiles, or at the very least, she is not the cheerful, servile secretary that he might nominate for the "old boys" to keep around (24). In a meeting, the same unnamed female co-worker accuses the Young Man of using "chauvinistic lexicon," and he immediately feels that her reprimand lessens his standing with his coworkers (24). Therefore, to preserve his masculine status with his male co-workers, he makes fun of her comments, and laughs them off at lunch. But he still feels like his female co-workers enjoyed his suffering, and this wounds his pride. The Young Man's pettiness turns ugly, however, when he discovers there will be lay-offs at work. More than likely, either he or his female co-worker will be fired. When a friend of the Young Man calls with a tip that the he is the one to be fired, he resorts to killing his daughter to receive sympathy from his employer and coworkers.

The Young Man's relationship to his body practices, his specific performed masculinity, is described perfectly (albeit inadvertently) by Carla J. McDonough as she reviews David Mamet's collection of essays "Some Freaks." While McDonough critiques Mamet here, we can imagine her speaking of the Young Man and his fixed ways:

> [His] ideas of masculinity [are often] in contrast to or defiance of women. Women are the objects against which male identity positions itself. Men's confusion and skepticism about women, which often borders on the misogynistic [...], stems from the fear that in losing the definition of women on which patriarchal market society is based, men have lost themselves. [This] drama addresses the confusion felt by men such as himself who no longer know where they stand in a patriarchy that is under revision; it also reveals that this ideal male community which offers acceptance, fun, and a sense of belonging is not readily available"[8]

LaBute's plays are once removed from Mamet's earlier questionings of masculinity. At least in his earlier plays like *Glengarry Glen Ross* and *Edmond*, Mamet stands with his characters in a sort of archetypal manly defiance. LaBute allows his characters to stand with a similar manly defiance, but unlike Mamet, LaBute leaves his characters to stand alone.

An important material component of the Young Man's masculine role of breadwinner is the lifestyle he provides for himself and his family. The Young Man's pride in attaining this lifestyle goes too far and contributes to his killing baby Emma. As he states, he worked in Salt Lake City and "commuted in from Orem every day because of the standard of living that area afforded us" (23). LaBute makes his family man live in the Provo/Orem area because it is consistently ranked as one of the most livable and crime-free cities in the nation. In this heterogeneous area, ninety percent of the citizens are conservative, Mormon, and white; and, those residents collectively refer to the area as "Happy Valley." Regrettably, the Young Man's desire to live well goes too far, and upon hearing he might lose his job his pride concerning his material possessions and luxuries cannot help but spill out: "I'm standing there, just taking in the VCR, and our big screen TV and one of the kid's bikes, I can see through the front window, the Pathfinder, "Wheel of Fortune's blasting on the TV in the family room," and "all these thoughts are swirling around in my head" (26). We discover that the suburban father has bowed under the pressures and expectations of his self-prescribed role. Wheel of Fortune is on the television (a reference perhaps to fortune and fate from Greek tragedy, but also to the riches spinning around the Young Man), but when the wheel stops, our hero, or anti-hero now, lands on (morally) bankrupt. LaBute lets his audience more fully see the details of the Young Man's enacted masculinity, and their complete view of his fallen masculine ideals, and of his crime, is chilling.

Just as in *iphigenia in orem*, LaBute plays with his audience's expectations in the next work from *Bash*, a one-act called *a gaggle of saints*. Akin to the Young Man in the previous act, John is a young Mormon male striving to live up to his socio-religious and economic masculine roles. John is a college student who tells the story of a weekend road-trip from Boston to New York where he and some others attend a prom-like bash. LaBute sets the action in a dual reality in which John and his girlfriend, Sue, describe and enact their special weekend. The pair lead the audience on their trip to a fancy hotel in New York City, and then on a stroll to Central Park. In the park, the conservative John encounters a gay couple kissing. For John, viewing a sexuality different from his own puts a damper on his perfect evening. He cannot erase from his mind the image of two grown men kissing. After the dance at the fancy hotel, the female members of the group are tired and go off to sleep. The young men are bored, so John suggests they all go for a walk. They horse around, kicking over garbage cans, and end up in Central Park where John and Sue had been earlier. Again, John and two other male Mormon youth see two older men kissing. John's chilling confession/reenactment continues as the three young men hatch a plan. John follows one of the gay men into a Central Park public restroom where a different sort of bash occurs. The three youth attack the gay man, one of them whispering "fag" while throwing a garbage can on his beaten body. They leave the man for dead. John's perceived masculinity — as defined by his religion, his relationship with his father, and his repressed sexuality — undergoes a questioning and resolution. Just as the Young Man in *iphigenia in orem* feels pressure from what he terms a "feminist" who spoils the way things "ought" to be, John cannot accept a different 'other,' a homosexual couple ruining his idyllic evening.

LaBute sets up a mounting tension within the John and Sue relationship. He names the second play *a gaggle of saints* because the pair are Latterday Saints by faith, but also, according to LaBute, "I got the idea from the beauty of a flock of geese [...] When you see them from afar in a field, they look great, but if you go out in the field, it's covered with shit. The geese are looking at that shit saying, 'Where did that come from?'"[9] Much like the Young Man initially establishes himself as an ideal suburban father, LaBute manipulates his audience by positioning John and Sue as the classic cute couple. The play relates a familiar "he says, she says" account of a night on the town, the biggest, most romantic bash of the year in New York City. But strangely, within the pair's dual monologue, or duologue, we are never sure if John and Sue are recounting their stories from the same room, or if one can hear the other as they tell their separate but chronologically parallel narratives. Like their relationship, something gradually seems askew. Nonetheless, for the first half of the play, the audience gets caught up in their good looks, big smiles, sheer All-American likeability, their prom story, their road trip excitement, and the history of their courtship. We think we know them. Again, LaBute has the pair address us directly and look us in the eye, gaining our trust as they tell their stories. This time there is not even an imaginary listener in the way. According to the audience's past experience with narratives, and with people and their body practices, we classify and define them as specific types: pleasant, energetic, good-looking college kids having a good time. This group of Mormon youth might be going "wild" for a weekend, but the audience thinks it is a wholesome, tempered "wild."

But as John and Sue talk more and more, like zooming in on a gaggle of geese, we see the pair is not as we had thought. We become aware of a new aspect of John's masculinity — a tendency toward extreme violence at a moment's notice. Sue emerges as an enabler and justifier, not seeming to mind his extreme action. The first inkling comes when John describes the moment he and Sue had their first kiss in high school. John thoroughly pummeled Sue's ex-boyfriend in order to win her heart, slamming the other boy's head against the high school track that he and Sue had been jogging around. This story is told to us in a dual reality, meaning that John reenacts moments from the past while he describes them to us in the present, as any good storyteller might do. John might even mime the action as he proudly, even smugly, declares, "I turn on him. Never spoke to him the whole time, just turned on him and flipped him over onto the ground and started pounding on his head" (51). Sue never questions what goes on; she merely says "I'd never seen this happen before" (51). In fact, she almost likes the idea of these two strong young men fighting over her. While Sue's girlishness is sweet and endearing, it also contains an innocence that is a decided naiveté, a convenient emotional absence, shielding her from responsibility at just the right moments. As we see in two more violent episodes in the play, John and Sue complement and enable each other's gender construction. John's fighting at the track foreshadows his violent attack on the homosexual man in Central Park.

John's concepts of his own masculinity are brought into question as he sees the two men kissing. This, in turn, makes the audience question his gendering specifically, and fixed masculinity in general. John thinks that by kissing in public the gay pair forces their sexuality on his ideal, and he senses that the interaction threatens his masculinity in some way. His sheltered upbringing has not prepared him to accept or tolerate an alternative to his own: ""I mean, come on, I know the scriptures, know 'em pretty well, and this is wrong" (62). There is a repression brewing inside John, too, but LaBute never fills in all the details. For instance, one of the older gay men reminds John of his father, and John mentions that fact a couple of times. John also takes a lot of time describing the details of the homoerotic interactions he sees in Central Park. An actor playing these moments certainly would not linger on the descriptions in an overtly sexual way, but their presence in the play does bring John's own sexuality into question. John describes what he says in great detail: "they were saying 'goodnight...' well, not saying it exactly. But kissing. Two men, grown men, standing in the park, public park in the middle of New York and kissing like something out of a Clark Gable film" (62). Most people would just let the situation go, even if homosexuality bothered them for some reason. But instead, John focuses even closer on what supposedly repulses him, noticing the pair have their "[t]ongues out, and the arms around each other, and nothing else in the world matters to these two" (62). It is easy to speculate that John himself has repressed homosexual feelings, especially when, moments later, LaBute brings the older gay man named Chet together face-to-face with John in the Central Park restroom. Although this is just before the three pals bash, Chet, John treats him like a lover: "I don't even bat an eye as he moves in, his lips playing across my cheek. Let his tongue run along my teeth and a hand, free hand, tracing down my fly" (64). John justifies his homosexual performance by informing us that he acts thus so that Chet will relax and open himself to attack more easily. But seeing John linger on those homoerotic details is evidence enough to trouble his masculinity. Because John and Sue obey their religion's tenets (if we conveniently skip over John's extreme violence), the pair do not indulge in any premarital sex. Therefore, after the prom-like bash they have attended that night, chaste Sue goes off to sleep in the hotel room with the other girls, and John goes outside to relieve his boredom. LaBute structures his play so that the gay bash is the climactic moment after the long, exciting buildup of the date. The chaste foreplay of the evening results in only the men's violent release.

There are two versions of *Bash* and one is more helpful to our line of analysis here because it more specifically positions John in a socio-religious context. The original edition of the play from 1999 is called *Bash: Latterday Plays*, but a second, edited version called *Bash: Three Plays* was published in 2001. As I mentioned before, LaBute himself is an LDS convert, and his church leaders asked him to edit out the majority of references to the LDS Church in *Bash*.[10] This editing hurts the work as a whole, stripping it of specificity, and detaching it slightly from a particular and poignant sociohistorical and religious context. It also lessens the resonances of masculinities in the *a gaggle of saints*' climactic moment. During the bashing in the Central Park restroom, in the 1999 version, while the gay man lies bleeding and broken, one of John's friends offers a blessing on Chet with consecrated, holy oil. In the LDS faith, the religious authority to offer such a blessing is called the priesthood, and is available to any worthy male member in the Church over eighteen years old. Such a blessing is administered with laying on of hands, wherein the man's body actually holds the power of God in that moment. The use of the priesthood, then, is the ultimate display of masculine power as it comes from the Father in Heaven. Because of their violent and hateful actions in Central Park, none of the men are worthy to act in the name of God or hold that priesthood. Their blessing is an absolute perversion of something potentially beautiful and holy. But the priesthood goes to the very core of Mormon masculinity. If a Mormon man honors that priesthood authority, he is a believer and doer of the highest order. He is the kind of man that most LDS women, like Sue back asleep in the hotel room, would want to marry and have as a father to her children. But by perverting their priesthood in such a manner, the three violators bring their entire performed and lived masculinities into question. In the 2001 edited version, John's friend does not offer a blessing, but a simple eulogy, which is less specific, less shocking, and less effective in revealing their hypocrisy.

The Shape of Things: Extreme Male Makeover

LaBute's next major play, *The Shape of Things* (2001), begins with the playwright playing God and updating Genesis: in the beginning of scene one Adam and Evelyn face-off under a statue at a contemporary art museum. Evelyn, like Eve, is the first to "sin." She holds a spray-can in her hand, ready to deface a sculpture that she dislikes. Adam, the young security guard, tries to prevent her from destroying this valuable art piece, which is a replica of a human body. After this inauspicious meeting, the nerdy Adam and rebelliously sexy Evelyn start to date, and their budding relationship is the main plot of the play.

Again, LaBute toys with the audience's expectations. As the plot unfolds, we might expect a modern-day *My Fair Lady* or reverse *Pretty Woman*, as Adam becomes more sexy, social, and cool under Evelyn's tutelage. But by the end of *The Shape of Things*, we discover that Evelyn is in fact a graduate student in art who shaped Adam into the man she wants because he is *literally* her master's thesis project. Her love is merely a means to an end, feigned for art's sake. He is her own private, living sculpture, and Adam transforms in order to embody the aspects of masculinity Evelyn finds most desirable: more muscle, less fat, different hairstyles, and more fashionable clothes. As per Evelyn's request Adam marks his skin with a tattoo on his penis: her initials (E.A.T.) brand his most central male appendage as her own. She is Pygmalion; he is her Galatea. His evolving masculinity, like a sculpture, is chiseled and changed onstage.

Importantly, the switches that Adam makes take place right before our eyes. We see him go from a dud to Evelyn's version of a stud, just like many makeover shows on television. No prosthetic fake muscles are used in the creation of this stud, however. He just dresses better, wears his hair differently, and other characters react to how much better he looks. Adam's biggest switches are the ways he carries himself, his flirting, and his overall confidence. With those changes, he also begins to act more aggressively with other women and the possibility that he cheats on Evelyn is presented. To make amends for his dalliance, he proposes marriage to Evelyn, unaware that he is her art project.

Of course, although Adam has willing consented to having his masculinity updated, he has not consented to being a thesis project. And, in sitting through a LaBute play, the audience consents to being artistically maneuvered too. Both Adam and the audience believe that love is blossoming until, with Adam present in the play's climactic moment, Evelyn unveils her master's thesis and gives a public lecture about Adam's transformed state. She holds up a large "after" photo and theorizes for everyone present:

> [A]nd yet open any fashion magazine, turn on any television program and the world will tell you ... he's only gotten more interesting, more desirable, more normal. In a word, better. He is a living breathing example of our obsession with the surface of things, the shape of them.[11]

Again, LaBute manipulates his audience and turns things on their head in the final moments of the play. But we are left pondering the fluidity of our gendering, its changeability and the implicit connection between who we are and how others want us to be. We might ask, how many of us try to get our lovers or friends or family to sculpt themselves in this way? No matter how well-intentioned our motives, even if we want them just to stop eating cookies or start listening to a certain band we admire? Surely we do not do so with darker motives like Evelyn. But, her ulterior motives aside, in a way, Adam is still a success story. After all, he changed for the better, did he not? The final image of *The Shape of Things* is of Adam alone watching one of the museum pieces about him: on a video screen, he and Evelyn whisper intimately back and forth. But, now that his muse has deceived him, all Adam can do is sit alone, watch his past on screen, and eat cookies.

A Pair of Taboos: *The Mercy Seat and Fat Pig*

LaBute's next two major plays, *The Mercy Seat* (2002) and *Fat Pig* (2004) are both controversial for different reasons, and both exhibit men adapting and reformulating their gender identity in relation to the women in their lives. *The Mercy Seat* was the first play to add a darker spin to the already dark September 11th tragedy. Set in Manhattan, Ben and his boss, Abby, are having an adulterous affair and are away from their place of employment, the Twin Towers, during the 9/11 attack. Throughout the play, as Ben's cell phone rings and echoes throughout the theatre, the audience grows slowly aware of Ben's masculine roles — not only as a boyfriend and employee to Abby — but also as a father and husband to the family we never see.

LaBute revises the tragic hero of September 11th. Those heroes include the firefighters, police officers, and ordinary workers who died in the rubble on that fateful day. They then became the celebrated, revered subjects of newspaper columns, magazine spreads, and primetime television specials. As mothers and fathers, daughters and husbands, their lives were noted and honored for many months after the Twin Towers fell. Although LaBute offers a characteristic final twist at the end of his play, his most straightforward but effective manipulation of the audience in *The Mercy Seat* is clear from the beginning as he reworks the lionized ideal of the September 11th hero. Holed up in Abby's apartment, Ben realizes that because of his current absence and lack of communication, his loved ones might mistakenly assume he has reached his demise at work, where he should have been during the attacks. With thousands dead only blocks away, Ben must decide between contacting his family to tell them he is safe, or literally playing dead. If he plays dead, he can be reborn as a new man elsewhere with Abby. In *The Mercy Seat*, LaBute detours the collective pathos from a memorable event, and uses that emotion to electrically charge the theater from his play's start. If only for a moment, the audience (almost sacrilegiously) wonders if all those September 11th heroes were really heroes, or if any of them were false constructions like Ben conspires to become.

Ironically, we discover it is Ben who has always felt like a false construction, mostly in his duties as father and husband. Ben is having an early midlife crisis, and admits that everything he has ever done in life, from his studies to work to marriage and fatherhood, has been a failure because he has always taken the "easy route":

> [D]o it faster, simpler, you know, whatever it takes to get it done, be liked, get by. That's me. Cheated in school, screwed over my friends, took whatever I could get from whomever I could take it from. My marriage, there's a goddamn fiasco. [...] The kids ... I barely register as a dad, I'm sure, but compared to the other shit in my life, I'm Doctor-fucking-*Spock*. No matter what I do or have done, they adore the hell out of me, and I'm totally knocked out by that. What kids are like.[12]

Ben wants out of his marriage, but his love for his children, and their unconditional adoration, makes faking his death a difficult decision. Furthermore, rebirth with Abby has additional complications rooted in Ben's concepts of his own masculinity: he cannot rid his mind of the idea that she, an older woman, is his boss *and* his lover. It bothers him so much that during sex, he can never look her in the eyes. The play ends with Ben still trying to decide which path he will take, which masculine roles he will choose to play during the next stage of his life.

A normally taboo subject, *Fat Pig* (2004) concerns the dating relationship of a "normal-sized" man and an obese woman. More than any of his works since *The Shape of Things*, LaBute focuses on the body and our expectations of masculine and feminine sexual desire in relation to another person. During the performance, as we watch intelligent, witty, pretty-but-obese Helen eat and eat some more, while her new love interest, Tom, chats and laughs and eats and watches Helen eat, we are entertained and touched by their banter and sincerity. Here is an example of their refreshing openness, taken from their first date:

> HELEN: Ummm, you probably couldn't guess, but I didn't date a lot when I was in school.
> TOM: Oh.
> HELEN: (*whispers*) I used to be a touch *heavy*.
> Helen chuckles. Tom joins in half-heartedly, then stops.
> TOM: Huh. (*Beat*.) And is that ... is it all right to talk about ... I dunno, your weight and everything, or should I...?
> HELEN: No, go ahead. It's not a shame thing for me. Not anymore. Not that I'm all *perfectly* adjusted, but ... you know. Whatever.
> TOM: "Anymore"?
> HELEN: Well ... it's all shame when you're younger, isn't it? You hate how you look or sound or, you know all that stuff that we go through. As kids. But I'm pretty all right with who I am now. The trick is getting other people to be okay with it!
> TOM: Right. And, so ... have you always been, like ... you know?
> HELEN: No. What?

TOM: Ummm, big ... boned, or whatever.
Helen laughs out loud at this one. Another beauty, which makes Tom giggle along. She takes his hand this time.[13]

As shown here, Helen is comfortable with her weight, to a point, and her size is an open topic of conversation. She knows she is overweight and jokes with Tom about it.

But, for Labute, the central dramatic question belongs not to Helen but to Tom. More specifically, LaBute zeroes in on Tom's masculinity. Simply, is Tom "man" enough to continue to date Helen? Tom starts to fall in love with her, despite disbelief from the superficial friends in his life that he would stoop to date an obese woman. Tom's best male friend, Carter, finally figures out that Helen is the woman Tom has been dating, and disbelievingly remarks: "I don't mean to be indelicate, so you're gonna have to forgive me here, but.... This is not her. You gotta tell me, tell me that much. This is not the ... *her* her. Is it?" (48). Tom admits that Helen *is* Helen, but admits to Carter he has been trying to hide the fact that he is dating an overweight woman. Their conversation succinctly captures Tom's dilemma in proving his masculinity:

TOM: Why didn't I just come clean, say that I was having dinner, out with a friend even, instead of making all that shit up?
CARTER: Because you're a pussy.
TOM: Man, come on...
CARTER: No, I say that in the best way. We all are — guys, I mean — if it comes right down to it. Very rare is the dude who stands up for the shit he believes in....
TOM: I know! I wanna be better at that sorta stuff, but a lot of the time I'm just ... yeah. A big wuss [51-52].

Even Tom's ex-girlfriend and co-worker, Jeannie, a skinny wisp of a girl, cannot understand Tom's new relationship either: "She's really *fat*, Tom! A fat sow and you know it. I can tell you're aware by the way you're acting, which is really the puzzling part..." (75). More than anything, self-absorbed Jeannie's sense of her own femininity is challenged, in fact, because Tom, her ex, might now love Helen. She wonders if Tom has a "thing" for fat girls, and if so, does that mean that she, Jeannie, is fat too? Despite all those factors, LaBute controls his audience by making us believe that perhaps this love story will work out, like so many other love stories that go against the odds. But, in the end, Tom is not man enough at all, as he puts it, "I am a weak and fearful person, Helen, and I'm not gonna get any better" (91). Their relationship ends.

Fat Pig questions specific aspects of masculinity and femininity within the realm of desire: our ability to love, others' expectations of who we love, our bodies during the acts of desire, and the extent that the media and other external sources influence our genders. In performance we even sense Tom's selves changing from scene to scene. He is a wholly different person when he is with his friend Carter, or his ex-girlfriend Jeannie, than with his new love, Helen. How he holds himself, his mannerisms, his musculature, his laugh, his reactions to the others in the room — all might vary from scene to scene within the concentrated time-span of the play script. Theatre compresses time and lets us see Tom as Toms, as alternating masculinities (or a variety of men), not just a sole masculinity or one man. Yet the same actor embodies Tom in the same theatrical space for the same audience.

Fat Pig, like all of the LaBute plays discussed herein, insinuates that our masculinity or femininity defines itself in relation to others. Gender changes from relationship to relationship, from day to day. Different aspects of one's masculinity show themselves at differing degrees and at different times. "Masculinity" or "his masculinity" means nothing on its own; masculinity only exists in comparison with someone or something else. Live theater shines a spotlight on the body's agency and continuous ability to change the practices and new realities we perform.

Notes

1. R. W. Connell, *The Men and the Boys* (Berkeley: University of California Press, 2001), 57.
2. *Ibid.*, 58.
3. Neil LaBute, *The Shape of Things* (London: Faber and Faber, 2000), back cover. John Lahr wrote it in a profile in *The New Yorker.*
4. LaBute's title comes from a David Mamet essay of the same name, found in the collection *Some Freaks* (New York: Viking, 1989).
5. Neil LaBute, "An Interview with Neil LaBute," by Rosalynde Welch. Times and Seasons Website. Posted January 19, 2005. http://www.timesandseasons.org/index.php?p= 1873 [accessed January 3–May 25, 2007].
6. I use Latter-day Saint (LDS) to refer to the religion itself (officially called The Church of Jesus Christ of Latter-day Saints). The members of the LDS church are nicknamed Mormons, and the adjective "Mormon" refers to the various aspects of the culture of the Mormon people.
7. Neil LaBute, *Bash: Latterday Plays* (Woodstock, N.Y.: Overlook, 1999), 14. All citations are from this text and will appear parenthetically. Republished as *Bash: Three Plays*, 2001.
8. Carla J. McDonough, "Every Fear Hides a Wish: Unstable Masculinity in Mamet's Drama," *Theatre Journal* 44 (1992) 195–205
9. Mary Dickson, "Who's Afraid of Neil LaBute?" *Salt Lake City Weekly*, September 21, 1998. Online: http://weeklywire.com/ww/09-21-98/slc_story.html.
10. LaBute discusses his disfellowship from the LDS Church in the Times and Seasons interview. He mentions that the Church asked him not to write any more Mormon characters. He also sanitized the *Bash* script after that point.
11. Neil LaBute, *The Shape of Things* (London: Faber and Faber, 2000), 121.

12. Neil LaBute, *The Mercy Seat* (New York: Faber and Faber, 2003), 32.

13. Neil LaBute, *Fat Pig* (New York: Faber and Faber, 2004), 31. All other citations will appear parenthetically.

Bibliography

Connell, R. W. *The Men and the Boys*. Berkeley: University of California Press, 2001.

Dickson, Mary. "Who's Afraid of Neil LaBute?" *Salt Lake City Weekly*, 21 September 1998. http://weeklywire.com/ww/09-21-98/slc_story.html. Accessed May 25, 2007.

LaBute, Neil. *Bash: Latterday Plays*. Woodstock, N.Y.: Overlook, 1999.

_____. *Fat Pig*. New York: Faber and Faber, 2004.

_____. *The Mercy Seat*. New York: Faber and Faber, 2003.

_____. *The Shape of Things*. London: Faber and Faber, 2000.

McDonough, Carla J. "Every Fear Hides a Wish: Unstable Masculinity in Mamet's Drama." *Theatre Journal* 44.2 (1992), 195–205.

Welch, Rosalynde. "An Interview with Neil LaBute." *Times and Seasons*. http://www.times andseasons.org/index.php?p=1873. Accessed May 25, 2007.

14

O.J. Simpson: Tabloidized, Sexualized, Racialized and Largely Despised

Elwood Watson

October 3rd was a paradoxical day for O.J. Simpson. A day that will be probably be permanently etched in his memory. On this date in 1995, he was acquitted of the double murder of his ex-wife Nicole Brown Simpson and her waiter, body builder friend, Ronald Goldman. Flash forward to the exact date thirteen years later — October 3, 2008, Simpson and his co-defendant were found guilty of attempted kidnapping and robbery in Las Vegas. A year earlier in October 2007, while supposedly attending the wedding of a friend, he and several other men busted into a Las Vegas hotel room brandishing weapons in an effort to recover items he believed belonged to him. The six minute dramatic confrontation ended in Simpson being arrested by Las Vegas police. Multiple other charges were levied against Simpson and his co-defendant as well. Several of the co-defendants were either granted immunity or much lighter sentences in exchange for their testimony. A year later, a decision was rendered against the former football great.

I was attending an academic conference when I heard the verdicts announced. Seeing Simpson on *Court TV* as the charges against him were being read made my mind flashback to the stark differences of the current trial and the previous one conducted thirteen years earlier. The frenzied media atmosphere that dominated trial number one contrasted with the virtual news blackout that greeted the more recent O.J. Simpson trial.

There is no question that O.J. Simpson provokes deeply charged emotions among supporters and detractors alike. Immediately following his arrest in 1994, he was no longer the neutral, mostly well-liked black man that everyone over 35 years old at the time knew. This fact itself was very difficult for Simpson to accept. During the height of the original trial in 1994, the former hall of fame player was distraught at the intense, salacious treatment that he was receiving in the mainstream media. He did hesitate to denounce such coverage and compared such treatment to carnival tabloidism. To quote Simpson "What hurt me the most is that in covering this story, the legitimate press became the "tabloid press."[1] Quite frankly, I do not know why Simpson was so taken aback by such a hostile reaction to his sudden predicament. This was after all, the same media that made him a megastar and portrayed him as a genial colorless pitchmen and superstar celebrity. He was a good black man who transcended race. These are the types of individuals that always descend from media sainthood into tabloid pariahs once they fall from public grace. This is not to say that Simpson made things any easier for himself, particularly given the retrograde behavior he frequently engaged in after he was acquitted in his first trial. Testy encounters and verbal altercations with neighbors, shameless attempts at marketing slackly packaged manuscripts and videos and brazenly dating young women who were young enough to be his daughter were just a few of his less than noble actions. He was either a proactive participant in making himself the object of infamous attention or a reactive subject who was the object of sporadic disdain.

Regardless of the position he was in, he was the focus of intense opinion. Mainstream, tabloid and cable media interest in the salacious, racial and gender factors of the first trial was intense. The same could be said for the publishing industry given the fact that more than three dozen books associated with the trial were published between 1994 and 2000. The initial Simpson trial was marked by racial paranoia and conflict and obsessive media coverage. While tense and somewhat irresponsible, it was an economically profitable bonanza for the media. On the contrary, the second trial produced no such level of media obsession. The truckload of media outlets, lines of adoring fans, former and dismissed jurors commenting about the trial on talk shows, jurors having their motives questioned and being criticized for their decisions on talk shows and ardent supporters and detractors and arguing in public with one another was virtually nowhere to be found. In fact, trial number two garnered very minimal attention. The intermediate period between trials for Simpson was marred with continued legal troubles, a number of controversies and shameless self-promotion.

The Act of Surrealism

It was almost too irrational to believe. A beloved football hero, Heisman trophy winner, prominent star of B movies, Hertz spokesperson (who can forget the commercial where the grandmotherly white woman is sitting in the airport screaming "GO O.J. GO!" as he ran through the airport). He was seen as a man who had it all. He had two, well-adjusted adult children from his first marriage, two other beautiful children from his second marriage, a beautiful trophy wife and a seemingly good relationship with his ex-first wife. He also had loving fans and an adoring public. He was sitting pretty well indeed. To quote one radical black journalist:

> At one time white people loved O.J. Simpson and he loved them. Like some kind of house pet one lets roam all through the house, being a "favorite negro" gained him access to any and everything white, including the most prized of White society, white women. White men who normally be looking to get a rope, would want an autograph instead. To them O.J. was "the man."[2]

But the O.J. we knew then came to a crashing halt in June 1994. The black Prince Charming had overnight become a big, bad, brutal "nigger."

From the outset of the trial O.J. was seen as the "negro who had fallen from grace." He had "betrayed" his fellow white citizens and was thus longer worthy of sympathy or the presumption of innocence. In the minds of many whites (and a few blacks) HE WAS GUILTY! He was no longer a distinguished gentleman, he was now another violent, sex obsessed black man. This fact was not lost on many black people. Distinguished Harvard University professor and public intellectual Henry Louis Gates argued:

> It's a cliché to speak of the Simpson trial as a soap opera — as entertainment, as theater — but it's also true, and in ways that are worth exploring further. For one thing, the trial provides a fitting rejoinder to those who claim that we live in an utterly fragmented culture, bereft of the common narratives that bind a people together.... Nor has it escaped notice that the biggest televised legal contests of the last half decade have involved race matters: Anita Hill and Rodney King. So there you have it: the Simpson trial — black entertainment television at its finest. Ralph Ellison's hopeful insistence on the Negro's centrality to American culture finds, at least a certain tawdry confirmation.[3]

The sudden transformation of the one-time football and hall of fame icon to black outcast was quickly seen in the initial coverage of the trial. Scenes of that famous or perhaps infamous Bronco chase are no doubt indelibly etched in the minds of millions of Americans. After a week of ambivalence as to his guilt or innocence the mainstream media declared O.J. guilty. He was convicted in the mind of the public who was being spoon-fed volumes upon volumes of information about his less than stellar behavior toward women in general and his wife in particular. He was cast as an ego-driven, jealous misogynist who would stop at nothing to maintain his relationship with Nicole Brown.

The original Simpson trial was a television spectacle with all the makings of a potential Hollywood movie. There was sex and violence, success and failure, interracial and religious issues, gender differences, allegations of sexual deviancy and other factors that made for a titillating spectacle. Intense coverage of the first trial made it difficult to avoid. Stories about the case became daily tidbits on the major three networks. Related networks such as *Headline News*, and *CNN* covered the trial for its entire duration. More than a decade after the original Simpson trial we have witnessed the likes of Paris Hilton, Lindsay Lohan, Britney Spears and others who have become perennial staples in the mainstream and tabloid press. Their personal lives are frequently front page news.

Since O.J. Simpson was already a famous celebrity, the trial became an even more intense fascination in the world of media. The fact that he had graced television and movie screens as an athlete, actor, commentator, movie star and spokesmen for numerous products provided him with the sort of visibility that the mainstream press loves.[4] His leap from the football field to acting behind the camera to reporting the news increased his visibility (as was the case with some other former athletes) and was successful in transforming him into multifaceted personality.[5] No one could argue that Simpson was a financial dream for the mainstream visual media. The fact that the trial was debated on sports channels, the big three networks and cable media. ESPN, CBS, CNBC and HBO demonstrated this fact. As cultural critic George Lipsitz argued:

> The Simpson trial became a story that was easy to sell, in part, because it seemed to replicate so perfectly the world of commercial television and its generic conventions. The /actor/celebrity defendant charged with murder could have come out of *Murder She Wrote* or *Columbo* while the details about his residence and vehicles might easily fir into segments of *Dallas*, *Dynasty*, or *Lifestyles of the Rich and Famous*. For experienced television viewers, courtroom confrontations enacted half-remembered episodes of L.A. Law, Perry Mason and Quincy, while the history of unheeded claims of spousal abuse evoked the concerns and conflicts often aired in the movie of the week.[6]

Imagine a real life trial that would most certainly be a novelist's dream. There was the sexy, black male former pro athlete who supposedly murdered his wife — a blond haired, blue eyed former beauty queen, Nicole Brown. There was the blond-haired beach boy who was a horrendously opportunistic human being, Kato Kaelin. Let's not forget about the Latin housekeeper, Rosa Lopez. We witnessed the Asian judge, Lance Ito; the white, Jewish female prosecutor, Marcia Clark; biracial people, Justin and Sydney Simpson; the black male prosecutor who was seen as a traitor by some blacks, Christopher Darden, the black defense attorney who was revered as a hero by many blacks, Johnnie Cochran; the Jewish lawyer for the defense team,

Robert Shapiro; and the legendary WASP attorney who represented the defense, F. Lee Bailey. You had searing allegations of adultery, bisexuality, illicit drug use, rampant alcoholism, recreational sex and a whole host of tantalizing details. It was theater of the surreal! Many people could not help but be riveted by such a spectacle. This being said, this did not (at least in my opinion and a large number of other people) justify the chronic (and in many cases, often one sided) level of coverage by the mainstream media. In an age of 24/7 coverage, no one should reasonably expect that an ever dependent financially driven media will refrain from pursuing salacious, tantalizing stories.

The story of O.J Simpson on trial was economically lucrative from many aspects. CNN presented 631 hours of televised coverage of the Simpson trial, garnering an average of 2.2 million viewers at any given time. During this time, networks ratings increased by more than 50 percent.[7] On October 3, 1995, the day the verdict was rendered, an abnormally high number of Americans took a respite from their regular activities to await the outcome of the verdict. In fact, for the entire week leading up to the verdict, the Simpson trial gave CNN fourteen of the fifteen most-watched cable programs. *Court TV*, which at the time, was in its infancy stage, saw its ratings soar during this time as well.[8] Industry experts credited the 25 percent increase in cable viewership between the fall of 1994 and fall 1995 to the Simpson trial.[9] Already popular newsmagazine programs such as *Inside Edition, Entertainment Tonight* and *American Journal* saw its viewership increase by more than 39 percent during this time period.[10]

Magazines such as *People, Time, US Weekly* and others devoted fifty-four cover stories to the Simpson case during the last half of 1994, and ninety cover stories to it during 1995. This was considerably more than devoted to talk show phenomenon Oprah Winfrey who was the second most covered individual during this period.[11] In January 1996, Simpson gave an interview with Black Entertainment Television (BET) that resulted in the highest ratings ever recorded for the then sixteen year old channel.[12] Prior to his first trial, the name O.J. Simpson was associated with products — Hertz Rent A Car, Chevrolet, Wilson Sporting Goods, and Royal Crown Cola. He served as an announcer of ABC *Monday Night Football* games, an actor in the *Naked Gun* movie series, motivational speaker at corporate events and was a personality for exercise videos.[13]

However, once the endorsements began to get cancelled, the very factors that enabled him to become a person that many people (especially men) aspired to be also made him the target of innuendo and racy gossip. John Fiske pointed out the manner in which tabloid newspaper accounts focused on such vices with stories like "Sex Secrets That Drove O.J. Crazy" and "Shocking

Truth About Nicole's 911 Call, O.J. Caught Her Making Love While Kids Slept in the Next Room."[14] Such stories pacified the carnal, voyeuristic desires of a public who crave information about celebrities. The media aggressively covered the private lives several individuals during the trial. We witnessed the Goldman family's anguish and pain. We saw Kimberly Goldman sob uncontrollably in her father's arms the day the verdict was rendered. We were also privy to information about her (Kimberly's) bouts with depression as well. We saw father Fred Goldman frequently release tirades of anger on both O.J. Simpson and Johnnie Cochran. We were given ambiguous hints of Ronald Goldman's sex life, including an implied relationship with Nicole and experimentation with bisexuality. Nicole, herself, was linked to several rumored affairs with other men and women, including Kato Kaelin and most notably close friend Faye Resnick. There was brief speculation about the sexuality of Simpson's oldest son, Jason that was quickly quashed by his mother, Marguerite, in the *20/20* interview.[15] Several weeks later, syndicated television program *Inside Edition* went so far as to show footage of Jason Simpson leaving a nightclub late one night with an unidentified woman. Such speculation about individuals associated with the trial further engineered the insatiable appetites of an ever inquiring public.[16]

Outside of a few miniature morsels fed to the public by the media, coverage of the second trial was minimal. Those who desired the same level of endemic coverage that ruled the first trial had to tune in to *Court TV* where the coverage was sporadic at best. CNN, Fox, NBC, ABC, CBS and other major news outlets provided minimal coverage of the trial. The same could be said for the mainstream and tabloid media. The black media was no different. O.J. Simpson had become *persona non grata*.

Race and the Media

Despite the ambivalence that a number of black Americans had toward O.J. Simpson during his first trial, many of them were convinced that despite his supposedly limited contact with the black community (especially the rank and file black community), that he was innocent of the charges being levied against him. In fact, poll after poll demonstrated the fact that an overwhelming majority of black Americans believed that Simpson was being framed. The conspiracy theory mindset ran rampant throughout the black community.[17] The mafia, Columbian drug dealers, Las Vegas gamblers, the LAPD, Los Angeles County District attorney Gil Garcetti, the Ku Klux Klan, the caretaker and even O.J.'s eldest son Jason, were probable suspects in the minds of many black people.[18] Immediately after his incarceration, a *Newsweek* magazine poll asked black Americans the same question; was Simpson the victim of racism?[19] Many blacks argued that the reason that O.J. Simpson was being framed was because he had amassed large gambling debts. He was seen as an uppity black man by powerful, bigoted whites. He was married to a white woman. He was having extramarital affairs with white women.[20]

CNN polls that were conducted in July and August of 1994 repeatedly found whites believed that the case against O.J. was strong. On the contrary 45 percent of blacks disagreed with this. The majority of whites believed that he would receive a fair trial.[21] The opposite view held true among many blacks. Unlike black male celebrities like Denzel Washington, Don Cheadle and Bill Cosby who are well known for their philanthropic contributions to the black community, Simpson was never known (at least publicly) to be heavily involved with the African American community. Indeed, one of the major criticisms of Simpson from some segments of the black community was that he rarely commented on racial matters and whenever he did his remarks were benign and designed not to offend white sensibilities.[22]

If white America was eager to embrace Simpson as their equal as they had done with fellow black media darlings, Bill Cosby, Oprah Winfrey and to a large degree, Barack Obama (well at least white liberals, progressives and a few moderates) into their homes and living rooms as supermen and women, many blacks were just as adamant to believe that he was a black man who, once he fell out of favor with whites, was also vulnerable to stereotypical, negative media coverage. It was this sort of protective paternalism that caused many blacks to rally around Simpson. A few months after the first trial concluded, a black journalist remarked:

> When Simpson reverted to being "just another black male under arrest," the African American community, as usual reclaimed its only prodigal son. They demanded that he be given a fair trial and all the rights of an innocent defendant until proven guilty by reasonable doubt. And in the end, it was reasonable doubt, according to the jurors, that allowed Simpson to go free. Across the country, an avalanche of Anti-Black sentiment quickly found a voice as angry Whites unleashed a verbal assault upon everyone from Johnnie Cochran for playing the "race card" that had been dealt to him by Mark Fuhrman to the Simpson jury for "freeing a murderer," to Black women in general, for betraying the movement against domestic violence.[23]

A common complaint that many blacks made was that the first trial was tinged due to the racial angle that the mainstream media employed in their coverage. Interestingly, some mainstream media outlets concurred with this sentiment. *Time* magazine agreed with Thelma Golden, a prominent arts curator and black woman who remarked "if Nicole had been black, this case would have been on the cover of *Jet* magazine and not much more."[24] Indeed, throughout much of the 1980s and 1990s the media has linked and viewed accumulation and securing of property, avarice, wanton sexual behavior and other related retrograde aspects through a racial lens.[25] We have all seen the mediated picture of crime, drugs and broken communities. More than often, they all have either a black or Latino face associated with them.[26] There seems to be no middle ground for black people. To quote cultural critic George Lipsitz, "On television, black people who do not belong on *The Cosby Show* belong on *Cops*.[27]

There has been very little room given to blacks to step outside the strictly defined parameters that have been historically defined as deviant or violent. This is why it was probably so easy for so many whites, as trial one progressed, to believe in the guilt of Simpson. The fact that many whites did not see the darkening of Simpson's face by *Time* magazine as offensive, whereas many blacks did and thus expressed their displeasure by crying FOUL exposed the high level of polarization that the trial had on both races.[28] The story of a supposedly guilty O.J. who was found not guilty by a majority black jury reluctant to take the word of a prosecution who had several glaring inconsistencies in their testimony was seen as unfathomable to many whites inside and outside the media.[29] Millions of Americans witnessed the virulent racism that was echoed by Mark Fuhrman on the infamous McKinney tapes. It became known that he had applied for disability due to his pathological hatred of blacks and other minority groups, including interracial couples. During the initial stages of the original trial, Fuhrman was able to successfully evade defense accusations that he was a rabid bigot who had potentially violent tendencies. Initially, the mainstream media seemed to buy into the notion that although Fuhrman was a bigot, his racism was "personal" and had nothing to do with the widespread racism of the Los Angles Police Department.[30]

Moreover, it was quite interesting that those in the media (and they existed) who initially argued tooth and nail that Fuhrman was not a racist and such information was fabricated, began to sing a different tune once his bigotry was exposed for all the nation to see. The tapes demonstrated a callous, vile, racist who voiced the word nigger at least 100 times. It was a revelatory moment for many journalists, particularly white journalists to witness. Despite such an odious revelation, there was no criticism of the prosecution for using him as a witness nor was there any effort to prosecute him for perjury.[31] In fact, as opposed to being outraged by such blatant racism, Judge Ito, informed the jury that there were at least "two instances" where detective Fuhrman had used the N-word on tape. Over the past decade, Fuhrman has been a frequent commentator on several networks giving his thoughts on various issues.

Ironically, many of these media types who had no problem absolving the prosecution of such careless behavior had no problem accusing the defense team led by the late famed attorney Johnnie Cochran of "playing the race card."[32] Some whites, media pundits and regular citizens had no problem tarring Cochran and other blacks as "reverse racists" due to the outcome of the Simpson verdict. Such an attitude prompted cultural critic Lewis Gordon to remark "What the aftermath of the O.J. Simpson case has shown about contemporary racial ideology in the U.S. is that it is considered bad taste, a violation of protocol, for blacks to identify racism where racism exists.[33]

The stark difference in public reaction to the juries in the first and second trial was notable as well. During the original trial, cultural critics Nikol Alexander and Drucilla Cornell discussed at length how the predominately black female jury was seen as harboring a "colored" perspective given the fact that they questioned and challenged various aspects of police misconduct and a possible violation of the constitution by the LAPD. By searching and trampling through Simpson's home without a warrant the Los Angeles Police department violated the fourth amendment of search and seizure.[34] Both women furthered argued that even those newspapers, commentators, radio hosts, tabloid magazines and independent authors who argued the "Black jurors decided to exonerate O.J. on their blind racial loyalty" conceded that there was a significant amount of evidence that Simpson's constitutional rights had been trampled upon. They pointed to an example of such infractions by citing a *New Republic* magazine editorial in which the neo-liberal magazine which has always distanced itself from traditional liberalism and had by this time moved notably further to the political right, upheld the viewpoints of many in the mainstream media and the general public that although there was some evidence of police misconduct and abuse of power such as lying on oath, that nonetheless, such violations were minimal and amounted to nothing more that "small lies and inconsistencies on the part of the police."[35]

Perhaps, it was inconceivable to the *New Republic* editorial page that most ethical juries — predominately white or black or racially mixed would condemn such unethical behavior by law enforcement and render a not guilty verdict. Instead, for many mainstream media observers such an explanation was not good enough. They saw the jury's decision as being poisoned by racial bias. Could it have been that many of these same journalists were guilty of the same transgression? It seems that the hypocrisy among many people was rampant.

There was also considerable attention given to the educational background of the jurors during the first trial. A large segment of the mainstream media did not hesitate to belittle the fact that many of the black women jurors had little more that a high school education. Several magazines repeatedly mentioned this fact. They were routinely criticized by faux liberal journalists such as Dominick Dunne as being unable to intelligently decipher the hard evidence presented by the prosecution. Interestingly, nothing was mentioned about the education level of the two white female or sole Latino male jurors. The fact is that several of these women had well respected government jobs. Some of them held administrative positions. This was a fact that the supposedly objective mainstream media conveniently ignored.[36] They (the rank and file media had already rendered its decision that the predominately black female jury had been seated with a pre-conceived mindset and that no evidence, no matter how compelling, would have changed their minds. Interestingly, no such analysis was given of the all white gender mixed jury for the second trial. In fact, the only information that was disseminated to the public was that two black female jurors were dismissed from the jury by the prosecution for legal reasons. No one, including "the prosecution is always right" commentator, Nancy Grace, feminist ambulance chaser attorney Gloria Allred or blindly opportunistic *FOX News* commentator Geraldo Rivera (who dedicated two years of his former CNBC program *Rivera Live* to the trial) or *The New Republic* made any effort to psychoanalyze the all white second trial jury or to probe into each juror's educational background. Ironically, it was Jeffrey Toobin, legal correspondent for *The New Yorker* magazine and current CNN legal analyst who informed the public during the first trial that lead defense attorney Johnnie Cochran would introduce a strategy known as "the race card" who came to Simpson's defense during his subsequent 2007 arrest.[37] Toobin argued (obviously incorrectly) that O.J. would likely have a credible case for acquittal given the fact that the sordid cast of characters he was involved with were obviously less than model citizens, had previous criminal records, were trying to set him up and that he (Simpson) was only attempting to collect his personal belongings. However, despite Toobin's analysis, it seems that in the eyes of many journalists, the second trial jurors two were competent individuals who did their job quickly and effectively.

A significant factor for Simpson during the initial trial was that he (in a perverse way) was a beneficiary of the times. During the year of his arrest, 1994, the mainstream, tabloid and cable media had a field day covering the trials and tribulations of black athletes and celebrities such as Michael Jackson, who were in trouble with the law. It was also during this year that Charles Murray and the late Richard Herrnstein published the controversial and racially tinged book, *The Bell Curve*.[38] This book pulled no punches in its brash, frank, polarizing rhetoric on racial distinctions. Parts of the book were quickly refuted by a number of prominent people including former President Clinton. The book also had its supporters, among them a number of politically right-leaning think tanks and policy institutes such as the Heritage Foundation.

The book was one of the most talked about in years and Murray and Herrnstein made the rounds of the media circuit and penned several op-ed pieces between them. It was also the year that a very conservative republican party led by Newt Gingrich took control of both houses of congress. Upon their inauguration in 1995, the 104th congress decided that they were going to dismantle affirmative action a policy that has been crucial in created a solid, stable black middle class. Given such a hostile climate, many blacks felt that they under siege by hostile larger culture. It was in such an atmosphere of mistrust and anger that Simpson found a large level of sympathy and support.

The myth of "Black man as villain" has long historical roots. One explicit example is the 1915 retrograde movie, *Birth of a Nation* which warned of lustful, oversexed black men who would ratify miscegenation laws in congress and rape white women if they were not lashed down and "put in their place." In commenting on the lurid August 1, 1994 issue of *Newsweek* magazine, social commentator Earl Ofari Hutchinson wrote:

> The truth is the pictures work. *Newsweek* successfully pushed America's oldest hot button: Black man+white+woman+scorned black woman=sexual brute. O.J. became an instant metaphor and warning to America of the menace posed by the abusive and sexually plundering black male. The myth has stirred deep fantasies and fear within much of American society. It is part of America's sordid and shameful history of racial and sexual stereotyping that has refused to die.[39]

There have been similar situations where black men have been targeted as deviant, perverted individuals. In 1989, a white man, Charles Stuart, frantically called Boston police alleging that his wife had been shot by a "raspy voiced black man."[40] Stuart's motive was to collect the insurance policy he had on his wife. Media coverage was intense. Five years later, in 1994, a similarly deranged person Susan Smith brutally drowned her two sons, Alex and Michael 3 years and 13 months at the bottom of a lake in Union, South Carolina, Afterwards, she went on national television and gave an "exact profile" of a black man with a ski mask. In the case of Stuart when it came to light that he himself was the actual murder of his wife, he jumped to his death in Boston Harbor. Under intense pressure from skillful law enforcement, Susan Smith confessed that she was in fact, the murderer of her own children.[41]

What was more telling in each of these cases is that the mainstream media did not revert to referring to Stuart as a "racist white," or Smith as a "typical white woman," rather they were seen as two psychopathic, abnormal social deviants. The real, hard core racism that a number of black and other some non -white Americans face everyday is either too parochial or mundane to garner adequate media coverage. However, in stories like Simpson's, where race is the central feature issues such as violence, sexual deviancy, drugs and other forms of perversion receive ample coverage.[42]

What made the seeming lack of public interest this time around so interesting was the critical absence of a response from many in the African American community during the second trial. To be sure there were some black people who avidly followed the trial, but they (like many whites and other non-blacks), appeared to have adopted a considerable level of indifference toward Simpson. The fact was that it was very difficult for many of his fellow brothers and sisters to rally around "the juice" the second time around. The mindset among many in the black community was that Simpson should have learned to — to paraphrase a popular saying "left well enough alone." As far as many blacks were concerned, he should have been grateful and counted his lucky stars that he was acquitted for the brutal murder of two people (particularly white, upscale Hollywood types) who were slaughtered and decapitated like animals and had the commonsense to keep a low profile. One journalist sarcastically, yet accurately made the following point:

> Everybody said it. You can't keep messing with white folk like that. Buying your freedom is one thing. Going out and getting another white woman that looked just like the one you were accused of killing, then proposing to write a book called, "*If I Did It*," is another.... The White man didn't do this to O.J. this time around, Simpson did it to himself.[43]

There were also some other blacks who felt that after his successful first trial despite making some brief overtures, that Simpson still largely "kept his distance" from the black community. To these blacks, he only associated with the black community when it was legally and politically convenient to do so.

Another problem for Simpson was that he had hardly moved to Florida before he was in trouble with law enforcement for assaulting a neighbor during a road rage encounter in 2001. Later, that same year, his home was raided by federal and local law enforcement officials after his name surfaced during wiretapped conversations with suspects in an international drug case.[44] While no drugs were found, television equipment was. In 2005, a judge in the sunshine state ordered Simpson to pay $25,000 for illegally stealing cable for the purpose of viewing Direct TV.[45] While a number of Simpson's decisions made the average person cringe, nothing did more so than the psychologically misguided decision to write a book about how he would have murdered his ex-wife and her friend. In addition to confirming to his adversaries that he was a potentially twisted narcissist who lacked any reasonable level of good sense, he further eroded, perhaps even forfeited, any reservoir of remaining good will he had among his diminutive number of supporters. More than a few people argued that Simpson had lost any and all sense of decency and that his arrogant decision further increased the tension that existed between him and the Brown and Goldman families.

If I Did It?!

Simpson's conflicts with the Brown and Goldman families continued well after the conclusion of the first trial. From a $33,000,000 civil judgment against him in 1997 in favor of Fred Goldman to an unsuccessful attempt to publish his side of the story in a tawdry book entitled *If I Did It*, published by Harper Collins and sponsored by publisher Judith Regan in the fall of 2006, Simpson has managed to keep himself in the public eye and earn the enmity of a large number of Americans.[46] The book was later changed by Fred Goldman to *If I Did It: Confessions of the Killer*.[47] It was the announcement of the planned publication of the book which was a hypothetical description of the murders of Nicole Brown Simpson and Ronald Goldman that sparked considerable public outrage. The original plan was to have the book promoted as a television special with Simpson being the subject of a major interview. The special was entitled *O.J. Simpson: If I Did It, Here's How It Happened*. Both the book and to be televised event were cancelled.

From the outset the book resulted in a torrent of controversy. Many people believed that Simpson was trying to profit from the two deaths for which he had been found liable. For some odd reason, it seemed to be lost on both Simpson and HarperCollins that in the mindset of a large section of the American public, Simpson was seen as guilty and such a move was seen as ruthless and callous. Sara Nelson, the editor-in-chief of *Publishers Weekly* decried the initial decision of Simpson and HarperCollins to publish *If I Did It*. Nelson saw such an act as one of greed on behalf of the publishing house and sadistic arrogance and pathetic narcissism on the part of Simpson.[48]

Former Colorado congresswomen and National Organization of Women (NOW) president Patricia Schroeder and current president and chief executive of the Association of American Publishers made her displeasure at the prospect of the forthcoming book known. She referred to such an act as sickening, yet potentially beneficial that such a book would get millions of people talking and would result in forcing American society to engage in a real self-examination toward its current condition of callous excess. Such an exercise Schroeder argued could result in a positive outcome.[49] It seems that Schroeder was too idealistic in her belief that many would read such a book and become enlightened to the dangers of the dark side of human violence and depravity. It should have been well known to many by this point, Schroeder included, that many Americans, certainly not all, had long surrendered to be concerned about the welfare of their fellow man. The "me, myself and I" mindset had long dethroned the "he ain't heavy he's my brother/we are the world" altruism that was the national anthem of the 1960s. A perverse satisfaction with other's misfortune was suddenly vogue. The normalization of deviancy has become more and more commonplace.

Nelson and Schroeder were not the only two individuals to make their opinions known to the public. The day following the announcement, the website O.J. book Boycott.com prompted a campaign that persuaded Americans not to purchase the book.[50] Similar acts of resistance took place in Australia and Europe.[51] The Goldman family got in on the petition act as well. The petition/boycott efforts resulted in a mild level of success. Within four days, almost 60,000 people voiced and signed their displeasure with the potential book deal.[52] What caused the tide to turn in favor of the Goldman family and the boycotter's was the rabid level of television coverage that followed the story. CNN, NBC, CBS, and FOX in particular, intensely followed the activities of Judith Regan, O.J. Simpson and Harper Collins.

The publishing world waged in on the controversy. Numerous bookstores were outraged by the prospect of Simpson profiting from a horrific tragedy that they refused to sell the book. National book chains such as Waldenbooks and Borders made it clear that they would donate any and all profits to charities that aid women who are the victims of domestic violence. The rationale for such a decision according to Borders spokeswoman Ann Binkley was that it was the belief of Borders that it was a First Amendment right for individuals to decide what to read or not read. Binkley also added the disclaimer stating that the company would not discount or avidly promote the book.[53] Interestingly, what seemed to get lost were the major ironies, contradictions and craven hypocrisy that personified the Simpson, Regan, *If I Did It* controversy. The fact that certain booksellers had no problem sharing the proceeds of a book that discussed in graphic detail the hypothetical gruesome murders of two human beings, one who was the victim of domestic violence with other real life victims of domestic violence was outrageous, hypocritical, disingenuous and in many respects, obscene. The fact that very few, if any, bookstore chains realized this fact was troubling.

The *If I Did It* saga became an issue for Canada as well as several Canadian bookstores declared that they would order the book for customers, but refused to carry it in their respective stores.[54] During the several day controversy, criticism of Judith Regan herself became the focus of vitriolic criticism from the Goldman family. Kimberly Goldman lambasted Regan as a shameless opportunist.[55] Her father Ronald Goldman, also enraged by the potential book and television interview made his feelings known:

> It is an all time low for television. To imagine that major network would put
> a murderer on TV to have him tell how he would murder the mother of his

children and my son is beyond comprehension. It's morally reprehensible to me ... to think you are willing to give somebody airtime about how they would murder two people.[56]

It is important to note that criticism of the project did not only come from the white community. A number of black Americans made their displeasure known as well. Celebrity attorney Star Jones, a woman who is controversial in her own right, made it clear in an appearance on the *Larry King Show* that had she been in the boardroom at the time that such a decision was being discussed, she would have made clear her deep outrage with such an abhorrent idea. Another well-respected African American journalist and MSNBC commentator, Eugene Robinson pulled no punches in his acerbic denunciation of both Simpson and Judith Regan:

O.J Simpson's forthcoming book, *If I Did It*, could launch a profitable new series for publisher Judith Regan and her parent company, Rupert Murdoch's media empire. Let me suggest that she follow up with another Snuff book, maybe "If I Shot My Wife in the Head," by Robert Blake, and then diversify into non-capital crimes with "If I Molested All Those Kids," by Michael Jackson.[57]

Robinson further denounced Simpson as a narcissist of the first order who was warped beyond redemption, was obsessed needing with being in the limelight and had forfeited any remaining morsel of decency he had left. He also admonished Regan by questioning her journalistic credibility as a former tabloid reporter, an ardent promoter of "satisfying humanity's bottomless appetite for slickly packaged trash" and urged both individuals to "go away" and drop out of the public eye for the greater good of mankind.[58]

Due to the fact that she was taking scathing verbal body blows from people of all races, colors and creeds, Regan decided to defend herself by announcing the fact that she herself had been the victim of domestic abuse and issuing the following statement.

The men who lied and cheated and beat me — they were all there in the room. And the people who denied it, they were there too. And though it might sound a little strange, Nicole and Ron were in my heart. And for them I wanted him to confess his sins, do penance, and to amend his life Amen."[59]

Whether she was sincere in her *mea culpa's* or desperately trying to salvage her deeply injured reputation by engaging in an ample level of intellectual dishonesty, one thing was for certain and that was Judith Regan had felt the rumbling fires tingling under her feet. Four days later, the forthcoming *If I Did It* book and television special had been cancelled and NewsCorp chairman and CEO Rupert Murdoch publicly apologized for the pain that they had unintentionally inflicted on the Brown and Goldman families.[60] Even Regan herself knew that by this point she was living on borrowed time. Her tenure at HarperCollins ended on December 16, 2006, when she was dismissed by the publishing house for allegedly making anti–Semitic comments about being the victim of a "Jewish cabal." A year later, she filed suit for wrongful termination alleging that her former employer dismissed her due to the fact that she had potentially damaging information on then republican presidential candidate Rudolph Giuliani and some of his associates.[61]

Several months later, the prosecuting attorneys in the original Simpson trial, Marcia Clark and Christopher Darden appeared on the *Oprah Winfrey Show* along with Kim and Fred Goldman. Passionate testimony and commentary dominated the hour. The hour concluded with Oprah turning to Fred Goldman with a copy of *If I Did It* in her hands denouncing the selling of the book as blood money and made a declarative pronunciation to her audience that she would not read it.[62]

Conclusion

No one can argue that the drama that firmly etched itself in the fabric of the first trial was all but absent the second time around. Once the sheriff's deputies handcuffed Simpson and led him from the courtroom, I began to think about what must have been running through his mind. Did he realize that he would not have found himself in such a predicament had he used better judgment in the first place? Judge Jackie Glass sentenced the former Heisman trophy winner to a minimum of nine years in prison. He may very well serve a longer sentence. Any appeal is likely to be rejected by a higher court. At this point, it is very likely that the 62 year old will spend a large portion, if not all, the remaining years of his life in prison. In his prime O.J., reveled in such coverage and was able to parlay such adoration into considerable wealth One can only speculate what he will do while in prison. Will he attempt to make amends for his past behavior? Will he become bitter old man? Will he think about the intense level of racial polarization that his first trial produced? Will he think about the indifference of his predicament that the second trial provoked from blacks and whites? Will he be reminded of the senseless murders of Nicole Brown Simpson and Ronald Goldman? Who knows how he will use his time? One thing is certain, he will certainly be thinking about the fact that he did not utilize commonsense in dealing with the media, a largely hostile public, his foes or in his own personal decisions — pre and post trial. He allowed himself to be tabloidized, sexualized, racialized, and largely despised.

Notes

1. O.J. Simpson, *I Want to Tell You: My Response to Your Letters and Messages* (Boston: Little Brown and Company, 1994), 76.

2. Anthony Asadullah Samad, "O.J. Did It! (to Himself)," *Black Commentator*, December 11, 2008.

3. Henry Louis Gates, *Thirteen Ways of Looking at a Black Man* (New York: Vintage, 1997), 115.

4. George Lipsitz, *"The Greatest Story Ever Told: Marketing and the O.J. Simpson Trial,"* in *Birth of a Nation'hood: Gaze, Script and Spectacle in the O.J. Simpson Case* edited by Toni Morrison and Claudia Brodsky Lacour (New York: Pantheon Books, 1997), 8–10.

5. Lipsitz, *"The Greatest Story Ever Told,"* 8–10.

6. *Ibid.*, 9.

7. Steve McClellan, "All Eyes on O.J.," *Broadcasting & Cable*, October 9, 1995, 6; Mandrese and Jensen, "Trial of a Century, Break of a Lifetime," 1.

8. Joe Mandrese and Thomas Tyler, "Simpson Shakes New TV Season," *Advertising Age*, October 16, 1995, 51.

9. *Ibid.*; Jim McConville, "Down Is Up for Cable Networks," *Broadcasting and Cable*, October 30, 1995, 71.

10. Cynthia Littleton, "Verdict Propels Tabloid Ratings," *Broadcasting and Cable*, October 9, 1995, 7.

11. Julie Johnson, "O.J. Scores Again on 95 Covers," *Advertising Age*, January 1, 1996, 4.

12. J.M. "O.J. Simpson Scores Big For BET," *Broadcasting and Cable*, January 29, 1996, 7.

13. Lipsitz, 13.

14. John Fiske, *Media Matters: Everyday Culture and Political Change* (Minneapolis: University of Minnesota Press, 1994), 19.

15. *20/20*, ABC (1994).

16. Lipsitz, 17.

17. *The Final Call*, July 20, 1994, 2.

18. *Ibid.*, 2

19. *Newsweek*, August 1, 1994.

20. *Ibid.*

21. Hutchinson 100.

22. *Ibid.*

23. Sylvester Monroe, "Race-Man," *Emerge Magazine*, January 1996, 33.

24. *Time Magazine*, October 9, 1995, 39.

25. Jimmie Reeves and Rich Campbell, *Cracked Coverage* (Durham, NC: Duke University Press, 1994): Herman Gray, *Watching Race: Television and the Struggle for Blackness'* (Minneapolis: University of Minnesota Press, 1995).

26. Gray, *Watching Race*, 23.

27. Lipsitz, 20.

28. *Ibid.*, 21.

29. *Ibid.*

30. *Ibid.*, 22–23.

31. *Ibid.*, 22.

32. A number of media commentators criticized Johnnie Cochran for engaging in what they saw were race-based tactics.

33. Lewis R. Gordon, "A Lynching Well Lost," *The Black Scholar* v 25, n 4 (1995), 37.

34. Nikol G. Alexander and Drucilla Cornell "Dismissed or Banished?: A Testament to the Reasonableness of the Simpson Jury," in *Birth of a Nationhood: Gaze, Script and*

Spectacle in the O.J. Simpson Case ed. by Toni Morrison and Claudia Brosky Lacour (New York: Pantheon, 1997) 72.

35. *Ibid.*, 72. "Reasonable Doubt," *The New Republic*, October 23, 1995, 8.
36. Alexander and Cornell, 73, 74.
37. Jeffrey Toobin, "The Race Card," *The New Yorker*, July 25, 1994.
38. Charles Murray and Richard Herrnstein, *The Bell Curve: Intelligence and Class Structure in American Life* (New York: Free Press, 1994).
39. Hutchinson, 7.
40. Margaret Carlson, "Presumed Innocent." *Time Magazine* January 22, 1990, 10–20. Larry Martz," A Murderous Hoax," *Newsweek Magazine*, January 22, 1990, 16–20. "Stranger Than Wolfe: The Charles Stuart Case: Gender and Murder," February 5, 1990, *Associated Press.*
41. Elwood Watson, "Black Men are Vulnerable Amid Others' Wrongdoing." *Portland Press Herald*, November 13, 1994.
42. Lipsitz, 25.
43. Samad, "O.J. Did It! (to Himself)," *Black Commentator*, December 11, 2008.
44. DeWayne Wickham, "O.J. Couldn't Break Away from Bad Judgments," *USA Today*, October 7, 2008.
45. *Ibid.*
46. Due to public outrage, plans to publish Simpson's book were initially cancelled. However, the Goldman family sued Simpson for the rights and were granted permission in June 2007 to publish the manuscript which they did.
47. *If I Did It: Confessions of the Killer* (New York: Regan Books/HarperCollins, 2007).
48. Sara Nelson, *Associated Press*, November 18, 2006.
49. Patricia Schroeder, *Associated Press*, November 18, 2006.
50. CNN, "O.J. Book Boycott," November 16, 2006.
51. Robert Lusetich, "O.J. Confession Book Boycotted." *The Australian*, November 16, 2006.
52. "Former lawyers Mum on Simpson's book," *Mercury News*, November 18, 2006.
53. Justin Grant, "Booksellers Mixed on Stocking O.J. Simpson Book." *The Washington Post*, November 18, 2006.
54. Canadian Retailers Divided Over O.J. Simpson Book." CBC. ca. November 17, 2006.
55. Michelle Caruso, "Gloves Off: Vics' Kin Blast O.J. Book," *New York Daily News*, November 16, 2006.
56. Robin Abcarian and Martin Miller, "Simpson to Tell How He Could Have Killed Pair." *Los Angeles Times*, November 16, 2006.
57. Eugene Robinson, "Blood Money," *Washington Post*, November 17, 2006, A 25.
58. *Ibid.*
59. "Regan Turns on O.J. Simpson." ABC News, November 16, 2006.
60. "Under Pressure, Newscorp Pulls Simpson Book, TV Show." *New York Times*, November 21, 2006.
61. "Regan Sues News Corp over Sacking." *Reuters*, November 14, 2007.
62. *The Oprah Winfrey Show*, September 14, 2007.

Bibliography

Abcarian, Robin, and Martin Miller." Simpson to Tell How He Could Have Killed Pair." *Los Angeles Times,* November 16, 2006.
Alexander, N.G., and Drucilla Cornell. "Dismissed or Banished? A Testament to the Reasonableness of the Simpson Jury." In *Birth of a Nationhood: Gaze, Script and Specta-*

cle in the O.J. Simpson Case, eds. Toni Morrison and Claudia Brodsky Lacour. New York: Pantheon, 1997.

"Canadian Retailers Divided Over O.J. Simpson Book." CBC. ca. November 17, 2006.

Carlson, Margaret. "Presumed Innocent." *Time,* January 22, 1990.

Caruso, Michelle. "Gloves Off: Vics' Kin Blast O.J. Book." *New York Daily News,* November 16, 2006.

Fiske, John. *Media Matters: Everyday Culture and Political Change.* Minneapolis: University of Minnesota Press, 1994.

"Former Lawyers Mum on Simpson's Book." *Mercury News,* November 18, 2006.

Gates, Henry Louis. *Thirteen Ways of Looking at a Black Man.* New York: Vintage, 1997.

Gordon, Louis R. "A Lynching Well Lost." *The Black Scholar* 25: 4 (1995).

Grant, Justin. "Booksellers Mixed on Stocking O.J. Simpson Book." *The Washington Post,* November 18, 2006.

Gray, Herman. *Watching Race: Television and the Struggle for Blackness.* Minneapolis: University of Minnesota Press, 1995.

Johnson, Julie. "O.J. Scores Again on 95 Covers." *Advertising Age,* January 1, 1996.

Lipsitz, George. "The Greatest Story Ever Told: Marketing and the O.J. Simpson Trial." In *Birth of a Nationhood: Gaze, Script and Spectacle in the O.J. Simpson Case,* eds. Toni Morrison and Claudia Brodsky Lacour. New York: Pantheon, 1997.

Littleton, Cynthia. "Verdict Propels Tabloid Ratings." *Broadcasting and Cable*, October 9, 1995.

Lusetich, Robert. "O.J. Confession Book Boycotted." *The Australian*, November 16, 2006.

McClellan, Steve. "All Eyes on O.J." *Broadcasting & Cable*, October 9, 1995.

McConville, Jim. "Down Is Up for Cable Networks." *Broadcasting and Cable*, October 30, 1995.

Mandrese, Joe, and Thomas Tyler. "Simpson Shakes New TV Season." *Advertising Age*, October 16, 1995.

Martz, Larry. "A Murderous Hoax." *Newsweek*, January 22, 1990.

Monroe, Sylvester. "Race-Man." *Emerge*, January 1996.

Murray, Charles, and Richard Herrnstein. *The Bell Curve: Intelligence and Class Structure in American Life.* New York: Free, 1994.

"O.J. Book Boycott." CNN, November 16, 2006.

"Reasonable Doubt." *The New Republic.* October 23, 1995.

Reeves, Jimmie, and Rich Campbell. *Cracked Coverage.* Durham, NC: Duke University Press, 1994.

"Regan Sues News Corp. Over Sacking." *Reuters*, November 14, 2007.

"Regan Turns on O.J. Simpson." ABC News, November 16, 2006.

Robinson, Eugene. "Blood Money." *Washington Post*, November 17, 2006.

Samad, Anthony Asadullah. "O.J. Did It! (to Himself)." *Black Commentator*, December 11, 2008.

Simpson, O.J. *I Want to Tell You: My Response to Your Letters and Messages.* Boston: Little, Brown, 1994.

_____. *If I Did It: Confessions of the Killer.* New York: Regan /HarperCollins, 2007.

"Stranger Than Wolfe: The Charles Stuart Case: Gender and Murder." Associated Press, February 5, 1990.

Toobin, Jeffrey. "The Race Card." *The New Yorker*, July 25, 1994.

"Under Pressure, News Corp Pulls Simpson Book, TV Show." *New York Times,* November 21, 2006.

Watson, Elwood. "Black Men Are Vulnerable Amid Others' Wrongdoing. *Portland Press Herald,* November 13, 1994.

Wickham, DeWayne. "O.J. Couldn't Break Away from Bad Judgments." *USA Today*, October 7, 2008.

15

Major League Baseball and the Cultural Politics of Sexuality

Rachelle Sussman

In late June 2001 the July issue of *Out* Magazine landed on newsstands in major urban areas across America. This particular issue contained a surprising admission from its Editor in Chief, Brendan Lemon. In his monthly Letter from the Editor column Lemon disclosed that "For the past year and a half, I have been having an affair with a pro baseball player from a major-league East Coast franchise, not his team's biggest star but a very recognizable media figure all the same." The letter went on to express the irony of the affair: that the senior editor of one of the most popular gay men's magazines in the country was carrying on an "illicit" affair with a closeted man. Lemon explains that he decided to write his very public letter to urge his lover to finally "come out and make my life easier." After intensive discussions about his lover's sexuality and relationship to his teammates, Lemon concluded that coming out would alleviate his lover's "psychic burden."[1]

Approximately one year later in May of 2002 rumors began to swirl within the baseball and gossip communities of New York City that Mike Piazza, the storied catcher for the New York Mets baseball franchise and poster boy for American masculinity, was romantically linked to a prominent gay man within the New York City area. This rumor prompted some to think that Piazza could also be the mysterious lover that Lemon spoke of a year earlier. Both *The New York Post* and *The Daily News* published front-page headlines referencing the rumors and Piazza's subsequent denial of them. However without any solid evidence to run with the rumors eventually cooled as the baseball chat rooms, sports magazines, and radio talk shows turned to other topics of the moment.

Following the Piazza incident the Associated Press broke a story involving a promising minor league player from Japan named Kazuhito Tadano who participated in a gay porn video several years earlier. The top pitching prospect was blacklisted in the Japanese leagues after rumors — later confirmed — of his participation in the video began to spread. In fact the Japanese commissioner of baseball publicly instructed teams not to draft Tadano, prompting him and his agent to set their sights on America. Once in the U.S. Tadano initially found himself scorned by teams until the Cleveland Indians decided to take a chance on him. After seeing Tadano pitch Cleveland concluded his past transgressions were worth the risk. Nevertheless Tadano felt compelled to "confess" his actions to his teammates who have at least publicly supported him. During a press conference about the "scandal" some of Tadano's first words through an interpreter were "I'm not gay. I would like to clear that up right now." He went on to explain that at the time the video was being made, he was a young and naïve college student who needed money.[2]

Broadly speaking these incidences point to a particular moment within the American gendered landscape and to professional sport more specifically. The significant numbers of gay men in professional sports, and in this case baseball, can only go publicly unacknowledged for so long. This essay argues that the continual and perhaps inevitable arrival of gay male baseball players onto the public stage reveals that hegemonic gender ideology so entrenched within American professional sport may be moving towards a significant "unmasking." The utilization of the metaphor unmasking points to the performative, slippery, and illusory nature of gender ideology, particularly when considering the link that is often made between masculinity and sexuality. Despite the continuous aura of solidified truth that surrounds gender and sexuality these forms of identity formation are in reality the result of an ongoing complex, socially constituted process within which values and beliefs necessarily shift over time for a variety of reasons.

This essay therefore explores the representations of these particular stories — Brendan Lemon, Mike Piazza, and Kazuhito Tadano — in the mainstream media in order to more fully understand how American masculinity negotiates the professional, gay baseball player. Primarily the article will focus on a variety of news media outlets and pundits that covered these stories as well as a popular internet baseball fan site entitled Bronx-Bombers.Com. Building upon the concept of unmasking that I identify this article argues that baseball's precarious dance with sexuality reveals how the seemingly rigid relationship between the gendered social norms of professional sport and sexuality are more fluid than perhaps often assumed. In fact the posturing that tends to accompany many of the prognosticators who claim, for instance, that major league baseball could never accept openly gay players, is perpetuated through its ability to exclude other points of view and evidence to the contrary. It is these excluded points of view that will be more pointedly discussed within this article.

I purposely focus on baseball in part because of what it signifies as America's Pastime. For many Americans baseball harkens back to a kind of pure and innocent America — a symbol of the good old days. Baseball has come to represent an important societal and cultural arena of demarcation between normal and unacceptable on a national level. From this standpoint the sport may be seen as a useful marker of current values, norms, and practices within mainstream culture as they are played out both on the baseball field and "behind the scenes"— in the locker room and the office. Ultimately my goal is to more fully comprehend the current state of American masculinity by exploring how the mainstream media represents gay culture and its relationship to America's pastime.

In order to frame this discussion I first briefly discuss some of the contemporary scholarship around gender and sexuality, including an analysis of the relationship between sport, media and sexuality. I then apply this analysis to the specific case studies mentioned above, paying particular attention to the media's role in framing and constructing the public discourses around Lemon, Piazza and Kazuhito. Finally I consider the possible outcomes of players' outings and what these outcomes imply about the state of American masculinity. It should be noted that this article does not necessarily advocate for professional baseball players to publicly come out or "stay in," but rather to use these instances as a way to explore the current American sexual and gendered terrain from the perspective of professional sport.

The Truth About Sex: Homophobia as Social Practice

In his introduction to the book *Herculine Barbin* Michel Foucault discusses the link that has historically been made in western culture between biological sex, sexuality and truth. As sexuality became scientifically identified and categorized within the modern western medical field, homosexual love was marked as a kind of sexual irregularity, representing an "error" of sorts within the realm of normal human desire. Foucault identifies this move as indicative of a mythic sexual landscape developed in the wake of modern psychology that sought to categorize human sexual behavior through a kind of moralistic spectrum. On one end of this spectrum lies the demarcation of "normal," heterosexual sexuality while the other end of the spectrum includes "abnormal," homosexual behavior. One of the modern results of this ideological practice is to use sexuality as a marker of one's essential nature, as a way to test the "truth" of one's character through his or her relationship to sexuality. Foucault explains:

> And then, we also must admit that it is in the area of sex that we must search for the most secret and profound truths about the individual, that it is there that we can best discover what he is and what determines him ... we now know that it is sex itself which hides the most secret parts of the individual: the structure of his fantasies, the roots of his ego, the forms of his relationship to reality. At the bottom of sex, there is truth.[3]

Drawing upon the psychoanalytic dream-world work of Freud and others, Foucault argues that psychoanalysis has rooted itself in this idea that "sex harbors what is most true in ourselves," and this truth may be revealed by uncovering the desires contained within one's sexuality. American cultural beliefs around sexuality perpetuate this link between truth and sex, a link that continues to play out in simplistic and binary formations, particularly around the relationship between sex and gender. To be a normal, "true" man, who does not err, one must display a particular kind of gendered "hegemonic masculinity" that includes, first and foremost, the desire to love a member of the other, "opposite" sex.

Foucault's notion of discourse is another important concept for this paper. Foucault demonstrates that much of what we believe to be the "truth" about particular subjects is the result of ideologically constructed ideas about these subjects that obtain value through their continued expression in verbal and written form. These ideas, or discourses, are indicative of the norms and values of a specific time and place rather than the result of any kind of universal, objective fact. Thus discourses actively produce knowledge and systems of meaning about "life, labor and language" in ways that may appear natural and logical rather than constitutive of ideological formations and systems of power. Discourses are a way through which people are objectified and constituted as subjects through processes of categorization and narratives of progress inherent within these knowledge disciplines.[4]

On the surface masculine discourses appear to be among the least penetrable or malleable within contemporary American culture. Scholar R.W. Connell discusses "hegemonic masculinity" as a social practice embodied within gendered discourse that legitimizes patriarchal values, including the superior status of men within society and the attendant subjugation of women. However hegemonic masculinity should not be thought of as a static process unchanging over time. Rather Connell suggests that masculinity is a practice shaped through ongoing social interactions and changing cultural landscapes. In reality American culture contains a number of different "versions" of masculinity or "masculinities," which helps explain how the presence of active, gay professional baseball players can go undetected, challenging contemporary notions of the masculine.[5]

Similar to Connell scholar Judith Butler characterizes gender construction as relational and predicated on interactions between socially constituted actors that alter and coalesce within a specific time and place. From this perspective masculinity and sexuality are shaped by socially acceptable signifiers that function to mark subjects within a realm of normal and unacceptable behaviors. As social actors men receive their "queue" from fellow actors caught in a hegemonic web of semiotic meaning so that the performance of masculinity is continually reinscribed through interrelated bodies of masculine knowledge.[6]

The "disciplinary regimes" of gendered performance are difficult to subvert because of their tendency to be naturalized within society through repeated exposure and authorization from a variety of mediums. In addition the performance and behaviors associated with gendered signs are valued along a spectrum of power, such that the enacted signs of masculinity and manhood are privileged over femininity and womanhood. Butler however locates an alternative space from which challenges to hegemonic masculinity may cohere. She states, "When the constructed status of gender is theorized as radically independent of sex, gender itself becomes a free-floating artifice, with the consequence that man and masculine might just as easily signify a female body as a male one, and woman and feminine a male body as easily as a female one."[7] Because gender is a social construction rather than an essential or static entity its predominant signifiers are subject to radical alterations and fraudulent exposures.

Athletic desire and acumen represent prominent hallmarks of hegemonic masculinity. The world of sport functions as an important space within which one can interpret and display some of the key masculine signs of our culture, including masculine initiation of young boys into American society. Hegemonic masculinity is expressed through sport by emphasizing physical prowess; brute strength, violence and an aesthetic of physical superiority. Football and boxing are perhaps the most visible and obvious markers of masculinity, whereas baseball and tennis may be considered somewhat less masculine. The difference is the degree to which a particular sport emphasizes physical manifestations of the signs of orthodox masculinity: toughness, dominance, aggression and ultimately violence. Sport enables men and boys to display acceptable masculinity through successful athletic performance and affirm physical/biological superiority over the female. The stylized violence of the professional athlete is one of the most effective examples of masculine interpellation, and the athlete is therefore understood to be among the most masculine of men.

So what happens when the exceptional athlete loves and desires members of the same sex? Does this knowledge allow the constructions of acceptable masculinity to be altered within society? Or has the grip of truth on sexuality become so strong that even the hallmark of masculinity cannot alter our conceptions of and belief in that truth? Can the unmasking of masculine illusion — the exceptional gay athlete — allow for an alternative, more holistic, and ultimately more progressive definition of masculinity? Or do the perceived threats of gay men and sport ultimately lead to some kind of violent expulsion, and an effort to more clearly demarcate the line between normal and unacceptable?

In his book *The Arena of Masculinity* Brian Pronger explores the meanings of homosexuality in our culture through the lens of gay athletic experience. While my focus is on the public, professional athlete Pronger is more interested in everyday athletics and the experiences, for example, of the high school athlete and ordinary citizen's relationship to the gym. In this way sport becomes his vehicle for exploring broader cultural issues related to homosexuality, sex and gender in American society. Thus the goal of Pronger's book is to critique what he believes are the "myths" of gender that permeate society and encourage the subjugation of the homosexual. In order to conduct his research Pronger interviewed thirty-four men from a variety of athletic backgrounds including high performance athletes, recreational athletes, coaches, and those uninterested in sports. Most of the interviewees identified themselves as gay and represent what Pronger describes as "contemporary North American middle-class culture."[8]

The gay athlete may be understood as a symbol of the experiences of the gay man in a straight world; a symbol fraught with paradox, power dynamics and illusion. Pronger asks, "What is it that's apparently so awful about homosexuality that boys with a personal knowledge of it, be it the product of unrequited desire or ambitions fulfilled, feel they should conceal it?"[9] Part of the reason for this fear and society's often violent reaction to gay culture may have to do with protecting predominant gender values and nodes of performance. Homosexuality undermines the ideology of "truth" around sexuality inherent within hegemonic masculine logic and challenges a central societal myth regarding the link between sexuality and gender identity. Pronger explains that "Because homosexuality and athletics express contradictory attitudes to masculinity, violation and compliance respectively, their coexistence in one person is a paradox, the stuff of irony."[10] This irony hangs over not only the gay athlete but society in general.

Despite the masculine contradictions that gay men must negotiate on a daily basis Pronger identifies a potential source of empowerment that stems from this subordinated positioning. He states that "To be a homosexual man is to have a special intuitive interpretation of the myths of our culture."[11] This enables gay athletes to understand homoeroticism as both a feared and desired element of athletic culture. Pronger asks "What is it about the homoerotic potential of the athletic world that is so fearful that it must be disguised by the assumption of heterosexuality?"[12] We are taught that sport is a gateway to manliness but homoeroticism is not even though homoeroticism is omnipresent within male athletic culture. Nevertheless its presence in sport goes largely unacknowledged because of its perceived threat to fundamental beliefs about gender and sexuality, demonstrating the salience of this relationship. Yet the relationship between gay men and sport is also strong and continues to be embraced within the gay community with each passing decade.

Sex, Media, and Sport: An Overview

If masculinity is a performative act constructed through dynamic interplay and normative behavioral codes then media may be understood as a major source of gendered semiotic display. It therefore represents a crucial space from which to analyze the representations of masculinity in general and sexuality within professional sport more particularly. In 1992 author Peter Lefcourt published a novel entitled *The Dreyfuss Affair*. His novel tells the story of two professional baseball players who fall in love during their championship season and are eventually outed through a peculiar chain of events. At one point Lefcourt was in talks with a variety of production companies to bring this story to the big screen. Not surprisingly the screenplay languished in "no man's land" as the film industry contemplated the risks involved in creating such a film. More significantly in 2003 the Broadway premiere of "Take Me Out" opened to positive reviews and eventually won a Tony award for best playwriting. The play centers on a major league baseball star who comes out to the press before the first game of the regular season, initiating a series of trials and triumphs following his pronouncement.

In both cases the story of the gay baseball player is narrated through three similar registers: the anguish of remaining in the closet until the moment of an intense public outing; the persistent threat of violence towards the outed player(s); and the creation of the gay star athlete. These stories are concerned with portraying the gay athlete as normal (i.e., talented) *and* gay — in other words, someone who may be easily "mistaken" for straight but happens to be gay. They point to an interesting turn within the realm of popular culture, gender and professional sport that indicates at the very least a curiosity among the general public regarding the relationship between masculinity, sexuality and professional sport. This curiosity is particularly evidenced through the need among the stories' creators to construct their narratives around an athletic star, demonstrating the ways in which athletic acumen is continually reproduced as a symbol of hegemonic masculinity.

In the book *Sportsex* scholar Toby Miller traces the impact of modern day consumer capitalism and corporate media on shifting gendered dynamics within the sports world. He illustrates the ways in which the once orthodox masculine bastion of sport is being transformed for the female and queer gaze in the name of marketing. Quoting Margaret Morse he writes, "The discourse on sports is like no other in our culture insofar as its object is the male body; its currency is statistical comparison of performances, of exchange rates and ownership, of strategies for deployment of bodies, and of the particular weaknesses, quirks, and gradual submission to injury, illness and aging of those bodies."[13] Indeed the gaze upon the male athlete has never been more focused from a larger source of consumers. Masculinity thus lends itself to this gaze and is transformed by it.

A good representative of the gendered dynamics present within the current culture of sport — or sportsex — is the English soccer star David Beckham. Beckham has become linked to the term metrosexual, a term made popular in America by Marian Salzman who is a chief strategy executive with the marketing powerhouse Euro RSCG.[14] Metrosexuals supposedly represent a new kind of masculinity in western culture, one that marketing strategists have become keen to capitalize on, particularly because the metrosexual is defined as a financially secure man who is concerned with grooming and fashion in a way that resembles traditionally female desires. Yet Salzman and others who have hyped up the metrosexual icon are quick to emphasize that he is primarily a straight male who displays gay tendencies. Beckham, who is married to a former "Spice Girl," is clearly a straight man who has been spotted in feminine style dress and represents himself as someone who is concerned with his outward appearance. Miller discusses a recent incident in which Beckham was photographed at a party in France wearing a sarong, prompting the English media to make fun of him while simultaneously questioning his manhood and patriotism.[15]

However the fluid nature of Beckham's masculinity has also helped to propel him into the stratosphere of stardom largely because he is perceived by female and gay populations as a strong yet sensitive male. This "female masculinity" is viewed by marketing strategists as a blessing rather than a curse because of the vast number of people that may be drawn to this ideal. Indeed consumers have begun to take notice. The fascination with Beckham's style of masculinity both challenges and supports Butler's assertions regarding the potential for political change within the signified realm. Although Beckham's metrosexuality has arguably widened contemporary notions of acceptable masculinity it has also been quickly co-opted by the advertising realm and is therefore vulnerable to becoming just another passing fad.

In the contemporary sports world Miller explains that "Beauty is as much a part of male sports discourse today as toughness, while grace is the avowed compatriot of violence.... Sports have become governed ... by venture capitalists, with the body their target."[16] Thus the gendered politics of sport reflect in part the complexities of the hegemonic nature of contemporary capitalism. Bodies of the elite athlete are not just for the masculine orthodoxy anymore; this audience is simply too limited in scope. While acknowledging the role that corporate America plays in the process of *sportsex* Miller believes in the subversive potential contained within this site as new spaces of gender performance and expression open up, a la Beckham.

Sportsex as a concept is important because it pinpoints a space within professional sport where hegemonic masculinity becomes more fluid. Arguably this space is quite vulnerable because of its reliance upon marketing and consumption fads of the moment. However as more women and gay men demand various forms of visibility within the professional sporting world this space may also be ripe for an outing. Miller states, "The present moment of change is a radical one, and I guardedly welcome it. Sportsex is everywhere — sold as such.... It is both a sign and a source of social change."[17] Amidst the *sportsex* context the emerging story line of the gay baseball star makes sense as a delicious tale that fills theatres, sells books or increases television ratings, and our gendered ideals are arguably altered and challenged through this exchange.[18]

In her book *The Rites of Men: Manhood, Politics and the Culture of Sport* Varda Burstyn takes a decidedly more critical view of the relationship between sport and media than Miller. She critiques the "hypermasculinity" that pervades today's sports culture and is promulgated through the media. She identifies the overarching nature of professional sports culture as a "sports nexus" which is defined as "that web of associated and interlocking organizations that include sports, media, industry, government, public education and recreation."[19] In this way we may think of sport as a cultural empire whose effects and influence are promoted through many important institutions within society.

Burstyn's goal, similar to Miller, is to explore the relationship between masculinity and capitalism but also to emphasize the ways in which "masculinism" expressed through the *sports nexus* encourages systemic inequality. She links the hyper-masculine ideal of sport to neoliberal economics, neoconservative politics and social relations of inequality. Thus where Miller finds cautious optimism within the climate of sportsex, Burstyn's *sports nexus* represents a space fraught with patriarchal ideals that can only have detrimental affects on society overall:

> Over the years I have been writing about sport, I have become increasingly disturbed by its profound and far-reaching commercial appropriation, and by the effects of this on gender relations and on political life. In this sense,

sport is a perfect example of neoliberal economics and neoconservative culture — a commercialized, gendered cultural enterprise, subsidized by the state,
that encroaches on and finally occupies and defines public space. As sport and
commerce fuse more closely, and expand more widely, it is more important
than ever to consider what kind of physical culture sport provides for society
and what kind of physical culture we really want to have.[20]

Burstyn is concerned with creating a different kind of sports culture, one
in which the more violent and chauvinistic aspects are discarded for an ultimately more pleasurable, egalitarian and progressive environment. In order
to achieve this we must consider, for example, the ways in which sport engenders young boys into the orthodox masculine social order and the forces at
work that aid in this process. Considering the arguments of Pronger, Miller
and Burstyn the next section explores how the presence of openly gay professional athletes might alter the contemporary discursive realm of professional sport.

Leaving the Door Slightly Ajar: Brendan Lemon

In his now famous June 2001 Letter from the Editor Lemon spells out
his motives for writing so openly about his affair with a closeted, professional
major league baseball player: the "irony" of being the editor of one of the
most popular gay men's magazines engaging in a secretive relationship with
"someone so deep in the closet" was beginning to take it's toll on his psyche.[21]
To make matters even more difficult his anonymous lover frequently called
Lemon in the middle of the night to discuss his sexuality "and the way it affects
his behavior towards his teammates."[22] Thus Lemon concludes that finally
coming out would alleviate the enormous pressures they were both feeling.
He was convinced that a public outing from the player would eventually be
met with more support than scorn. Perhaps there would be some initial abuse
from the media, bleacher bums and a handful of adolescent teammates. Ultimately however Lemon is confident that the necessary support from teammates and fans would prevail in the end. After all, he explains, "Their prime
concern is winning, not who you're sleeping with."[23] Lemon further believes
that in this day and age coming out does not equate to career suicide while
suppressing one's true self is more harmful than any reaction from narrow-
minded individuals.

Although Lemon's letter seems fairly optimistic it nevertheless reveals the
primacy of hegemonic and heteronormative masculinity expressed through
the anguish of his lover. The elite athlete fears being openly gay at the same
time that society does not want to acknowledge the professional, gay athlete.

There has never been a professional male athlete to come out during his professional career. Lemon however believes that space may finally be here to inhabit. His letter arguably seems to approach the matter somewhat simplistically in that he considers the possible backlash to gay baseball players with a cursory sentence or two. He also assumes that it is on the burden of this one player to come out on his own without the backing of major league baseball, the player's union, or fellow teammates.

For the brief moment that the letter was in the public eye it was a topic of conversation on the lips of many in the sports world and the gay community. Lemon was besieged by requests for interviews from sports talk radio shows and a variety of media, stating "Whenever you combine sex with sports ... you are going to touch a nerve."[24] Billy Bean, a former major league player and current author who came out after he retired in 1996 reacted to Lemon's letter by stating "I think it's easy to say those things when you are the editor of a gay and lesbian magazine. But if I were that ballplayer, I'd have cold sweats right now."[25] Bean explains that while he is proud of gay athletes, "this is not about pushing people out on a plank and saying, 'Jump and lead us.'"[26] Clearly then, members of the gay community close to this issue vary widely in their opinions of how it should be dealt with. For Bean as for scholars such as Miller, the burden of integration should not fall on the shoulders of one person. According to his friend and colleague, it is this very kind of burden that eventually killed the first African-American major league baseball player Jackie Robinson.

Miller's article in the *Chronicle of Higher Education*, "Out at the Ball Game: the New Look of Sports" discusses the public reaction from "newspaper column ranting, populist talk-radio guessing, Matt Drudge Internet dredging, and ESPN polling" that occurred immediately following Lemon's letter. The article compels us to re-think the current state of professional sports in which neoliberal market values, the sports-media complex, and the explosion of sexuality in the public realm have perhaps altered the landscape of acceptable masculine behavior. Echoing *Sportsex* he states, "What used to be thought of as an exclusively jockish, male audience for sports now includes gay men and straight women, who have become targets for marketers."[27] And marketers seek to target this fairly new population of consumers with the sex appeal contained within athletic male bodies.

Miller argues that the late twentieth century marks significant developments in advertising for the gay consumer. Certain segments within the gay community increasingly seek to promote themselves as upwardly mobile and able-bodied consumers. Meanwhile companies have begun to notice them, creating subtle and not so subtle marketing ploys to attract the gay consumer. Television advertisements are often created "to make queers feel special for being 'in the know' while not offending straights who are unable to read the codes."[28] This way advertisers can appease both gay and straight consumers.

Advertising has become but one vehicle to showcase the rise of the gay consumer in the media. The late '90s and early twenty-first century have witnessed the broadcast of unprecedented gay-oriented programming including NBC's prime-time, enormously popular situation comedy "Will and Grace"; Bravo's "Queer Eye for the Straight Guy"; Showtime's "Queer as Folk"; and the emergence of significant gay characters on shows such as "Six Feet Under." While these shows may differ rather significantly in content and character portrayal, the creation and popularity of these shows demonstrates media and advertising executives' willingness to appease the gay consumer and tap into this expanding market.

Theatrical entertainment however differs from sports entertainment, which often works by a different set of cultural rules. Thus Miller believes that if Lemon's lover indeed were to come out it would be "a threshold issue for contemporary American masculinity" because major league baseball still serves as a primary vehicle for expressing and solidifying hegemonic manhood.[29] Even if we look to the programmatic changes within theatrical entertainment the majority of television programs mentioned above tend to contain portrayals of gay men as stereotypically, over-the-top, feminized buffoons. The gay professional baseball player poses a significant challenge to this kind of portrayal because of his disciplined bodily comportment which must conform to heteronormative masculine ideals within the field of play. Thus public knowledge of a gay player who can easily conceal his sexuality through performance necessarily exposes the falsified link between performance and truth, sexuality and masculinity.

Enter Mike Piazza

So just how would the mainstream media come to terms with the gay baseball star in the prime of his career? Enter Mike Piazza, the celebrated baseball star who now plays for the Oakland Athletics baseball franchise. Even by baseball standards Piazza is a looming presence, standing over 6 feet tall and possessing a body builder's physique. For most of his career Piazza played in what is considered to be one of the most grueling positions on a baseball team. The starting catcher crouches behind home plate for the duration of a baseball game night after night, often getting beaned in the head by baseball bats and high-speed baseballs. For protection he dons imposing and awkward equipment that harkens back to the era of the Roman gladiator. On the field he is at the center of action as the one who often dictates how a pitcher will throw to an opposing hitter. By virtue of his positioning he is able to keep track of what is happening on the field in a way that no other position player can do. In this way the catcher is a team leader, intimately involved with the developments of a particular game. As a catcher for the New York Mets for many seasons Piazza was on the brink of breaking the major league record for the most homeruns by a catcher. He is known as a power hitter, a home run king who dominates the baseball diamond every time he steps up to the plate. He is considered one of the best at what he does and has thus become a New York athletic icon.

In June of 2002 it was rumored that he was going to step up to the plate in a different kind of way by coming out as a gay man during his playing career. The rumors started circulating after his former manager Bobby Valentine was interviewed by *Details* magazine. During the interview Valentine stated that "Major League baseball is probably ready for an openly gay player." After this interview became public the *New York Post*'s famous and powerful gossip column Page Six picked up Valentine's quote and ran with it. One of their headlines that summer titled "In and Out with the Mets" called Valentine's remarks a possible "pre-emptory strike" before "one of his big guns [players] is outed."[30] The article further explains that "There is a persistent rumor around town that one Mets star who spends quality time with pretty models in clubs is actually gay and has started to think about declaring his sexual orientation."[31] Piazza has often been photographed with models and "playboy bunnies" in clubs and out on the town. In some ways the Post article infers that perhaps these women — as the ultimate, feminine symbols of masculine conquest — are actually a ruse for Piazza's "true" sexual preference. Predictably it didn't take long before the sports media outlets got wind of the Post article and quickly assessed to whom it was referring.

The media's response to the Post mirrored the response that Lemon had received a year earlier. The fact that this story came out of the heavily saturated New York media market only added to its ability to circulate widely and draw a good deal of interest on the national level. Various sports pundits considered the evidence, recalled the Lemon incident, and weighed in on the controversy. King Kaufman of *Salon.com* wrote an article entitled "The gay Babe Ruth" with a cartoon image of a metrosexualized Piazza featured next to the headline. The article began "The list of great gay baseball players is long and distinguished. It would astonish you to know who's on it. Of course, nobody knows who's on it."[32] Perhaps, Kaufman thinks, "A century from now we'll be able to put together a team of openly gay stars; I have no doubt."[33] But not now.

ESPN commentator Jim Litke also weighed in after Piazza felt compelled to issue a statement to the press in which he said "I can't control what people think. That's obvious. And I can't convince people what to think. I can only say what I know and what the truth is and that's I'm heterosexual and I date women. That's it. End of story."[34] Playing off the Post story Litke described this statement by Piazza as "a pre-emptory strike of his own" to "clear" his name. However Piazza also pointed out in his statement that he doesn't think open homosexuality would be a big deal for a fellow player, stating "If the guy is doing his job on the field ... I don't think there would be a problem at all."[35] Mets general manager Steve Phillips echoed Piazza's sentiments explaining that statistically speaking every team has gay players. Once again the idea that strength and athleticism can trump "deviant" or unacceptable social behavior is utilized to assess the openness of the sport community.

Litke thinks that the decision to come out as a gay baseball player is a very big deal and would result in career suicide. In response to Lemon's statement regarding the relatively minor negativity such an outing would produce Litke writes "You have to wonder what planet Lemon is on. Much as we might like to think locker rooms have changed in these enlightened times, experience tells otherwise."[36] He also quotes Billy Bean who in an earlier article stated that "the media scrutiny is so much greater now" that the openly gay player "would face a more daunting challenge than [the first black player to enter the major leagues] Jackie Robinson" concluding that "it would become a circus" and he hasn't yet met the person who would be up for the challenge. Bean alludes to the fact that the player to come out would need to embody a certain character to withstand the harsh treatment. Playing ability would simply not be enough. These statements point to a number of anxieties the gay baseball player producers within the American imaginary. Litke specifically discusses the locker room as the space within which homosexuality would not be accepted while Bean focuses on the media. Inherent within their statements is a concern with the reactions of others to the transgression of norms in both the private (locker room) and public (media) sectors.

In order to emphasize his opinion more strongly Litke interviewed the manager at the time of the Philadelphia Phillies, Larry Bowa, who stated "If it was me, I'd probably wait until my career was over."[37] Yet even Bowa echoes the sentiment that if the player is an exceptional athlete it would be easier for him than if he were a minor factor on the team. On the contrary Miller believes that "a player below superstar status would improve his marketability by becoming a niche hook for queers."[38] In Jackie Robinson's case his athletic acumen was key to his acceptance by players and fans alike though subsequent black players did not need to measure up to Robinson's athletic talents in order to be accepted and integrated. Although it is somewhat problematic to attempt to directly compare the dynamics of race and sexuality Robinson's legacy does perhaps point to a reason why several in the sports community believe that athletic acumen can overcome the excluded status of the Other. Not just sport, but American society itself is marked by an ethos of competition that places a premium on excellence and winning.

Both the Lemon letter and the Post article prompted a modern day witch hunt by fans and the media to discover the mysterious gay baseball player(s) in question. Fan sites such as the major league franchise New York Yankees fan site Bronx-Bombers.com devoted pages of commentary from passionate fans who posted email after email speculating on who Lemon's mysterious gay athlete could be. Mobilizing the performative nature of gendered constructions fans drew upon outward appearance, marriage status, and the rumor mill to determine the identification of the gay player. Some posts listed entire rosters of various teams and eliminated possible players one by one until they had determined the right man. Other posts dedicated pages of analysis regarding Piazza's sexuality, listing possible clues such as his changing hair color, single status, and personal grooming habits to argue for or against his homosexual status.

Here the work of Foucault, Butler and Connell become particularly salient to consider. What kinds of truths are the fans of the baseball site drawing upon to make their decisions regarding sexual status? Instead of professing surprise at the potential deviant behavior of this masculine icon many fans instead reinterpreted his identity through the twin spectrums of gender and sexuality. Piazza's body became feminized through a kind of ideological maneuver that enabled fans to create a gay man instead of reconcile the orthodox masculinity that Piazza displayed with his possible "gay-ness." From this perspective it would seem that the assumed heteronormativity of individual bodies may be easily challenged and altered within the public sphere but the ideals of hegemonic masculinity still triumph. Instead of viewing a homosexual Piazza as a challenge to hegemonic masculinity these fans could only accept Piazza as gay by re-coding his mannerisms, actions and outward appearance as homosexual in nature.

The Case of Kazuhito Tadano

The witch hunt mentality that surrounded Mike Piazza stands in contrast to the actions of the Cleveland Indians baseball franchise and their decision to rally around one of their minor league players despite his admission of engaging in a homosexual porn video as a college student in his native Japan. Kazuhito Tadano characterized this decision to his new teammates and the public as a mistake and asked for forgiveness. Reading from a prepared statement during a press conference specifically designed to address his past Tadano remarked "All of us have made mistakes in our lives. Hopefully you learn from them and move on."[39] He continued "It was a one time incident that showed bad judgment and will never be repeated. I was young, playing baseball, and going to college and my teammates and I needed money. Frankly if I were more mature and had really thought about the implications of what I did, it never would have happened."[40] The "implications" of what he did most likely refer to the way in which the video could have cost him his baseball career given the homophobic nature of sport.

The video caused Tadano to be completely blacklisted in Japan specifically on the instructions of its baseball commissioner. However during the press conference Cleveland players and coaches alike issued supportive comments towards Tadano. One of his fellow teammates explained that after Tadano confessed his actions nobody thought anything more of it. Describing Tadano as nervous during his "confessional" the player concluded "He's a great guy and a great pitcher."[41] Echoing these sentiments another teammate stated "We have good guys here. Everybody has done something they regret in their lives. He's a person just like everyone else."[42] In the book *The History of Sexuality, Volume One* Foucault discusses the role of confession within the history of western culture as a way to both produce and establish truth around taboo subjects such as sexuality. Within the Judeo-Christian tradition the confession is indicative of an admission and purging of guilt or sin and is also a way to obtain forgiveness. After his confession players felt compelled to stress Tadano's good character, even reassuring the public of his humanity and their willingness to grant him a clean slate. Yet other than his confessional act how can we account for the support Tadano received in comparison to the reactions against Lemon and Piazza?

The answer may partly lie in Tadano's early experiences as a baseball pitching prospect. Initially he was blacklisted by American teams because as one baseball scout explained Tadano did not pitch well enough in try-outs for teams to ignore the "scandal." Eventually Cleveland decided that "the upside was well worth the risk, energy and time to support him."[43] Ironically the Cleveland Indians baseball franchise has been repeatedly criticized for its brazenly offensive name and logo, the latter of which features a literal red-faced caricature of what one is supposed to assume is a Native American "mascot" smiling profusely, reminiscent of the old south "sambo" caricature. Despite protests and pleas from the Native community to remove the logo and change their franchise name altogether the Cleveland ownership has refused to budge on these issues. They are not willing to risk the anger of their fan base that have grown up with the Sambo character. Management is willing however to welcome Tadano into the fold — as long as his pitching does not disappoint.

The baseball scout's admission that Tadano's acceptance was based at least in part on his potential as an athlete points to Miller's and Burstyn's observations regarding the impact of commercialization on baseball and sports culture in general. Good teams bring bodies and revenue to the ball park and good pitching in particular is essential for lasting success. Once Cleveland management made a decision to draft Tadano its players fell in line with that decision, publicly supporting him and stressing his athletic ability. Ironically it is Tadano's ability to display a hallmark of acceptable masculinity — athletic acumen — that also opens up the space for him to display deviant forms of acceptable masculine behavior.

Conclusion: Unmasking Masculinity

Perhaps one of the more positive fall outs from the Piazza incident took place a few months later when Ed Gray, a storied sports reporter for the *Boston Herald* came out as a gay man in one of his columns. His reasoning pertained to the "unabashed homophobia" in elite and amateur sports. He felt dismayed by the open tolerance of homophobia in the sporting world and decided it was time to speak out about this issue. By doing so Gray hoped that "major league sports address the issue of homophobia and people who make overt homophobic remarks or actions be held accountable."[44] His column was titled "Out and Proud" and gained the immediate support of his sports editor. Gray's remarks sparked discussion and debate on local Boston radio programs as people wondered whether his admission would make him an outcast within the sports community.

For Gray the most important thing was to be able to be true to himself and work freely and openly as everyone else. He encouraged professional athletes to come out and be supported by their teammates, believing as Lemon did that the initial frenzy around such an act could be quickly diffused with the public support of one's team. Some gay sports columnists characterized Gray's article as an opportunity to dispel the myth that gay people are not appropriate for the world of sports. For example a journalist from the *Atlanta Journal-Constitution* stated that "The more visible, everyday, average, non–'Queer Eye for the Straight Guys' who come out, the more diverse [the gay community] appears."[45] The public assertion of orthodox- masculine gay men helps to diffuse essentializing notions of queerness by mainstream culture. Additionally orthodox-masculine gay men can function as a kind of rupture between hegemonic masculinity and heteronormative behavior, exposing the illusory link between these processes of identity formation.

Gray also discusses the smoking gun excuse that homophobic athletes use against supporting the gay athlete: the locker room. What if a gay athlete, goes the argument, takes advantage of a locker room situation by using this safe space to steal glances at naked male bodies? Or worse, what if he tries to turn the locker room into a cruising expedition? Gray counters this fearful mindset by explaining "Any man secure in his heterosexuality should not have a care in the world when a gay man is present in the locker room. He is there only to earn a living, not to infiltrate the locker room ... to 'convert' straight athletes."[46] After all, Gray argues, a healthy gay man is not interested in testing the powers of his sexuality in a room full of straight men. What he may also be alluding to is the utilization of the locker room by athletes as one of the key sites in the policing of hegemonic masculinity.

Various sports scholars have discussed the locker room environment and its ritualized effects on male bonding through sexist and homophobic language. The irony of this phenomenon is that the male locker room itself can be quite homoerotic, whether it is full of straight men or not. Simply put, hard, naked bodies in an enclosed space will most likely produce erotic energy. Perhaps it is for this very reason that the locker room can engender such vicious language towards women and gay men, as a way for athletes uncomfortable with the erotic nature of their environment to channel their angst into sexist and homophobic language.

As sports scholar Michael Messner explains "Sexist jokes are often used as a way to mediate the sexual tension boys feel for each other."[47] There is a social function to jokes in that they can reinforce normative values, desires and anxieties. The locker room is a way for athletes of all sexualities to prove their manhood by outdoing their fellow teammates in derogatory banter towards each other and subjugated communities. Thus the gay man can use the locker room to pass by engaging in this banter (perhaps even more viciously then straight men) in order to hide his sexual preferences from the group. Elite athletes tend to draw enormous self esteem and shape their identity from their acceptance by peers and public adulation of fans. Additionally athletes depend on endorsements and the popularity of their public persona. To jeopardize this in the locker room or other settings by not performing up to acceptable masculine standards is far too risky *financially* for many athletes to flirt with.

Gray states that public support by one's team can go a long way in acclimating the openly gay player to the public. People predicted utter disaster for both Jackie Robinson and the game of baseball before he entered the league. Robinson did endure unending abuse during his career at the same time that he became a revered hero, something that fewer people predicted. Since his arrival onto the public stage baseball has changed immeasurably for the better and now includes players and fans from all over the world.[48] However baseball's desegregation did not cause significant structural changes for African Americans in this country despite the fact that Robinson became a tremendous inspiration for large numbers of people.

The legacy of Robinson and the experience of Tadano both indicate the possibility of "acceptance" of a gay player once the initial media buzz dies down. Perhaps however this question of acceptance overshadows a greater issue. Even if the player or players in question were to be shunned or unsupported by teammates the internal and external questioning of hegemonic masculinity will have already begun. This is especially true if a group of players were to come out at the same time. Thus whether or not society ever learns the identity of Lemon's lover, or whether his claims were even true, is almost beside the point. As Piazza, Lemon and Tadano have illustrated the decision to go public by gay players can re-position the dominant discourse so that the more significant outing becomes the slippery nature of masculinity rather than the sexuality of individual players. The experiences of Lemon, Piazza and Tadano demonstrate the gendered hypocrisies and jagged trajectories that each of these case studies proceeded along, particularly around the question of "acceptance." What cannot be questioned however is the flurry of discursive activity that opened up in their wake and will continue to swirl with each passing innuendo, rumor and subsequent unmasking.

I would like to thank professor Toby Miller for his encouragement, scholarship and sound advice during the writing of this paper.

Notes

1. Brendan Lemon, "Letter from the Editor"; available from http://www.out.com/html/edletter90.html 2001; accessed January 2002.

2. "Minor Leaguer: It was a 'One-Time Incident'"; available from http://sports.espn.go.com/mlb/news/story?id=1720362; accessed February 2004.

3. Michel Foucault, *Herculine Barbin*, trans. by Richard McDougall (New York: Random House, 1980), x–xi.

4. Paul Rabinow, ed., *The Foucault Reader* (New York: Pantheon, 1989), 9.

5. R.W. Connell, *Masculinities* (Berkeley: University of California Press, 1995), 77.

6. Judith Butler, *Gender Trouble: Feminism and the Subversion of Identity* (New York: Routledge, 1990).

7. *Ibid.*, 6.

8. Brian Pronger, *The Arena of Masculinity: Sports, Homosexuality and the Meaning of Sex* (Toronto: Summer Hill, 1990), xi.

9. *Ibid.*, 2.

10. *Ibid.*, 3.

11. *Ibid.*, 8.

12. *Ibid.*, 10.

13. Toby Miller, *Sportsex* (Philadelphia: Temple University Press, 2001), 7.

14. Michael S. Rose, "Metrosexual Goes America"; available from http://www.newox fordreview.org/article.jsp?did=0704-rose; accessed August, 2004.

15. Miller, *Sportsex*, 8–9.

16. *Ibid.*, 9.

17. *Ibid.*, 14.

18. ESPN's 2003 short-lived drama series entitled *Playmakers* about the National Football League was a ratings hit in part because of one major story line featuring a gay (in the closet) player. The show was cancelled as pressure mounted from NFL officials and players who disapproved of the show's "negative" portrayals.

19. Varda Burstyn, *The Rites of Men: Manhood, Politics and the Culture of Sport* (Toronto: University of Toronto Press, 1999), 3.

20. *Ibid.*, 6–7.

21. Brendan Lemon, "Letter from the Editor"; available from http://www.out.com/ html/edletter90.html 2001; accessed January 2002.

22. *Ibid.*

23. *Ibid.*

24. Available from http://www.advocate.com; printed on September 21, 2002.

25. *Ibid.*

26. *Ibid.*

27. Toby Miller, "Out at the Game: The New Look of Sports"; available from http: //chronicle.com/weekly/v47/i49/49b01401.htmchronicle.com; accessed August 2002. 1.

28. *Ibid.*

29. *Ibid.*, 3.

30. Neal Travis, "In and Out with the Mets"; available from http://pqarchiver.nypost. com/nypost/advancedsearch.html; printed on May 20, 2002.

31. *Ibid.*

32. King Kaufman, "The Gay Babe Ruth."; available from http://www.salon.com/ news/sports/col/kaufman/2002/05/23/gays/index.html; accessed February 2003.

33. *Ibid.*

34. Jim Litke, "Piazza Denies Rumor as Gay Player Issue Resurfaces"; available from http://espn.go.com/mlb/news/2002/0522/1385446.html; accessed March 2003.

35. *Ibid.*

36. *Ibid.*

37. *Ibid.*

38. Miller, "Out at the Ballpark," 2.

39. "Minor Leaguer: It Was a 'One-Time Incident'"; available from http://sports. espn.go.com/mlb/news/story?id=1720362; accessed February 2004.

40. *Ibid.*

41. *Ibid.*

42. *Ibid.*

43. *Ibid.*

44. "Sportswriter for *Boston Herald* Comes Out"; available from http://advocate. com/news_detail_ektid09568.asp; accessed on February 2004.

45. *Ibid.*

46. *Ibid.*

47. Michael Messner, *Taking the Field: Women, Men and Sports* (Minneapolis: University of Minnesota Press, 2002), 47.

48. Baseball has seen a precipitous drop in African-American players over the last five to ten years. See Dave Winfield's *Dropping the Ball: Baseball's Problems and How We Must Solve Them.*

Bibliography

Burstyn, Varda. *The Rites of Men: Manhood, Politics and the Culture of Sport.* Toronto: University of Toronto Press, 1999.

Butler, Judith. *Gender Trouble: Feminism and the Subversion of Identity.* New York: Routledge, 1990.

Connell, R.W. *Masculinities.* Berkeley: University of California Press, 1995.

Foucault, Michel. *Herculine Barbin.* Trans. Richard McDougall. New York: Random House, 1980.

_____. *The History of Sexuality.* Trans. Robert Hurley. New York: Vintage, 1978.

Gauntlett, David. *Media, Gender and Identity.* London: Routledge, 2008.

Messner, Michael. *Taking the Field: Women, Men and Sports.* Minneapolis: University of Minnesota Press, 2002.

Miller, Toby. *Sportsex.* Philadelphia: Temple University Press, 2001.

Mirzoeff, Nick, ed. *The Visual Culture Reader.* London: Routledge, 1998.

Pronger, Brian. *The Arena of Masculinity: Sports, Homosexuality and the Meaning of Sex.* Toronto: Summer Hill, 1990.

Rabinow, Paul, ed. *The Foucault Reader.* New York: Pantheon, 1989.

Sturken, Marita, and Lisa Cartwright. *Practices of Looking.* New York: Oxford University Press, 2001.

Weedon, Chris. *Feminist Practice and Poststructuralist Theory.* Cambridge, U.K.: Blackwell, 1997.

About the Contributors

Daryl A. Carter is an assistant professor of history at East Tennessee State University and specializes in twentieth century United States, political, and African American history. He has written on race, class and Robert Kennedy, and his current project is a book on President Clinton and his relationship with African Americans.

Daniel Mudie Cunningham is an independent scholar based in Sydney, Australia. In 2004 he completed his Ph.D. on the aesthetics of whiteness and "white trash" at the University of Western Sydney, where he also worked for a decade as lecturer and senior research associate in art history and visual culture. He is also active as a curator and arts writer with a track record for work that primarily negotiates the queering of visual histories, popular cultures and oppositional identity politics. His recent publications include essays in the anthologies *Queer Popular Culture: Literature, Media, Film, and Television* (Palgrave Macmillan, 2007) and *Everyday eBay: Culture, Collecting, and Desire* (Routledge, 2006).

Marc DiPaolo, an assistant professor of English at Alvernia University, is a specialist in British literature and film studies. He is the author of *Emma Adapted: Jane Austen's Heroine from Book to Film* and is the co-editor of the literature anthology *The Conscious Reader*. Formerly a reporter for the *Staten Island Advance*, DiPaolo has contributed chapters to the books *A Century of the Marx Brothers* and *The Amazing Transforming Superhero!* and writes the autobiographical blog "The Adventures of Italian-American Man" for I-Italy (http://www.i-italy.org).

Debbie Epstein is a professor of education at Cardiff University. She has published widely on questions of gender, sexuality and race and their intersections in educational sites and in popular culture. She has written extensively on higher education and was the lead editor for the *World Yearbook of Education 2208: Geographies of Knowledge, Geometries of Power: Framing the Future of Higher Education*. Together with Rebecca Boden and Jane Kenway, she is author of *The Academic's Support Kit*.

Alina Haliliuc is a doctoral candidate in the department of Communication Studies at the University of Iowa.

Kristin Jacobson joined the Richard Stockton College of New Jersey's faculty as an assistant professor of American literature in 2005. She teaches courses in American literature and women's studies. Incorporating feminist geography and literary analysis, she is writing a book titled "Domestic Geographies: Neodomestic American Fiction," which investigates late twentieth-century and early twenty-first-century manifestations of "domestic fiction." She has published articles in *Genre, Tulsa Studies in Women's Literature,* and *Legacy.*

Ruthann Lee is a doctoral candidate in the graduate program in sociology at York University in Toronto, Canada. Her dissertation examines the production of racialized masculinities in North American popular culture. She has previously published in *Women and Environments: Embodying Asian/American Sexualities* (edited by Gina Masequesmay and Sean Metzger, Lexington Books, 2008) and collectively edited and contributed to the anthology *Han Kut: Critical Art and Writing by Korean Canadian Women* (Inanna, 2007).

David Magill is an assistant professor of English at the Longwood University where he teaches courses on American literature, African American literature, film, and popular culture. He is revising his manuscript "Modern Masculinities: Nostalgia and Jazz Age White Manhood" for publication. He has published articles on race and masculinity in several collections, focusing on 1920s celebrity culture, John Wayne, Joss Whedon's *Firefly,* and Tim O'Brien.

Heather Mendick works as a senior research fellow at the Institute for Policy Studies in Education at London Metropolitan University and as a lecturer in the education department at Goldsmiths University of London. Before becoming an academic she was a mathematics teacher. She has researched a range of subjects including, most recently, the role of television drama in young people's career aspirations. She is the author of *Masculinities in Mathematics* (published by Open University Press).

Marie-Pierre Moreau is a research fellow at the Institute for Policy studies in education at London Metropolitan University. Her research interests are education and employment policies in relation to social justice, with a particular focus on gender and its discursive construction. Particular areas she has researched recently include: graduates' employment, teachers' careers, equal opportunities policies in schools, and young people's relationship with mathematics.

Valeria Palmer-Mehta is an assistant professor of communication in the Department of Communication and Journalism at Oakland University in Rochester, Michigan. A sampling of her publications can be found in such journals and books as *Text and Performance Quarterly, Communication Teacher, Women's Studies in Communication, Journal of American Culture, The Oprah Phenomenon* (ed. Jennifer Harris and Elwood Watson), and *Black Women's Intellectual Traditions: Speaking Their Minds* (ed. Kristin Waters and Carol Conaway).

Jane E. Rose is an associate professor of English at Purdue University North Central in Westville, Indiana, where she teaches courses in American literature, gender, and ethnicity. Her publications include articles on nineteenth-century conduct books for women, on Elizabeth Oakes Smith's domestic and feminist writings, and on Annie

Proulx's *Brokeback Mountain*. She has also published pedagogical essays on Toni Morrison's *The Bluest Eye* and on post-secondary correctional education.

Jesse Scott is an assistant professor of English and African American studies at the University of Mississippi.

Marc Shaw is an assistant professor of theater and literature at Hartwick College. His research concentrations include contemporary British and American theater, Harold Pinter, twentieth-century acting techniques, masculinities in theater and popular culture, and solo performance. His writing appears in *Theatre* journal, *Shakespeare Bulletin*, and has a forthcoming work from Rodopi Press entitled *Modern Drama and Theatre Topics*. He has presented his research at many national conferences.

Bradley Smith is a lecturer in the first-year writing program at Columbia College, Chicago. He has presented at regional and national conferences, including CCCCs, and has an article forthcoming in *Mosaics: A Journal for the Interdisciplinary Study of Literature*.

Rachel Sussman is a Ph.D. candidate in the Department of Media, Culture, and Communication at New York University, where she also serves as an instructor for the course Gender and Communication.

Helena Wahlström works as an assistant professor in English at Gävle University, where she also teaches gender studies. She has a Ph.D. in American literature. Her dissertation was *Husbands, Lovers, and Dreamlovers: Masculinity and Female Desire in Women's Novels of the 1970s* (as Helena Eriksson, 1997). Her publications also include articles on gender and genre, on masculinity in texts by Gloria Naylor and John Irving, and on fatherhood in texts by Caryl Phillips, Michael Cunningham and Paul Auster, as well as on the relationship between masculinity studies and feminism. A collaborative book project, "Making Home: Orphanhood and Agency in Contemporary American Novels," is funded by the Swedish Research Council.

Elwood Watson is full professor of history, African American studies and gender studies at East Tennessee State University. He is the co-editor of two anthologies *There She Is, Miss America: The Politics of Sex, Beauty and Race in America's Most Famous Pageant* and *The Oprah Phenomenon*. He is the sole editor of *Searching the Soul of Ally McBeal: Critical Essays*. His book *Outsiders Within: Black Women in the Legal Academy After Brown v. Board* was published in 2008 by Rowman and Littlefield. The author and co-author of several award winning articles, he is currently working on an anthology that explores performance and anxiety of the male body and a monograph that explores the contemporary race realist movement.

Index